Harvard Historical Studies • 160

Published under the auspices
of the Department of History
from the income of the
Paul Revere Frothingham Bequest
Robert Louis Stroock Fund
Henry Warren Torrey Fund

The Betrayal of Faith

*The Tragic Journey of a
Colonial Native Convert*

Emma Anderson

HARVARD UNIVERSITY PRESS

Cambridge, Massachusetts

London, England

2007

Library of Congress Cataloging-in-Publication Data

Anderson, Emma.
  The betrayal of faith : the tragic journey of a colonial native convert / Emma
  Anderson.
    p. cm.—(Harvard historical studies ; 160)
  Includes bibliographical references and index.
  ISBN-13: 978-0-674-02608-7 (alk. paper)
  ISBN-10: 0-674-02608-X (alk. paper)
  1. Pastedechouan, Pierre-Anthoine, b. 1608.   2. Montagnais Indians—Saint
Lawrence River Valley—Biography.   3. Montagnais Indians—Missions—Saint
Lawrence River Valley.   4. Indian Catholics—Saint Lawrence River Valley—
Biography.   5. Catholic converts—Saint Lawrence River Valley—Biography.
6. Franciscan Recollects—Missions—Saint Lawrence River Valley.   7. Religion
and culture—Saint Lawrence River Valley—History.   8. Racism—Religious
aspects—Christianity.   9. Saint Lawrence River Valley—History.   10. Saint
Lawrence River Valley—Religious life and customs.   I. Title.
  E99.M87A46 2007
  971.4004'97320092—dc22
  [B]   2007008169

To Mark
with all my love.
Without you, this book
could never have been written.

And

to Sophie and Danny
with infinite tenderness.

Contents

Illustrations

Acknowledgments

This attempt to glimpse into the interior religious world of a young Innu man in seventeenth-century Canada would never have been possible without the kind support of my mentors, colleagues, and family, to whom I owe an extraordinary debt of gratitude and the financial generosity of a number of institutions whose aid I gratefully acknowledge.

I am profoundly indebted to my mentors at Harvard, particularly David Hall, who shepherded this project from its inception, invariably providing trenchant yet gentle criticism. His patience and magnanimity with his time during the writing of this book have been extraordinary. Robert Orsi provided his energy and insight to the developing work and the inspiration of his own attempts to understand religious actors and the scholars who study them. John O'Malley was also a pivotal contributor. Having inadvertently gotten himself roped into the project, he was, thankfully, too polite to extricate himself. I am grateful for his entanglement.

To their invaluable help was added that of my new Canadian colleagues at the University of Ottawa and beyond, who have graciously extended to me their warm welcome and kind help. Though I approached him as a complete stranger, Cornelius Jaenen, one of the finest historians of early Canadian contact, generously read multiple drafts of the work and made many helpful suggestions. Allan Greer kindly invited me to share my research with his Early Canada Forum at the University of Toronto and, through his own scholarly example, challenged me to come to a more complex, nuanced understanding of the phenomenon of aboriginal conversion. Mike DeGagne, Executive Director of the Aboriginal Healing Foundation, shared with me his expertise on Canadian aboriginal residential schools and their deleterious contemporary effects: I am grateful to him for contributing both his professional knowledge and personal insights. I would also like to thank Kim Cheena for sharing with me her experiences, and those of her family.

I would also like to acknowledge the invaluable assistance of those who helped me during my research in France. Father Anthoine Ruais of the Cathédrale Saint-Maurice in Angers greatly aided my evocation of Pastedechouan's seventeenth-century baptism. Armed with Jean Louvet's eyewitness report, he personally escorted me through his imposing church, pointing out where each of the ritual actions would have occurred and helping me to understand how the space has changed over more than three hundred years. Bernard and Monique Bourgeois and Yolande Stern of La Baumette were equally gracious, allowing me to tour their home, formerly the Recollet convent of La Baumette, in which Pastedechouan stayed during his five years in France, and providing a wealth of anecdotal information regarding its past. To their assistance was added that of the archival community. Jacques Maillard and Scott Marr obligingly provided their expert guidance in navigating the Anjou archives. Elisabeth Verry and Myriam Favreau of the Archives Départmentales de Maine-et-Loire were most generous with their time and expertise, as were Sylvain Bertoldi and Sandrine Monnier of the Archives Municipales d'Angers. I am grateful also to the staffs of the Bibliothèque Municipale d'Angers, particularly Marc-Edouard Gautier and the Bibliothèque Municipal d'Orléans, in particular, Anne Monginoux. I would also like to thank the staff of Le Musée Amérindien de Moshteuiatsh in Quebec, particularly Denise Robertson, for sharing their insights on contemporary Innu religion and culture.

Finally, I would like gratefully to acknowledge not simply my family's patience and support during the long years of this book's gestation, but their active contributions to it. Our constant discussion of the events of Pastedechouan's life and his reactions and motivations were critical in engendering within me an invaluable sense of distanced yet engaged empathy with the young Innu man who is at the heart of this work.

To this wealth of intellectual and moral support was added the generous financial backing of a number of institutions, which made the protracted process of research and writing possible. The University of Ottawa provided generous funding for research in France, which allowed for a much richer evocation of Pastedechouan's experiences there. My research and writing was supported by Harvard University's Frank Knox Memorial Traveling Fellowship, by the Canadian Government, and by the Whiting Foundation, through their Fellowship in the Humanities. I would like to extend to each of these organizations my sincerest thanks for seeing the value in this study of religion, culture, and identity in early modern Canada and for so generously supporting this project.

The Betrayal of Faith

Prologue

Pierre-Anthoine Pastedechouan, Voyager between Worlds

Wet and naked, he stood shivering, conscious of the hundreds of eyes fastened upon him. The holy water with which he had been drenched streamed in rivulets down his limbs to pool in puddles on the cold unevenness of the cathedral's stone floor. Standing with his back to the ornate altar of the miracle-working St. Serene, the young boy self-consciously circled himself with his arms, which, stripped of their traditional, colorful body paint, seemed pitifully denuded. His nostrils assailed by the sweet smoke of the incense, and his ears by the baritone pealing of the cathedral bells, the boy stared at the nightmarish depiction of the momentous struggle of Christ and his angels against the Beast and his demonic animals, vividly portrayed in the elaborate tapestries that adorned the church's dimly lit walls. Still puzzled, despite his mentor's lengthy explanations, at what seemed to him the impious treatment of animal "relations," and as unnerved as much by the images' frozen violence as by the crowd's steady gaze, the eleven-year-old boy ran his fingers through the unfamiliar sparseness of his once-long hair, while he silently repeated to himself the name which had just been bestowed upon him—Pierre-Anthoine. Sumptuously robed clerics then held out for him a white robe, softly glowing in the diffuse light, and crowned his cropped head with a baptismal bonnet. Accompanied down the nave by his noble godparents and missionary mentors and jostled by the rowdy, gaping crowd, the white-clad aboriginal boy slowly mounted the stairs of the ornate pulpit. Surrounded by a corona of candlelight, he sat alone, silently displaying himself as a newly won Christian soul, for the edification of all present.

It was April 1621. The imposing cathedral was that of St. Maurice, in

1

the walled French town of Angers. The young boy who was the mute center of the ceremony's opulent ritual, the newly renamed Pierre-Anthoine Pastedechouan, was an Innu, a Native American youth from the St. Lawrence River valley of distant Canada. Voluntarily surrendered by his people, who expected him to serve as their trade ambassador, he was brought from thence by gray-robed Franciscan Recollet missionaries eager to intimate the bright future of their newly established mission in New France. Through such young converts, they argued, the aboriginal societies of the New World could be transformed from mere trading partners into colonial strongholds loyal both to the Gallic king and to the embattled Catholic Church.

This book tells the story of the momentous meeting of two very different cultural and religious worlds, as experienced by this young boy, Pierre-Anthoine Pastedechouan, whose life bridged the fragile yet tenacious traditionalism of his Innu people, long adapted to congress with European traders, and the determined devotion of the early seventeenth-century French missionaries, who sought to transform forever their way of life. A sprawling narrative of cultural and religious negotiation, misunderstanding, and coercion on two continents, it explores, through the intimate detail of a single life, the struggle of colliding cultures to retain, control, and impose their respective religious identities during a period of unprecedented global change. This book traces the sweeping trajectory of Pastedechouan's brief life, from his 1608 birth in the vast, rugged hinterlands of the Canadian Shield, to his initial encounter with newly arrived Recollet missionaries, to his five years abroad in the austere, sun-drenched cloisters of their cliff-top convent, La Baumette. Documenting his accelerating alienation from his natal culture and his difficult readjustment once back on Canadian soil, it explores Pastedechouan's agonistic struggle, in the latter years of his life, to discern and assert his identity in the face of contradictory pressures both within and outside himself. Simultaneously vulnerable to the tug of his maternal society, in which, as a misfit, he contended for acceptance, and the fear-filled dictates of the rigid Catholicism with which he had been indoctrinated, the youth's key relationships with his eldest brother, Carigonan, a shaman, and with Paul Le Jeune, the Jesuit Superior of New France, each evinced a curious mixture of defiance, desperation, and deference. Pastedechouan's youthful encounter with French Catholicism had engendered within him a fatal religious ambivalence, which, by stranding him in the liminal space between childhood and adulthood, conversion and apostasy, and his natal and adopted cultures, eventually estranged him, with deadly results, from both his native community and his missionary mentors.

Pastedechouan's people, the Innu of early seventeenth-century Canada, were (and are) a migratory indigenous nation living along the north shore of the St. Lawrence River in what is today Quebec and Labrador. Dubbed by the Europeans who began, in the mid-sixteenth century, to encounter them as "les Montagnais" or "mountain people," because of their hilly homeland, they seem to have referred to themselves as the "Innu," meaning simply "the people." Not to be confused with their traditional northerly enemies, the culturally, religiously, and linguistically distinct Inuit, the Innu were (and struggle to remain) a society of nomadic hunter-gatherers. The Innu were precluded from the large-scale, semi-sedentary agriculture which characterized their westerly Wendat allies and southerly Mohawk enemies, both by their terrain, which was largely unsuitable for farming, and by their deep sense of sacred dependency upon the animals whom they hunted.

For the Innu, religion was inescapably relational, as the human and nonhuman community was envisioned as coextensive and interdependent. Both human and animal beings were considered "persons," who differed only in their outward appearance and in the degree of their power, sharing souls, personality, volition, and intelligence in common. The central preoccupation of Innu religious life was the continuous prevention and assuagement of illness, dearth, and death through the ritual establishment and maintenance of respectful, reciprocal relationships between persons, both human and nonhuman. Ritual persuasion of animals selflessly to surrender themselves for the slaughter ensured their human relatives' endurance in the face of an unforgiving environment. Without the cordial relations between hunter and prey carefully fostered in their elaborate ritual and art, the Innu's impressive arsenal of weapons and traps, would be, they felt, simply so much flint and wood.

As is apparent from their transspecies definition of their community, for Pastedechouan's people, identity was behavioral rather than biological. Any individual—be he European, a member of a rival aboriginal nation, or of the icy, inhuman race of the windigo cannibal giants—who was ritually incorporated into the community and who consistently respected their behavioral codes was seen as a bona fide Innu. At the heart of Innu diplomacy was the desire culturally to incorporate other groups, whether through the peaceful means of intermarriage, trade, and military alliance or the martial means of war, torture, and forced integration. When real or potential enemies adopted their social contract, the Innu successfully expanded their own collective safety zone during a period of unprecedented conceptual, economic, and military upheaval.

In sixteenth-century North America, a series of events unfolded which pushed Innu traditional mechanisms for maintaining and disseminating their corporate identity into overdrive. The emergence of powerful new military alliances amongst native groups and first contact with European traders accelerated Innu attempts to incorporate, either maritally or martially, potential threats or rivals.

Innu relations with southerly enemies in this period demonstrate the militant side of Innu identity politics. The increasing influence, unity, and cultural cohesiveness of five distinctive Iroquoian nations, who had begun, in the sixteenth century, to form themselves into the famed Iroquois League, prompted the simultaneous formalization of traditional alliances north of the St. Lawrence and exacerbated long-standing animosities between the Innu and their most tenacious adversaries, the Mohawk. Locked into a heated, protracted struggle for cultural supremacy, economic superiority, and geographical dominance, the Innu and Mohawk increasingly sought, through warfare and the after-battle treatment of captured prisoners, to render deadly foes into peaceful members of their respective communities. Through complex, violent rituals of adoption and assimilation, these rival cultures sought forcibly to transform war prisoners into living repositories for the returning souls of their beloved dead, effectively replacing the members of their communities lost to raiding, starvation, and childbirth.

Innu relations with their increasingly frequent European visitors during the same period, however, illustrate the friendlier face of Innu policies of cultural incorporation. For at least sixty years before Pastedechouan's 1608 birth, his people had been in intermittent contact with a ragtag group of European traders, who became their itinerant clientele for furs and in turn supplied the Innu, with weapons, utensils, and decorations. Such transactions were part of a worldwide economic revolution, in which the exploitation and redistribution of global resources was becoming both increasingly frequent and lucrative. European exploration throughout the sixteenth century had opened up fiercely competitive trading routes all over the world, notably to the "Spice Isles,"

linking disparate cultures through the medium of often profoundly un-
equal exchange.

From their first contact with European traders—who were compellingly described by Pastedechouan's grandmother as "bone-eating,
blood-drinking, metal bodied beings"—the Innu attempted emphati-
cally to convey their social and religious expectations, effectively inviting
these bizarre strangers to become part of their community. Though
French explorers and merchants were often unaware of the social and religious resonance of their actions in Innu terms, the two groups nevertheless gradually evolved mutually acceptable rules of cultural engagement.
This process was facilitated by aboriginal numerical dominance and control of sought-after natural resources, and by European recognition that
their financial success depended upon continued aboriginal cooperation.
In this, their first, economically driven encounter with Europeans, the
Innu successfully utilized traditional strategies of cultural assimilation
and economic diplomacy to negotiate a relationship that preserved rather
than threatened their key cultural values. Rapprochement with European
traders, then, though it affected Innu material culture and destabilized already fraught relations between rival aboriginal alliances, ultimately reinforced rather than challenged traditional Innu views of themselves and
their world.

Onto this established Innu-European "middle ground," forged in trade,
French Recollet missionaries marched in 1615. This conservative offshoot
of the protean Franciscan movement founded by St. Francis of Assisi in
1223 harbored an agenda in encountering native peoples of the Americas,
that could not have been in starker contrast to that of their merchant
countrymen. Influenced more by the religious revolution which had
rocked sixteenth-century Europe than by radical economic developments
within the same period, the Recollet eschewed commercial accommodation for religious imposition, cherishing the dream that aboriginal nations could be systematically reconfigured to become vanguards of
Catholic civilization. The religious unity and exemplary piety of these
utopian societies would then serve as an implicit rebuke to the disorder
and confessional heterogeneity of the Recollets' Gallic homeland.

Like the Innu, these Franciscans were responding to the disorientation of a century of accelerated social change by defiantly reaffirming
their religious and cultural identity whilst simultaneously seeking to impose it upon others. In sixteenth-century Europe, long held ideological,

religious, and spatioconceptual ideas regarding the nature of reality were shattering even as Catholicism's hegemony was eroding. Traditional assumptions about the nature of the earth's relationship to other heavenly bodies (and the theological realities with which they were reflexively conjoined) were being questioned. Moreover, heretofore unexplored areas of the globe were being encountered for the first time by Europeans. Columbus's fateful meeting with the inhabitants of the West Indies during his failed quest to find a superior trade route to the East Indies commenced an age of military, economic, and religious engagement between Europeans and the diverse inhabitants of a "new" hemisphere. Only twenty-five years later, Luther's defiant display of his Ninety-Five

Following the fracturing of European Christianity, Catholic missionaries saw the native peoples of North America as ideal "compensatory converts" to make up for the masses lost to Protestantism in Europe, cherishing a vision of New France as an ethnically diverse but confessionally united Catholic colony. (Courtesy of the National Archives of Canada.)

Theses on the doors of the Schlosskirche in Wittenberg sparked the Protestant movement, engendering a period of intense religious and political destabilization across Europe. In tandem with the disequilibrium produced by changing geographical realities and the questioning of dominant theological verities, this period also saw the emergence of a heliocentric worldview. The geography of the earth and its connection to the larger universe, and the nature of humanity and its relationship to the divine, then, were all systemically questioned within only two generations.

Whether geographical, astronomical, or theological, these revolutionary ideas and discoveries faced a violent backlash as sacred and secular authorities colluded to reassert conventional wisdom. Utilizing symbolic, ritual, or physical coercion, the Catholic Church and its allies attempted to force agents of change—be they scientists, Protestants, or the inhabitants of previously unknown continents—to abjure their "otherness" and conform to traditional European roles and realities, which the very existence of these agents seem to belie or challenge. The heliocentric reorganization of the universe was condemned as heresy, and its principal exponent, Galileo, chastened with the threat of excommunication. Luther and Calvin's novel and divisive theologies caused former neighbors, friends, and kin to regard one another with deepening suspicion across a widening confessional divide. Protestants and Catholics increasingly perceived the other as dangerously alien and politically nefarious, prompting an orgy of religiously motivated war and destruction across Europe. In France, the Huguenot minority intermittently faced the forced recantation of their faith, the kidnapping of their children to be raised in the "true church," and determined campaigns by Catholic authorities which sought nothing less than their utter extinction. Such phenomena were the European equivalents of the tortuous reinvention of postwar personal identity employed by aboriginal adversaries during the same era. Like their Native American contemporaries, Europeans sought to destroy what they could not transform into their own image.

Even as the Catholic Church impotently strived to reinstate its vanished hegemony in Europe, it searched, as if in restitution, for fresh cultural contexts in which to assert itself, sending its missionary representatives into parts of the map long marked "terra incognita" or "here be monsters." Like the Innu in their treatment of Mohawk prisoners of war, French missionaries to North America sought to transform the identity of those they encountered. Fresh from their battle with intransigent Protestants, Catholic missionaries pursued, in the "new" world, compensatory converts and the recreation of a shattered Catholic dominance.

Missionary dreams of imposing their embattled Catholic ideals upon the ancient cultures of early modern North America, while never realistic, were all the more quixotic given their tiny numbers. The first contingent of Franciscan Recollets to the St. Lawrence River valley in the days of Pastedechouan's youth could be counted on the fingers of one hand, numbering only four men. Unlike the colonial contexts of New Spain or New England, in which European invaders were militarily or demographically dominant, in seventeenth-century New France the small number of European settlers were vastly outnumbered by the aboriginal nations who surrounded them. Even by the 1670s, some sixty years after the 1608 foundation of Quebec, the European population of New France was, it has been estimated, only six hundred souls, clustered in a few modest communities along the fluvial arteries leading to the continent's heart.

Their lack of human resources, coupled with their commitment to conversion as exclusivistic rather than relativistic, quickly forced the tiny cadre of Recollets to miniaturize their original grandiose ambitions in the persons of aboriginal children. Perceiving the young as more amenable to religious influence than their elders, long "steeped in sin," the Recollets began day and boarding schools for native students and transported some children overseas for intensive religious reeducation in the French heartland, an ocean away from their native culture. In so doing, they fervently expected that such child converts, reunited with their families and communities, would ferment devotional revolution within their natal cultures, leading to their reorganization along European Catholic lines.

Recollet requests for youngsters to educate translated well into Innu terms, as children were traditionally given to cement important new alliances. Moreover, young Innu had previously traveled across the Atlantic to negotiate military or economic pacts with the highest echelons of French society. It was likely with little trepidation and with high expectations, then, that the Innu would have entrusted Pastedechouan to Recollet care, fully expecting that this young boy would return home with a wealth of relevant military and economic insights.

It was only upon Pastedechouan's belated return that the degree of the cultural misunderstanding which had occurred became evident. Unlike earlier Innu visits to France, arranged by traders eager to cement their ties with their aboriginal trading partners, Pastedechouan's had been a religious immersion, designed to transform completely his identity, allegiances, and religiosity. This transformation, however, provided his people none of the strategic benefits they had come to expect from such overseas endeavors. Pastedechouan's new religious sensibilities, moreover—by precluding his participation in the cycle of reciprocal relationships which characterized Innu social and religious life and by perpetuating his reliance upon religious authority figures—were seen as undermining his development into a responsible, mature Innu man. His people's astonished, dismayed apprehension of Pastedechouan's radical transformation fostered their belated recognition that these gray-robed missionaries cherished objectives far different from those of the more familiar traders, with whom they had long had congress.

Pastedechouan's experiences, then, illuminate critical, symmetrical patterns of change, struggle, and the strategic retrenchment of religious identity on both sides of the seventeenth-century Atlantic. His natal Innu culture and his adopted Gallic Catholicism each attempted to categorize, confront, and transform enemies on their own soil, replicating the dynamic of these experiences of attempted incorporation (with Mohawks and Protestants respectively) into their unfolding relationships with one another.

But while epic in its sweep and international in its setting, Pastedechouan's is also a very personal story of one individual's attempt to negotiate terrifyingly destabilizing change, within and without. His short, eventful life provides us with an unequalled glimpse into the mentality of a young convert subject to the extraordinary demands of the prevailing missionization models of his time, which emphasized the extraction and isolation of the vulnerable child from his home environment and coupled "francization" with conversion. By casting the boy's impressionable religious consciousness into their exclusivist mold, his Recollet mentors had sentenced him to a lifetime of religious confusion and cultural anomie as he sought to reconcile their demands with the cultural imperatives of his own family and community.

Pastedechouan's struggle to discern and assert his individual identity in the face of contradictory social and religious pressures is relevant to many today, particularly his own people, the Innu, who face a renewed assault upon their traditional way of life. Though this work focuses intimately upon the religious journey of a single early seventeenth-century Innu man, it is my hope that its examination of the Gordian knot of religion, culture, and identity will illuminate not simply a remote corner of the early modern Catholic world but, potentially, our own contemporary struggles with these issues during the current era of disorienting global change.

Q: What is a
Gordian knot?
Religion, culture + identity

1

"Thy God Has Not Come to Our Country"

Innu Childhood

The newborn's bawling abruptly broke the predawn stillness. Outside, in the wide, damp silence of early morning, the first hints of gray light appeared on the hilly horizon and glinted on the wide expanse of river. Inside the crowded birch-bark structure the smoky air was filled with excited murmuring and laughter following the long night of stoic suffering and vocal encouragement. After the women of her band had cut the umbilical cord and swaddled the baby in a comforting mantle of caribou hide, Pastedechouan's mother might have cuddled the youngest of her four sons close to her body and begun to nurse him.[1] While the pair, exhausted from their joint ordeal, would have lain, half-asleep, in the warm embrace of the fire, protected from the dew and chill of the early morning, the rising sun would have illuminated "The Breasts," the gentle twin slopes that had given the Innu summer gathering place of *Tadoussac* its name.[2]

As he peered at the surrounding world from the safe confines of the moss-lined bag in which his mother carried him during his early months, little Pastedechouan was beginning the long and complex process of "becoming Innu," observing, absorbing, and mirroring the religious and social practices of his people and imbibing, with his mother's milk, a sense of himself in relationship to the Innu culture that surrounded and defined him.[3] He would have learned, with each successive year of his passing childhood, how to relate to the human and nonhuman "persons" who constituted this Innu "us," as well as the sometimes threatening, sometimes benign "others" who existed outside of its firmly drawn physical and conceptual boundaries, others it was his personal destiny to intimately encounter.

This chapter seeks to accompany Pastedechouan through his process of conceptually apprehending the "us" and "them" who formed the dyadic heart of seventeenth-century Innu self-understanding. Consequently, our exploration of Innu religious and cultural life in this chapter will consider both intra- and interrelations. Evoking the holistic, diffuse, and highly gendered process of Innu education, we will attempt to view the contours of early modern Innu culture from a child's perspective. The preponderance of social and religious behaviors to which the Innu sought gradually to introduce their children involved the ritual articulation of an ethic of mutual respect and reciprocity between the relational agents who were together seen as constituting the Innu community. What Europeans classified as inanimate objects—plants, animals, rushing waters, heavenly bodies, atmospheric phenomena, or seasonal changes—were seen by the Innu as sharing what Europeans would deem exclusively human attributes.[4] The needs and desires of these "other-than-human persons," the Innu believed, must be discerned and respected so that in turn they would favorably dispose themselves to human beings.[5] Other-than-human persons were seen as honored relations who, sharing the human qualities of personality, volition, and a moral power, were deserving of the same etiquette as their Innu kin.[6]

Innu collective identity was also shaped by its diplomatic, economic, and military relations with rival human groups who, because of their refusal to observe Innu behavioral norms, were often perceived as potentially dangerous "others." Accordingly, this chapter will also address Innu relations with the Mohawk, their long-standing aboriginal foes, and with the European traders who had become, since the mid-sixteenth century, increasingly important players on the Innu stage. Relations with each of these groups sharpened and strengthened the distinctive Innu sense of self even as they challenged entrenched intra-Innu relational norms. Both the inward- and outward-looking aspects of Innu life, then—the community's collective attempts to introduce their children to their worldview and way of being, and their attempts conceptually and diplomatically to deal with outsider groups who failed to conform to their cherished relational ideals—provide key insights into Innu collective identity in the years of Pastedechouan's childhood.

Pastedechouan's People: The Contours of
Everyday Innu Life in Seventeenth-Century Canada

The egalitarian and cohesive nature of early modern Innu social and religious life can be intimated from its myth of origin, which posits that Paste-dechouan's people were descendents of Messou, a human culture hero, and his wife, a female muskrat who had once helped him to reconstitute the world after a disastrous flood.[7] Inaugurated by this primordial

An Innu family of seventeenth-century Canada. Dubbed by the French "les Montagnais" because of their hilly homeland, Pastedechouan's people were nomadic hunter-gatherers who had established an economic and military alliance with the French. (Courtesy of the Bibliothèque et Archives Nationale du Québec; photo: Pierre Perrault.)

marriage of human and nonhuman persons, Innu religious life took as its primary objective carefully to maintain cordial, reciprocal relationships between human beings and the animal relations from whom they were descended. Just as the maintenance of collective cordiality within the human community required that all its members follow behavioral prescriptions, such as the avoidance of antagonism and the redistribution of resources amongst community members, so the personhood of the animals upon whom the Innu were dependent necessitated the extension of this relational dynamic outside the intrahuman realm. The Innu felt that animals and all other-than-human-persons—which included mythological beings such as the *acten* (feared cannibal giants), animals, spirits, fish, plants, and powerful actors such as the *Manitou*—must continually be entreated to act benevolently toward the supplicatory community. In particular, game animals must be persuaded to sacrifice themselves for their human brethren by the latter's exemplary ritual behavior before, during, and after the hunt.

Though animals in particular were approached and propitiated as individuals, they were also thought to exist in familial relationships with one another. Each member of a species, whether beaver, bear, or moose, was believed to be represented and protected by its "elder brother" or "master," an unusually large, powerful member of the species who served as its diplomat to the human community, appearing in the dreams of hunters, much as shaman individually personified the human collective in their ritual dealings with animals.[8] Just as a shaman was distinguished from his fellow Innu by his degree of spiritual power rather than any coercive authority, so each animal master functioned as an advocate for rather than a governor of the individual member of his species. Such animal elders were often thought to be former human beings who had intermarried with a member of the species and who could assume human guise at will.

Innu beliefs regarding the architecture of living beings further reinforced the perception of human beings and animals as being, despite differences in their appearance, fundamentally similar. Both human beings and animals were seen as possessing souls which allowed the preservation of their individual identity in the shadowy land of the dead or their return to this world in another physical form following their demise.[9] Thus, recognition of the inevitability of human reliance upon animals colored Innu perceptions of the life to come as one in which, with some variations, community life continued relatively unchanged.

The contours of Innu life were definitively shaped by the regal, seasonal movements of Pipounoukhe and Nipinoukhe, other-than-human persons whose celestial perambulations, known as Achitescatoueth, betokened, respectively, the commencement of winter and the dawning of spring. With the advent of Nipinoukhe, winter slowly relaxed its brutal grip, and the great alluvial arteries that facilitated Innu transportation and communication once more began to flow. With their thaw, small, scattered bands of Innu, widely dispersed in kin-based winter hunting parties, would begin to congregate in considerable numbers at traditional centers such as Tadoussac and Quebec for fishing, trading, and socializing with one another and with allied groups.[10] The summer months, though short, were abundant with the teeming fish and eels of the St. Lawrence and its tributaries, the sun-warmed wealth of wild fruit, and cornmeal obtained through trade with agriculturalist allies, which supplemented reliance upon hunting, making it possible for larger groups to cohabitate without exhausting the available environmental resources. After Pipounoukhe had turned the leaves from green to gold, and the brusque breezes of October had blown them far and wide, the Innu would likewise scatter to the four winds. Breaking into smaller, mobile bands during the difficult winter months lessened the possibility that overpopulation would exhaust the game reserves in any one area.

Technology, adornment, and housing around the time of Pastedechouan's birth around 1608 were still largely traditional.[11] Though the Innu had freely adopted many European goods in the years since their first contact with these strange outsiders, they generally adapted new articles to long-standing customs.[12] Though many preferred to rely upon their forefathers' tried-and-true hunting technology, spectacularly noisy European firearms were intermittently available and became a regular, if modest, part of the Innu's formidable panoply of death.[13] Sturdy, sharp European knives found a range of domestic and martial uses, and durable new metal pots found a favored position at Innu hearths alongside traditional basketry and pottery.

The Innu also selectively utilized European clothing and decorative items, eclectically adapting them to their own ascetic norm and preferred uses. Pastedechouan would have worn the traditional caribou-hide clothing of his ancestors, its detachable sleeves and fringed leggings likely sporting traditional painting and dyed porcupine-quill embellishments, as well as glass beads bartered by the French. As it was a mark of respect to their prey to wear only their finest clothing whilst hunting, the Innu ornately decorated not only their outerwear and accessories but also the wide pack-straps used to carry or pull large quantities of meat homeward after a successful hunt. This penchant for elaborate beautification extended to the Innu toilette. Both tattoos and multicolored makeup were used by both sexes to make their faces and bodies as bold and colorful as their garments and personal effects. All ages and sexes wore their tresses long and pulled back from the face, greased, dressed, and decorated in elaborate styles.[14] The Innu regarded facial hair as ugly, prompting its removal by those men unfortunate enough to possess it.

Innu housing at the dawn of the seventeenth century was ideally suited for a small-scale, migratory society involved in intense, if intermittent, guerrilla warfare with a proximate foe. Homes were designed for quick collapse and easy transportation during a long winter's day of trekking and for rapid reassembly upon arrival at a new site, as the lengthening of blue shadows over the snow signaled the early onset of winter twilight. Constructed of stripped poles planted deep into the ground or snow which were then lashed together at the top, their exteriors were covered with large sheets of birch bark carefully sewn together, which the women were charged with transporting from site to site. The replacement of snow in the new home's interior with a thick layer of fur-covered boughs, the jerry-rigging of a leather or cloth door, and the starting of a fire in the center of its circular floor were all that was needed to ensure the safety and comfort of the dozen or so kinsmen of all ages that such a structure would house.[15]

Innu society was organized around the extended family and was notable for its fluidity, dynamism, and adaptation to the environment. Winter hunting bands were typically composed of twenty to forty men, women, and children related by blood, adoption, or marriage. Though the culture appears to have been matrilineal—an Innu man would see his sister's children rather than his own, as his heirs—Innu society was not uniformly matrilocal, nor was it matriarchal.[16] New couples appear to have had a great deal of freedom in choosing to winter with the husband's or the wife's relatives, depending upon where their skills would be most useful, though it seems to have been customary for newlyweds to spend at least one of their first three years together with the bride's family.[17] Accordingly, the constitution of hibernial bands was in a state of constant flux from year to year, as new marriages, births, adoptions, and deaths occurred. Even whilst in the hinterlands, these amorphous entities could double or halve in size, depending upon weather and hunting conditions, as groups came together to share bounty or splintered upon encountering dearth.

Though spouses in a union were generally both members of the Innu community, this was not necessarily the case. Potential partners could also come from neighboring, allied groups, such as the Kichesipirini, Algonkian, and Etchemin, with whom the Innu shared linguistic and cultural ties, or from the ranks of European seasonal traders or colonials. Such mixed marriages, whether intra-aboriginal or aboriginal-French, were an invaluable way of cementing amicable ties between peoples and provided the Innu with a forum in which gently to introduce new members of their group to its core ethics. Innu women appear to have exercised a great deal of autonomy in selecting their marriage partners. New couples often met and courted during the summer's large, riverside congregations, with their motley mixture of ingathered Innu, their economic and military partners, and European traders. Marriage prospects might also come from the ranks of their Mohawk enemies, as prisoners of war of both sexes were often spared death in order that they might be integrated, through ritual and marriage, into the ranks of Innu society. Through a series of elaborate ceremonies, war captives left behind their status as despised representatives of a hostile culture and came to be regarded as the newly reborn relatives of the bereaved Innu community.[18]

Before marriage, and in childless unions, the extramarital sexual liaisons of both husbands and wives were apparently regarded with complacency. However, a new mother's successful parturition both cemented her role as an adult woman in Innu society and considerably strengthened a couple's marital bond. The dissolution of fruitful unions was negatively perceived and was consequently less common, as most young Innu did not care to endure the barrage of shaming and shunning behaviors which enforced their culture's social norms. However, while serial monogamy appears to have been the norm for most seventeenth-century Innu, polygamy was also practiced, as this ensured the continuing well-being of widows and female orphans in a society highly dependent upon hunting, considered a male skill and prerogative, for survival. Though Innu ethics demanded the equitable redistribution of resources throughout the entire community, in practice ties of blood or marriage helped to keep potentially vulnerable individuals from social marginalization and subsequent privation.[19]

The Replication of the Community:
Innu Traditional Education

As much a part of everyday Innu life as gathering firewood or construct-ing traps and lures was the education of the rising generation. In the oral Innu culture, the mentoring of young children took place in the context of daily life and was a community affair. Virtually from infancy, children of both sexes were introduced to their society's key social and religious values: respect for the persons—human and otherwise—who consti-tuted their kin group; the fostering and maintenance of internal group harmony; the use of one's skills and resources in the service of collective rather than merely individual survival; and the exhibition of physical and emotional stoicism in the face of suffering. Pastedechouan, like other early modern Innu children, would have absorbed these cultural and religious ideals as the result of his careful mentoring by the adults of his community, his observation of their conduct toward himself and one another, and from his own engaged participation in social and ritual life.

Though the Innu regarded all persons as possessing a degree of amoral personal power, which they could chose to use for the community good or for asocial ill, they perceived the youngest members of their society as possessing this power in its weakest, most attenuated form, without the necessary preconceptions as to its optimal deployment. While European ideas about children during this period emphasized their purity and in-nocence, intimating their moral superiority to their corrupted elders, the Innu posited that children, while winsome, were undeveloped beings who needed to be mentored by their wiser elders to maximize their po-tential as adult members of the community. Children's increased power and the wisdom to use it correctly was seen as coming only with age, careful instruction by their elders, and exposure to and liaison with other-than-human persons, accrued through childhood ritual contact and crowned with the mentorship won through the youth's vision quest.

Innu attempts to form the developing characters of their children, to enhance their awareness of the ubiquity and power of other-than-human persons, and to equip them with both the practical and relational skills necessary for survival in the personalistic Innu world were tasks imperceptibly interwoven into the rhythms of day and night, work and recreation. Characterized by oblique methods and eschewal of formal, step-by step-instruction, Innu educational methods stressed children's informal observation and imitation of adult experts, such that seventeenth-century Innu children, "often did not realize that they had, in fact, been educated and trained by adult society."[20]

As well as being unobtrusive, Innu pedagogy was multifaceted, even paradoxical, combining demanding, hard-edged realism, exuberant, permissive affection, and an omnipresent sense of respect for children's individuality and personal autonomy. In mentoring their community's children, adults displayed a constant awareness of the challenges that they would face and a consequent desire to help them learn to bear with bravery and dignity the hunger, cold, and illness which invariably accompanied life in an unforgiving climate. Europeans noted with some astonishment the stoicism of even very young children, who struggled to demonstrate self-mastery under sometimes harrowing conditions. One observer commented, "A child having asked for something to eat, when he was told there was nothing at all, the poor little fellow's eyes filled, and tears as big as peas rolled down his cheeks and his sighs and sobs filled me with pity, although he tried to suppress them. One lesson they teach their children is to be brave in time of famine."[21]

When possible, adults sought to make a virtue of necessity, turning daily challenges into occasions for fulfilling competitive play for their children. Whether male or female, Innu youngsters were encouraged to vie with one another in feats of strength and endurance. On the long winter treks between hunting camps, Pastedechouan would doubtless have competed with his snowshoe-clad peers in marathons designed to showcase their courage and determination: "These little ones have their load, or their sledge to accustom them early to fatigue; and they try to stimulate them to see who will carry or drag the most."[22] Such contests wisely harnessed individual ambition, even in childhood, to serve the common good.

Even as they taught their children to face with equanimity the harsh realities of life in the boreal woodlands and encouraged them to view difficulties as stimulating challenges to their developing physical prowess and mental endurance, Innu adults regarded children with affectionate, playful, and permissive indulgence. Doted on by the many members of their extended families, children were denied nothing, parents going so far as to take food out of their own mouths should their youngsters express a desire for it. Childish pranks were generally regarded with amused tolerance. Even when Innu youth contravened their society's behavioral norms, they generally faced only indirect correction, such as oblique ridicule or the recounting of relevant cautionary tales. As mild as it was by seventeenth-century European standards, Innu social discipline, expressed both through the gentle teasing of childhood and the more forthright shaming practices of adulthood, seems to have been remarkably effective in enforcing individual adherence to the psychologically demanding renunciations necessitated by the Innu social contract.[23]

No matter how egregious the childish crime, physical punishment of young culprits was not a socially acceptable option. For the Innu, who saw violence as morally permissible only outside their social covenant, recourse to corporal punishment, particularly in the service of pedagogical goals, was as unconscionable as it was intellectually incoherent. Consequently, they regarded French recourse to the corporal punishment of children as both perplexing and shockingly cruel. The Jesuit missionary Paul Le Jeune records an incident in which French authorities, intent on punishing an "insolent" young Innu boy with a whipping, were confronted by one of his adult male relations, who, throwing a blanket over the child to protect him from the imminent blows, requested that he be permitted to bear the punishment in the boy's stead.[24]

Encouraged to be stoic in their endurance of environmental insults and indulged within the heart of their extended families as its lovable dictators, Innu children were seen from a young age as autonomous agents whose freedom to develop and learn must be unimpeded. As the Innu saw true wisdom as the product of direct, personal experience, they placed a premium upon children's autonomy in their individual learning process. Such was their faith in the pedagogical power of personal experience that Innu adults allowed children wide latitude to experiment and make mistakes so that they could learn from both failure and success how best to manipulate their physical and social environment. Recognizing that adults could not provide an education for their children, but merely help them to discover critical truths for themselves, the Innu extended to the youngest members of their society the same respect that characterized their relationship to all others, both human and nonhuman, whom they saw as constituting their community.[25]

"And for the Needle She":
The Gendered Nature of Innu Traditional Education

Though described by Europeans who encountered them as living in a raw state of nature, the Innu had evolved elaborate conceptual means to demarcate and dissolve differences within their society, particularly the dyads of male and female, young and old. Their unanimity as to what constituted their culture's most treasured values—illustrated by the assiduous cultivation, in children of both sexes, of a spirit of competent self-reliance, generous concern for others, and stoicism in the face of cold, privation, and pain—took place concurrently with children's education into sharply defined and powerfully enforced gender conventions. Age and gender roles were the chief means of articulating an ethic of complementary differences within Innu society, forming the basis for their division of labor: "The order which they maintain in their occupations aids them in preserving peace in their households. The women know what they are to do, and the men also; and one never meddles with the work of the other."[26]

The male domain consisted of the manufacture of weapons, hunting, fishing, diplomacy, religious leadership, and war. Female prerogatives included the care of young children; the production and decoration of shelter, clothing, and cooking implements; the ritual dismemberment and cleaning of game; the gathering, cooking, and preservation of food; the transportation of necessary items between camps; the procurement of firewood; and the maintenance of the central hearth.[27] The taboo around men performing women's work was, however, probably stronger than the converse. Paul Le Jeune recounts in 1633 that Manitougatche, an elder forced by his wife's lingering illness to gather firewood, did so at night so that his shamefully "womanly" actions would go unnoticed.[28] The Innu applied their own highly gendered expectations around the performance of daily activities to their observation of other peoples. For example, they perceived French missionaries as womanly because of their inability to hunt and their willingness to do "women's work" around the camp.

Like their broader cultural education, the sex-specific training of chil-

dren took place during the regular course of daily activities and intensified at puberty, when Innu young people were on the cusp of assuming
fully adult responsibilities and relationships. Ceremonies celebrating her
first menses marked the collective recognition of a girl's new, womanly
status. The termination of a boy's childhood education was marked by
the twin traumas of vision quest and war.

Because of Innu commitment to sex-specific vocational training, children spent much of their time in the company of their own gender. After
his initial two or three years spent in close proximity to his mother,
bonded by the intimate tie of breast-feeding, Pastedechouan would have
been abruptly thrust into a predominantly male venue, psychologically
and emotionally separated from his mother's influence at much the same
time as he was physically weaned.[29] Boys were encouraged to build
strong relationships with their male peers and adult mentors, such as
their brothers, fathers, and uncles. Just out of toddlerhood, Pastedechouan would likely have tagged along with his three older brothers, absorbing in an attenuated, age-appropriate form the skills and attitudes of
Innu male adulthood. Included in many community ceremonies, such as
those designed to find game, heal the sick, ritually distribute meat, and
punish enemy war captives, Pastedechouan would have been sheltered
from some of the more dangerous ceremonies, such as burials, which involved exposure to the newly liberated souls of the dead. Like other children of both sexes, Pastedechouan would have been excluded from
some feasts restricted to adult males; his presence at such occasions
would become acceptable only upon his physical maturation and passage through the rituals which recognized and sanctified it. Through the
ubiquitous games of childhood, such as tag and hide-and-seek, as well as
the more culturally specific pastimes of play hunting and lacrosse, Pastedechouan would have learned the speed, strength, and hand-eye coordi-
nation that he would need in his future career as a warrior and hunter.[30]
Male childhood education, then, was grounded in the Innu traditional
means of production and sought to foster competency in the cultural
and religious techniques necessary to the provision of game.

To read of the complexity of early modern aboriginal hunting methods
is to respect the ingenuity and skill of those who taught them and the difficult task of those who sought to master them. The Innu hunted a wide
variety of animals, utilizing an impressive range of tools and techniques,
including trained dogs, for their capture. The use of guns in seventeenth-

century Canada was not initially widespread, as the Innu preferred their own traditional methods for capturing animals. Early modern firearms were impractical for hunting, as they were noisy and inaccurate, and ammunition was only sporadically available from European traders. Moreover, guns may not have been seen as religiously acceptable substitutes for traditional methods of capture. An integral part of any Innu boy's childhood would have been his apprenticeship in the construction of assorted traps, nets, spears, lures, blinds, and runs and the acquisition of enough practical experience to utilize them effectively.[31]

But this panoply was just the technology of death. No matter how cunning their construction or skillful their utilization, these items were utterly useless if employed without entering into the correct ritual relationship with the sought-after animal. To train young boys in the use of this equipment without endowing them with the correct relational and religious tools to facilitate their affiliation with the animals they sought would have been, from the Innu perspective, an exercise in futility as well as irreverence. Accordingly, children of both sexes were taught from a young age the wide variety of religious techniques for encountering and influencing other-than-human persons and for correctly predicting their wishes, movements, and behavior.

All Souls: Innu Conceptions of Personhood

At the marrow of all the religious rituals to which the Innu assiduously introduced their children were core beliefs regarding the existence and behaviour of souls, which underlay their understanding of the nature of dreams, and human and animal experiences of life, death, and the afterlife. The Innu believed that all beings were endowed with a life essence, which at once enlivened and animated its possessor and, upon the destruction of its physical form, survived it. Souls, then, were not the sole prerogative of humans but were thought to be possessed by all persons sharing the characteristics of individual personality, intentionality, and power: mythological beings, animals, the seasons, heavenly bodies, plants, and objects conceptually grouped by Europeans under the heading "inanimate." Jesuit missionary Paul Le Jeune reported, with characteristic sarcasm, "the Savages persuade themselves that not only men and other animals, but also all other things are endowed with souls, and that all the souls are immortal; they imagine the souls as the shadows of the animate objects."[32] Unlike European Christians, who saw their endowment with a soul as separating them from the brute beasts, Innu soul beliefs asserted that both human and nonhuman persons were similarly and wonderously made, possessing endowments that allowed communication between soulful beings, just as they facilitated the extension of life after death. Innu words for "soul" and "shadow," *atca'k,* are the same.[33] While capturing their incorporeal, wraithlike conceptualization of a soul's physical appearance, such a characterization gives a misleadingly insubstantial impression of what was for the Innu the source and seat of all personal volition, emotion, and power. Like modern depth psychology, to which the Innu soul concept has been compared, an individual's soul was (and is) seen as encompassing not simply his or her conscious awareness and capabilities but a deeper strata which is both, paradoxically, self and nonself, at once familiar and unsettlingly foreign. The concept of the soul as being simultaneously the most profound, authentic version of oneself and an enigmatic internal stranger is one of the foundational concepts of Innu religious life. Rituals implicated the soul in one of two ways, as one either plumbed one's own inner depths to discover solutions to individual and collective problems or utilized one's soul to contact and negotiate with those of other beings.[34]

Dreams were seen as communication from one's inner "Great Man," or soul. Through dreaming, the conscious self could receive messages from this secret source or core of the self, which concerned the soul's communication with those of its animal counterparts. For the Innu, as for many other aboriginal cultures in the seventeenth century, dreams were a critical part of their spiritual economy—providing clues as to the reasons for collectively experienced dearth, disease, and death; suggesting ways to resolve interpersonal conflict within the group; facilitating demands upon the group's collective resources, particularly on behalf of the ill or bereaved; and giving glimpses into the future.[35] Dreams were valued as a venue through which nonshamans could communicate with elusive other-than-human persons on a one-to-one basis and served as the inspiration of much Innu art, as the designs carefully stitched onto hunting clothing and pack straps were often inspired (or demanded) by dream events.

As heightened forms of personal experience that represented a profound encounter with the personalistic forces upon which life depended, dreams were anticipated and carefully interpreted and shared. Dreams were a sort of internal form of scapulimancy, the diagnostic reading of partially burnt animal bones, and as an integral part of the Innu collective's attempts to understand and control reality, motivated many of their ritual actions. Invalids' dreams of a particular object or person were seen as valuable clues to what or who might cure them. A hunter's dream of a particular animal being was seen as predicting the imminent capture of members of that species: "If anyone, when asleep, sees the elder or progenitor of some animals, he will have a fortunate chase; if he sees the elder of the Beavers, he will take Beavers; if he sees the elder of the Elk, he will take Elks, possessing the juniors through the favour of their senior whom he has seen in the dream."[36] Dream landscapes, particularly visions in which particular areas of terrain were selectively illuminated by the sun, were seen as indicating clues as to where elusive prey, whether fish, fowl, or beast, might be found. Dream weather was also seen as accurately indicating future meteorological events.[37]

To fail to heed the messages encoded in one's dreams was felt to be a direct affront to the forces, both within and outside the self, which had produced them. To ignore dreams was to eschew the guidance of one's "Great Man" and the clues that animals afforded attentive hunters to their whereabouts. The seriousness with which the Innu took their dreams and visions is evident from the comment of Europeans, so common as to be almost ubiquitous: "Our lives depend upon the dreams of a Savage; because, if they dream that they have to kill us, they will surely do it if they can."[38] European fears of dream-inspired violence greatly exaggerated the threat, however, as they assumed an Innu literalism regarding what were often layered, ambiguous dream contents. Innu dreams were rarely simple imperatives, rather, they were glimpses into a still maleable future.

During the years of Pastedechouan's childhood, he would have been taught the Innu religious art of remembering and interpreting his dreams. The fact that he reportedly still did so in the latter years of his life, many years after his Catholic baptism, is testament to the power of his people's beliefs in dreams and their pivotal role in Innu religious communication and collective ritual life.[39]

The Survival of the Soul:
Death, Reincarnation, and the Afterlife

The Innu did not see the death of a human being or an animal as terminating the vitality of its soul. Though separated from the physical forms they had long animated, liberated souls, as shadowy doubles of the corporeal body, retained the deceased individual's distinctive identity and ability to affect the lives and fortunes of the Innu community.[40] Indeed, the soul of a newly deceased animal or human being was thought to have almost incalculable power. The Innu believed that a dispatched animal's spirit lingered near an Innu encampment for days to observe the human treatment of its corpse, motivating the scrupulous performance of elaborate after-kill rituals. If pleased with the prudent treatment of its remains, the animal's spirit would once again take on physical form and return to succor the community, beginning anew the cycle of propitiation, killing, thanksgiving, and reincarnation. If displeased, however, the animal's soul could prevent the capture of others of its species until it received suitable ritual reparations from the human community. Newly liberated human souls were considered so powerful that exposure to their presence was thought to risk the lives of vulnerable young children. Though not actively malicious, the deceased were seen as being lonely, fearful of the difficult journey to the Innu afterworld, and longing for reintegration back into the community from which death had newly severed them. As death in the midst of life, moreover, such souls were matter, powerfully and dangerously out of place.

As a child, Pastedechouan probably mourned the death of at least one of his grandparents. In deference to his youthful vulnerability, he would have been carefully protected to ensure that exposure to the deceased's newly escaped soul did not kill him. He may have watched, however, from a safe distance, as his deceased grandparent was taken out of the family shelter through a specially made door in its birch-bark covering, a measure which protected the aperture used by the living. Mourning, the young boy might have witnessed his grandparent's corpse being gently curled into the fetal position, laid in a bark-lined grave, and surrounded by the gendered implements he or she had utilized in life.[41]

Though lacking the moral dualism which characterized Christian heaven and hell, Innu conceptions of the soul's fate after death were dyadic in a different sense. Pastedechouan's people appear simultaneously to have believed both in a geographical afterworld and in a form of reincarnation in which liberated souls, both human and animal, returned to their former communities in new physical forms. Seventeenth-century Innu conceived of the land of the dead as an actual physical location, where newly released souls would be reunited with relatives who had predeceased them and where they would continue a lifestyle similar in most respects to that of terrestrial Innu life. Like many other aboriginal groups, they associated their afterlife with both the west (the direction of the sun's daily demise) and the celestial realm, leading some Innu to associate deceased souls with the stars and to equate the blazing yet ephemeral northern lights with the souls' joyous celebration. Envisioning the soul's journey to this distant land as long and treacherous, the Innu buried with the deceased a range of everyday implements, believing that the "souls" of these objects would aid the beloved relative on his or her perilous journey across the Milky Way or the *Tchipaï meskenau*—the celestial "path of souls." Once in the land of the dead, the soul, surrounded by family and friends, would be comforted by the familiarity of the daily and seasonal round, which continued with only minor inversions. In the afterworld day and night were reversed: the dead slept with the dawn and began their nightly stalking of the souls of game with the twilight, as "their day is the darkness of the night, and their night is the light of the day."[42]

It is clear that even as they envisioned a celestial afterlife, the Innu also believed in the reincarnation of both human beings and animals. Long overshadowed by European analysis, which stressed aboriginal conceptions of the afterlife in geographical terms, a view that had something in common with Europeans' own preconceptions, early modern Innu belief in reincarnation has been poorly understood, perhaps because the doubleness of Innu afterlife concepts can make them appear contradictory, even incoherent. How can a single belief system hold that the afterworld is a distant, westerly land while simultaneously positing that human and animal souls, enrobed in new flesh, can and do return to the land of the living? Pastedechouan's people, however, evolved a number of sophisticated means of yoking the two concepts together in intellectually and emotionally satisfying ways. Reincarnation answered the wrenching question of what happened to souls, such as those of the very young or extremely aged, who might be too inexperienced or too feeble to make the dangerous, demanding journey to the Innu afterlife. Moreover, the shadowy western world of the dead could be thought of as an intermediate stage for souls between earthly gambits, a sort of celestial waiting room.[43]

Though the Innu conceptually separated names and souls, the two were intimately linked both to one another and to their concept of reincarnation. Saying the name of the deceased was believed to gain the (possibly dangerous) attention of his or her soul. Moreover, in bequeathing a living person with the name of the beloved deceased, one effected, in some sense, their presence in that person. A young child named for a powerful ancestor in some sense "became" or was protected by that ancient figure. Likewise, an enemy captive who ceremonially received the name of a newly deceased Innu casualty of war was no longer perceived as a belligerent stranger but as a beloved friend or relation returning to the Innu body politic.[44]

When examined from a slightly different analytical angle, it is immediately apparent that Innu beliefs in both reincarnation and an afterlife, though seemingly contradictory, both served the function of maintaining community cohesion, perhaps the central social value of Innu culture. While in one sense beliefs and practices surrounding death emphasized the disjuncture between living and the dead, as seen in the community's fears that exposure to the liberated spirit might harm the living, their belief in reincarnation kept open the possibility that the dead would once again return, suitably fitted out with a new earthly form, either that of a newborn baby or that of an enemy captive.

The way in which the Innu envisioned their afterworld also displays the value of community cohesion through its marked continuity with earthly life and its promise that there, families long separated by death would finally be reunited. Because they believed in the community distribution of justice during an individual's lifetime, the Innu did not fear, as did so many of their Christian contemporaries, that a final separation of the wheat from the chaff and the sheep from the goats would split husband from wife or child from parent. The arduous journey to the land of the dead along the path of the Milky Way, while certainly a test of determination and physical courage, was not one of moral fitness. For the Innu, one's earthly behavior did not determine one's fate in a dualistic afterlife.

Innu children were thus taught that their relationship with animals— ancient kin who, like them, possessed powerful souls—was profound, the fundament of their experiences in this life and that of the world to come. Children were encouraged to analyze their dreams to help their elders, particularly parents, to locate game and to anticipate and avoid relational difficulties with other-than-human persons. Elders introduced children to a range of rituals to be employed before, during, and after the hunt, to ensure that relational integrity between the human and nonhuman world was maintained and strengthened through predictable, amicable transactions.

Innu Hunting Rituals

As hunting was, for the Innu, a "holy occupation," prehunting ceremonies served two goals: to propitiate and to locate animals.[45] These, however, were not exclusive categories but rather two aspects of a single goal, as it was believed that animals' revelation of their whereabouts to human hunters signaled their willingness benevolently to surrender themselves on behalf of the Innu community. Conversely, animals' refusal to disclose their location communicated their dissatisfaction with the ritual status of their would-be hunters or their disgust with the breaking of critical taboos in the past. Thus, inquiry into an animal's location was also, inevitably, an investigation into the status of relations between human and other-than-human persons.

In addition to the daily propitiation of animals with which Innu children started their day, shouting as they emerged from their shelter, *Cacouakhi, Pakhais Amiscouakhi, Pakhais Mousouakhi, Pakhais* ("Come, Porcupines; come, Beavers; come, Elk"), the youngest members of the community were taught a variety of techniques to divine the wishes, intentions, and movements of animals.[46] Along with his siblings, Pastedechouan would doubtless have witnessed his parents' attempts to discern animal location and to predict future weather patterns through the interpretation of the family's dreams and through "scrying" or "sculpimancy," the ritual interpretation of animal bones.[47] Small markings on the ritually burnt bones were felt to contain a wealth of information on animals' disposition toward their would-be hunters. When such individual, ad hoc practices failed, however, the Innu turned to ritual specialists to perform dramatic public ceremonies, in which the other-than-human persons of the Innu pantheon became demonstrably present to the entire community.

The most important of these collective sacraments was that of the "shaking tent."[48] While all Innu rituals, in one way or another, provided a venue in which the human and nonhuman, the living and the dead could meet and interact, most rituals were envisioned as the trespass of human souls, through dreams or trance, into other-than-human enclaves. The shaking tent ceremony, on the other hand, represented the human community actively inviting other-than-human persons to come into their midst. Generally held in the difficult circumstances engendered by dearth or illness that remained stubbornly unassuaged by individual attempts at amelioration, these prolonged rituals allowed the communion of human and nonhuman ritual actors and the ritual remediation of human problems.

For this ceremony, a special temporary lodge was erected. Like ordinary Innu homes, it was constructed of long stripling poles placed at regular intervals, tied together at the top and covered with furs or bark. The ritual specialist known as a *Kakushapatak,* having retreated alone into this enclosure, would be secured within it, and the door would be sealed. Shaking tent ceremonies were generally held in the evening, with the community congregated in a circle around it, attentively awaiting the advent of other-than-human personages inside the enclosure.[49] For a long time, only the low voice of the Kakushapatak could be heard entreating and invoking the beings, whose individual arrivals were signalled by a violent shaking of the tent, the gyrations of which were described by the confounded Europeans who witnessed them as being unattributable solely to the actions of the ritual leader inside it:

> At first, as I have said, he [the ritual specialist] shook this edifice gently, but, as he became more animated, he fell into so violent an ecstasy, that I thought he would break everything to pieces, shaking his house with so much force and violence, that I was astonished at a man having so much strength, for, after he had once begun to shake it, he did not stop until the consultation was over, which lasted about three hours.[50]

Following their dramatic appearance, the identity of each actor would be immediately apparent to the assembly from the timbre of its voice or the jocularity of its comments (the turtle, popularly perceived as a joker, rarely failed to intrude a note of levity into what were otherwise solemn, life-or-death proceedings). For the early modern Innu, other-than-human persons were not disembodied, abstract concepts but fully formed individual personalities who could be readily distinguished one from another because of their characteristic forms of self-expression.

After all of the participants, human and nonhuman, had been assembled, the ritual leader would engage in a dialogue with them, posing the questions and concerns of the group as a whole, which ranged from the general to the particular: Why was the community being punished by the illness, discord, or dearth? By whom? What must be done to recover the favor of the affronted party? What would the snows be like this winter? In what direction would game be found? Would an invalid recover or die? Having received answers to their queries, whether merciful or harsh, the ritual would conclude with the performance of tremendous feats by the empowered Kakushapatak. One of the most common and, to European observers, the most puzzling of such feats was the ritual specialist's walking on top of the shaking tent, without losing his balance on its steep pitch or falling through the bark or furs which covered it. Such actions led Jesuit missionaries to question whether aboriginal ritual specialists obtained their powers from diabolical forces. Le Jeune, the Superior of the Jesuits from 1632 to 1639, wrote in 1633, "I am inclined to think that there are some of among them [the Innu] who really have communication with the Devil, if what the Savages say is true; because some are seen to walk upon their huts, without breaking them down."[51]

The shaking tent ritual, undertaken to ameliorate the interpersonal relations upon which a successful hunt depended, dramatically demonstrated the interpenetration of human and nonhuman in the Innu universe. The Kakushapatak, in hosting and questioning other-than-human beings, made dramatically real for the whole community the presence and personality of these animal actors, who so affected the contours of their daily life.

Having located animals through dreams, scapulimancy, or the shaking tent ritual, thus ascertaining their willingness to be killed to succor the community, the Innu would commence their hunt, sporting their specially decorated clothing and accoutrements, which either memorialized dream events or, honored the souls of slain animals. From these animals, chief amongst them beaver, porcupine, moose, and caribou, the Innu sought the most basic elements of their survival: food and clothing. Though they had nothing as critical to offer in return, nevertheless hunters sought to make this fundamentally unbalanced human-animal relationship more reciprocal by promising their prey rich presents, a quick death, memorialization in paint or thread on their ceremonial hunting clothing, and, most critically, the prudent collective use of their body. Often, just before an animal was killed, it would be addressed as a revered grandparent and explicitly asked permission for its life to be taken. Immediately after its slaying, hunters presented their prey with compensatory presents. Doubtless Pastedechouan would have witnessed, at the site of a fresh kill, his father reverently placing offerings of tobacco into the dead animal's mouth. Indeed, it was customary at a kill site for Innu hunters to reverently smoke their own tobacco, keeping the animal's newly released soul company as it simultaneously enjoyed its own gift.[52]

In their postmortem treatment of each animal species, the Innu scrupulously followed ritual rules they believed had long ago been set by the animal master or elder of each species. Adherence to the letter of this compact was monitored by none other than the slain animal itself, as its soul hovered near the kill site, observing the treatment of its remains. The Innu respected the stipulations of some species that their entire body must be put to use: hide, bones, flesh, and entrails. Their adherence to this request led to the fashioning of bone implements even after European metal substitutes became available, and inspired some to acts of ingenious creativity (for example, caribou scrota were tanned, decorated, and utilized as small storage bags for food and sundries).[53] They also strictly adhered to animal specifications regarding what portions of their bodies could be eaten by the various gender and age cohorts of Innu society. For example, a bear's head could be consumed only by the most elderly male of the group, and the rest of its flesh could not be eaten, or even touched, by the immature, defined in Innu terms as the children and uninitiated youth of both sexes. Moreover, Pastechouan's people honored each animal's specific preferences for internment: beavers wanted their bones returned to the water, bears desired their skulls elevated in trees so that they could continue to observe occurrences in their sylvan home, and caribou, quite inconveniently, wished their antlers transported from camp to camp by the mobile Innu.[54]

Certain actions were felt to dishonor all animals, regardless of species. Eating a female animal's embryo was thought to signal a wanton disregard for her maternal feelings.[55] Wasting an animal's flesh, failing to treat and dress its hide and throwing its bones to dogs were all actions which were felt to connote a lack of respect for the animal's self-sacrifice. The Innu believed that failure to adhere to the strict rules surrounding the ritual dismemberment and handling of animal remains invited punishment upon the whole group by the offended animal: "Before the Beaver was entirely dead, they told me, its soul comes to make the round of the Cabin of him who has killed it, and looks very carefully to see what is done with its bones; if they are given to the dogs, the other Beavers would be apprised of it and therefore they would make themselves hard to capture."[56] The breaking of such taboos, whether inadvertent or deliberate, was looked upon as being a deeply horrifying, antisocial act which imperiled the group's most treasured objective: its collective survival.[57]

Innu boys, then, in being taught to hunt, were being instructed not simply in the manipulation of technological devices to capture animals but in the art of establishing and maintaining cordial relationships with these powerful other-than-human persons before, during, and after their ritual slaughter. Their goodwill must be secured, their location determined from dreams and prognostication, and their physical forms captured, appeased, killed, and utilized in a respectful manner that would allow their released souls to be reborn, so as to facilitate the continuation of this symbiotic relationship. "Success" in hunting, then, did not entail merely the slaughter of animals, for if one acquired or utilized them in an illicit or disrespectful way, the short-term gain of a few days' meat would pale in the face of the possible privation these powerful agents could wreak in response. Though the childhood education of both male and female children would have engendered in them a similar attitude of respect for these other-than-human persons, boys, as young hunters-in-training, would likely have felt an intensified identification with their would-be prey.

Embracing Adulthood

In addition to defining each gender in terms of the other and demarcating their complementary responsibilities in the shared project of collective survival, the education of Innu boys and girls also encompassed their graceful transition from childhood to maturity. The Innu greatly valued the wealth of knowledge brought by accumulated experience, respecting the elderly of both sexes as repositories of wisdom. Because age brought with it increased social status, youth eagerly sought ritual experiences which would cement their new status as respected and independent adults.

In the female sphere, it was physiological indicators that provoked community confirmation of a girl's new adult status. Ceremonies surrounding her first menses marked a girl's initial recognition as a mature, and hence marriageable, woman; however, her reception as a fully adult member of the community was contingent upon her successful reproduction.[58] For a young boy, achievement of adulthood hinged on his successful demonstration of competency in the twin diplomatic roles of male adulthood: hunter and warrior. To prove himself as a hunter, a youth had first to secure a personal animal patron through a period of volitional, ecstatic starvation. To become a respected warrior, the boy must demonstrate his commitment to the group's collective safety and honor through his engagement with the Innu's traditional aboriginal rivals, the Mohawk.

Ontological realities and pedagogical imperatives intersected during the paramount experience of an Innu youth's life: his vision quest.[59] The apex of a boy's education, this was not simply a celebration of his physical maturation, as the timing of his ritual initiation was not tied to involuntary physiological indicators. Rather, a boy's mental preparedness and religious attunement were seen as indicating his readiness to encounter the other-than-human agents who would help him to achieve his new status as a respected adult male in Innu culture. Nevertheless, vision quests were generally undertaken after the onset of puberty but before the commencement of sexual relations. After extensive preparation, the youth would walk, bereft of supplies, alone into the wilderness, traveling a considerable distance from his family encampment. Eschewing all necessities—food, shelter, and sometimes even water for a period of days—the young man would besmirch his face with ashes to make his suffering appear all the more pitiable to other-than-human onlookers, whom, it was hoped, would thus be moved to aid him. Unlike rituals that attempted to create or demonstrate reciprocity between the Innu and their nonhuman kin, the vision quest eloquently acknowledged the fundamentally unbalanced nature of the human-animal relationship, encouraging human beings to present and experience themselves as wholly dependent upon their powerful other-than-human patrons, whose generous gifts of their knowledge and their very bodies made Innu existence possible. In this period of starving isolation, a postpubescent youth would, through his epiphanic dreams and waking visions, identify and bond with an animal patron, who would impart to her young charge gifts of hunting prowess, speed, strength, wisdom, or healing powers, founding a relationship that would endure for the remainder of his life. In return, however, the guardian animal demanded special consideration from her protégé, which probably included his lifelong abstention from her flesh. Imparting a sense of mature identity and a personal connection to the other-than-human world, the completion of a successful vision quest would have marked a critical transition in a young boy's life.

Following the isolation and privation of their vision quest, male adolescents sought opportunities to demonstrate publicly their ability to avenge and protect their community through battle. Indeed, the highly stylized practice of warfare and enemy capture was, for both the Innu and their antagonists, a key means of forging their next generation of leaders. Along with the recently bereaved, young men were the chief instigators of the continuous, small-scale skirmishes that characterized Innu–Mohawk conflict. The impatient youth of one or the other rival cultures often provoked conflict to gain opportunities to display their bravery and worth to their male peers and elders. Warfare in early modern Innu society, then, was as much a culmination of the male educational process as were the vision quests of late puberty.[60]

Though its methods were seamlessly integrated into the daily round of life and often took the form of play and contest, education of the community's boys had a serious aim: to bequeath the cultural skills, mental outlook, and religious attunement that would produce responsible, self-sufficient men capable of shouldering the burden of providing for and defending themselves, their families, and their wider community in a context in which the margin between survival and disaster was often distressingly thin. Each of these experiences provided an opportunity for an Innu youth to assert himself on the key relational vectors integral to the articulation of Innu collective identity. Through his visionary experiences, a boy took his place as a diplomat in the ongoing, critical negotiations between human and animal communities, who together constituted the wider Innu "us." In his battle experiences, the boy proved himself a warrior committed to the forceful assertion of Innu cultural priorities in the face of a hostile "other."

"Persons, Power, and Gifts": Key Innu Social and Religious Imperatives

As we have seen, the Innu of early modern Canada lived in a personalistic universe in which social and religious imperatives were mutually reinforcing, and thus cannot be examined separately without conceptual distortion. The Innu systemically extended the close kin relationships of their small-scale society into their dealings with nonhuman beings, enshrining as the common aim of their social and religious interactions the maintenance of harmonious, mutually beneficial relationships among codependent human and nonhuman entities. Innu assumptions that the other-than-human actors they daily encountered possessed intelligence, personality, and volition analogous to their own allowed them to extend to these agents the same relational covenant which had brought them the high degree of security and stability they enjoyed within the strictly human community. By creating standards of behavior that reflected their core values and by seeking to persuade others—whether animal prey, other aboriginal groups, or wholly foreign elements, such as Europeans, to adopt their "rules of engagement"—the Innu sought to make their world more predictable. Binding their own to an etiquette which stressed cooperation, generosity, and reciprocity forged a community in which exacting expectations for conduct were uniformly known and observed, creating an island of safety in a world fraught with change and hardship. By ceremonially extending this social ethic to the human and nonhuman "others" that they encountered, the Innu hoped that the respect and benevolence they telegraphed would be mirrored back to them, thus expanding this "comfort zone."

To express such views about ideal personal relationships was to articulate larger concepts concerning the nature of "persons, power, and gifts."[61] Because the Innu saw reality in familial terms, mapping onto their experience of the larger world the kin relationships that constituted their intimate face-to-face society, all outcomes—good fortune in hunting, a successful birth, safe voyage, devastating illness, or persistent privation—were seen as being the result of relational transactions. Their characteristic response to any propitious or unfortunate event was therefore not to ask "What happened?" but rather "Who did this?" While persons differed in their capabilities, all persons, large and small, human and nonhuman, were thought to possess a degree of personal power which could be employed either to thwart or to aid collective objectives. Consequently, Innu socioreligious interactions consistently aimed to persuade persons to employ their amoral power for the attainment of socially beneficial ends: human beings were encouraged to follow Innu behavioral norms, which valued the collective above the individual; animals, to sacrifice themselves to succor their human relations. Persuasive articulations as to why they should do so were often accompanied by the sharing of resources or giving of gifts. Potential allies, as well as animal prey, were urged to enter into a reciprocal relationship with the Innu in order that the basic physical and psychological needs of each could be continuously met through cooperative, mutual provision.

Though contemporary anthropologists and historians have often applauded the optimism and idealism of the Innu interpersonal ethic and the egalitarian cultural forms which it generated, in fact Innu behavioral rules betray a profound caution regarding the nature of persons and their power. The formality and guardedness with which human and nonhuman agents within and without the community were approached, and the repetitiveness with which they were enjoined to display benevolence, illustrates Innu perceptions of the unpredictability of persons and the fundamental amorality of their power. Power in Innu terms was apprehended as the ability decisively to influence events: its moral coloration was determined exclusively by the results of its operation.[62]

That the Innu perceived power in fundamentally amoral terms becomes readily apparent when we examine their perception of those within their society who were thought to possess the highest degree of human potency: shaman and other religious specialists such as Kakushapatak. Shaman healed the sick, led collective ceremonies, diagnosed and ameliorated relational problems, and aided in the propitiation and detection of game. Each shamanic function, in the broadest sense, was shared by every member of the religiously egalitarian Innu society. As we have seen, the Innu believed that dreams enabled each person to communicate both with their own deeper selves and with a range of other-than-human persons, from whom they could obtain prophetic knowledge of current and future events. Shaman, however, were believed to be able to enter into such alternate states of consciousness virtually at will. A shaman's superior ability in controlling the composite parts of himself to investigate and remediate the community's ills through dialogue with the Innu pantheon was the principle source of his considerable prestige in Innu culture.

Despite their status, however, ritual specialists inspired ambivalence in the communities they served, as their higher degree of personal power and wider range of religious abilities provoked disquiet as well as reassurance. Shamans' role as a liaison between the human and nonhuman worlds gave them a degree of influence in an otherwise egalitarian society, which could easily lead to their resentment by the independently minded Innu. The healers in their culture, shaman were paradoxically seen as being at once the source of and cure for human illness. In keeping with Innu ideas regarding the fundamentally amoral nature of personal power, ritual specialists were believed to have the ability to inflict as well as to ameliorate suffering and to deal death as well as protecting life.[63] An individual's accrual of power, then, was as unnerving as it was comforting—provoking anxiety that the powerful would utilize their personal potency against the community rather than on its behalf.

Just as the Innu blended grateful awe with resentful fear in their attitudes towards their religious specialists, their traditional narratives combined optimism regarding their culture's ability to persuade the most aberrant beings to adopt their social conventions with an unsettling awareness of ever-present asocial tendencies within the group. Innu moralities tales involving the *atcen* or *windigo,* frightening giants from the icy north who sought to eat human flesh, impressed upon children the inevitable triumph of Innu social norms.[64] The consistent theme of such stories was the "taming" of the atcen by Innu values of respectful, generous, community-oriented behavior. Supplementing children's personal experience and observation of adult Innu behavior, the elaborate recitation of such tales encouraged youngsters cautiously to extend respect and generosity even to apparently unreceptive, antisocial strangers, thus emulating the domestication of the fearsome acten by the friendly formality of the stories' protagonists.

While the happy endings of many of these windigo stories, which feature the "Innuification" of cannibal giants, display Innu faith in the power of the community's adaptive mechanisms to contain outbursts of immoral, predatory selfishness, the ubiquity of cannibal themes in traditional narratives indicates that primal anxieties regarding personal power, self-assertion, and privation nevertheless remained strong in the Innu psyche. Windigo tales paradoxically expressed and assuaged fears that Innu socialization would prove inadequate to prevent the breaking of critical taboos in situations of extreme duress. The fact that these inhuman, wintry beings were thought to have the ability to assume the form of a beloved family member starkly expressed deeply held Innu fears of being killed and consumed by kin desperate to survive famine or, worse still, of themselves perpetrating such an unthinkable crime.[65]

Windigo stories at once reflected and distorted this aboriginal group's tragic historical experiences with starvation-induced cannibalism. Heavily dependent upon animals for their survival, the Innu knew that starvation always loomed as a chilling possibility during the periods of scarcity which inevitably punctuated the seemingly endless months of a Canadian winter. Narratives of the acten giants effectively recast the actions of those who, pressed by fearful privation, had killed and eaten their own family members, suggesting that it was not they who had committed these actions but rather the windigo who possessed them. Even as they gnawed the bones of their beloved deceased, Innu cannibals would realize that, even if such tactics kept their bodies alive, they would simultaneously effect their social death. Many of those whom, in desperation, turned to intra-Innu cannibalism were unceremoniously excised from their communities. The cannibals' horror at their own actions, however, often exceeded even that of their punishers: Innu who had tasted the flesh of their kin, unable to live with their subsequent guilt, frequently took their own lives. Those who refrained from this ultimate expression of regret nevertheless typically regarded themselves with utter loathing. Having nourished themselves with forbidden flesh, aboriginal cannibals often regarded themselves as having effectively abdicated their personhood, relinquishing any claim to be perceived and treated as a human being by others: "Although I still exist, I cannot any longer consider myself a human being."[66]

Nowhere can the strength of the Innu distinction between "us" and "them" be seen in starker relief than in their cultural attitudes to cannibalism. Cannibalism was not taboo in Innu culture for the apparently obvious reason, that it involved the eating of human flesh. While repulsed by those who ate their own when forced to do so by extreme privation, the Innu embraced ritual cannibalism of their enemies as an expression of revenge, a test of the enemy warrior's endurance, and as a means of assimilating the positive characteristics of fallen captives for themselves. Even as a very young child, Pastedechouan would have participated in the nightlong ritual torture of captured Mohawk prisoners, seeking to have his enthusiasm rewarded with a piece of a captive's heart. As he swallowed the raw flesh, Pastedechouan would doubtless have treasured the hope that, in time, he would come to emulate the enemy warrior's exemplary courage.[67]

That Pastedechouan's people forbade privation cannibalism whilst simultaneously valorizing ritual cannibalism suggests that the cultural and religious identity of the victim was central in determining the validity of the action. Cannibalism of Innu by Innu was taboo because it violated the culture's most treasured values, which elevated collective above individual survival. The fear that starvation might so unhinge someone as to kill and eat one of their own—the fundamental selfishness of that act—was what so horrified and appalled early modern Innu, not the mere consumption of human flesh.[68]

Innu Valuation of Collective over Individual Survival

As already intimated, Innu culture by necessity valued the collective over the individual. The harsh physical setting of their homeland—with its long, extreme winters, its engrained tradition of incessant intra-aboriginal conflict, and with the advent of Europeans the specter of epidemic—dictated that the Innu privilege community over individual survival. The genius of their culture and religion was to make the individuals who constituted Innu society themselves concede, not merely intellectually but emotionally, the wisdom and necessity of such a valuation. The Innu set about this task of physical and social self-preservation both by establishing clear cultural guidelines to be followed when the trajectories of individual and group survival clashed and, perhaps more importantly, by creating a system in which the natural desire for competitive self-assertion was harnessed to serve rather than endanger group well-being.

Although cannibalism of one's kin was seen as an abomination, euthanasia was practiced when mobility in search of food meant the difference between the community's collective survival and its demise. In his youth Pastedechouan likely would have witnessed the mercy killing, during periods of extreme privation, of the terminally ill, immobile aged, and occasionally his own childish peers, the very young. When long hunger came to debilitate those who habitually dragged their sick or immobile relatives on stretchers through the woods, the latter were either killed or left to die, thus allowing the remaining strength of younger family members to be used in the service of their own survival. "They kill him, as much to free him from the sufferings that he is enduring, as to relieve themselves of the trouble of taking him with them when they go to some other place."[69]

Similarly, nursing infants and toddlers who had lost, with the death of their mothers, their primary source of nourishment, were also slain when a suitable wet nurse was unavailable and the child was as yet unable to consume the the traditional Innu diet. Though the Innu doubtless saw such actions as profoundly merciful, as they prevented the further suffering of such individuals by hastening the blissful release of their all-but-inevitable death, the primary purpose of such practices was to ensure the survival of as many of the remaining members of the hard-pressed group as possible.[70]

As well as setting up clear rules privileging communal survival should the preservation of individuals collide with group's best interests, the Innu sought in their daily life to make the twin goals of individual and collective endurance synonymous by channeling the individual instinct for self-preservation and competitive self-display into the service of collective perpetuation. As already explored, adults wisely utilized childish competition to make the difficult realities of transporting life's necessities through the northern woods an anticipated pleasure for their children rather than a dreaded inconvenience. But it was the ability of Innu culture to harness adults' desire for competitive self-assertion to serve, rather than thwart, collective ends that was perhaps the most critical factor in the endurance of the community. The reciprocal dynamics of Innu social and religious life enhanced individual social prestige even as it maximized collective benefits. Feasting and gift giving maintained a relationship of mutual dependency between community members, which, while it rewarded individual initiative with social prestige, ultimately worked to benefit the whole community.

Though their society has been described as "egalitarian" and hierarchically "flat," it is important to note that early modern Innu culture did recognize differences in human ability, power, and prestige.[71] The Innu power continuum placed children in its lowest ranges, initiated adults at its center, and elders and shaman at the highest human extreme, surmounted only by the superior potency of other-than-human persons. Moreover, Pastedechouan's people acknowledged that human beings displayed different levels of skill in food acquisition, war and diplomacy, physical and cultural reproduction, and religion and rewarded the superior performance of gifted hunters, warriors, artisans, mothers, and shaman with enhanced social prestige. The fact that outstanding ability in gender-appropriate pursuits conferred considerable influence upon its prodigies should always modulate descriptions that seek to depict Innu society as completely devoid of any social hierarchy.

Innu ethics of reciprocity and respect for individual autonomy and its traditions of noncoercive leadership, however, made such individuals' prestige contingent upon the socially responsible deployment of their skills. It was the gifted hunter's equitable distribution of his spoils, the shaman's benevolent deployment of his power, and the artisan's generosity with her handiwork that gave each of them a claim on collective admiration. The contingency of community respect upon the responsible use of special talents helped to stymie the inappropriate use of personal prestige. Should a warrior admired for his skill in battle attempt to parlay his prestige into coercive power, or an artisan hoard rather than freely give her creations, each would instantly nullify the basis of his or her own regard. By stepping outside the acceptable boundaries of Innu behavior, such an overweening individual would exchange prestige for withering ridicule. Strong mutual agreement as to what constituted collective priorities ensured that the influence of individuals remained within culturally acceptable limits and met culturally appropriate ends. Thus, individual attainment of a high degree of competency in socially approved pursuits reinforced rather than upset collective ideals. As long as individual competition was aligned with strictly defined social goals, differences in ability fostered rivalry which enhanced rather than undermined collective security.

Rhetorical persuasion of animals voluntarily to offer themselves on behalf of the dependent human community was similar to the appeals made to humans to follow Innu behavioral ethics, in that they judiciously blended entreaties for noble self-sacrifice with blatant manipulation of the animal's presumed self-regard. Just as they did with their own sick and weak, the Innu implored the generosity of animal persons by asking them to surrender their individual lives for the sake of their human kin's collective survival. As with their petitions of their own young and strong, however, the Innu also played upon animals' assumed desire for social prestige by emphasizing, in their entreaties, the gifts of tobacco, memorialization in art, and widespread public recognition and gratitude that their self-sacrifice would occasion.

The complexity of early modern Innu relational dynamics meant that their rituals were multivalent, simultaneously appealing to the disparate needs and motivations of both human and nonhuman participants even while quietly fulfilling the pragmatic aim of sustaining life. For example, an "eat-all" feast, held in response to an animals' presumed wishes that its entire body be utilized by the community, simultaneously celebrated the capture of a large animal, thanked her for so magnanimously allowing herself to be caught, and raised the cultural "currency" of the successful hunter who hosted the feast. The hunter's status as the "giver" was underlined by his abstention from, or mitigated participation in, his own feast. "The one who gives the feast and who serves it never takes part therein, but is satisfied in watching the others, without keeping anything for himself."[72] Even as it affirmed both the hunter and the prey's desire for community validation of, respectively, his skill and her sacrifice, the feast actualized Innu social values of sharing, reciprocity, and generosity.

Innu feasting practices encouraged participants to eat past the point of satiation and were ideally adapted to the difficult realities of life in a harsh and unforgiving climate. Though frequently chided by Europeans for their apparent improvidence with dietary resources, aboriginal communities realized that the immediate, generous distribution of food through feasting, rather than the hoarding of food by individual hunters or families, would nurture strong bonds of mutual dependency and a powerful sense of reciprocal obligation in participants.[73] Such expectations were, in fact, made explicit in the feast's closing words, spoken by its host: *Egou Khé Khicouiecou* ("Now you will go away; return this feast when you please.")[74] Hosting a feast for others was a self-interested act, as it reflected the pragmatic reality that when the plenty of today was followed by the privation of tomorrow, one's guest might well gain the critical resources necessary for survival.

Innu Amelioration of Relational Problems

Innu desire to make the behavior of both human and nonhuman persons more predictable led to the enshrinement of collective over individual survival and institutionalized the drive for prestige and self-assertion in the service of the communal good. Despite Innu attempts to control social behavior, however, things could and did go wrong. Discussion of the optimal theoretical functioning of social and religious interactions, then, must be supplemented by consideration of how the Innu handled conceptual and pragmatic challenges to the ethics that they had evolved.

The explanatory power of the Innu belief system was such that it was able to apply the same relational logic it employed in the ritual pursuit of collective health, well-being, and happiness to account for and ameliorate personal, social, and environmental problems. Innu analysis of misfortune utilized the same categories of persons, power, and gifts as did their theoretical construction of optimal relationships between human and nonhuman persons. Though Innu explanations of misfortune were complex, illness, privation, and violence within the community were all seen as indicating disturbances in interpersonal relationships that required simultaneous recourse to a range of diagnostic and ameliorative rituals.

Illness is a particularly good case in point. An individual's experience of ill health could be attributed, variously, to malevolent bewitchment by a fellow human being, the just revenge of an other-than-human person for the breaking of a key ritual taboo, the presence within the body of an insalubrious foreign object, or to the sufferer's own antisocial emotions. In this last explanation the early modern Innu reveal themselves as astute psychologists. Aware that their social and religious values of collective survival, intragroup harmony, and physical and emotional stoicism made onerous psychological demands on those whom it shaped and guided, the Innu posited that illness could arise from the psychological maladjustment of the invalid, particularly his or her experience of negatively perceived emotions. Anger, jealousy, and depression in particular were affects that were felt to pose a significant threat to the Innu social equilibrium, as they diminished an individual's ability to work productively with their kin—anger by prompting violence, jealousy by promoting covetousness, and depression by diminishing an individual's ability to contribute to community life. Anger was also thought to signal the individual's loss of his or her closely guarded emotional self-control, adding the perception of personal failure to the individual's fiery burden of rage. Anger's close association with violence, taboo within the close confines of the Innu community, made it seem that much more dangerous in the Innu imagination.[75]

Such a range of diagnosis led inevitably to a multiplicity of cures. Attempts to identify and confront the responsible witch or ritually to appease the offended other-than-human agent could occur simultaneously with the administration of purgatives, bleeding, sweating, and collective attempts to alleviate the invalid's negative emotional state by identifying and fulfilling their antisocial wishes.[76] With the license of illness, invalids were encouraged, through direct expression or the analysis of their dreams, to vent negative emotions and reveal thwarted desires by demanding special foods, ritual performances, illicit sexual contact, or envied personal items, such as decorative clothing, cooking implements, or weapons. At the bedsides of ill relatives and friends, Pastedechouan would doubtless have joined in the collective dances often held to encourage the invalid's recovery.[77]

Curing the Innu invalid was thus a carnivalesque communal endeavor which affirmed Innu social ethics even as it appeared to challenge or negate them. Efficacious participation of the collectivite rites ultimately affirmed Innu values of communal cooperation and generosity even as it indulged and rewarded the patient's ritual expression of antisocial emotions and impulses. Thus, while the Innu had multiple explanations for illness and utilized a number of different ritual approaches to assuage it, each of the multiple approaches and treatments utilized the triad of person, power, and gift, thus reinforcing rather than challenging their personalistic social and religious system.

Innu social customs and religious practices, then, both created and reflected a strong sense of Innu collective identity and were oriented toward the supreme aim of group survival. Their understanding of the amoral nature of personal power led the Innu to formulate a system of social ethics which persuasively argued that utilization of one's talents in the service of the group was ultimately in one's own best interest. Both the social and religious aspects of Innu collective life involved the constant ritual maintenance of community cohesion through reciprocal practices involving both human and nonhuman agents, and the continual discernment and ritual remediation of relational problems that could manifest themselves in a variety of different ways.

Relations with "Them": Innu Conceptualizations of Non-Innu Groups

Like many other human ideations, Innu cultural and religious precepts emerged from the warp and woof of perceived similarities and differences, affiliations and animosities. Just as the cultural vectors of gender and age provided a sense of distinction and difference within an intra-Innu context marked by a high degree of cultural unanimity, so the dynamics of Innu encounters with "them"—non-Innu groups who remained impervious both to diplomatic courtship and forceful incorporation—played a key role in the emergence of a distinctively Innu collective identity. Indeed, a central aspect of Innu conceptual adjustment during the liminal period of early contact, with its attendant economic, social, political, military and religious disruptions, was their careful articulation of an increasingly self-conscious sense of their *comparative* collective identity.

The articulation of this communal sense of self involved the systematic classification of anomalous social entities into the overarching category of "them" and the initiation of an Innu campaign to insist that "they" become more like "us" through cultural alliance and assimilation. While Innu social and religious practices attempted primarily to preserve the group's internal cohesion by promoting careful and respectful interactions between and amongst its human and other-than-human constituents, they also sought, secondarily, to persuade potentially hostile "others," both aboriginal and European, to conform to predictable standards of Innu behavior. That being an Innu was a behavioral rather than an ethnic or racial definition is apparent from the fact that Europeans or members of other aboriginal nations who entered the community through adoption or marriage were perceived as being as much a part of the group as those born into it. The Innu thus attempted to neutralize threats from outside the group in very much the same way that they addressed potential dangers from within—by demanding universal adherence to the ethic of generosity, reciprocity, and social harmony.

Pastedechouan's people employed an incorporative agenda for those who responded favorably to their diplomatic overtures, such as allies, sharing with them economic, human, and military resources. They reserved an aggressive response for those who forcefully and repeatedly rejected or ridiculed their advances. In their relations with these resistant groups, the Innu reversed intra-Innu behavioral norms in sometimes spectacular fashion, indulging in behaviors that would have been met with appalled repulsion had they occurred within the Innu community. While the Innu strongly discouraged intragroup antagonism, expecting their own members to ameliorate rather than aggravate conflict, aggression forbidden amongst their own was positively encouraged in Innu external relations with unrepentantly obdurate "others."

In the aftermath of conflict, however, the Innu impulse toward incorporation reasserted itself, as the Innu included surviving foes in their body politic, transforming yesterday's enemy captives into today's long-lost kin. Attempts to force outsider groups to recognize Innu social norms had a strongly pragmatic element, given both the protection that behavioral predictability brings and the demographic boost that war captives would have given the Innu community. Their characteristic strategy of culturally incorporating outsiders suggests that, despite their cultural and religious relativism, the Innu perceived their own ways as superior to those of their aboriginal friends and foes and to the bizarre customs of the European strangers whom they had recently encountered. Independent of their practical advantages, attempts to incorporate other groups reflected the sincere Innu belief that their cultural dynamic was the best means of ensuring individual and collective happiness and longevity. Though the Innu would themselves become the targets of intense evangelization by missionary Europeans, their own outlook was not wholly devoid of the desire to culturally transform other groups to make them more closely approximate their own social ideals.

Death or Assimilation:
The Dynamics of Innu-Mohawk Relations

The Innu had a category of unassimilatable "them" long before their contact with Europeans, in the persons of their intimate enemies, the Mohawk.[78] Much more is known about how the dynamics of the Innu-Mohawk encounter perpetuated their mutual antipathy than about how the conflict originated. Scholars concur that their rancor in all probability related to competing ambitions regarding territorial expansion and the economic and military dominance of their shared region, factors which considerably predated the appearance of Europeans in North America in the mid-sixteenth century, though these new pressures undoubtedly deepened their rancor. In addition to the low-grade nature of aboriginal warfare, the relatively equal strength of the Mohawk and the Algonkian alliance against them (spearheaded by the Innu), meant that their antagonism could smolder for decades without either participant gaining the definitive upper hand. Though the Innu of the late sixteenth and early seventeenth centuries enjoyed considerable intra-aboriginal political influence and, by virtue of their enviable control of the strategically situated port of Tadoussac, economic dominance of the region, their preeminence was continually challenged by the more southerly Mohawk, who appear to have enjoyed martial superiority.[79] Only with their military alliance with the well-armed French, initiated in 1603, did the Innu achieve an edge over their intractable foe.

The Mohawk were the eastern "door" of five linguistically and politically linked entities, which together comprised the powerful Iroquois League. Though they were intimately connected to the Innu through an ongoing, mutually comprehensible dynamic of violent confrontation and forced incorporation, the Mohawk differed fundamentally from their Innu antagonists in their language, social organization, and means of production.[80] In contrast to migratory northern groups, such as the Innu, who congregated in large groups by rivers or lakes only in the summer months spending their winters in atomic, kin-based bands, the Mohawk were a semi-sedentary nation living in large, palisaded towns of up to two thousand residents, and were dependent more upon agriculture than hunting for their primary dietary staples.[81] Mohawk reliance upon corn, squash, and beans, commonly referred to as the "three sisters," and their conceptualization of farming as the joint prerogative of human and other-than-human females has been interpreted as underlying their development of a distinctively matrilineal clan structure and as facilitating the comparatively high status of women in Mohawk culture. In contrast to the hunting-dependent Innu, who defined and valorized the roles of hunter, warrior, and shaman in largely male terms, the agricultural, matrilocal Mohawk offered women leading roles in religious life and considerable power in the collective decision-making process. As the daughters of Atahensic, a primordial mother figure in Iroquois mythology, Mohawk women were instrumental in most rituals related to soil fertility, seeding, and harvesting. Moreover, they were critical, in their roles as influential elders and as bereaved widows, sisters, and daughters, in instigating and enacting the characteristic dynamics of Mohawk-Innu warfare.[82]

The mighty St. Lawrence River appears to have delineated the unofficial boundary between the Innu sphere of influence along its northern shore and the southerly realm of the Mohawk, this easternmost Iroquois group. The tantalizing proximity of their foe proved a constant, irresistible provocation to the Innu to assert their own cultural identity and to subdue, incorporate, and transform that of their antagonists, through battle and the series of intricate rituals which followed the capture of enemy prisoners.

Innu-Mohawk conflict was dissimilar from war in larger-scale European societies, differing both in its methods and motivations. Engagements were usually of relatively short duration as aboriginal antagonists favored the guerilla tactics of surprise confrontation, and both sides sought to limit their own casualties whilst gaining as many war captives as possible. Furthermore, though the Innu and Mohawk, like their European counterparts, fought in self-defense and in an effort to effect political, military, and economic dominance, warfare for both these aboriginal groups also served far more personal purposes, mirroring the contours of their small-scale, face-to-face cultures. Ongoing low-grade conflict was precipitated on both sides by life-cycle politics and the dynamics of what Daniel Richter has christened the "mourning-war complex."[83] Thus, sporadic engagements could be occasioned either by the impatience of young men to gain the wisdom and courage that could only came from battle or by the desire of the bereaved to wreak revenge for slain family members whilst simultaneously obtaining prisoners who could serve as human reparations for, and effective replacements of, their murdered kin.

The ritual torture of captured prisoners of war appeared to the Europeans who witnessed it as the apotheosis of savage cruelty and the ultimate expression of aboriginal anarchy: "There is no cruelty comparable to that which they practice on their enemies . . . they make them suffer all that cruelty and the Devil can suggest."[84] Such evaluations, however, utterly failed to comprehend the underlying logic and symbolism of aboriginal war and postwar practices.[85] Torture of prisoners at once affirmed cultural distinctions between "us" and "them," provided an outlet for aggression that was taboo within the society's own behavioral boundaries, punished enemies for their stubborn refusal to submit, and dramatically affirmed key cultural values, such as courage, held in common by the antagonistic groups, even in their calculated destruction of one another.[86]

The ritual torture of prisoners acquired in battle involved all segments of Innu society: men, women, and children. Doubtless young Pastedechouan would have rushed to inflict a childish beating upon the Mohawk prisoners arriving at his family encampment, following his kinsmen's triumphant return from battle. He would have taken his place in the gauntlet composed of both sexes and all ages.[87] When the enemy captives were dragged into camp, all were made to pass through this motley assembly, who would threaten, kick, punch, and beat them, before their ultimate fate of death or assimilation was decided. The prisoners knew that they faced either slow destruction by a series of brutally inventive tortures or a shorter ordeal followed by assimilation into a grieving Innu family. Though both the Innu and the Mohawk habitually spared women and children, incorporating them into the victorious community, it is likely that the Innu, because of their cultural definition of hunting as a male prerogative, spared more male prisoners. Those intended for incorporation were tenderly nursed back to health after their ordeal so that they could become replacements for deceased Innu husbands and fathers. The saving of selected Mohawk men meant that the burden of providing for a larger number of incorporated women and children did not fall solely to the original males of the Innu community.

Either outcome, death or assimilation, followed highly stylized ritual rules which were recognized as legitimate and scrupulously observed by both torturers and the tortured. Each recognized that, were the circumstances reversed, they themselves could be either victim or assailant. The torturers, consequently, mixed intense psychological and physical torment of their captives with occasions for rest and food and politely commended the victim on his courage and endurance. These periods of respite, however, also had another motivation. Because Innu and Iroquoian torture often took place at night, anthropologists have speculated that these groups attempted to inflict the most egregious punishment possible while still ensuring that their victims lived to see daylight, in homage to the sun, an important other-than-human person in both cultures. The doomed prisoner, for his part, sought to demonstrate his bravery by loudly singing his death song under torture and by defiantly taunting his captors, refusing to beg for a mercy he knew would not be forthcoming. The supreme postmortem compliment to a captive's exemplary death was to eat his flesh, in order to subsume something of his provocative courage.

The ritual treatment of prisoners marked for integration, though gentler, was equally equivocal. While such captives were welcomed as the new family members they would shortly become, they too were made to feel the intensity of Innu anger for the suffering of the slain kin they would soon replace. Though the taunting and physical mistreatment they received was generally fairly mild, in keeping with their impending status as fellow Innu, it would have been—in concert with the triple shocks of sudden separation from their own society, probable recent bereavement, and their likely witnessing of the deadly assaults upon their male kin—a shattering, terrifying experience for the men, women, and children who endured it.

Death-or-assimilation treatment of prisoners in the aftermath of war illustrates the existence of a second, grimmer set of Innu relational rules that effectively inverted intra-Innu ethics in its treatment of unregenerate "others," one in which the communal ethic of nonprovocation was lifted, and injunctions upon expressions of rage and violence annulled.[88] Such behavior also suggests the omnipresence of Innu incorporative aspirations, revealing the community's determination to effect the cultural reproduction of its values and the replacement of its slain family members, by force if necessary. Innu contact with aboriginal enemies thus had as its basic motivation the self-same goals that underlay friendly contact. While diplomatic initiatives sought to persuade aboriginal "others" voluntarily to accept Innu behavioral norms, warfare attempted violently to force the incorporation of intractable "others" into the Innu body politic.

The European "Them": Innu-French Relations

Pastedechouan's generation, like that of his parents, lived in a postcontact world decisively impacted by the presence of a tiny but influential cohort of Europeans. During his parent's lifetime, what had once been the seasonal intrusion of these strange outsiders had become a permanent though numerically small presence. Initially lured to Canada by the possibility of finding trade routes to the Far East and subsequently distracted by the luxuriant abundance of its fish and furs, the French had become residents in their midst. Of all the members of his large family, only Pastedechouan's elderly grandmother could remember a time before their ubiquitous and occasionally unsettling presence, and recall the shock of first contact:

> Pierre Pastedechouan has told us that his grandmother used to take pleasure in relating to him the astonishment of the Natives, when they saw for the first time a French ship arrive upon their shores. They thought it was a moving Island; they did not know what to say of the great sails which made it go; their astonishment was redoubled in seeing a number of men on deck. The women at once began to prepare houses for them, as is their custom when new guests arrive, and four canoes of Savages ventured to board these vessels. They invited the Frenchmen to come into the houses which had been made ready for them, but neither side understood the other. They were given a barrel of bread or biscuit. Having brought it on shore they examined it; and, having found no taste

in it, threw it into the water . . . Having sent some one to investigate the character and appearance of the men brought by that great house of wood, the messengers reported to their master that these men were prodigious and horrible; that they were dressed in iron, ate bones, and drank blood. They had seen them covered with their cuirasses, eating biscuits and drinking wine. Our Savages said the Frenchmen drank blood and ate wood, naming the wine and the biscuits.[89]

With its note of caution regarding the powers and propensities of unknown cultural actors, coupled with the optimistic assumption that the Innu social ethic would soon tame them, Pastedechouan's grandmother's narrative recapitulates aspects of the familiar atcen tales. Attribution to the French strangers of a propensity towards cannibalism—neatly explained by the French interpolator who relates her story as the comic misapprehension of hardtack and wine—reveals the profound Innu tendency to interpret these new "others," with their novel food, transportation, and clothing, in terms of traditional (though hardly flattering) cultural paradigms.

The women's reflexive recourse to hospitality illustrates the strength of Innu incorporative tactics: as modeled in windigo stories, they extended a welcoming response even to apparently blood-guzzling, metal-bodied strangers. But, far from being the simple and openhearted gesture expressing of an untouched, precapitalist society, such reflexive generosity was intended to inaugurate a lasting and *mutually* beneficial relationship. Innu magnanimity, as already noted, was not devoid of strategic considerations: by modeling their own standards of civilized behavior, the Innu hoped their benevolence would be mirrored back to them, forming the foundation of a long-term social and economic relationship.

Generosity was thus accompanied by marked caution: even as they prepared graciously to receive their guests, the Innu also sought further information on the capabilities and intentions of these unknown people by sending a contingent to "investigate the character and appearance of the men brought by that great house of wood."[90] The tactic of closely scrutinizing the French, when possible in their own milieu—inaugurated by the first canoeload of Innu men boarding the unfamiliar Gallic vessel—would culminate in the coming decades with the sending of agents, such as Pastedechouan himself, across the Atlantic to the French motherland to perform similar reconnaissance on European soil.

Even as the Innu recoiled from the unexpected advent of these grotesque strangers, then, they began the process of groping toward a mutual understanding with their increasingly entrenched European guests. The two groups, over successive decades of contact, would struggle to articulate mutually intelligible linguistic and cultural means of interaction with one another in the service of what would become mutually acceptable goals.

Their political, economic, and demographic strength, as well as their effective control of the rich physical resources that the Europeans wished to exploit, meant that the Innu were initially the dominant partner in this encounter and thus were able to significantly contribute to an evolving Innu-European "middle ground."[91] Unlike the experiences of indigenous cultures in Mexico and South America, the Innu's first encounter with Europeans was not at sword point, nor was it punctuated by the devastation and terror of cannon fire. Though incidents of misunderstanding, coercion, and violence did occur, given the propensity of early European explorers, such as Jacques Cartier, for kidnapping aboriginal peoples, the Innu were never the victims of an overwhelming European military onslaught.[92] On the contrary, they welcomed French military prowess and successfully sought to parlay what was initially a trading liaison into a full military alliance, so as to appropriate French resources, manpower, and weaponry for their continuing struggle against the Mohawk. Neither epidemic nor European settlement seriously threatened the ability of sixteenth- and early seventeenth-century Innu people to live in their traditional manner upon their traditional lands.[93]

At the time of Pastedechouan's birth around 1608, the Innu were at perhaps the apex of their economic influence and territorial dominance, controlling the north shore of the St. Lawrence River from Tadoussac to as far west as Quebec, and perhaps beyond. By contrast, European settlements were in their barest infancy. Until the nativity of Quebec, born, like Pastedechouan, in 1608, Europeans had been merely a sporadic, seasonal trading presence in the St. Lawrence River valley, as regular in their migratory movements as their Innu hosts. Coming in droves with Nipinoukhe and his late-spring rains, these exotic strangers departed overseas when Pipounoukhe began to paint the autumn leaves. As competition between merchants for lucrative North American furs increased, however, traders began to risk earlier spring crossings and left later and later in the fall. Eventually, French appreciation of the advantages of a permanent Canadian trading site overcame their misgivings regarding the climactic challenges of what was for them a culturally and geographically remote setting.

Their fears initially proved well founded, as French attempts to establish a permanent presence on the St. Lawrence River met with bitter and repeated failure. The first small contingents of Europeans who attempted a year-round stay experienced decimating casualty rates, as the long, cruel Canadian winter trailed disease and starvation in its icy wake. Cartier's disastrous 1541 attempt to winter near Cape Rouge was followed by the equally discouraging experiences of the fur trader Pierre de Chauvin, whose endeavor to establish a permanent European trading center at Tadoussac in 1600 resulted in the loss of eleven of his sixteen men. Even the founding of Quebec seemed initially to follow the same ill-fated trajectory, as Samuel de Champlain's party was more than halved when his poorly equipped men likewise fell victim to illness and privation.[94]

The survivors of both early seventeenth-century contingents had the Innu to thank. As both Tadoussac and Quebec were within their sphere of influence, Innu hunting bands in keeping with their social emphasis on generosity supplied the pitiable Europeans as best they could, instructed them in the preparation of herbal medicines such as cedar, and introduced them to the art of survival in the boreal forest. The tragic incompetence of the French in the most rudimentary aspects of life in Canada probably led the Innu initially to dismiss them as a serious challenge to their own political and economic dominance of the St. Lawrence's northern shore.

What had started around the 1550s as an intermittent trade liaison between the Innu and European fishermen seeking additional profits from a few traded furs became, by the early years of the dawning seventeenth century, a pivotal economic and diplomatic relationship for both parties. Innu delegations, sponsored by wealthy fur merchants, traveled to France to reinforce economic ties and secure royal assent to the deployment of French military resources in the service of Innu interests. Innu presence in the areas the French found most desirable for settlement and defense—and the symbiotic economic, political, and military ties between the two groups—meant that the Innu served as the prototypical aboriginal group in the French imagination. Tellingly, the French referred to the Tadoussac Innu as simply "the Canadians."[95]

Innu-French Trade

Innu-French trade relations as they emerged in the late sixteenth and early seventeenth century are best understood as a mutual projection, by each group, of their own cultural assumptions onto their of ally's behavior. The Innu initially intuited the economic behavior of European "others" through their own cultural categories of persons, power, and gifts, seeing the exchange of actual physical items as symbolizing the more important intangibles of trust, religious and cultural affirmation, and military and economic alliance. The French, however, while they utilized complex, nuanced systems of symbolic gift exchange within their own culture, did not initially apply these principles to their congress with aboriginal groups. Rather, influenced by their perception of North American peoples as culturally and technologically backward, the French viewed native ignorance of the value of unfamiliar European goods as a welcome opportunity to apply capitalistic rather than gifting models to this encounter.[96] Much of the conflict and confusion between French traders and their Innu hosts, then, originated in the mistaken assumption of each group that their counterpart understood their mutual activity (imagined as "trading" and "gifting" respectively) in similar terms and approached it with similar motivations.

Innu trade with European newcomers was conceptually predicated upon long-standing pan-aboriginal patterns that recognized economic exchange as merely one expression of a more diffuse political and military alliance between autonomous groups. The exchange of goods was envisioned not as an economic activity carried out by individuals but rather as a formal political compact intended to cement alliances between independent aboriginal polities, as trade never took place between enemies but only actual or potential affines. Trade was thus inseparable from diplomacy, as the exchange items themselves, however vital to survival, were merely the material representation of allies' mutual approval, accord, and alliance.

Intra-aboriginal gift exchange had several different ritual contexts. Gifts could be used to maintain cordial relationships or to repair those badly damaged by distrust or violence. Just as feasts were the ordinary means of maintaining community cohesion in the intra-Innu context, so the exchange of goods was the usual way to reaffirm mutually beneficial ties between aboriginal societies. Just as murder within the Innu community called for immediate and elaborate ritual remuneration to stave off further, retributory violence, so strained intra-aboriginal relationships required more extensive ritual and economic remediation, including escalated, lavish gift giving.

Gifting at such critical junctures could include the bequest of children. A human gift encapsulated many messages, evincing the desire that the two societies become one and expressing trust in the benevolence of the host culture. When children were given as reparative gifts by the aggressor culture after incidents of violence, the recipient society was reassured that the child's donors would behave more peacefully in the future. As a "goodwill hostage," then, the child's presence precluded provocative actions against the community that held him or her.[97]

Because the exchange of gifts was freighted in the intra-aboriginal context with a wealth of significance, the size, nature, and quality of the gifts given and received were carefully considered. Gifts represented both the essence of the group giving them and the donor's evaluation of the recipient's worth. The decision to accept a gift expressed its recipients' desire to establish or maintain peaceful relations with its provider. Conversely, the refusal of a gift represented a snub to its giver, whom it effectively symbolized. Thus, while the exchange of mutually acceptable gifts inaugurated or reaffirmed alliances, thwarted gift exchanges could trigger diplomatic breakdown, inaugurating a dramatic shift from alliance to antagonism. Gifts also represented the giver's evaluation of the receiver, because lavish presents signaled great respect and a strong desire for affiliation, whereas small or inferior gifts were a calculated insult, as they tele-graphed a slighting evaluation of the recipient's importance. As aboriginal gifts symbolized military, political, and economic accord, their giving was a zero-sum game. Barter or negotiation did not occur, as such a practice would have run contrary to the communication of mutual respect that gift exchanges encoded.

French conceptions of the nature and meaning of their economic dealings with aboriginal peoples were quite different. In her magisterial survey of early modern French gifting practices, Natalie Zemon Davis notes that the nuanced, judicious diplomacy that characterized intra-French gifting did not form the model for their developing economic relationship to the native peoples of North America, because of French perceptions of a cultural and technological chasm between themselves and their aboriginal trading partners. Though a few aspects of the French-aboriginal exchange *did* mirror traditional gifting patterns between the hierarchical strata of French society, Gallic perceptions of the "primitive" level of Innu technology substantially altered the substance and meaning of these holdovers. In the European context, the giving of small metal "trinkets" or "trifles" by social superiors to their economic dependents was intended to supplement extant compensation and to soften what were often exploitative relationships. In the French-aboriginal context, however, these small, supplementary gifts became "the *substance* of European gifting and bartering with the peoples of the Americas." Bartering small metal objects allowed French traders to obtain valuable furs for a pittance.[98] Merchants gleefully argued that both the "primitive" nature of Innu material culture and the ignorance of "savages" as to the true value of European trade goods justified their continuing economic exploitation. In contrast with their cautious, diplomatic maneuvering through the loaded symbolic world of French gift exchange, then, traders in the New World perceived their congress with aboriginal peoples as a free-for-all, both with their native hosts and their European competitors, in which the self-evident goal was to obtain as many lucrative assets with the smallest possible outlay of resources.

The Clash of Innu and French Perceptions of Economic Congress

This mind-set ill prepared European traders to appreciate the religious, political, and diplomatic nuances of Innu gifting practices or to understand the complex implications of their own participation in trading or feasting with their aboriginal hosts. First, Innu perceptions of trading as a group activity clashed with the individualist preconceptions of the French. Gallic traders appear to have assumed that their Innu counterparts likewise perceived themselves as atomistic individuals competing with their fellow tribesmen for trade with Europeans. However, Innu conceptualizations of "benefit," given the decidedly collective emphasis of their environmentally adaptive social ethos, differed dramatically from European notions of competitive personal enrichment. An offended Innu elder related to a sympathetic Recollet missionary that his appeals for fairer prices for his people's goods were interpreted by French traders merely as questioning his own personal treatment:

He complained that we sold our goods too dear when the Indians came to trade, and he asked that they should be sold cheaper in the future. Our factor for the merchants, seeing his importunity, told him that he would sell cheaper to him, but not to the rest. This Indian then began to say to this factor in a disdainful way: "You make fun of me to say that you will sell cheap to me and dear to my people. If I did I should to be hung and beheaded by my people. I am a chief; I do not speak for myself, but for my people."[99]

The merchant's attempt to redress the elder's grievance on an ad hoc basis shows that, as late as the third decade of the seventeenth century, some Europeans had still not grasped either the fundamentally collective nature of Innu economic, social, and religious priorities or the conceptual interrelationship between the three.

Innu perception that gifts were merely the material indicator of the desire to inaugurate mutually beneficial relationships also clashed with French conceptualizations of goods as being simply objects of barter and exchange. French who attempted to negotiate for furs by opening with low bids, which they then expected to raise to achieve a mutually acceptable price, were surprised by the vehemence of the Innu response. Gabriel Sagard reported in 1624,

> The principal chief of the savages, whom we call La Forière, having come to visit us on our pinnace and being dissatisfied with the small present of figs that our captain made him when he left the vessel, threw them into the river in anger and counseled his savages to come on to our ship one after another and carry off from it all the goods they liked, and give in exchange as few peltries as they liked, since we had not given him what satisfied him.[100]

Unaware that their paltry initial "gift" had communicated a provocative lack of respect, bemused Europeans, afraid to intervene lest they compound their offence, could only watch as the incensed Innu, having destroyed the offending item, absconded with trade goods that they judged to be more suitable presents.

Gradually, the Innu came to discern that their French trading partners were motivated by a set of relational rules and assumptions inimical to their own. As we have seen, when outsider groups, whether intentionally or unintentionally, signaled their determination to withstand incorporation, the Innu responded with an alternate set of relational rules, those reserved for "them." Thus, the Innu evolved a dual-track ethic in their re-lations with the French that was conceptually similar to that which they employed in their interactions with their traditional Mohawk foes. Hav-ing come to understand the rules of competitive negotiation and the dy-namics of intra-European trading rivalries, the Innu adroitly manipulated the supply of furs to obtain maximum trading leverage, often refusing to enter into trade negotiations until numerous European ships were pres-ent, so as to inflate prices for their goods.

The Innu's effective reversal of their traditional collective ideals in their congress with the French has been taken as evidence of the European per-version of Innu social ethics or as reflecting their capitulation to the se-ductive ethos of individualistic mercantile capitalism. In contrasting the Innu with the Wendat of the 1620s, for example, Bruce Trigger suggests that Innu collective values and identity had been undermined by their decades of trade with Europeans, implying that Innu behavior toward the French can be seen as reliably reflecting of their internal relationships and core values.[101] Such a view, however, fails to understand that the Innu were able simultaneously to hoist the French by their own conceptual petard whilst safeguarding traditional exchange practices within their own cultural parameters.

When French merchants failed to understand or obey Innu relational imperatives, Pastedechouan's people began to interact with traders on their own terms, effectively punishing them by selectively adhering to their European model of individualistic, competitive trading rather than to the Innu ideals of gifting and affiliation. Their sophisticated applica-tion of European rules to European agents, however, was accompanied by a continuing preference for traditional codes of behavior in the intra-Innu context. Thus, while not hesitating to use what they saw as the shortsighted selfishness of European traders against them, the Innu did not condone the emulation of such individualistic egotism within their own culture. Arguably, just as in the Innu-Mohawk dynamic, the ritual contravention of Innu norms of behavior in congress with outsider groups strengthened rather than weakened the Innu sense of compara-tive, collective selfhood.

Innu selective adoption of European trading practices existed along-side an ongoing but largely ineffective campaign to educate their Euro-pean partners as to the benefits of Innu-style economic interactions. Writing in 1634, Jesuit Superior Paul Le Jeune noted that it was the

French failure to respond to Innu invitations to "live like brothers" that was responsible for their pointed exclusion of the French from the more favorable terms they accorded the in-group:

> They are very grateful, very liberal, and not in the least importunate toward those of their own nation. If they conduct themselves thus toward our French, and toward other foreigners, it is because, it seems to me, that we do not wish to ally ourselves with them as brothers, which they would very much desire. But this would ruin us in three days; for they would want us to go with them, and eat their food as long as they had any, and then they would come and eat ours as long as it lasted; and when there was none left, we would all set to work to find more . . . but, as we know nothing about their mode of hunting, and as this way of doing is not praiseworthy, we do not heed them. Hence, as we do not regard ourselves as belonging to their nation, they treat us in the way I have described. If any stranger, whosoever he may be, unites with their party, they will treat him as one of their own nation . . . but if you carry on your affairs apart from them, despising their laws or their customs, they will drain from you, if they can, even your blood.[102]

This passage clearly reflects the adaptation of a precontact dual-track ethic to a novel social situation. Le Jeune explicitly states that the Innu continued to use traditionally generous rules for themselves and close affiliates, while denying the French the benefits they had so frequently been offered in the past.

Innu recourse to European trading rules represented, then, not cultural capitulation but their resort to a less generous set of rules reserved for stubborn "others" who resisted their efforts at diplomatic incorporation. Far from buckling under the ideological pressure of European mercantile capitalism, the Innu utilized European trading norms to punish Europeans for their failure to understand or obey the more generous terms continually offered to them under the rubric of Innu relational ethics.

Pastedechouan, as a young child, was the product of this rich seventeenth-century Innu culture. Beginning with his birth and safe ensconcement in the soft moss lining of his mother's carrying bag, his orientation to the world would have been woven upon these subtle warps and woofs of similarity and difference, incorporation and distinction. Surrendered at the time of his weaning to an all-male social venue, Pastedechouan would have begun, literally and figuratively, to follow in the footsteps of his father and his three older brothers. Imitating his older male kin, Pastedechouan would have attempted, in his childish way, to mimic his future adult duties: provision for his family, through hunting, and defense of his community, through warfare. Whether he was shouldering his modest load during a long winter day's march, witnessing the mercy killing of an orphaned infant, or crouching to watch his father tenderly speak to his dying prey, the little boy was beginning his Innu education, which gradually and indirectly inculcated in the rising generation critical Innu values. Pastedechouan's people, in response to their unique cultural and geographical environment, cherished emotional and physical stoicism, valued the survival of the collective over the individual, and took as their life's work the establishment and maintenance of cordial, reciprocal relationships with human and other-than-human entities, even whilst holding to the necessity of reversing cherished Innu behavioral norms in their congress with intransigent "others."

Embedded at the heart of his extended family, Pastedechouan would have watched his parents ritually burn bones to discover animals' disposition and location and would have carefully remembered and recounted his own dreams, a habit he apparently retained all of his life. Witnessing the ceremonial slaughter of animals and likely the death and ceremonial internment of one or more elderly family members, the young boy would have absorbed his culture's understanding of the soul and its double destiny, which encompassed both a perilous journey to a shadowy western world and a return to the land of the living. Attending the shaking tent ritual, the child would have experienced the drama of other-than-human persons in the Innu midst, heard the distinctive timbre of their individual voices, and perhaps laughed at the scatological antics of the irrepressible tortoise.

During the years of his childhood, Pastedechouan also would have gotten his first glimpses of the "others" who, classified collectively as "them," loitered at the fringes of the secure, cohesive Innu community. Lining up to help form the feared gauntlet that greeted newly arrived Mohawk war prisoners, Pastedechouan would have wreaked his childish worst on their straggling cohort, as, bloody and restrained, they limped into his familial camp. Staring, he would have curiously regarded the strange, hairy "dog faces" of Europeans first identified by his grandmother in terms adopted from the windigo-haunted Innu oral tradition, unaware as of yet that he would spend five critical years of his life in their exclusive company.

Understanding the complex and highly adaptive social and religious culture into which Pastedechouan was born around 1607 or 1608 is essential to understanding his identity prior to his period of intensive contact with French missionaries, the degree of culture shock that he likely suffered upon his removal from Innu society, and his lifelong difficulties in establishing himself as a respected adult male in Innu society.

For, however rich, Pastedechouan's was an interrupted Innu childhood. In analyzing the subsequent events of his life, it is essential that we recognize that the timing and duration of his absence from his own society had a number of deleterious effects independent of the actual content of anything he was taught by French missionaries. The young man's absence from his natal society during his critical early teen years meant that he was deprived of the knowledge he would have acquired with the dramatic escalation of Innu traditional education that began with the advent of puberty. The dual occupations of Innu manhood— hunting and war—though they manipulated the technologies of death, had, as their core goal, the persuasion of human and nonhuman others to accommodate themselves to the primal priority of Innu collective survival. If, as appears likely, Pastedechouan was too young to undertake the twin Innu rites of passage, vision quest and battle, before his departure for France at the age of twelve, his transformed religious mentality would certainly have precluded his participation in them following his return. Uninitiated into these ultimate mysteries of Innu religious culture, Pastedechouan, as a newly returned sixteen- or seventeen-year-old, would have been stranded in the liminal space between child and adult, fatally cut off from the traditional sources of male competency and status, and bereft of the relational sensibility and resources he would need to succeed and thrive in Innu terms.

2

"Do Not Take Me Back to Those Beasts Who Do Not Know God"
Transformation in France

Glancing up from the letter he was writing across the table to the handful of small Innu children with whom he was sharing its rough surface, Father Joseph Le Caron might have smiled.[1] Having already led them through their catechistic lessons and corrected them as they parroted, in French, the short prayer he had composed for them, he now would have watched with some amusement as his young charges, who may have included Pastedechouan in their number, laboriously copied the exemplary alphabet he had penned for them.[2]

Here, in the rough day school for Innu children which he had established at Tadoussac during the winter of 1617–1618, Le Caron, a thirty-two-year-old Recollet missionary, might have written his own letter to his religious superiors in France whilst simultaneously teaching the rudiments of French literacy to his young students. Presenting his two personal preoccupations—the conversion of aboriginal peoples and the containment of Protestant influence at this easternmost port on the St. Lawrence River—with a combination of plaintiveness, indignation, and sly humor, Le Caron lingered upon the subject of his young students, whom he likely observed as he wrote: "I would have had a great many children to instruct in the mysteries of our holy faith, if I had anything to give them to eat. I have taught the alphabet to some, who begin to read and write pretty well. Monsieur Hoüel can show you a specimen which I have sent him."[3] Perceiving his students' innocent amenability to his influence as being like the blankness of the empty page upon which he recorded his fervent hopes for their future as Christians, Le Caron opined that such an outcome would depend upon their cultural and linguistic reshaping into little Frenchmen: "Thus I have kept open school in our house at Tassoudac, in order to attract the Indians and render them sociable with us, to accustom them to our ways of living. If we knew their language perfectly I do not know what progress could not be made with these people."[4] As their spiritual mentor and self-appointed schoolteacher, Le Caron expected them painstakingly to imitate his own religious example just as they struggled to approximate the letters he had drawn for their childish emulation.

The lesson and his letter concluded, Le Caron would have dismissed his young charges, perhaps with a few raisins each, to encourage their attendance of lessons the following day. Having let the ink of both his missive and the children's imitative efforts dry fully in the drafty interior of the small, hewn-log convent, he might have enclosed them together, sending the children's work to his religious superiors as evidence of his progress in impressing his young charges with something of the Gallic stamp.

"First Establishment of the Faith":
The Recollet Advent in Canada

Recollet focus on the transformation of Innu society through the education of its youngest members was the fruit of their previous two years of missionary work along the shores of the St. Lawrence River. They had first come to Canada in May of 1615, in answer to the call of that indomitable exponent of European colonization, Samuel de Champlain.[5] Champlain approached Jacques Garnier de Chapoüin, Provincial of the Recollet province of Saint-Denis, and asked the religious leader to provide him with dedicated missionaries to assist in the "francization" and Catholicization of native Canada.[6]

The "Recollets," so called "because of their stress on meditation or recollection" were a reform-minded subgroup of the larger Order of Friars Minor, or the "Franciscans," as they were popularly known, a religious group founded by St. Francis of Assisi in the thirteenth century.[7] All the heirs of St. Francis believed themselves faithful to their founder's triple emphasis upon poverty, mendicancy, and popular preaching. However, even during Francis's lifetime, disagreements emerged as to the degree to which the idealistic saint's vision of communal life could be implemented in practice. The stigmatic saint's spiritual children split into two main camps: the Observants, who sought rigorously to adhere to his holy example by clinging to a literal interpretation of his Primitive Rule, and the Conventuals, who championed a more practical interpretation of his legacy. As Moorman drily remarks, "One of the things which every Observant firmly believed was that his half of the Order was very much better than the other."[8]

In late sixteenth- and early seventeenth-century Europe, reforming Franciscan factions, who wished to restore the original marginality and purity of Francis's vision from what they saw as its corruption by wealth

Gray-robed Recollet missionaries first came to the St. Lawrence River valley in 1615. Observant Franciscans, they shared with Samuel de Champlain an ambitious plan to transform the religious lives of its aboriginal peoples through the religious reeducation of native children such as Pastedechouan. (Courtesy of the Bibliothèque et Archives Nationale du Québec; photo: Pierre Perrault.)

and worldliness, were in the ascendancy. The Recollets, who had established themselves in France only in 1597, were at the forefront of this movement towards greater austerity. Accordingly, it was "on foot and without money, in the manner of the apostles, in the vestments of the true Franciscans" that they made their journey to the port of Honfleur, from which, on the twenty-fourth of April, 1615, they departed for Canada.[9] Such behavior ostentatiously advertised their fidelity to the *Regula Non Bullata*, which forbade the riding of horses and mandated that mendicant Franciscans should, like Jesus, take to the road "carry[ing] nothing . . . neither purse, nor bag, nor bread, nor money, nor staff."[10] The Recollets' "true vestments" consisted of a natural-wool habit with a long, pointed hood, or *caperon*; a long, corded belt; wooden-soled sandals; and tonsured hair. In imitation of their beloved patron, the Recollets would cling to this garb, despite its impracticality in the harsh Canadian climate.[11]

Champlain had recruited these uncompromising, otherworldly friars to help him achieve his dream of Canadian colonization. Sensitive to the contemporary critique that large-scale immigration to New World colonies inevitably led to the economic and military weakening of the mother country, Champlain had long argued that contested French rights to northeastern North America could be secured through the cooperation of those already resident there. Using logic curiously similar to that of the Innu whom he wished to colonize, Champlain speculated that if aboriginal peoples could be persuaded to become "like us"—French-speaking, Catholic, and loyal subjects of the King—then a host of tactical and political objectives could be met without the necessity of a potentially enervating French influx. A key component of this francization process, in Champlain's estimation, was the religious conversion of aboriginal peoples to Catholic Christianity, the settlement of traditionally migratory groups, and their introduction to the pacifying, civilizing effects of agriculture. Over the next fourteen years, Champlain, a probable convert to Catholicism, and the "good friars" he had chosen to assist him would together refine, develop, and advocate this powerfully influential agenda for the civic and religious future of New France.[12]

At the time the Recollets first set their sandals on Canadian soil, the French "colony" itself existed more on paper and in the dreams of its ambitious founder than it did in reality. Though the tiny outpost of Quebec had been established some seven years earlier, around the time of Pastedechouan's birth, Champlain's dream of an agricultural colony com-

posed of both pious Old World settlers and converted, "civilized" aboriginals remained strictly in the realm of fantasy. Entrenched patterns of
aboriginal-European economic interaction, established for over a half
century, continued largely unchanged. Numerous European entities, licit
and illicit, continued to vie with one another to trade with established
aboriginal intermediaries along the St. Lawrence for valuable furs gathered in the continent's jealously guarded northern interior. Champlain's
repeated attempts to impose a modicum of order upon this chaotic
scrum by enforcing trade monopolies and diversifying the colony's economic base were resisted and resented both by European traders, who
sought to defend their stakes in a lucrative business, and by aboriginal
groups such as the Innu, who benefited from fierce European competition for their furs.

Champlain's championing of the aboriginal adoption of settled agriculture, moreover, was resisted and ridiculed, both by traders, who had
a vested economic interest in the maintenance of aboriginal traditional
life ways, and by aboriginal peoples themselves. The Innu saw their lack
of reliance upon agriculture as a key cultural and religious feature dis-
tinguishing them from their farming rivals, the Mohawk, as an anecdote
related by Jesuit Superior Paul Le Jeune in 1634 makes clear. Le Jeune relates a conversation in which he attempted to dissuade the Innu from
their complex series of rituals following the hunting death of an animal,
by arguing that the Iroquois, though they did not follow the same taboos
were still rewarded with hunting success. His comments were met with
derisive laughter on the basis of the incomparability of Iroquois and
Innu means of production: "You have no sense," they replied. "Don't you
see that you and the Hiroquois cultivate the soil, and gather its fruits,
and not we, and that therefore it is not the same thing?"[13] Adopting an
agricultural economy would have radically changed the way that the
Innu related to one another, the land, and the other-than-human persons
with whom they saw themselves connected by complex and reciprocal
bonds of obligation. While the Innu were interested in engaging with
Europeans for purposes of acquiring useful goods, they had no interest
in discarding their environmentally and militarily adaptive cultural, religious, and economic system and embracing a way of life they associated
with their enemies.

The Recollets, then, came to Canada in the service of what was an un-
popular and largely unrealized agenda: one which sought to shift the

purpose of European interactions with aboriginal peoples from lucrative economic exchange to spiritual and civic congress and to replace its laissez-faire ethos of cultural accommodation with the imposition of religious and political authority. Appreciation of this fact is critical for understanding Recollet interactions with the motley European merchants and their aboriginal hosts, with whom they had over the years established a rough modus vivendi. The incompatibility of the Recollet program with the interests of the vast majority of the Europeans present on the St. Lawrence created a strong animosity between missionaries and merchants, even as the missionaries' uncompromising Catholicism exacerbated already extant confessional tensions. Moreover, in contesting the agenda of their countrymen, the Recollets also allied themselves against Innu economic self-interest and ancient, treasured notions of collective identity—hardly an auspicious beginning for an enterprise whose success rested on the amenability of those whose interests the Recollet were imperiling. Thus, though these newly arrived Recollets cherished grand dreams of the conversion of northeastern North America, hoping to emulate the success of their brethren in New Spain, their fundamental opposition to what had come to be shared Euro-aboriginal assumptions about how interactions between the two cultures should be conducted, their lack of understanding of aboriginal religious and social realities, and their paucity of human and financial resources would greatly impede their effectiveness.

"Apostolic Labors": The Evolution of Recollet Missionization Strategies

Upon their arrival in the spring of 1615, the tiny cadre of four Recollets—Superior Denis Jamet; two youthful Recollet priests, Jean Dolbeau and Joseph Le Caron; and Pacifique Du Plessis, a lay brother—initially established their headquarters at Quebec before fanning out to seek first-hand experience of aboriginal life.[14]

The small group differed considerably in their backgrounds, talents, and outlook. Their most senior member, Jamet, was a seasoned, politically astute leader who had previously held administrative positions in the Recollet province of Saint-Denis and had been handpicked by the influential Jacques Garnier de Chapoüin to preside over the establishment of the Recollet mission in Canada. The most junior, Du Plessis, the only unordained member of the delegation, utilized his secular training as an apothecary to minister to the bodies as well as the souls of French colonists and the majority aboriginal population, at both Trois-Rivières and Quebec.[15]

Jean Dolbeau and Joseph Le Caron, who were both born in 1586 and who were each entrusted with an individual mission, present a study in contrasts. Resident since 1605 at Jacques Garnier de Chapoüin's cliff-top convent, La Baumette, Dolbeau was a mystic: having immersed himself in theological and philosophical studies, he then prevailed upon his superiors for an overseas missionary posting. It is likely that Dolbeau, even as a twenty-nine-year-old, possessed, if only in embryonic form, the gift for spiritual direction that would, in his later years, make him a much-sought-after confessor in France. The clarity of Dolbeau's reputed spiritual insights, however, was in sharp contrast to the fragility of his corporeal vision: the weakness of Dolbeau's eyes would impede his ability to reside in the smoky cabins of his native hosts.[16]

Le Caron, as fractious and charismatic as Dolbeau was calm and contemplative. Though only an intermittent presence at Tadoussac, the Innu summer gathering place, Le Caron was held in high regard by some segments of its seasonal population, prompting a local leader, Choumin, to name his newborn son "Père Joseph," after the missionary.[17] A fierce defender of the Recollet presence in Canada, Le Caron frequently clashed with the Recollets' merchant underwriters, whom he regarded as undermining rather than facilitating the work of God. Le Caron intermittently left the mission field to return to France, with the double aim of more firmly entrenching Recollet prerogatives in Canada and of contesting the counterclaims of their Huguenot antagonists. Such was the extent of Le Caron's emotional involvement with the Recollets' mission in New France that some historians have attributed his early death to his heartbreak at Cardinal Richelieu's 1632 decision to restrict the Canadian mission field solely to the rival Jesuit order.

While Jamet and Du Plessis remained behind at the tiny European enclave of Quebec to supervise the building of the Recollet convent and to cater to the religious needs of its small French community, Dolbeau and Le Caron commenced their immersion with, respectively, the Innu of the Tadoussac area and the Wendat further west along the St. Lawrence.[18]

These two aboriginal groups represented, in the eyes of these new European interlopers, the patterns of the past and the way of the future. Like the traders, with whom they were almost always at odds, and Champlain, with whom they usually agreed, the Recollets sought access

to more westerly indigenous groups, such as the sedentary, agriculturalist Wendat. The military allies and commercial rivals of the Innu, the
Wendat were Iroquoian in their language and many of their cultural and
religious practices, but stood with the Innu and their Algonkian allies
north of the St. Lawrence against their linguistic and cultural kinsmen
on its south shore.[19] Ironically, the substantial, palisaded villages of the
Wendat, with their lovingly tended fields of crops and carefully constructed longhouses, were more attractive to the newly arrived Franciscans, vowed to poverty and mendicancy, than was the lifestyle of the
Innu, which in some ways more closely resembled the itinerant Franciscan ideal. While the motivations of European traders for seeking congress with the Wendat were largely mercantile, arising from a desire to
undercut aboriginal monopolies (including that of the Innu), which artificially inflated the price of goods, the Recollets were motivated by an
inchoate but powerful equation of agriculture with "civility" and "dis-
positions less estranged from Christianity." Though their missions in the
West would, for a number of reasons, be delayed until 1623, the agriculturalist Wendat or "Huron" as they were called by the French, remained
a powerful symbol to the Recollets, who continually contrasted the
Wendat's incipient "humanity" and imagined tractability to catechistic
overtures with the realities of the "errant and vagabond" Innu, with
whom they had much of their early religious commerce.[20]

"Relapsing into Their Indifference for the Things of Salvation": Recollet Reactions to Aboriginal "Apostasy"

In the spring of 1616, following their winter immersion within these diverse aboriginal societies, Dolbeau and Le Caron reconvened with their
comrades at Quebec to swap stories and forge a coherent missionization
policy. Comparing notes on their experiences, the two immediately isolated a common, disturbing theme in their interactions with both the
Innu and the Wendat. Despite the care taken with their religious education, many aboriginal adults upon whom the Recollets had ceremonially
conferred the sacrament of baptism during this initial encounter "immediately relapsed into their ordinary indifference for the things of salvation . . . profaning the sacrament."[21] The Recollets saw this "apostasy" as
a horrifying sin that threatened not simply the salvation of its perpetra-

tors but also that of the priest who had so unwisely administered baptism to its subsequent profaner.

The Recollets' perception that baptized converts' "regression" to "barbaric" ways had "exposed" the sacrament demonstrates the contrasting religious orientation of these early modern missionaries and their aboriginal targets. The Recollets conceived of conversion to Christianity as a one-way, exclusivistic decision, which by its very definition implied a radical reordering of converts' interior sensibilities and their utter repudiation of traditional religious and social norms. The Recollets sought to precipitate a wholesale cultural shift in which Catholic Christianity would become the singular touchstone of aboriginal life, triumphing over its rivals: indigenous traditional beliefs and the "heretical" errors of Protestantism, to which some Innu had intermittently been exposed. Accordingly, in their preaching to aboriginal groups, the Recollets sought to invoke conversion as a decisive and irrevocable choice that had eternal ramifications. They stressed that continued allegiance to traditional beliefs could lead only to infernal torment, whereas personal and social conformation to both the strictures of Roman Catholicism and to French cultural norms would be rewarded by the attainment of celestial bliss. Because of their linguistic deficiencies the Recollet often attempted to demonstrate these eternal verities with pedagogical artwork. Gabriel Sagard, a Recollet lay brother, describes a picture of the "Grand Jugement," which the missionaries would display for aboriginal audiences "so that they [could] understand the final destiny of man, the glory of the saved, and the punishment of the evil doers."[22] Though, following their initial experiences in the winter of 1615–1616, the Recollets' collective commitment to the wholesale religious transformation of aboriginal society remained unwavering, their categorization of native reactions to the Recollet religious message as "apostasy" would lead them to formulate a far more cautious, defensive, and gradual approach to the achievement of this sacred goal.

The exclusivism of Recollet religious expectations defied the established aboriginal-European relational dynamic, which was generally characterized by mutual accommodation. Judging from what we know about Innu behavior toward the Recollets, it seems likely that they initially perceived these new French interlopers, despite their unusual appearance, as being, like other Europeans, economic agents with whom mutually beneficial relations should be established. Many Innu "apostates" who had accepted baptism for themselves or their children during their initial winter encounter with Recollet missionaries probably did so because they saw this intriguing ceremony as inaugurating their political and economic affiliation with this new European subgroup.[23]

Even when the Innu discerned the specifically religious nature of Recollet claims, its exclusivistic demands were blunted by Innu relativism. In a report home, Joseph Le Caron wryly noted this strong cultural propensity: "They will believe all you please, or, at least, will not contradict you; and they will let you, too, believe what you will . . . No one must come here in hopes of suffering martyrdom, if we take the word in its strict theological sense, for we are not in a country where savages put Christians to death on account of their religion. They leave every one in his own belief."[24]

Innu religious relativism was particularly effective because it had both incorporative and defensive capabilities. Christianity, apprehended in an incorporative manner, offered a new repertoire of rituals, images, and ideas that, like the European trade goods with which the Innu were more familiar, might provide novel means of addressing traditional goals. In its defensive mode, however, Innu relativism overtly challenged Recollet cultural and religious exclusivism by highlighting French alterity, as Le Caron impatiently reported: "As they believe that the French live in a different world from theirs, when we wish to disabuse them of their folly by telling the real creation and restoration (of the earth) they say that this seems to be true of the world we inhabit, but not of theirs. They often ask even whether there is a sun and moon in Europe, as in their country."[25] Such questioning implicitly suggested that, as missionary claims reflected only French realities, their didactic prescriptions could claim merely societal rather than universal scope.

Having identified "apostasy" as the chief obstacle to the successful acquisition and retention of aboriginal souls for Christ, the Recollets, in concert with Champlain and other lay supporters in the spring of 1616 devised a comprehensive missionization strategy to combat such tendencies. This three-pronged policy reiterated the need for the sedentification and francization of aboriginal groups, strongly advocated the religious homogenization of the European population, and crafted a new evangelization strategy targeting aboriginal children rather than adults.[26]

The Recollets' experiences amongst the Wendat and Innu only confirmed missionaries' already extant suspicions that the "civilization" of aboriginal peoples must precede their Christianization. In order to reinvent Canada—transforming it from a contentious site fraught with economic and religious rivalries in to an economically diverse but religiously unified colony—traditionally migratory, hunting-and-gathering peoples such as the Innu must be persuaded to settle and emulate the agricultural techniques of their more "civilized" aboriginal neighbors and the small, agrarian French population. In short the Innu and others migratory groups must be "made into men" before they could be "made into Christians." Persuading peripatetic aboriginals to adopt what the French saw as the culturally and morally superior practice of agriculture was a necessary precursor in preparing them to accept, and voluntarily to retain, the yoke of Christ. Joseph Le Caron, writing back to his superiors in France stated, "It must be hoped that as the colony is peopled we shall civilize the Indians. This is necessary first; their mind will open and their good sense, of which they have the base. They will be regulated by French laws and modes of living, in order to render them capable of understanding such profound mysteries; for all that concerns humane and civil life is a mystery for our Indians in their present state."[27]

As the Recollets saw the conversion process as a form of socioreligious mentoring, they wanted to bolster the presence of those whose influence they perceived as benign, whilst excising those whose example could only prove pernicious. The Recollet claimed that Huguenot merchants continuously undermined missionary attempts to catechize the Innu population, both by their presence, which gave the lie to the missionaries' presentation of their universally acknowledged religious authority, and, more seriously, by the Huguenots' active, hostile interference with Recollet catechistic efforts, as summarized by Le Caron, with his characteristic combination of bombast and understatement: "Those who say derisively that what our priests consecrate at the altar is a White John, that his Holiness is the Antichrist, that if they could get their hands on the God of the papists, they would strangle him . . . and on the last monk, they would eat him . . . are not suited to . . . plant the Catholic, Apostolic, and Roman religion."[28] While Champlain had long pursued a trade monopoly for economic reasons, the Recollets now sought a religious monopoly for spiritual reasons. By arguing for the exclusion of Huguenots from New France, the Recollets were fighting the softening of royal policy, exemplified in the 1598 Edict of Nantes, on the shores of the New World.

"We Could not Risk the Sacraments to Adults":
The New Focus on Aboriginal Children

Along with their pleas for increased Catholic settlement, advocacy of the sedentification of aboriginal groups, and demands for Protestant exclusion from Canada, the Recollets in 1616 advocated the aggressive targeting of children for religious reeducation. Disturbed by their encounters with aboriginal adults, who embraced and transformed Christianity whilst simultaneously retaining their own cultural and religious worldview, the Recollets decided to limit baptism to those whom they saw as being under their absolute control. The Recollet initially made this decision on the basis of their own firsthand encounters with aboriginal religious relativism. In 1618, however, they consulted with theologians at the University of Paris and the Sorbonne "on the difficulty they felt in administering the Sacrament of Baptism to the Indians." These consultations reaffirmed their original decision to restrict reception into the Catholic Church to adults on the brink of death and to "those who, by long practice and experience, seemed touched, instructed, and detached from their savage ways, or to those habituated among our Frenchmen, brought up in our way of living, and humanized after being well instructed."[29] Though theoretically these "habituated" aboriginals could be adults, in practice missionary efforts quickly came to focus upon the isolation and instruction of young boys, whom the Recollets perceived as being less egregiously "steeped in sin" than their more obdurate elders. Having them absorb the French language, culture, and religion, the Recollet hoped to deploy these young converts as influential missionaries to their own people.

The Recollet decision to target the youngest members of aboriginal society initially appeared to have a number of pedagogical and financial benefits. The focus upon children allowed recourse to a wider range of familiar European educational techniques, including corporal punishment. From the beginning, Recollet-established schools in New France attempted to isolate children from their families and communities in order that this form of pedagogical "encouragement" could be utilized without the interference of indignant aboriginal parents. In Canada, corporal punishment could be used only sparingly, in secret, and on minors.[30] The Franciscans had utilized coercive methods in their catechism of adult neophytes in New Spain, sometimes to appalling excess.[31] However, the circumstances of French colonization along the St. Lawrence—characterized by a small, initially seasonal European presence which was dependent upon indigenous goodwill for the achievement of its economic, political and military goals—largely precluded the public physical coercion of aboriginal adults in the service of their salvation. Indeed, French desire to maintain cordial relations with their aboriginal allies led them significantly to alter their punishment methods in the civic arena, even for what would have been capital crimes in France.[32]

The Recollets' new child-focused policy was also well suited to the missionaries' dismally meager human and capital resources. The very evangelical poverty that lent the Recollets credibility in Europe put them at a practical disadvantage in North America. Without the consistent financing or manpower necessary to attempt the wholesale cultural and religious transformation of aboriginal societies, the Recollets effectively "miniaturized" their aspirations in the persons of these young children.

The new Recollet program of limiting baptism to moribund adults and culturally alienated children, while stemming aboriginal "apostasy," did so at a heavy cost, swelling the ranks of the Church triumphant at the expense of the Church militant. Converts who died shortly after the administration of the sacrament were of no help in persuading their fellows to embrace the Church: indeed, the practice of deathbed baptism only strengthened aboriginal suspicions of a causal link between the sacrament and the individual's demise, which almost invariably followed.[33]

Moreover, in selecting children as the preferred recipients of their attention, the Recollets made another strategic error. While they came to be skillful at successfully altering the religious and cultural identities of children artificially isolated from their homes and families, these young believers, without exception, failed to convert their native societies once repatriated. The Recollets' strategy greatly underestimated the pressures that would be brought to bear upon such children when they returned to their own milieu. Moreover, they fundamentally misjudged the direction of child-adult influence in aboriginal societies, which associated age, not youth, and experience, not childish ignorance, with wisdom. For the Innu, as for other early modern aboriginal cultures, children, though beloved, were perceived as culturally and spiritually unformed. Thus, even if converted children remained faithful to Christianity following their reimmersion into their native culture (in itself no mean feat), they nevertheless lacked the status to promulgate their new religion. In designing a child-focused missionary strategy, then, the Recollets squandered all their spiritual capital upon the least influential members of aboriginal society.

Despite their serious disadvantages, however, these child-focused Recollet policies would prove to be an influential model for successive waves of missionaries in the seventeenth century and beyond. The Recollet strategy of excising children from their native milieu and indoctrinating them with a novel set of religious and social practices far from home was thus the progenitor of the modern aboriginal residential school.

Pastedechouan's First Encounters with the Recollets

It is likely that Pastedechouan first encountered the Recollets in 1615, at the age of seven or eight, when Father John Dolbeau, who was to take him to France some five years later, first accompanied Innu bands on their winter hunt, assiduously excising the sign of the cross into the living wood of the northern forests as he went. Pastedechouan may have participated in the new Recollet program of child-focused evangelization several years later, when Joseph Le Caron established his modest day school at Tadoussac. There the young boy, then aged nine or ten, may have been one of Le Caron's students, learning his catechism and copying his lessons with laborious care. Indeed, Pastedechouan's efforts might have been among the examples of aboriginal penmanship that Le Caron so triumphantly enclosed with his own missives to his superiors and potential donors to the mission.

Such rudimentary, underfunded day schools were already, in 1618, felt to be wholly inadequate to the task of forming young "shock troops" bent on the religious reformation of aboriginal society along Catholic lines. Though the Recollets initially wished to found a series of local seminaries at all the important trading centers in New France, hard economic reality forced them to narrow their aspirations to a more achievable aim: an endowed theological school at Quebec, which would introduce its young boarders to Christian mysteries, inculcate French and possibly Latin literacy, and serve as the seedbed for a native clergy. Such an institution would effectively shelter its young charges from the insalubrious influences of both their unconverted families and hostile

Protestant traders, thus facilitating full Recollet control of the children's cultural and religious transformation.[34]

The Recollets' Reasons for Sending Pastedechouan to France

Young Pastedechouan's journey to France was intimately entangled with the foundation of the Recollets' new educational institution in Quebec. Indeed, the young boy appears to have been viewed as something of an economic agent both by the Recollets who procured him and by the Innu who surrendered him. While the Recollets' primary motivation for acquiring Pastedechouan was doubtless the salvation of his soul and the desire to equip him as a missionary to his own people, they also hoped that the young boy's presence in France, by attracting the attention of both the curious and the devout, would marshal new sources of financial support for their mission, particularly the new aboriginal seminary. Writing to the school's generous patron, Charles Des Boves, the Vicar General of Pontoise, Recollet Superior Denis Jamet stated that he was sending him Pastedechouan as something of a human progress report, a prototype of the devotional product the De Boves' investment capital would make possible.[35]

Pastedechouan's 1620 voyage came at the culmination of a particularly strenuous period of Recollet self-promotion in France, during which the missionary order was campaigning for stronger political and economic support for their presence in the New World and royal ratification of the increasingly detailed and ambitious agenda for Canadian development. Since their departure from France five years earlier, the Recollets had suffered the ignominy of being financially dependent upon the very trading interests whom they had bitterly antagonized. Though initially the merchants of Rouen and Saint-Malo committed themselves to underwriting the free passage and support of six Recollet missionaries a year, even in the first year they sent only four, who, virtually unaided, would form the nucleus of the Recollet presence for years to come. Not surprisingly, the merchants, many of whom were Protestant, resisted and resented their contractual obligation to underwrite missionaries who espoused an agenda contrary to the merchants' own immediate and long-term interests, who strongly objected to their business practices, and who doggedly questioned the legitimacy of the Protestant presence in the New World.

Though the Recollets were relentless in attempting to bring their plight to the attention of the court, their appeals often went unheeded.[36]

Though it initially appeared that the aboriginal seminary would prove to be a happy exception to the Recollets' bleak financial fortunes, in the end it too was blighted in the bud. Despite some generous initial donations, which would have enabled Pastedechouan to witness the June 3 ceremonial of the future seminary's cornerstone by his mentor Jean Dolbeau shortly before their joint departure for France in 1620, the scarcity of funds that had dogged the Recollet mission since its inception would eventually kill this young initiative in its infancy. Originally envisioned as a center capable of housing fifty aboriginal boys, the Quebec seminary became, after the 1623 death of underwriter Des Boves, merely a "halfway house, an antechamber, so to speak," for students, the majority of whom, like Pastedechouan, were destined for France.[37]

Given the chronic lack of funding and the decreasing number of aboriginal children offered by the Innu for education, the option of sending students to France, which was originally a means to an end, gradually came to be an end in itself. Like the seminary that it effectively replaced, expatriation of children performed the same functions of isolating a child from alternative religious influences and engendering in him or her a profound identification with Catholic Christianity.

"Observe Things for Us and Report Them": Innu Motivations for Consenting to Pastedechouan's Journey

Even as he was being groomed as a potentially lucrative fund-raising tool by the Recollets, Pastedechouan was also seen as an economic agent by his own people. It is a virtual certainty, given the economic, political and military interdependence of the Innu and French in 1620, that Pastedechouan's departure was, unlike Jacques Cartier's infamous kidnapping of aboriginal hostages some ninety-six years earlier, voluntary rather than coerced. Though Pastedechouan himself may not have been consulted about his fate, he doubtless boarded the France-bound ship only with the express permission of his family and larger society. Moreover, his journey made sense, in Innu terms, to those who had authorized it.

The Innu decision to allow Pastedechouan to travel to France was informed by a number of precedents in their relationships with both aboriginal and European groups. As we have seen, the intra-aboriginal exchange of young children had long been customary in cementing economic and military alliances. Adapting this custom to their commerce with Europeans, several aboriginal groups had welcomed young *trouchemens,* or *truchements,* for linguistic and cultural instruction and sent their own juvenile representatives to France. Children, as already noted, could also serve as human reparations and "goodwill hostages," effectively signaling the group's determination to smooth over relations marred by violence and suspicion. In 1618, two years before Pastedechouan's journey to France, the Recollets were given two young Innu boys, Nigamon and Tebachi, as reparations for the murder of two French traders by disgruntled Innu. While the Recollets vociferously objected to French compliance with this traditional aboriginal reparative practice, breaking with their ally Champlain in calling for the harsher measures of retributive French justice, when overruled, they made the best of a bad lot by recasting the young hostages as seminarians and sending the more "amenable" of the two, Nigamon, to France for theological training.[38]

While all of these precedents would likely have influenced how the Innu perceived Pastedechouan's journey overseas, the available evidence suggests that they saw him primarily as a political and economic agent. Eighteen years earlier, in 1602, two young Innu from Tadoussac, sponsored by the fur merchant François Gravé Du Pont, were presented at the court of Henri IV during the course of their year in France. Repatriated the following year, they gave an account of their successes, including the king's personal promise to help them in their ongoing military campaign against their Iroquois enemies, to a large crowd of Innu and their allies, assembled at Tadoussac. As related by Samuel de Champlain:

> One of the savages whom we had brought [to France] began to make his oration, of the good reception that the king had given them, and of the good entertainment they had received in France, and that they might feel assured His Majesty wished them well, and desired to people their country, and to make peace with their enemies . . . or send force to vanquish them. He also told of the fine castles, palaces, houses, and peoples they had seen, and of our manner of living. He was heard with the greatest possible silence.[39]

The resultant military alliance between the French and the Innu, the result of the young ambassadors' initiative, arguably established a strong precedent, decisively shaping how the Innu would perceive such junkets in the future. In the short term, it also resulted in a rash of Innu travel to France. The boys' triumphant return in good health, their successful negotiation of military assistance, and their wealth of relevant firsthand observations of the workings of French society prompted the influential Innu warrior and leader, Bechourat, to give his own son to Du Pont with the request that he "use him well, and let him see what the other two savages had seen." Five other aboriginals, including three other Innu, eventually accompanied this 1603 contingent. Around the same time, the Innu successfully placed a young representative at the heart of the French court, in the care of the young dauphin, but the Innu child died, likely the victim of a European disease, after only one year in France.[40]

By bringing young aboriginal delegates to France, traders sought to curry political favor with the court, to enhance their own prestige, and to gain an advantage over their trading rivals by forging personal and linguistic ties with their aboriginal guests. The Innu, for their part, appear to have welcomed their access to the pinnacle of French power in order to investigate for themselves the social, political, and economic lives of their trading partners on their home soil, the better to understand their intentions and capabilities.

The opportunity in 1620 once again to send an Innu agent to France proved irresistible. During Pastedechouan's childhood, Innu economic supremacy on the St. Lawrence had gradually been eroded by French incursions westward and their establishment of secure trading relations with rival aboriginal groups such as the Wendat. The Innu had long sought to forestall these developments by refusing repeated French requests for guidance in navigating the northern interior by means of the Innu-controlled Saguenay River, killing members of rival aboriginal groups who attempted to trade with the French without Innu mediation, demanding tariffs from those who traveled along Innu-dominated portions of the St. Lawrence, and engaging in elaborate whisper campaigns that sought to spread alarming rumors about the French, thus discouraging rival indigenous nations from establishing commerce with them.[41] The Recollet request to take another lad to France was probably seen by the Innu as the felicitous opening of a potential new front upon which they could fight their ongoing battle to retain their tenuous economic dominance. By placing an agent in the heartland of their sometimes inscrutable French ally, the Innu probably hoped to learn, as they had in

1602 and 1603, firsthand information that might help them to regain something of their former power.

The Innu decision to surrender Pastedechouan to Recollet guardianship should not be taken as indicating their ratification of the Recollet religious program or their consent to the profound spiritual transformation that these priests hoped to affect in their young charge. Indeed, even the Recollets acknowledged that Innu provision of young children for instruction was motivated more by their interest in maintaining cordial relations with Europeans rather than by their attraction to or acceptance of the Recollets' spiritual message. As Le Caron glumly noted: "They offer us their children and wish them baptized, but all this without the least sentiment of religion."[42] Thus, though both the Recollets and the Innu sought to utilize Pastedechouan's presence in France to their own economic advantage, Recollet success in their primary purpose—the transformation of Pastedechouan's religious mentality and sense of cultural identity—would prove to be a shocking, unprecedented, and unwelcome surprise to the Innu who had sent him as an economic ambassador. Upon Pastedechouan's return they gradually perceived that the Recollets had undermined the very sense of Innu identity and agency that would have made his mission a success in their terms. For, after five years abroad, Pastedechouan was no longer recognizable as "one of us."

Pastedechouan's Arrival in France

Pastedechouan left Canada for France at the age of "twelve or thirteen," accompanied by Father Jean Dolbeau. The two departed in the late summer or early fall of 1620, sometime after Dolbeau's ceremonial laying of the cornerstone for St. Charles, the aboriginal seminary that Pastedechouan's overseas trip was to promote. Following their long Atlantic crossing, the pair set off, probably on foot, for La Baumette, a fifteenth-century convent founded by Duke René of Anjou on cliffs overlooking the Maine River, within the sight and sound of the massive bell towers of the Cathédrale Saint-Maurice downstream in the larger center of Angers. Probably arriving by boat, the pair would have ascended the still-extant stone staircase from the river's edge into the interior of the imposing convent, which comprised four stone-built wings around a square inner courtyard rich with flowering trees, ringed with cloisters, and capped

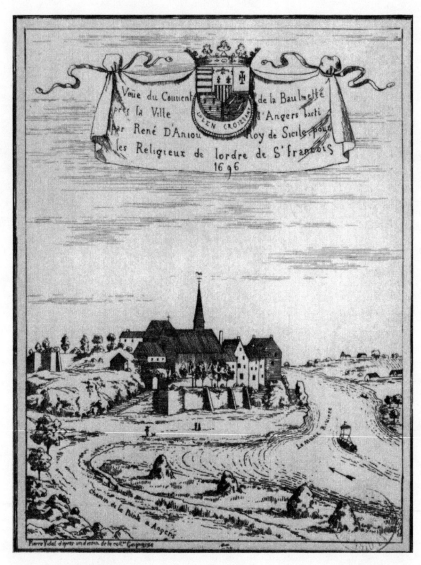

The cliff-top Recollet convent of La Baumette, near Angers in France, Pastedechouan's home from 1620 to 1625. A local pilgrimage site revered for its reputedly miraculous statue of Mary Magdalene, the convent was described as being
located in "a spot so beautiful that it ravished the eyes of all beholders and cured
the sick in soul." (Courtesy of the Archives Départmentales de Maine-et-Loire.)

with turrets. Named for the Provençal mountain upon which Mary Magdalene was said to have performed her famous penitential exercises, La
Baum, the convent had been excavated from the cliff's heart, and was
perched above the slow, lazy flow of the Maine River. As rhapsodically described by a sixteenth-century visitor, La Baumette was "a spot so beautiful that it ravished the eyes of all beholders and cured the sick in soul."[43]

Initially deeded to the "Cordeliers," as the Recollet's rival Franciscan
order was colloquially known, because of the three wide sashes or "corde-
lières" around their waists, the complex was ceded to the more rigorous
Recollets by Henri IV when its original inhabitants apparently failed to
approximate the Magdalene's austerity. The monarch's choice of the Recollets as replacements apparently hinged upon his pivotal conversation

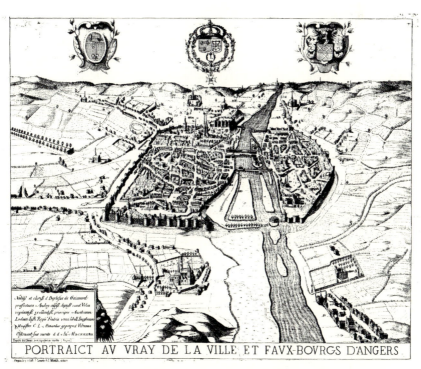

PORTRAICT AV VRAY DE LA VILLE ET FAVX-BOVRGS D'ANGERS

Seventeenth-century Angers. The Recollets of La Baumette, Pastedechouan's
mentors, were an integral part of the city's rich ritual life, which included the
Sacre d'Angers, a spectacular religious parade during Holy Week. (Courtesy of
the Archives Municipale d'Angers; photo: Bruno Amiot.)

with Recollet Provincial Jacques Garnier de Chapoüin. Asking the devout Franciscan what he wished for most in the world, the king was so impressed with the Provincial's austere answer, "poverty and reform," that he promptly arranged for the Recollets to inhabit the deserted La Baumette, staunchly backing them in their subsequent legal disputes with the disgraced Cordeliers.[44]

From its aerie above the Maine, La Baumette commanded an excellent view of the adjacent town of Angers. Clearly visible from the convent's lush cliff-top gardens were the massive fortifications of their own royal founder's hereditary castle and the twin spires of the great Cathédrale Saint-Maurice whose baritone chimes the convent met with the higher, more ethereal peals of its chapel bells, intimating with this sonorous exchange something of the intertwined nature of the educational and devotional life of the university town and her outlying hamlet. In the 1620s Angers, a walled city split down the center by the river Maine, was an ecclesiastical, legal, and educational center less renowned for trade or government than for its university, with which La Baumette, as a *studium generale,* or Recollet "house of studies" was closely connected.[45] In addition to its university, founded in 1431, Angers was noted for its impressive number of professed religious, its celebrated relics and religious treasures, and for the splendor of its annual cycle of devotional spectacles and processions. Though punctuated by sumptuous religious parades on the major feast days, the ecclesiastical year at Angers culminated with the magnificent *Sacre* on Corpus Christi, a daylong procession of the town's many religious orders, secular clergy, and twelve "torches": splendidly realized waxworks of violent, emotional scenes from the Hebrew Bible and life of Christ. Inaugurated at the cathedral with an early mass and punctuated by periods of alfresco preaching, the solemn procession of these realistic tableaux, each borne by more than a dozen men, together with the mobile display of the amassed treasures and relics of the respective religious community, was a pivotal local event, drawing pilgrims from throughout the region and well beyond.[46]

La Baumette, Pastedechouan's home for his five-year interlude in France, was both an integrated part of the Angers community, participating in the city's rigorous scholarly community and lavish ceremonial life, and a religious powerhouse in its own right, enjoying "considerable prestige and a reputation for piety."[47] A satellite of the larger center's centrifugal force, La Baumette also had a certain gravity of its own. Its status as its province's *studium generale,* its involvement in the Canadian mission, and its proprietary education of a young colonial prize—the aboriginal adolescent now living in their midst—prompted the curiosity and respect of the other local orders that had no such exotic overseas connections. Moreover, La Baumette's wooden statue of the Magdalene, clothed only in her long hair, was reputed to be miraculous, motivating a constant trickle of lay and religious devotees who wished to beseech her saintly intervention. While the Recollets of La Baumette ventured downstream throughout the year to take their appointed place in the festal processions that marked religious observance in Anjou, on July 22, the feast day of La Baumette's patroness, the Magdalene, the tide of humanity reversed. Angers "virtually emptied" as its religious communities and secular populace flocked up the river to touch the reputedly thamaturgical statue of the naked saint during the annual festivities in her honor.[48]

Adjusting to life in the Franciscan enclave was likely a lonely, exhausting, and jarring process for Pastedechouan. From his first ascent up the stony cliff-cut steps, Pastedechouan's days and nights would have begun to approximate the austere Observant model. In answer to the pealing bells, Pastedechouan would have quit his small cell or abandoned his work in study or stable, hurrying through the shadowed cloisters to join the larger community for their traditional eight daily periods of communal worship in their intimate chapel.[49] Whether lit by the pale candles of matins, or dappled in the lozenges of light created by the bright noon sun streaming through its stained glass, the chapel's clean, austere lines were interrupted on one side by a large outcropping of natural stone, which prompted visitor Abraham Golnitz, writing in 1631, to remark that La Baumette was a better place to visit than to live, as its "church, cloisters, and dormitory were practically in the rock."[50] Ostensibly there to harbor a grotto for the sacred image of the Magdalene, the presence of a dramatically naked, untooled rock face in this most sacred space distracted attention from its less imposing altar even as it threatened to destabilize the equation of civilization with Christianity and nature with barbarism which was the foundation of Pastedechouan's education at La Baumette.

Punctuated by these frequent interruptions for collective prayer, Pastedechouan's daily activities would probably have reflected his ambiguous status as lowly child, colonial trophy, and catechumen, comprising everything from homely domestic errands, high-level fund-raising meetings, and ongoing linguistic and theological preparation for baptism. Pastedechouan probably earned his keep by participating in the less-exalted daily routine of La Baumette, the corporeal counterpoint to its prayerful life of the spirit, by helping out in the kitchens or stables. In so doing, he followed in the footsteps of François Rabelais, the Franciscan literary giant famous for his coarse, subversive, and often anticlerical humor, who was a student at La Baumette early in the sixteenth century.[51] Like generations of boys before and after him, Pastedechouan would have been initiated into the deliciously ambiguous custom surrounding the fetching of the wine for cooking and meals. Contrary to common French practice, wine at La Baumette was stored not in a cool, musty cellar but at the top of one of the turrets enclosing the courtyard. In keeping with apparently long-standing tradition (which probably originated from the time of the rowdier Cordeliers), the boy sent to fetch the wine would intone one word of the Paternoster for each step of the winding staircase, arriving at "la cave" with an exultant "Amen." (Rabelais, however, apparently found this an insufficiently irreverent practice and supposedly inverted the prayer so as to arrive at the top step with the word "malo" of the phrase "Deliver us from evil," which simultaneously indicated his low opinion of the local wine and his willingness to play fast and loose with the words of Christ.)[52]

Even whilst adapting to the point and counterpoint of his daily devotional and servile obligations, Pastedechouan had to contend with the other demands of his Recollet hosts, who expected him to be both a crack fund-raiser and a model student. A key player in the Recollets' high-stakes public relations campaign, Pastedechouan met, throughout his first winter in France, with key members of the local clergy and nobility to persuade them of aboriginal religious and cultural amenability and to loosen their purse strings for the Recollets' Canadian cause. In fulfillment of Jamet's promise in his August 1620 letter, Pastedechouan would have met with Charles Des Boves—"an ecclesiastic of great piety . . . father and founder of our mission by his care and liberality"— the most generous donor to the newly established aboriginal seminary at Quebec and honorary "General Syndic" of the Recollet mission to Canada.[53] Pastedechouan also would have spent time with his godfather, Pierre de Rohan, the Prince of Guémenée, a powerful local noble and generous donor to the Recollets, probably at Rohan's palatial Chateau

Vergers. Apparently charmed by the young Innu, the prince, who was to finance Pastedechouan's education for the next five years, was an enthusiastic if informal teacher, instructing his godson in how "to know and love God and to say his paternoster in French and in Latin."[54]

"*Cathécumène Margajat*": Pastedechouan's Baptism

While Pastedechouan would likely have become accustomed to being the object of intense individual European scrutiny in his fund-raising role, embodying for interested donors the salubrious effects of Recollet missionization, nothing could have prepared him for the near mayhem that greeted his baptism on April 25, 1621. Even in a region well accustomed to extraordinary religious spectacle, Pastedechouan's ceremonial reception by the church appears to have excited an unusual outpouring

Cathédrale Saint-Maurice, the site of Pastedechouan's spectacular April 1621 baptism. Eyewitness accounts attest the church's courtyard was so thronged with those eager to catch a glimpse of the young Innu boy that "it was impossible to turn around." (Courtesy of the Archives Départmentales de Maine-et-Loire.)

Interior of the Cathédrale Saint-Maurice as it would have appeared in the
seventeenth century. It was here that Pastedechouan was stripped naked, baptized
by aspersion, dressed in white, and exhibited, holding a candle in the cathedral's
pulpit. (Courtesy of the Archives Départmentales de Maine-et-Loire.)

of interest, as the people of Angers and the surrounding area sought, that late spring evening, to catch a glimpse of the exotic youngster. According to Jean Louvet, a local diarist who recorded his impressions of the event, the Cathédrale Saint-Maurice was jammed with hundreds of onlookers, and its front courtyard was so tightly packed that it was "impossible to turn around." Most present hoped at least to catch a glimpse of the young cathechumen, whom, they had heard, hailed from the icy wastes of distant Canada.[55] Ecclesiastics, nobles, and commoners alike thronged the nave and choir galleries and, jostling, stared as Pastedechouan, accompanied by a coterie of clerical officials, his noble godparents, and an entourage of

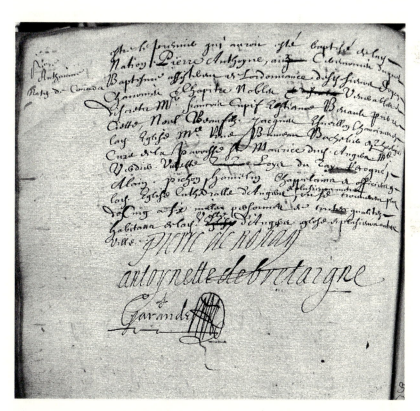

Official registry of Pierre-Anthoine Pastedechouan's April 1621 baptism, signed by his noble godparents and namesakes, Pierre de Rohan, the Prince of Guémenée, and Antoynette of Bretaigne, his wife. (Courtesy of the Archives Municipale d'Angers; photo: Bruno Amiot.)

servants, preceded through the exterior cloisters and down the nave, dwarfed by the centuries-old Tapestry of the Apocalypse hanging on the towering walls around them, its angels and demons transfixed in their struggle for ultimate ascendancy. Flowers and incense scented the dim, stone-vaulted interior of the church, and candlelight from the many white tapers winked on the rich, ornately inlaid cross held aloft in advance of the grand procession and glinted on the silver vessels of holy oil borne by the score of pages. The party emerged from the main church building through its massive, brass-studded wooden doors surmounted by the austere figure of Christ in judgment and passed through the cathedral's echoing gallery into the mild evening air. There in the public square in front of the cathedral, in full view of the assembled crowd, the Prince and Princess of Guémenée effected their godson's civic rebirth by wrapping him in a green cloth "in the French manner" and bestowing upon him their own names: "Pierre-Anthoyne, because the Prince was called Pierre and madam the Princess, Anthoynette." Reentering the crowded church, Pastedechouan was stripped of his clothing just within its massive front doors, liberally anointed with holy oil, and then baptized by aspersion at the adjacent altar of a local saint, *Serene*. Redressed all in white and given a lit white candle to hold, he was crowned with a snowy white baptismal *cresmeau,* or bonnet.[56] Following a sermon, Pastedechouan was taken "ceremoniously to the choir and the nave to show him to the people who wanted to see him." To appease those whose curiosity was unsatiated, Pastedechouan was elevated to "the pulpit, where he was for a long time with the *cresmeau* on his head and a lit candle in his hand, where he appeared completely relaxed."[57]

Aboriginals in Europe: Sixteenth- and Early Seventeenth-Century Precedents

Aboriginals exhibited in Europe had long had the power to draw a crowd. For over a hundred years before Pastedechouan's baptism, European explorers had brought aboriginal people from both North and South America to serve as living proof of their successful voyages, to sell as slaves, to give as human gifts to patrons, or to display as animate artifacts to a public who indiscriminately devoured tales of real and imagined voyages to distant and exotic lands. Whether they were spectacular, large-scale displays of entire aboriginal groups, such as the elaborate Brazilian scene evoked to celebrate the entry of Henry II into Rouen in 1550, or the amateurish exhibition of a smaller numbers of captives, such as that of a kidnapped Inuit woman and her child in the Netherlands in 1566, the sixteenth-century presentation of these living "curiosities" invariably emphasized the spectacular "otherness" of aboriginal people.[58]

Most sixteenth-century aboriginal captives taken to Europe died there: some of wounds inflicted during their capture, some of diseases to which they had no immunity, some from rough treatment or the unfamiliar diet, some simply from the trauma of being violently plucked from their own society and thrust into one in which their freedom of movement and ability to communicate were severely restricted. Though repatriation of living aboriginals did occur, it was relatively rare.

At the turn of the seventeenth century, however, motives for bringing aboriginal peoples to Europe began to change, as the volitional exchange of political and economic ambassadors gradually came to rival the chaos and fracture of forced kidnappings. Particularly for French traders in northeastern North America, a lack of permanent European settlements and a fiercely competitive intra-European trade situation necessitated the establishment of mutually acceptable relationships with their aboriginal trading partners. With so much to lose, Europeans could ill afford to alienate their powerful hosts, as had Jacques Cartier some seventy years earlier. Typical of this changing climate of increasing mutuality was the visit to the French court, some eighteen years before Pastedechouan's own journey, of the Innu contingent of 1602 and the similar, subsequent visits which its success inspired.

While it is true that a considerable number of aboriginal people were baptized in Europe prior to the 1620s, particularly in the Spanish empire, neither the sixteenth-century coerced capture and display of New World peoples nor early seventeenth-century voluntary trade exchanges were primarily in the service of religious objectives. Though the royal permissions given to the explorers of northeastern North America were often couched in religious terms, this verbiage, derided by Trudel as a "ridiculous pretense," was generally empty political rhetoric.[59] Moreover, though professional religious (generally priests, but occasionally Protestant ministers) sometimes accompanied the whalers and fisherman who haunted the coasts of North America in the summer months, they generally confined their religious duties to the spiritual care of their European shipmates rather than extending them to the edification of New World "savages."

Nor did the imagination of the sixteenth-century public appear incorporatively inclined, perceiving North American aboriginal peoples as being so alien as to belong, almost, to a different order of beings. Early modern broadsheets advertising the exhibition of captured aboriginals played to this strong sense of "otherness" with wild allegations of gigantism and cannibalism and by invariably contrasting the God-fearing piety of European audience members with the benighted savagery of the "barbarian" captives that they had paid to see. One such advertisement reads, "Let us thank God the Almighty for his blessings, that he has enlightened us with his Word, so that we are not such completely wild people and man-eaters as are in this district, that this woman was captured and brought out, since she knows nothing at all of the true God, but lives almost more wickedly than the beasts."[60] The religious conversion of Canadian aboriginals in the sixteenth and early seventeenth centuries was thus only a peripheral concern of the French kings who authorized New World trade and exploration, the agents who carried out their orders, and the flotilla of illegal whalers and fisherman who sought illicitly to purloin the resources, including, occasionally, the human resources of this new world. Their essential disinterest in the religious transformation of aboriginal peoples was reflected by the crowds who flocked to see captives or ambassadors. For the throngs who jostled one another in their desire to gawk at these exotic strangers, religion remained a primary marker of fascinating but inexorable human difference rather than a potentially unifying and transformative force.

The eyewitness description of Pastedechouan's baptismal ceremony thus reveals both continuity and change in the way in which aboriginal peoples were perceived in France and the European motivations for effecting their presence. His baptism was a striking blend of publicity stunt, religious rite, and freak show. The baptism's official purpose—rendering the exotic, dangerous "other" familiar and comprehensible—and the obvious interest of the crowd in just these suppressed elements. For the Recollets who had brought the young boy to France and their noble benefactors, who underwrote his education, this ceremony remade Pastedechouan into their own European image, both politically and religiously, and celebrated their power in being able to effect these momentous changes. For them, Pastedechouan's sacramental transformation was the prototype of a much more ambitious project: the systematic religious reconfiguration of aboriginal culture and the establishment of an ethnically diverse but religiously uniform colonial society in distant Canada. For the spectators, however, conditioned to expect exotic display, Pastede-chouan was intriguing because of rather than in spite of his differences from them. Jean Louvet, the French layman who so carefully described Pastedechouan's baptism, appears to have seen the boy's "otherness" as essentially unaltered by the ceremony, given his repeated description of him as a *cathécumène margajat,* a "second class" or "marginal" catechu-men, and his fascination with Pastedechouan's exotic appearance: "He was very black, his nose was wide, and he had a big mouth."[61]

Nonetheless retaining elements of spectacular exhibitionism (and, con-sequently, its wide popular appeal), Pastedechouan's public display during his baptism represented an essentially new focus in early seventeenth-century France on the extraction, isolation, and radical religious transfor-mation of young aboriginal children. While earlier exhibitions of captured aboriginals had indulged their audiences' craving for the fantastic by em-phasizing, often artificially, aboriginal "otherness," this religious ceremony proposed something quite novel: that "one of them" could be transformed into "one of us." The mutation of what had been an essentially secular genre of aboriginal exhibition, based on an assumption of radical "other-ness," to a religious genre of transformation, based on a new and illusory perception of aboriginal religious tractability, epitomized the permeation of late sixteenth-century Catholic revivalism into the disparate enclaves of colonial policy, overseas trade, and popular entertainment, venues that had long been largely impervious to its influence.

Goals of Pastedechouan's Recollet Education

Pastedechouan's baptism both symbolically epitomized and initiated an inexorable process that, in the four years following, would radically trans-form his cultural, religious, and linguistic identity. As dramatically enacted in the ritual symbolism of his baptismal ceremony, the Recollets sought to effect his transfiguration from "savage" to Frenchman, from "Godless hea-then" to devout Catholic, and from "one of them" to "one of us."

Pastedechouan's new civic identity was ritually marked by his effective rebirth into a noble French family, that of Pierre de Rohan, and signaled by his public reception of a new name, fashioned from those of his god-parents. The Recollets wished formally to link religious and civic affilia-tion, (vainly) arguing that the rite of baptism should confer upon all new aboriginal Christians the right to French citizenship.[62] The success of Pastedechouan's ability to assume and retain a French identity would thus have been evaluated by his host society in cultural as well as religious terms, as he represented in microcosm a compelling argument for the civic as well as the spiritual future of New France.

The most fundamental goal, however, both of the baptism itself and the additional years of theological education that it presaged and initiated, was Pastedechouan's religious transformation. On one level, the white candle given to Pastedechouan to hold during his exhibition in the pulpit of Cathédrale Saint-Maurice was a pragmatic response to the vocal desire of the jostling crowd for a better look at the object of their fascination. But it also signaled his emergence from the darkness of "superstition" and animist "ignorance" into the gospel light of Christ.

Recollet aspirations for Pastedechouan's religious transformation were also encoded in the baptismal ritual's performative language of stripping and reclothing. This dramatic and highly unusual ritual gesture was not contemporary French custom but rather evoked the practice of early Christian evangelization, recapitulating in a sense the transformation of the Franks from pagan to Christian centuries before. His Recollet mentors did their assiduous best, for the remainder of Pastedechouan's tenure in France, to make this ritual promise of transformation a fully realized, living reality.[63]

By 1620, when Pastedechouan departed for France, the Recollets, having accrued five years of mission experience, had reconsidered their initial impression that, as the Innu lacked the familiar accoutrements of religion, "they acknowledge no divinity."[64] Rather, as their grand plans to effect a total cultural and religious reorganization of native society stalled, Recollets were forced to acknowledge the extent to which everyday Innu life was permeated with the sacred.[65] The act of symbolically stripping Pastedechouan of his garments signaled Recollet determination entirely to divest him of his native religious conceptualizations and to vitiate the devastatingly effective Innu strategy of religious relativism. Indeed, perhaps chief among the goals of the Recollets who trained Pastedechouan and his fellow aboriginal children in France was the desire to impress upon them that their conversion, ratified by the baptism that symbolically received them into Christ's mystical body, was an exclusivistic, unalterable and one-way choice that necessarily entailed the renunciation of most aspects of their previous way of life. To that end, the Recollets isolated their young neophytes not only from their families on the other side of the Atlantic but also from their juvenile compatriots in France. The Recollet policy of widely dispersing visiting aboriginal children, while maximizing the fund-raising opportunities that their presence afforded, also ensured that newly arrived boys could not reinfect their Christianized brethren with the contagion of traditional beliefs.[66]

Though the stripping of a young neophyte of his garments at baptism was highly unusual, Recollet insistence on Catholic exclusivism was not peculiar to the missionaries' congress with the aboriginal nations of early modern North America. The determined tenacity the Catholic Church displayed in grappling with aboriginal beliefs mirrored its aggressive re-action to threats to its supremacy within the European context. The re-ligious formation of children had long been the battleground upon which Catholicism had struggled to reassert its broken hegemony. In the religiously divided, battle-scarred France of the sixteenth and seventeenth centuries, Catholic orders were not above kidnapping the children of prominent Protestants in order to raise them in "the true Church."[67] The Recollets' intent eradication of Pastedechouan's tradi-tional Innu beliefs was similar in most respects to their elimination of the Protestant preconceptions of the Huguenot children they sought to indoctrinate. The Recollets' "scorched-earth policy" of replacing extant aboriginal beliefs with the strictures of post-Tridentine Catholicism should not be understood primarily as expressing cultural ethnocen-trism but rather as indicating the Recollets' radical intolerance of alter-native religious beliefs and practices, be they aboriginal or European.

Recollet Pedagogy and Spiritual Direction

Every minute of Pastedechouan's days at La Baumette would likely have been crammed with individual devotions, catechism, collective religious observances, spiritual direction, language lessons, and the visual assim-ilation of religious information. The mere fact that this young boy, the product of an oral culture, apparently learned, between his arrival in the fall of 1620 and his departure in the spring of 1625, to speak, read, and write both French and Latin testifies to the circumscribed, studious, and pious manner in which he must have spent his days.

But how Pastedechouan was taught during his five years in France ar-guably affected his developing personality and religious mentality as much or more than what he was taught. The informal mentoring of his Innu childhood contrasted in almost every particular with the authoritarian rigors of his theological and linguistic education in France. Though both systems had as their overall aim the reproduction of cultural and religious knowledge, the two differed sharply in their overall orientation, purpose, and methods. As we have seen, in Innu society the teaching of young children took place within the context of daily life. Innu children learned kinetically, through a process of observation and imitation, and at a level appropriate to their age, the gendered skills and behaviors that were required of them. Aboriginal discipline of children usually took the form of gentle teasing or the recounting of cautionary tales: harsher taunting was reserved solely for adults who had failed to master the adaptive set of skills and behaviors that would befit them for social and physical survival. Physical punishment of children was not tolerated: the Innu regarded French recourse to such methods as both perplexing and cruel. Though Innu education was a lengthy, informal process of pragmatic and unstructured tutoring, it intensified in the late preteen years, as Innu young people approached physical maturity. The fundamental goal of the Innu mentoring process was the production of self-sufficient cultural actors capable of shouldering the burden of providing for themselves, their families, and their wider community. Rather than demanding children's submission to the authority of the adults who mentored them, Innu education aimed to bequeath the cultural skills, mental outlook, and religious attunement that would foster adolescents' skilled self-reliance and adherence to the social ethics of respect, cooperation, and stoicism.[68]

French formal education in the early seventeenth century was, by contrast, a discrete process divorced from the regular activities of daily life, a process that emphasized academics, took place in a specialized setting, utilized a formal syllabus, entailed highly prescribed behavior, and involved the rote memorization of both theological and linguistic concepts. Fear of physical coercion and deprivation, as well as the actual employment of these practices, were routinely utilized both to facilitate students' mastery of prescribed information and to impress upon them the awesome authority of their teachers. While the aim of Innu mentoring was the child's achievement of mature independence, Recollet education sought to erode aboriginal children's "proud" freedom and to curb their "willful" autonomy, both by conditioning "docile" behavior more in keeping with the Franciscan ideals of humility and obedience and by implanting a deeply internalized sense of dependency upon and subservience to religious authority. Though Pastedechouan became a man during his five years in Recollet custody, he remained, to his religious superiors, a mere "child in the faith," whose spiritual progress was entirely contingent upon their continuous watchful guidance.[69]

As his education and spiritual formation appear to have been in the hands of Jean Dolbeau during the entirety of his time in France, the strictness and austerity of Pastedechouan's formal linguistic and theological training may have been mitigated somewhat by more individual, personalized spiritual direction. After his return to La Baumette with Pastedechouan in 1620, Dolbeau was appointed, in recognition of his gifts for discernment and individual spiritual counseling, as a master of novices, to direct the education and religious formation of both children given to the Recollets for education and incoming novices in the Recollet provinces of St. Denis and St. Marie-Magdalene.[70] Judging on the basis of his celebrated spiritual direction of Anne de Pichery many years later, Dolbeau's style of individual direction appears to have emphasized development of an interior spiritual life through the encouragement of contemplative apprehension of the Trinity. Dolbeau's mystical propensities, though particularly intense, illustrate the long-standing Franciscan preoccupation with mental prayer and individual spiritual development, an aspect of their movement that is often eclipsed by scholarly attention to their collective evangelical ethos. Even after the Franciscans at La Baumette adopted elaborate liturgical celebration after 1518, they continued to stress the necessity for individual, internal reflection as well as collective, external celebration.[71] Dolbeau's possible perception and treatment of Pastedechouan as a religious actor with his own relationship to the divine, a relationship which should be guided but not determined by outside influences, may have given the boy some sense of himself as a spiritual subject rather than encouraging him to view himself as malleable clay passively awaiting the impress of his Catholic education.

Conversely, the Franciscan concern for inner transformation as well as outer conformation would have made this highly individual form of pedagogical contact a double-edged sword. Close attention to the nature and orthodoxy of his inner spiritual life would have made it more difficult for Pastedechouan to create his own idiosyncratic religious ethos through orthopraxic participation in ritual actions that left much of their theological import implicit. The Recollets' "rigorous program of personal transformation," would have used meditative and disciplinary exercises to fundamentally reform his sense of self, with the goal of making inner inclination and outward behavior perfectly congruent.[72] It is unclear, then, whether his relationship with Dolbeau would have empowered Pastedechouan by giving him a sense of ownership of his own religious subjectivity or further weakened his sense of self by further facilitating his internalization of essentially foreign norms and expectations.

Classroom of the Eyes: Education by Images

In addition to his formal pedagogical instruction and his more personalized guidance by his mentor Dolbeau, it is likely that iconography was part of Pastedechouan's education, particularly in its early stages, when his grasp of French was imperfect. Early modern religious orders, both in Europe and overseas, relied upon graphic depictions of their faith's central mysteries to help bridge conceptual and linguistic barriers between themselves and their target populations, be they the rural illiterates of Europe's backwaters, the religiously unenlightened "pagans" of Asia, the unlettered "savages" of North America, or even urban French parishioners. Indeed, the famous Sacre d'Angers, which featured the procession of intricate religious tableaus, was itself a form of mobile religious education. The "torches" eloquently, if mutely, related in their frozen action the epic of the fall and redemption of man—graphically depicting sin, suffering, and atonement. For many attendees, wordless gazing at such spectacles may have replaced the verbal homilies that were intended to accompany and supplement them. McManners, in his book on the ritual life of eighteenth-century Angers, states of such noonday sermons,

> The bishop placed the Sacrament in the central arcade . . . from whence . . . one could see the whole city spread out below. There was a halt here for two hours, a motet was sung, and a sermon preached from the open air pulpit in the cemetery adjacent to the chapel. According to strict liturgical theory, the people remained here, worshipping like the Israelites at the foot of Sinai; in practice, there was a general adjournment for lunch . . . so the sermon was rather wasted.[73]

Abroad, among the most frequently requested items in missionaries' letters to their European superiors were elegant, impressive, and systematic visual depictions of major Christian personages and ideas, which were required as much for their didactic utility as for their sacramental and possibly thaumaturgic value.[74] While still on Canadian soil, Pastedechouan would have become familiar, likely through exposure at Le Caron's humble day school Tadoussac, with the visual attributes of the infant and suffering Christ, his mother, and the patron saints of Jesuit and Recollet missionaries. By gazing at these imported images Pastedechouan would have arrived at a provisional understanding of Catholic sacred geography, both infernal and celestial, and grasped the missionaries' central message, to fear hell, depicted as a place of fearful physical and psychological torment, and to seek, through Christ's sacrifice, the blessed assurance of heaven.[75]

With Pastedechouan's arrival in the Old World, opportunities for his visual education would have increased exponentially. La Baumette, liberally adorned with frescos, was a treasure trove of Christian iconography.

Images were often used by Catholic missionaries to North America to communicate their theology nonverbally. This detail shows "The Worship of the Beast," from the nightmarishly vivid Tapestry of the Apocalypse, to which Pastedechouan was doubtless exposed. Its strongly dualistic rendering of the final battle between good and evil couched the latter in bestial terms, presenting the religious appreciation of animals, the benchmark of Innu religion, as diabolical. (Courtesy of MONUM, centre des monuments nationaux; photo: Caroline Rose.)

Pastedechouan would have taken his meals in the convent's refectory, under the sorrowful gaze of the Virgin of the Deposition, mournfully clutching the body of her Son before a backdrop of contemporary Angers. Frowning saints would have silently supervised his studies in the convent's library. The arrested beating of angels' wings, lovingly depicted in all their feathery perfection, would have urged him down the sunlit corridors to mass. Once in the chapel, Paste-dechouan would have contemplated, in her stony grotto, the chaste nudity of Mary Magdalene, his new home's accidental patron.

The Cathédrale Saint-Maurice, site of Pastedechouan's 1621 baptism and home of the Sacre, presented further possibilities for his iconographic education. Its principal treasure, the nightmarishly vivid fourteenth-century Tapestry of the Apocalypse, encompassed within its sixty-seven panels an evocative rendering of the Revelation of St. John.[76] Commissioned in 1377 by Louis I of Anjou, it was owned by each of the dukes of Anjou until Roi René, the founder of La Baumette, deeded it in his will to the Cathédrale Saint-Maurice. Double-decker, its panels were divided into serene upper sequences—which depicted, in their predominant palette of celestial blue, the otherworldly peace of heaven and the triumphant reign of Christ—and lower panels whose scarlet tones presented scenes of rampant carnage and destruction.[77] The archetypal theme of the battle between the forces of God and the Devil for possession of an individual soul, evident in the modest etchings of Pastedechouan's provisional Canadian classroom, here metastasized into massive, violent depiction of the end-times war between Jesus and Satan. The Canadian miniatures and the larger-than-life tapestry both vividly urged the necessity of definitively allying oneself with the forces of righteousness, as the dire consequences of rejecting Christ's sovereignty were all too vividly portrayed. The damned are masticated alive by infernal monsters, broken under the hooves of the Apocalypse's four horsemen, or drowned, burning, in a fiery sea. With its threatening double message of alluring peace and nightmarish torture, the tapestry visually asserts the necessity of becoming a foot soldier against the forces of sin and Satan. The message of the tapestry would doubtless have been reinforced by Pastedechouan's Recollet educators as they led the white-gowned boy through his baptismal preparation and procession.

It is particularly interesting to try to imagine how Pastedechouan, the product of culture that valorized animals as "other-than-human" persons would have interpreted these emblazoned panels, in which beasts both real and imagined played a central and generally malign role. With the exception of the symbolic winged animals of St. Mark and St. Luke (the lion and the ox respectively) and the depiction of Christ himself as a slain yet triumphant Lamb, the beast's tapestry embodies satanic pride, deceit, and malice. Accompanied by more anthropomorphic symbols, such as Death (a skeleton mounted on his "pale horse") and the accursed Whore of Babylon, these powerfully muscled, many-headed beasts repeatedly receive the mistaken worship of the uninformed and wreak bloody war on the brave, beautiful armies of angels.[78]

While it is impossible to conclude how Pastedechouan himself may have viewed such images, it is likely that they influenced his lifelong tendency to think of religious allegiance in strongly dualistic terms, even as they reinforced his hosts' assertions that conversion represented an decision simultaneously to embrace the one true church and actively to fight the forces of delusion and disorder. The tapestry's repetitive images of the worship of bestial gods validated the Recollets' claims that those who, blinded by and enslaved to Satan, clung to false deities would face a horrifying chastisement. It is likely that both Pastedechouan's later description of his own people as "beasts who know not God" and his lifelong preoccupation with the pains of hell were nourished by the rich depictions of idolatry and its consequences realized with such care in the silken red-and-blue threads of the tapestry.[79]

Interruptions to the Pedagogical Program: Illness and Death

The regularity of Pastedechouan's theological, linguistic, meditative, and iconographic education during his five years at La Baumette, which was likely as orderly as his systematic declension of Latin and French verbs, was at several junctures interrupted by intimations of mortality. Though Pastedechouan, unlike his predecessor Rabelais, did not encounter the plague at Angers, at some point during his La Baumette sojourn the boy apparently experienced a major, possibly life-threatening illness, likely a European ailment to which he lacked immunity.[80] We know little of the details of Pastedechouan's illness. Indeed, we would not even know that it had occurred had he not, years later, bitterly remarked to Jesuit Superior Paul Le Jeune, "Would to God that I had died when I was sick in France, and I would now be saved."[81] Given the statistics on aboriginal survival in the Old World, Pastedechouan's illness comes as no surprise: it was his ability to cheat death that was somewhat unusual. Almost every aboriginal visitor to Europe in the seventeenth century experienced some sickness, and many, especially those there for some time, died of exposure to foreign viruses. Lacking immunity to virulent European diseases such as measles, mumps, chicken pox, and scarlet fever, aboriginal ambassadors to Europe faced an appallingly high mortality rate. Compounding biological vulnerability were the psychological

Pierre de Rohan, Pastedechouan's noble godfather, who underwrote his five-year French education and "taught him to pray his paternoster in French and Latin." (Courtesy of the Archives Municipale d'Angers; photo: Bruno Amiot.)

factors of loneliness, depression, and culture shock. During Pastedechouan's illness the Recollets would have nursed him and, concerned
more for his soul than his body, prepared him for death, judgment, and
burial in an unmarked grave in the small cemetery immediately adjacent
to the chapel. Like other invalids at La Baumette, the young man might
have witnessed Mass from an honoured place in a specially constructed
gallery for bed-bound invalids in the convent's chapel.

Perhaps, having dodged his own fate, Pastedechouan owed God a
death. Certainly, the outcome he had so narrowly avoided redounded
upon the head of his noble godfather and namesake, the Prince of Guémenée. Although relatively young, the prince in December 1622 would
meet his own terrifying and unexpected end, only nineteen months following his triumphant appearance at Pastedechouan's baptism. The no-
bleman's breathless, apoplectic death-dance horrified all who witnessed it.
Gripped by violent, shuddering convulsions, Pastedechouan's patron col-
lapsed at his sumptuous home of Vergers, frantically gasping for breath
and clawing at the air as if attempting to fend off approaching demons. His
education secure due to special provisions in Rohan's will, Pastedechouan,
as his godson, would certainly have attended the subsequent, elaborate fu-
neral, the somber double of his own baptismal procession.[82]

Only in the linguistic arena of Pastedechouan's education was his
transformation deliberately left incomplete. To facilitate his ability to
convert his fellow Innu following his repatriation, his teachers alternated
the young man's thorough instruction in French and Latin with opportunities for him to converse in his native language. While the Recollet saw
French as the eventual lingua franca of Canada, they realized that their
ability to communicate the Gospel in aboriginal tongues would be critical in the intervening years.[83] Accordingly, Pastedechouan, while yet a
student of Latin and French, became the Innu language instructor of eager lay brother Gabriel Sagard.[84] Sagard's interest in aboriginal linguistics
had been simultaneously stimulated and thwarted by his exposure to the
cryptic scribbles of his fellow Recollet missionaries, and he regarded the
opportunity to converse with a native speaker as heaven-sent. It is unclear for how long Pastedechouan tutored Sagard, but when the latter departed for Canada in March of 1623, besandled and penniless, he broke
with the Primitive Rule of St. Francis enough to take with him a "small
dictionary" of the Innu language, "composed and written in the clear
hand of Pierre-Anthoine, our Canadian."[85]

The Recollet decision to allow Pastedechouan to hold onto a modicum of his former cultural identity, in the form of his mother tongue, did not endanger their larger project of effecting his total religious transformation. Indeed, so complete was Pastedechouan's identification with the French Catholic identity modeled for him by the Recollets that, in the latter years of his sojourn, he apparently claimed to have forgotten the Innu language. It is unlikely that such a claim was factually accurate, as Innu was Pastedechouan's maternal language and, at least until Sagard's 1623 departure, he had ample opportunity to speak it. The fact that Pastedechouan repeatedly made such statements seems to indicate not the true loss of competency but rather his repudiation of his former linguistic, cultural, and religious identity.[86]

"Send Me Not Back":
Pastedechouan's Reluctant Return to Canada

Pastedechouan's claims of his deteriorating ability in his maternal language had unexpected results, precipitating events that he seems to have experienced as a devastating crisis in his young life. His individual religious transformation, while an important end in itself, had always been envisioned by his Recollet mentors as the necessary means to a yet greater goal: the conversion of his native society. Pastedechouan's comments triggered Recollet concerns that, by lingering in France, he might become unfit for the remainder of his religious task. In attempting to voice his affinity with the Recollet agenda, Pastedechouan had unwittingly provoked his missionary hosts to demand his immediate repatriation. "As Pierre-Anthoine was more advanced, having made five years' stay in France, which he did not wish to leave, Father George and Father Joseph thought proper to persuade him to make a voyage home. As he was tractable and docile, he yielded to their entreaties from a pure motive of God's glory."[87] On April 24, 1625, one day short of exactly four years after his magnificent baptismal ceremony, Pastedechouan was shepherded aboard a ship bound for Canada, accompanied by Recollet Father Joseph de la Roche Daillion and a small contingent of Jesuits, an order with which his future was to be fatefully intertwined.[88] In answer to Recollet requests to help their ill-funded, ill-manned mission, the group included Jesuit's Charles Lallemant, Enemond Massé, and Jean de Brébeuf, the famous linguist and martyr.[89]

Le Clercq's presentation of Pastedechouan's "docile" and "tractable" yielding to Recollet requests notwithstanding, it is clear that the young man sought to challenge, evade, and delay his repatriation at every turn. Even aboard ship, racing westward across the Atlantic, when return to his community must have seemed a fait accompli, Pastedechouan planned a way to delay the inevitable. Rather than eagerly rejoining his family at Tadoussac, the ship's initial port of call, the young man successfully pleaded with his missionary mentors for permission to continue upriver to Quebec to winter at the Recollet headquarters. Described during this period as "a naturalized Frenchman, and very devout," Pastedechouan studiously "avoided intercourse with the few Indians who came" to the missionary outpost.[90] This maneuver probably bought him another nine or ten months. But the advent of spring brought renewed Recollet demands that he re-embrace his family and community. Even now, far from being reconciled to his fate, Pastedechouan "long showed repugnance" and "begged the father Superior, with tears in his eyes, to dispense him from this, saying: 'My Father, how could your Reverence want to send me back to the beasts who do not know God?' But the Fathers said to him that it was so they would know God and so that he would relearn his mother tongue to help in saving his family and all his nation, after which he obeyed and prepared himself to go."[91]

Pastedechouan's reported fear of return, first to Canada and then to his family at Tadoussac, can be seen as a response to the Recollets' totalistic missionary model, which postulated that children's removal from their "contaminated" culture was the best way they could become and remain Christians. Though chilling in their profound cultural alienation, Pastedechouan's reported words and the fears they so eloquently express were eminently logical within the central premise of this model: that one's individual identity is largely predicated upon the nature of one's surrounding environment. Having labored for five years to transform himself culturally, linguistically, and religiously from an Innu to a Frenchman, Pastedechouan may have been concerned that this fragile new identity would be lost once its enabling environment was removed. His characterization of his own family as "beasts who know not God" powerfully illustrates the way in which he had been taught to think of his maternal and adopted cultures in deeply antithetical terms. Such a characterization, in fact, betrays a double alienation. At the most obvious level, Pastedechouan is demonstrating his distance from his family and community by describing them in such terms. But his very choice of the word "beasts," used in a derogative sense, also indicates his profound alienation from the broad Innu concept of community, in which animal beings are seen as being "like us,"—as having shared "personalistic" characteristics of will, intent, and power.

Pastedechouan's already palpable fear of his people as a source of sinful corruption would only have been intensified by the elaborate rules of engagement impressed upon him by the Recollets before his departure for Tadoussac. His mentors sought to armor their young convert for contact with the unconverted in a hostile, religiously heterogeneous environment by instructing him "in how he must conduct himself amongst these people without risk to his salvation," thus heightening the youth's preoccupation with religious purity and contamination.[92] It is clear that the Recollets' exclusivist model of conversion and cultural conformation demonstrably influenced how Pastedechouan regarded the relationship between religion, culture, and identity for the remainder of his life, decisively lessening his ability flexibly to combine European and native elements in any religiously meaningful or psychologically helpful way, as was eventually done by several other members of his large aboriginal family.

"The *Manitou* Is Good for Nothing": Typical Reactions of Aboriginal Child Converts

Pastedechouan's apparent cultural and religious alienation from his own people—expressed in his effective disavowal of his own linguistic background, his reported expressions of repugnance toward native beliefs and practices, and his fearful aversion to contact with other aboriginals— were typical of the response of many seventeenth-century indigenous children removed from their society and forced into a relationship of dependency upon and identification with the language, religion, and culture of the French. Whether they were young seminarians voluntarily given by their families for education, goodwill hostages surrendered as insurance for the lives of French missionaries venturing into the interior, or female orphans taken on as servants by overseas convents, many of Pastedechouan's fellow "reluctant ambassadors" experienced and expressed a similar response. Indeed, Pastedechouan's agonized and alienated words were echoed by a young aboriginal girl's apparent assertion, in 1630s Dieppe, that "the *Manitou* was good for nothing [and] that she no longer wished to return to Canada."[93]

Five factors appear to have been critical in promoting aboriginal children's identification with French culture: the degree of their cultural isolation, their precise life circumstances, their age when taken, the nature of their host institution, and the amount of time they spent in French custody.[94] Those children who were mostly likely to experience profound cultural, religious, and linguistic alienation from their own cultures and a concomitant identification with French ways and ideals were those who, like Pastedechouan, were unable to dilute the overwhelmingly French influence upon their lives by maintaining strong connections with their own communities; those who were wholly dependent upon European care due to the death of their parents or guardians; those who were taken by the French at a young age, before their status as adults in their own societies had been ritually affirmed; those who were taken to France by missionaries, and those who were held for long periods.[95] By contrast, children who were able to maintain many aspects of their religious and cultural integrity had intact families to return home to, were taken by the French during less vulnerable developmental periods, were hosted by explorers or traders rather than missionaries, and spent only limited amounts of time in exclusively French custody.[96]

Though both responses did occur, it was the pattern Pastedechouan experienced, which combined rejection of the child's maternal culture with the fervent adoption of that of the French, that was promoted and recorded by early modern European missionaries with undisguised relish. Recollet and Jesuits alike saw children's changing attitudes as evidence that their young charges were beginning to mirror their own evaluation of aboriginal religious and cultural practices as "sinful" and "barbaric." Their embarrassed rejection of their own culture was seen as a necessary precursor to children's embrace of a profound Christian spirituality, which was often described in hagiographic terms. The achievements of child neophytes, such as Pastedechouan's own fervent piety, were presented both as an indication of missionary success and as an explicit rhetorical rebuke of the tepidity of contemporary European devotion. Thus Christian Le Clercq, writing about Pastedechouan's religious transformation for a European audience, reproachfully wrote: "He [Pastedechouan] was a Christian, and so devout as to shame many who laid claim to piety." Moreover, European missionaries saw the spiritual intervention of deceased child converts as being particularly powerful. In 1622 a Recollet missionary, describing a particularly dangerous voyage, credited prayers addressed to a recently deceased young aboriginal convert, whose body had been consigned to the raging waters, with saving all aboard their ship from imminent disaster on the stormy St. Lawrence:

> This precious deposit which our Fathers . . . had placed in heaven was not useless to them. He acted as their intercessor in a storm which surprised them in the river . . . They were all in extreme peril, when several of the passengers on board cried to God for mercy, and begged it in the name of that soul which He had just received . . . He received the intercession of that glorious soul, for there suddenly appeared in the evening a light by which they saw that the vessel was about to be wrecked on some rocks, and veered off.[97]

Converts' immersion in the devotional hothouses of early modern French convents, then, led many young aboriginals to express negative evaluations of their cradle cultures, perceiving and presenting themselves as wholly French and as entirely Catholic. Their hosts generally encouraged and ratified such self-perceptions, suggesting that these youthful prodigies, through their innocent ardor, the tireless efforts of their missionary mentors, and the grace of God, had not merely attained spiritual parity with their European counterparts but far exceeded them.

Developments at Tadoussac in Pastedechouan's Absence, 1620–1626

The six years of Pastedechouan's absence from Tadoussac, first in France, then at Quebec, had been tumultuous and stressful for his people as they sought to adjust to a series of military, economic, and religious shifts. Though their nearly continuous war of attrition with their traditional Mohawk foes, which had been raging since at least the turn of the century, had ceased with a peace treaty in 1624, the end of hostilities merely caused new tensions to rise to the surface. The temporary neutralization of their trenchant aboriginal antagonists to the south led to an Innu reconsideration of their alliance with the monopoly-holding French colonials at Quebec.

Innu economic and political influence had received its first rude shocks years prior to Pastedechouan's journey, with the opening of direct

French trade with the Huron in 1612, a move that the Innu had long foreseen and attempted to thwart. Innu predominance received a further blow with the establishment and vigilant enforcement of a French trading monopoly in 1614, which, by reducing the amount of illegal trading, dramatically drove down the prices that the Innu were able to demand for their furs. During the second and third decades of the 1600s, the Innu went from holding a virtual monopoly on pelts gathered to their north to supplying only one-third of the total furs traded along the St. Lawrence.

The waning of Innu economic dominance coincided with the community's increasing dependence on European goods. At the height of their preeminence, the Innu had been able to act as intermediaries between the French and their inland allies, the Etchemin, Algonkian, and Kichesipirini peoples, effectively trading the furs trapped by others. But with the collapse of the Innu monopoly, the aboriginal groups who had formerly supplied them now dealt directly with the French. Innu participation in European trade, as a result, became far more difficult, as they now needed to supply a greater percentage of their furs through their own trapping efforts. As these activities took their attention from traditional subsistence activities, the Innu became reliant upon European foodstuffs to make up the difference, just when they could least afford to purchase them.[98]

In addition to their continuing involvement in the "legitimate" fur trade, the Innu of the 1620s increasingly indulged in illicit barter with the Quebec monopolists' illegal rivals. Tadoussac, downriver from Quebec, the French administrative center, became the center of Protestant disaffection with the stringent enforcement of the trading monopoly further upriver and the increasingly Catholic complexion of French colonialism along the St. Lawrence.

From the beginning, the low-grade intra-European conflict, ostensibly over trade, had economic, political, and religious aspects. Attempts to preserve trading monopolies for commercial reasons and efforts to police the confessional identity of the colony for religious reasons, while conceptually distinct goals, were often linked in practice. In Acadia, the more easterly of the two Canadian colonies, a Protestant minister and Catholic priest living in the same small community apparently so despised one another that they repeatedly came to physical blows. When both died within days of one another, the Acadians apparently buried them in a common grave, "to see if they would continue to argue after death."[99] Protestants in the St. Lawrence River Valley, who initially dominated the Canadian trade, had long had their religious activities restricted, being forbidden to bring ministers or to establish their own churches. Such interdictions did not stop them from defiantly and lustily singing psalms and hymns, or gathering informally for prayer. However, though the Recollets had initiated their campaign for a Canadian ban on Huguenot immigration in 1616, Protestants were barred from New France only in 1627, one year after Pastedechouan's return to Tadoussac and one year before this critical stronghold would fall to the Calvinist Kirke brothers, invaders in the service of the English crown.[100]

The 1615 advent of the Recollets heightened already extant powerful confessional tensions between Catholic and Huguenot contingents in New France, each of whom perceived the other as the more favored and powerful. Le Caron complained that Protestant-dominated trading companies got their way because of their economic clout, describing Huguenots as having "the best share in the trade," and feared that "the contempt they showed for [Catholic] mysteries would greatly retard the establishment of the faith."[101] For their part, French Protestants, long remembering their persecution both before and after the 1598 Edict of Nantes, were understandably defensive and wary when the legality of their entrenched place in the New World was brought into question by these missionary upstarts.

During the summer of 1620, just as Pastedechouan was preparing to leave Tadoussac for France, Champlain complained of the antics there of two renegade vessels from Protestant La Rochelle. "Notwithstanding the King's prohibition" and numerous attempts to apprehend them, these illegal traders had allegedly "carried off . . . a quantity of peltries and had given the savages a large supply of firearms . . . a most pernicious and mischievous thing thus to arm these infidels, who might on occasion use these weapons against" the colonial presence at Quebec. Champlain continued, "These rascals, moreover, coming into this country suborn the savages and talk about our religion in a very pernicious and spiteful manner, or order to render us the more odious in their eyes." In relating the escapades of the lately escaped "Rochellais," Champlain conflated their Protestant confessional identity with their political disloyalty: "'What can you expect?' people say—'they are Rochellais, that is to say, very bad and disobedient subjects, in whom there is no such thing as justice.'"[102]

Later in the year Champlain would discover further evidence of the degree of the bootlegging, and the determination of the illegal traders to defend their illicit trade with the Innu, using both physical barriers and ideological weapons against monopolists who were seeking to enforce their legitimate title. Once again heeding calls that there were renegade vessels around the Tadoussac area, Champlain pursued the lead, only to grimly remark that "it was too late . . . The birds had flown . . . Nothing was found but the nest, a kind of palisade that they had erected to guard against surprise while they were trading."[103] While the defensive palisade was easily destroyed, diffusing the escalating confessional tensions would prove to be more difficult. In 1622 Champlain reported a bitter dispute about worship aboard a confessionally divided ship. Three years later, angry Catholics burned inflammatory anti-Jesuit pamphlets. In 1626 Huguenot sailors anchored off Tadoussac and, in defiance of legislation banning their public worship, sung their shipboard psalms so lustily that they could be clearly heard by shore-bound Innu and pained Catholics alike.[104]

Innu exposure to the defiant Protestant theology of these loudly sung psalms was symptomatic of their increasing subjection to a cacophony of clashing European religious ideations and interests in the 1620s. Because ancient Innu summering places around Tadoussac continued to host a substantial Catholic missionary presence, even as their distance from Quebec attracted covert Huguenot traders, each European confession attempted to erode Innu confidence in the religious and economic claims of their rivals, while loudly promoting their own. Though some Tadoussac Innu continued to give their children to the Recollets as a means of affiliating themselves with the missionaries' increasingly powerful ally, Governor Champlain, Protestant merchants discouraged Innu accord with Catholic missionaries by suggesting that Catholics were responsible for outbreaks of illness among aboriginal peoples. Reporting his conversation with a prominent Innu, Gabriel Sagard wrote, "La Fourière . . . said, too, that the priests, who prayed to God with the form and ceremony they used, were the cause of many of their companions dying . . . with other impious words from the talk of men of the Reformed religion, who had put such notions into their heads, besides a lot of other such things concerning our faith."[105] Protestants made frightening allegations about the nature and intent of the Catholic baptismal rite, leading to incidents of real and threatened violence against Recollets, Jesuits, and their young charges.

Innu reliance upon Champlain's military aid early in the seventeenth century initially thwarted the development of an "unholy alliance" between the Innu, bitter at their economic eclipse, and rogue merchants smarting from their exclusion from the Canadian fur trade. But with the succession of intra-aboriginal hostilities in 1624, long-standing attempts of Protestant merchants to play upon Innu economic discontent to provoke their uprising against colonial authorities began to bear fruit. Some Innu began openly speculating that if they killed all the French at Quebec trade would once again become more competitive and European goods would become cheaper. A large Innu expedition would have had a good chance of success, given the small number of European residents of the St. Lawrence River Valley. Encouraged in such aspirations by Huguenot traders, who supplied them with European arms, the Innu began to be regarded by colonial officials as a significant threat to ongoing peaceful trade. Though large-scale conflict was successfully averted, in 1617 and a decade later in 1627 several French monopolists were murdered by Innu in the course of trade disputes. Champlain's heavy-handed response to these instances only increased Innu resentment.[106]

Pastedechouan's Reception by the Innu

Pastedechouan's return to Tadoussac in the spring or early summer of 1926 took place in this turbulent and unsettled atmosphere. Though Recollet writers paint a rosy picture of his reintegration, somewhat vaguely claiming that the young man "rendered great service to the mission under the guidance and direction of our Fathers," Pastedechouan's short stay at Tadoussac may be an indication of how profoundly his "mission" had failed there.[107] Pastedechouan appears to have taken a leadership role among the young Innu boys whom the Recollets already had under instruction and with whom he probably lived. While his relationship with his grey-robed mentors and other French remained close and cordial, outside that charmed circle, where he was regarded as something of a celebrity, his reception was markedly cooler. Dramatic changes in his appearance, behavior, and identity and his apparent unwillingness or inability to resume a traditional Innu lifestyle caused considerable confusion and disquiet among the Innu.

But why should Pastedechouan's assumption of a distinctive new identity be so disturbing to his erstwhile community? After all, the complete and sometimes abrupt ritual transformation of an individual's very self was not unknown in Pastedechouan's cradle culture. Indeed, Innu religious expectations countenanced dramatic shifts in an individual's identity, loyalties, and capabilities. The central ritual drama of male adulthood, the vision quest, transformed a green boy into a mature man in a period of days, impressing his freshly minted adulthood with the stamp of an animal mentor and bequeathing him with a new name, abilities, and skills.

Moreover, the complex dynamic of Innu-Mohawk hostility in early seventeenth-century Canada was one in which the politics of identity transformation were central. As we have seen, captured Mohawk prisoners became part of the Innu body politic and vice versa. Those killed in nightlong, tortuous rituals were incorporated literally, through the ceremonious ingestion of their physical remains. Those spared—generally all of the women and children and a significant percentage of the men—were culturally assimilated, becoming valued members of the Innu community. Initially ill treated upon their arrival into the Innu camp, those kept alive were seen as potential family members who would become, through their ritual reception of a foreign soul, the walking embodiments of the beloved dead, receiving from them the social roles which the dead had played during their earthly lives. As familial incarnations, the newly adopted were seen as unimpeachably Innu and were expected, as such, to display absolute loyalty to their new community. Captured women took their place in the sexual economy of their new families: becoming wives and mothers. Men fought as Innu beside their new compatriots, often against their former kin and communities.[108]

In Innu as well as Catholic terms, then, an individual's cultural and religious identity and allegiances were seen as fluid and potentially transformable. Just as Pastedechouan's Recollet mentors had sought, through baptism, to change a young "savage" into a pious Catholic, Pastedechouan's Innu community confidently asserted that they could remake a captured enemy into a respected and loved family member, indulging, like their Catholic counterparts, in dramatic ceremonies thought to utterly eclipse an individual's former identity and allegiances. At first glance, then, Pastedechouan's radical transformation at the hands of his Recollet mentors should have been readily comprehensible in the religious terms of his own community. In spending five years in France, Pastedechouan, like a young Innu prisoner of war, had undergone abrupt removal from his cradle culture and the total reshaping of his identity and loyalties. Why, then, did Pastedechouan's transformation so appall his community?

Because, in short, the surface similarities between these two forms of social transformation were belied by their yet deeper differences. Innu-Mohawk warfare helped to forge a shared, mutually comprehensible ethic by providing similar functions within each culture. Through low-level, constant antagonism with one another, each group gained a training ground for young men seeking to assert their competency; an outlet for the aggressive impulses strictly repressed within each culture; and a ritual venue for expression of the shock, anger, and grief of bereavement. Warfare itself and, more particularly, rituals surrounding the transformation of foe into kin, which were at the heart of postwar incorporative practices, paradoxically affirmed and strengthened the deep cultural and religious similarities between the two indigenous groups, as can be seen by the fidelity with which each side adhered to the rules of engagement, whether in the role of victor or vanquished. Innu-Mohawk antagonism was a ritual drama that paradoxically depended for its meaning and efficacy upon shared religious and cultural values and assumptions, locking the antagonists into an embrace as fecund as it was violent.

In contrast to interaboriginal hostilities, which reinforced deep cultural and religious congruencies between very different aboriginal societies and tempered bitter animosity with palpable respect, missionary indoctrination of young children sought to engender in them a profound sense of contempt for and alienation from their cradle cultures, teaching them to see their families and communities, living in the vast darkness outside baptism's holy circle of light, as "beasts who know not God." Far from cementing new familial ties between antagonists, this form of religious transformation was predicated upon the complete repudiation of one's cradle culture and the replacement of one's biological family with one's new family in Christ.

Moreover, the two transformative processes, Innu and Christian, were predicated upon wholly different understandings of the adult role. While capture by and reintegration into a rival aboriginal group was doubtless traumatic, it did not significantly disrupt a child's process of cultural maturation, as early modern aboriginal groups generally held congruent ideals of adulthood, characterized by an emphasis upon self-sufficiency, responsibility for family and community, and adherence to the gendered arts of survival. Reeducation by an early modern Catholic order, by contrast, substituted spiritual dependency, even in adulthood, upon missionary authority for the intellectual and economic self-sufficiency that ideally accompanied the achievement of aboriginal maturity.

Thus, despite the fact that both the Innu and French missionaries utilized identity-transforming ceremonies such as captive adoption and religious reeducation, critical distinctions in the way each envisioned the dramatic change that such rituals encoded meant that the Innu reacted to Pastedechouan's religious transformation with astonishment. Expecting the return of a confident Innu man who, like his 1602 predecessors, could shrewdly relate to them new insights into French capabilities and intensions, they found only a boy whose ethos, outlook, and priorities were virtually indistinguishable from those of his missionary mentors. Innu shock at his frighteningly undeveloped skills in the adult male arts of hunting, diplomacy, and war was matched only by their horrified realization of the extent of Pastedechouan's dependency upon and deference to the gray-robed Recollet interlopers. The young man's seeming inability to provide his people with the crucial economic and military information that they had awaited, coupled with his pronounced difficulty in achieving or exhibiting a mature Innu perspective, provoked in sectors of his community intense feelings of disappointment, suspicion, and anger.

The nature of the Innu response to Pastedechouan's transformation (and to the place of child converts in Innu culture more generally) is illuminated by events that occurred during Pentecost of 1627, more than a year following the young man's forced encounter with the Innu community at Tadoussac. The occasion was the contentious baptism of another young boy, Naneogauachit, a ten-year-old Innu whom Pastedechouan appears to have tutored in the Christian faith, advising him to remain faithful to his missionary mentors in the face of familial opposition to his religious reeducation.

In many ways, Naneogauachit's story is a Canadian echo of Pastedechouan's own childhood experiences in France. Like his adolescent mentor, Naneogauachit was exposed to artwork that depicted salvation and damnation, finding his own version of the Tapestry of the Apocalypse in a large engraving of the Last Judgement in the Recollet convent, which the missionaries used specifically to illustrate for aboriginal visitors the contrast between the happiness of the saved and the suffering of the damned. Poignantly, Naneogauachit asked to see this schematic representation of Catholic sacred geography the better to pinpoint the destination of a friend who had recently died.[109]

Naneogauachit was isolated from his family, living at the Recollet convent in Quebec rather than further east, near his band's traditional summer camp. His experiences eloquently demonstrate how missionary practices of isolating and reeducating young children on Canadian soil "fractured families and split Innu society." Recollet documents demonstrate that the boy's mental health began to deteriorate alarmingly as he was caught between the contrary urgings of Pastedechouan and the Recollets, who sought to preserve him in the Catholic faith, and the often violent attempts of his apparently Huguenot-influenced father, Choumin, to force him from their convent.[110]

In contrast to Pastedechouan's magnificent public ceremony in the packed cathedral at Angers seven years earlier, a ritual which publicly displayed missionary power and piety, Naneogauachit's baptism at the preeminent Canadian center of European influence was a hurried and furtive affair, illustrating the degree to which Catholic religious rituals had become suspect in the Innu community. As the intransigent opposition of Choumin to his son's baptism provoked Recollet fears of its possible violent disruption, the ritual, coperformed by Recollet and Jesuit missionaries, was witnessed only by the pillars of French Catholic society and a handful of "reliable" Innu, including, of course, Pastedechouan, their model convert. In a brief homily delivered to the larger Innu assembly at a goodwill feast the missionaries had prepared, Joseph Le Caron sought to disperse the palpable cloud of Innu suspicions surrounding the event in particular and Recollet presence and intentions more generally. The former Tadoussac schoolteacher, now Recollet Superior, reiterated the urgent necessity for wholesale Innu religious and cultural change, presented baptism as its seal and symbol, and urged all present to follow the lead of Naneogauachit and Pastedechouan by accepting religious instruction. While his words were favorably received by some segments of his Innu audience, Le Caron's comments prompted a very different response from an Innu leader named Mathican Atic. Rather than directly challenging Le Caron's arguments, however, Mathican Atic instead addressed Pastedechouan:

> Pastedechouan, . . . it is true that you are not very smart because you haven't told us what you learned in France. We sent you there in order

for you to observe things for us and report them, but you have been here for more than a winter and you haven't told us anything. I don't know if it is because you are not smart enough, or because you are too shy, or because you don't care about what's in France, but when you are talking with us about France you are too childish. You must be a man and speak with confidence and wisdom, telling us the things you have seen and learned, in order that we should know them too.[111]

Mathican Atic's words illustrate the profound frustration that comes from confounded expectations. It is clear that his negative evaluation of Pastedechouan's performance abroad was informed by his comparison of it with that of previous Innu contingents, who had traveled overseas in the service of their people's military, political, and economic aspirations. Mathican Atic, reiterating that the Innu had consented to Pastede-chouan's journey so that he could "observe things for us and report them," expressed his deep disappointment with the paucity of usable information obtained during Pastedechouan's long years abroad. Previous Innu contingents had been able to report that the trade goods given to aboriginal peoples were of inferior quality, giving them the inside information they needed to negotiate for better products. Others, such as the 1602 Innu contingent, had successfully brokered critical, still-extant military alliances.[112]

Mathican Atic's personal expectations for Pastedechouan's trip would only have been heightened by the fact that the elder's family had long supported such endeavors. His father, Anadabijou, an influential Innu leader, had been intimately involved in the reception of the returning 1602 Innu contingent. It was his enthusiastic endorsement of the military and political gains that had been made by these young Innu agents and his personal satisfaction with their treatment while abroad that encouraged other prominent Innu headmen, such as Bechourat, to send their sons on similar missions.[113]

Though Mathican Atic complained that Pastedechouan had not "told" the Innu "anything," this accusation probably indicated the Innu leader's deep dissatisfaction with the information the young man had provided rather than its total absence. The Catholic doctrine that Pastedechouan doubtless attempted to promulgate upon his return had none of the pragmatic, strategic value that the Innu were seeking: indeed, in the tense and poisonous atmosphere of 1626 Tadoussac, such religious information would immediately have been associated by his audience with a host of controversial political and economic positions. Mathican Atic's complaint, then, was fundamentally that the Recollets had highjacked a useful though rarely used weapon in the Innu arsenal, the foreign trade delegation, and refashioned it without Innu consent into an instrument of individual religious transformation. Such a result, however, had none of the military or economic benefits that the Innu had come to expect from their engagement in this form of commerce with Europeans.

In addition to stating that Pastedechouan had failed in his mission because of his unwillingness or inability to gather, interpret, and disclose useful knowledge, Mathican Atic also contended that Pastedechouan's agency and development had been seriously undermined by his long tutelage by the Recollets. Mathican Atic's long speech, addressed to Pastedechouan, implicitly answered Le Caron's call for the Innu assembly to accept Christianity by pointing out that the religious transformation the Recollets were advocating at the societal level had had devastating results, from the Innu perspective, at the individual level. Mathican Atic implied that Pastedechouan's peculiar dependency upon the Recollets had thwarted both his successful completion of the tasks entrusted to him and his acquisition of the wisdom and independence he needed to assume his rightful place as a mature man in Innu society. Mathican Atic's reservations about the degree to which Pastedechouan's Recollet education had made him unfit both mentally and physically for Innu life would prove to be eerily prescient. For the remainder of his short life, Pastedechouan would struggle fruitlessly to acquire Innu survival skills, leading to his humiliating dependency upon the other male members of his family and eventually to his untimely death. By describing Pastedechouan's current behavior as "childish" and urging him to "be a man," Mathican Atic challenged the youth to recognize and reverse the detrimental effects that his French sojourn had had upon his personal development and social acceptance. By appealing to Pastedechouan, Mathic Atic expressed the still-extant hope of Innu leaders that this youth could yet provide them with valuable information, based upon his unprecedented exposure to French society, during a period in which their economic dependency upon their sometime ally was only deepening.[114]

Pastedechouan's failure to acknowledge or address Mathican Atic's complaints would have only reinforced his challenger's arguments in the minds of the attentive Innu crowd watching the exchange. Though it is unclear from the evidence available whether Pastedechouan, unwilling to answer his interrogator, voluntarily deferred to his mentor or whether he was prevented from responding by Le Caron, who replied on his behalf, either scenario would have confirmed Mathican Atic's portrait of Pastedechouan as inappropriately dependent on Recollet authority. Moreover, the Recollet Superior's impatient response makes it clear that such complaints and queries were common. Expressing his exasperation with Innu "distrust" of his protégé's previous reports of his experiences overseas, Le Caron responded to Mathican Atic's trenchant questions by reciting a list of the young man's religious achievements while in France: "He learned French, he learned how to pray to God, how to read and write, and a lot of other things that you don't know, that we will, if you would like, teach you and your children."[115] Le Caron's exasperated remarks betray his genuine ignorance of how Pastedechouan's experiences had dashed the powerful expectations set by previous Innu economic contingents to France in the premissionary era.

It is important to note that Pastedechouan's challenger, Mathican Atic, and other community leaders, such as Naneogauachit's father Choumin, were not Innu "traditionalists" adamantly opposed to the presence or program of the French. Rather, these men were among the most "French-identified" members of the Tadoussac-based Innu community. Both were deeply implicated in Gallic efforts to control Innu politics from the outside by influencing the fortunes of their favorites. Mathican Atic had only five years before received Champlain's help in achieving a position of considerable power within the Innu community. Choumin had also assiduously courted French connections. As we will recall, during the early years of the Recollet presence, he had gone so far as to name one of Naneogauachit's brothers "Père Joseph" after the very missionary performing the baptismal ritual to which he was now so vehemently opposed.[116] Neither man, then, can be characterized as merely anti-French. Their objection to the Recollet conversion of young Innu boys appears to have been motivated by the fact that such dramatic religious changes did nothing to advance Innu economic or social interests and had a pernicious effect upon the independence, agency, and maturity of those it touched. Pastedechouan, then, was not rejected because his community objected to the actual content of his new religious views but rather because the manner in which his new religious identity had been impressed upon him had negatively affected the fulfillment of his Innu mission in France and undermined his achievement of Innu standards for adult male behavior.

Like the laypeople crowded into Cathédrale Saint-Maurice on the late spring evening of Pastedechouan's baptism, these pillars of Innu society appear to have been taken aback by the recasting in religious terms of patterns of engagement and identification between Europeans and aboriginals that had become more familiar with the passage of each successive decade. Just as the French crowd, conditioned by their earlier experiences of encounters with aboriginal peoples, brought to the new religious setting a readiness to shamelessly gawk at one of "them" rather than solemnly to witness the incorporation of one of "us," so the Innu at Naneogauachit's baptismal feast expected Pastedechouan, as "one of us," to disclose critical information needed to deal with an increasingly intrusive and ambitious "them." Mathican Atic's expressions of frustration with what he perceived as Pastedechouan's secrecy regarding his experiences in France clearly demonstrate that the young boy's repeated protestations regarding the religious nature of his experiences were deeply disappointing to the Innu. Equally alarming was the apparent slippage in his sense of ethnic and religious identity. Far from gaining the insights of a trusted Innu agent, repeated interrogations of Pastedechouan had resulted only in the reiteration of French perspectives from a boy who now considered himself "one of them."

In isolating, baptizing, and reeducating young Pastedechouan, the Recollets had done the unprecedented. Unlike their secular successors, who had brought aboriginals to Europe to display as living artifacts of mysterious distant lands or as trade ambassadors, the Recollets had successfully transformed Pastedechouan's consciousness to closely resemble their own, inculcating in Pastedechouan a Catholic exclusivism that made him regard other religious systems, be they Protestant or Innu, as dangerous contaminants. Indeed, they had instilled in him such a fear of and contempt for his culture that he was unable effectively to communicate with, let alone reintegrate into, Innu society. Challenged by a leading Innu elder to justify his actions and explain his experiences in France, Pastedechouan remained mute, leaving his puzzled Recollet mentor, who ill understood the perspective of his questioner, to reply for him.

His people's essentially negative perception of Pastedechouan upon his return was heightened by a series of events during his five-year absence, which had made Tadoussac a center for illegal trade and a fulcrum of anti-Catholic propaganda. Huguenot success in linking Catholic religious rituals with what were widely perceived by the Innu as unfairly monopolistic trading practices meant that Pastedechouan, as an agent of Catholicism, was probably seen as defending these despised policies.

In addition to inculcating in Pastedechouan a strong commitment to his new identity and a desire to defend and preserve it, the Recollets also imparted to him a powerful sense of its fragility, emphasizing the omnipresent danger to his faith from contact with the unconverted aboriginals and dangerous heretics who surrounded him upon his return to Canada. Their sense of this danger, encoded into a lengthy set of rules Pastedechouan was to observe while in the presence of these twin threats, represented their evaluation that his fragile new persona as a French Catholic could be quickly and easily undermined.

As his consequent behavior would demonstrate, Pastedechouan appears to have internalized this sense of his identity as weak and fragile and to have seen French colonial society, with which he identified himself, as permanent and enduring. Both perceptions, however, were wildly inaccurate. Pastedechouan's commitment to his French identity and alliances was to prove remarkably strong, such that he was willing not only to brave the rejection of his people but, out of loyalty, decisively to refuse alliance with the rival European powers who would soon shatter the proud illusion of French dominance in the St. Lawrence River valley. Pastedechouan's destiny was to be decisively shaped, not simply by his exposure to an imperious early modern Catholicism, but by the clash of the French and the English for control of Canada.

3

"I Have Not a Mind Strong Enough to Remain Firm"

Religious Ambivalence

Squinting against the bright June sunlight, Pastedechouan might have stared intently downriver to where the wide St. Lawrence met the sea. His attention, like that of the rest of the small crowd assembled on the sandy shores at Tadoussac that early summer morning in 1632, would have been distracted from the beauty of the rounded blue hills and broad expanse of harbor by the small flotilla of French ships, now only an indistinct speck on the distant horizon.

It had been a long time since Pastedechouan had looked upon a European without considerable trepidation. Some four years earlier, in the late spring of 1628, while walking along these same banks, Pastedechouan had innocently saluted a passing ship flying the English standard and ended up the unwilling guest of its captain. The presence of such a vessel was not at all unusual—quite the contrary. Far enough east of the French colonial center of Quebec to escape frequent patrol, Tadoussac had come to be something of an unofficial headquarters for Protestant merchants, English and French, who were bent upon defending their stakes in the lucrative illegal fur trade in defiance of the official monopoly. Those on board this vessel, however, had a rather more ambitious agenda. Its captain, David Kirke, accompanied by his four younger brothers, would capture Quebec the following spring, forcing the repatriation of the fledgling colony's entire administrative, missionary, and trading personnel for some three years.[1] Though the Kirkes' father was English, their French mother, their nativity in Dieppe, and above all their Protestantism led to their acid description by those they defeated as "renegade and Anglicized French."[2] French feelings ran so high against the Kirke brothers after their initial successes against colonial targets that they were officially deemed "public enemies" and ceremoniously burned in effigy in the streets of Paris.[3] English reactions, as recorded in a popular ballad, were rather different, celebrating the Kirkes as impeccably English heroes avenging the noble Protestant cause against French religious and political enemies:

> Three Ships that lancht forth lately
> (Vessels tall and stately)
> Under the command of brave Captaine *Kirke,*
> Hath had such auspitious chance,
> Against our vaunting foes of France,
> *That all true English may applaude this worke . . .*
> Thus our valiant Captaine *Kirk,*
> Did the *French* men soundly jerk,
> And pur[ch]ast honor *unto* h's native land
> Oh had we many like to him,
> Then *England* would in credit swim,
> And *France* nor *Spaine* could not against us stand.

The work concluded with a rousing call for human and divine defense of Hugenot stronghold La Rochelle, then being besieged by Catholic forces:

> Our gracious King and Queene God save,
> With all the Privy Counsell grave,
> And send reliefe to *Rochel* in distresse,
> Oh now when earthly means doth faile,
> Let Heavenly power at last prevaile,
> *Amen, cry all that doe true Faith professe.*[4]

English eyes had turned late to the St. Lawrence River valley. Preoccupied with his more southerly holdings in Virginia and Massachusetts, King James I regarded the successive failures of Cabot, Cartier, Frobisher, and Champlain in their shared quest to find the Northwest Passage as confirming long-held English assessments that this cold, benighted territory should be left unchallenged to the shivering French.[5] Gradually, however, both the burgeoning profits of the fur trade and a heightening of French-English religious, economic, and political tensions seemed to demand a reevaluation of this tacit policy. While the 1625 marriage of the newly crowned and fiercely Protestant Charles I of England to Henrietta Maria, the equally devout Catholic sister of France's Louis XIII, was designed to quell French-English political and religious disaffection, their union would only exacerbate it. Far from softening his stance on the practice of Roman Catholicism within his realm, Charles banished most of his new wife's "Papist" entourage in August of 1626. This and other insults did not go unnoticed by the French: repeated attacks on their vessels by English merchants prompted the seizure of all English goods in Rouen and elsewhere, causing further English retaliations. These chronic antagonisms flared as Louis, on the advice of his closest advisor, Richelieu, in the spring of 1627 moved to crush the remaining Huguenot dissenters at La Rochelle, prompting Charles to send thirteen thousand troops to lend the embattled Protestants support. Defeated, the English monarch cast about for a suitable vengeance and hit upon the notion of an English conquest of "Canaday." Such a victory would be doubly sweet, as the seizure of this prize would not only rob the French of what had come to be the source of considerable income but would also revenge the exclusion of Protestants from this nascent colony, which had been effected in May of 1627. Congratulating himself on having let his French rivals fund the foundation of a number of small colonial centers along the St. Lawrence, Charles sent the Kirkes in the spring of 1628 to probe carefully for weaknesses and quickly force a French surrender.[6]

Pastedechouan, turning to hail the Kirkes' ship, was identified by a French deserter on board as a rare and valuable commodity: an aboriginal Christian who possessed critical linguistic skills. Procuring reliable translators knowledgeable in both native and European languages was critical to the Kirkes' ambitions of securing economic and political alliances with local aboriginal groups. Such alliances were a key component in their plans to defeat the French and reap for their English sponsors the exclusive rewards of aboriginal trade.

Captured, Pastedechouan was interrogated at length in French and Latin, each of which he feigned not to comprehend.[7] When this ruse failed, the young man sought to win his freedom with a combination of flattery and guile. Disingenuously protesting his willingness to serve the "brave" and "honorable" David Kirke, Pastedechouan protested that his religious debt to the French precluded his overt service to the English invaders: "I have all the wishes in the world to serve you and to leave the French . . . but I thought that, as you are a man of honor, that you would do me the favor of not betraying me to the French, especially to the Recollets, to whom I owe the obligation of holy baptism. They would be very unhappy with my revolt, and would have nothing more to do with me . . ." Pastedechouan suggested that this delicate difficulty could be overcome by assigning him a secret mission to the trading center of Trois-Rivières. Impressed by the youth's eloquent promises to "bring his nation down to trade," the Kirkes entrusted Pastedechouan with several canoes filled with clothing, alcohol, and assorted foodstuffs. Having decamped with the valuable supplies, he enjoyed them in liberty with his three brothers, "feeding well and mocking the English." For the next four years, Pastedechouan was wanted by the English for this capital offense, as, learning of his betrayal, the humiliated Kirkes promptly put a price on his head.[8] In winning his freedom, Pastedechouan signaled his unwillingness to work as a political agent for the English invaders, affirmed his loyalty to his French allies (still, at the time of the incident, firmly ensconced at Quebec), and provided his family with a memorable "eat-all" feast, doubtless temporarily improving his always tenuous social standing.

In targeting Pastedechouan for capture, the Kirke brothers had made a reasoned decision. The young man's French and Latin was far more comprehensible than the standard St. Lawrence trading jargon, a slippery pastiche of Innu and French, making communication with him refreshingly easy. Further, the Kirkes' rudimentary knowledge of the political and economic situation of the various indigenous peoples of the St. Lawrence might have suggested to them that Pastedechouan, as an Innu, might prove amenable to their pitch for closer economic relations and possible joint military action against the French monopolists at Quebec. After all, as we have seen, Huguenot appeals to the Innu, which coupled economic and political grievances with lurid allegations regarding the nature of Catholic sacraments, had proven deeply influential upon considerable segments of the Innu community.[9]

In seeking to make Pastedechouan their agent, however, the Kirkes failed to appreciate the fundamentally religious nature of Pastedechouan's linguistic talents. The youth's abilities in French and Latin were merely the philological expression of his Catholic identity and allegiances. The context in which Pastedechouan had acquired these valuable skills had shaped his distinctive religious identity, which was as inimical to that of the Protestant Kirkes as it was to the religious commitments of his own people: he had been steeped in a defiant and defensive post-Reformation Catholicism that defined itself in large part by that which it opposed. His Recollet mentors had, in effect, shaped Pastedechouan's religious literacy so that it would prove useless should he fall into Protestant hands. To use his linguistic skills against the French colonial society with which he was allied and upon which he was dependent would have been an unthinkable betrayal of his still-strong religious loyalties, as Pastedechouan himself had reportedly protested.

Pastedechouan's Abandonment, 1629–1632

It is doubtful whether Pastedechouan could have fully appreciated the implications of his decision, hastily hatched as a captive aboard the Kirkes' vessel, to cheat the English and remain true to his French mentors. To do so, he would have had to anticipate the Kirkes' successful siege of Quebec more than a year later and their subsequent deportation of virtually all French colonial and missionary personnel. Abruptly deprived of the economic and psychological support of the French and of the sacramental affirmation of his assumed Catholic identity and having burned his bridges with the furious English, Pastedechouan's only recourse now lay with the family and community that, as a would-be missionary, he had rejected, ridiculed, and attempted to reform. From the moment of the forced departure of his Recollet mentors in September of 1629 to the return of the French ships, which he now he awaited with mixed emotions on this bright June morning in 1632, Pastedechouan had been compelled to seek succor and alliance with the people he had been taught to regard as his religious and cultural inferiors.[10] Estranged from and inept in Innu ways, Pastedechouan, during these three years, came to an uneasy reckoning with the culture of his childhood, forging, with the invaluable assistance of his elder brothers, a provisional if anomalous new Innu identity.[11]

Though our knowledge of this period of Pastedechouan's life is fragmentary, we can speculate that his attempts at cultural reintegration, forced upon him by the new political situation and his own decisive actions against the English, would have been thwarted by a number of factors. Pastedechouan's behavior toward his own people since his return from France in 1625 had probably not made him many Innu friends. His preference for Quebec over Tadoussac after his return, his failure to obtain helpful information while in France, his disturbing immaturity, his unwillingness as a Catholic, to participate in traditional religious ceremonies, and his defiant loyalty to the French, whose economic policies and religious rituals had engendered the open hostility of many in his Huguenot-influenced community—all these factors would have hampered his acceptance by his own people. But the fact that Pastedechouan's rapprochement with the culture of his childhood had been forced upon him rather than freely chosen would likely have been the final straw. His social acceptance, mitigated as it might have been, appears to have been possible only through the loyal generosity of his three older brothers, Carigonan, Mestigoit, and Sasousmat.

Carigonan, the eldest of the three, had likely established himself by the time of Pastedechouan's 1626 return to Tadoussac as a respected shaman among the Innu people, well on his way to being acknowledged as "the most famous sorcerer or *manitousiou* . . . of all the country," as he was described by Jesuit writer Paul Le Jeune in 1634.[12] Possessed of a compelling, dominant personality, a sharp wit, and a competitive streak, Carigonan was the undisputed religious leader of his three brothers, their families, kin, and affines. It was likely he who spearheaded Pastedechouan's religious reintegration into his community and who set the tone for his family's treatment of its youngest member—treatment that combined affectionate, amused derision with generous provision and advocacy.

Mestigoit, in his early thirties, was the second eldest. Though he shared little of his older brother's often ostentatious charisma, he was also widely respected within the close-knit Innu culture. In contrast with Carigonan's religious preeminence, Mestigoit drew his social credibility from his close conformity to Innu ideals of emotional stoicism and his deep competence in the arts of Innu manhood. Soft-spoken, thoughtful, and more conciliatory than Carigonan, Mestigoit appears often to have taken the role of family peacemaker. It would have been he who was saddled with the thankless task of attempting to reawaken his apprehensive sibling's long-dormant hunting and survival skills.

Sasousmat, who, in his early twenties, was the brother closest in age to Pastedechouan, is the most obscure of the fraternal trio. Though the vagaries of the European record omit more than they reveal, hints remain that Pastedechouan may have enjoyed a more egalitarian relationship with Sasousmat than with his more dominant elder brothers and perhaps even enjoyed a degree of influence. Significantly, Sasousmat was the only one of Pastedechouan's three brothers to emulate his younger sibling by converting to Christianity, accepting the Catholic sacrament of baptism shortly before his death in January 1634. Indeed, in asking the Jesuits at Quebec for catechistic instruction, Sasousmat apparently reproached them for their negligence in not replicating his brother's earlier experience with the Recollets: "Take me to France to be instructed, otherwise you will be responsible for my soul."[13] Moreover, Sasousmat and Pastedechouan each married into the family of prominent, French-identified Innu headman Manitougatche, who served as a father-in-law to each brother.[14]

It was this trio of brothers who, during the interregnum period, attempted to integrate Pastedechouan into his Innu community and who provided for him when he could not support himself. It was they who found him prospective brides after each of his successive marriages failed. In facilitating their brother's marital happiness, the trio would have been voluntarily accepting responsibility for yet another dependant, given Pastedechouan's apparently incorrigible incompetence at hunting.

The three-year absence of his missionary mentors would have had a number of important implications for Pastedechouan's religious identity. With the banishment of the French, Pastedechouan would have been denied the formal opportunity for any collective, sacramental affirmation of his Catholic identity, as the collective, participatory nature of post-Tridentine Catholicism made it difficult for an individual to function in the absence of the sacramental superstructure.[15] The open hostility of the English occupiers to the modest evidence of Catholicism at Quebec, as evidenced by their plundering and burning of Recollet and Jesuit residences and their alleged harassment of aboriginal neophytes, would have made this center a dangerous arena for the expression of Catholic sympathies.[16] We can only speculate whether Pastedechouan and the small cadre of young aboriginal converts for whom he may have been responsible made any attempts to maintain a modicum of Catholic practice after the last French boat had sailed, secretly chanting their rosaries in the cold, despoiled church. Whatever their strategy for persevering in the French faith, at some point encounter with the traditional religious life of their peoples would have been inevitable.

Any hunting instruction that Pastedechouan received from his brothers would have had inescapably religious overtones, as hunting was for the Innu an essentially relational exercise in which the hunter attempted to capture the pitying attention of his powerful prey. Pastedechouan would thus have been reimmersed in these ancient rites of reverent supplication even as he was retaught his childhood facility with lance and bow, snare and trap.[17] His apparently pronounced difficulty in mastering these arts would doubtless have been interpreted by his fellow Innu in religious terms.[18] Because hunting success was seen as ultimately dependent upon an animal's positive evaluation of the moral and ritual status of her hunter, Pastedechouan's record of abysmal failure was likely seen by his community as indicating animals' collective disapproval or suspicion of him rather than resulting from merely technical ineptitude. Such an interpretation would have lent a note of real gravity to his derisive dismissal as an "idiot," "blockhead," "know-nothing," and "dog," an evaluation that was wholeheartedly seconded even by the brothers whose generosity kept him tenuously tied to the community, preventing his social and physical death.[19]

Something of Pastedechouan's liminal status within his natal society can be glimpsed through the lens of aboriginal oral narrative. The Cree, with whom the Innu share many cultural and linguistic features, tell a story of "the man who could not kill anything." Despite the enthusiastic instruction of his father and other adult male mentors, this unfortunate lad had never managed to capture the smallest living creature. His lack of hunting success had brought him social ridicule and an inability to marry. When his predicament was brought to the attention of the Lady of the Caribou, however, the situation was quickly rectified. In short order, animals presented themselves to him, from smallest bird to largest mammal, and urged him to sacrifice them. Soon the presence of other family members in the camp was required to help clean, cook, and treat the flesh and hides of these slaughtered souls. The man quickly became sought after as a husband, but, remembering the women's cruel ridicule of his previous incompetence, he spurned their advances. The Lady of the Caribou eventually took him for herself. In marrying her, the young man became a benign protector of his new animal family and benefactor of pious hunters. Though it is a Cree, rather than an Innu narrative the story of "the man who could not kill anything" demonstrates how disturbing and anomalous those who defied age and gender expectations were to aboriginal communities.[20].

Certainly, the issue of Pastedechouan's disturbingly anomalous gender, age, and religious identity would have been somehow addressed during this lengthy period of negotiation with the culture of his childhood. However, the silence of the European sources and the complexity of the issue itself do not permit us to do anything more than speculate about how Pastedechouan's people resolved the troubling issue of his varigated identity. As previously explored, gender and age distinctions were one of the chief means by which the Innu articulated a sense of complementary differences within their society. Male and female roles were demarcated by largely separate spheres of influence and association, symbolized by the different responsibilities of each sex in ensuring collective survival. While gender distinctions remained largely constant throughout the life cycle, advancing age was seen as bringing a wealth of improvements to an individual's character and capabilities. Many of these changes were affected or recognized by religious rituals. Young, foolish boys were melded into mature, wise men in the forge of intense religious experience and the furnace of war. Through these rites, their childish dependency on adult family members was replaced by a salutary relationship with a powerful animal patron, and their reliance upon the protection of others supplanted by their own successful defense of the women, children, aged, and infirm of their community.[21]

Pastedechouan's probable failure to pass through these fiery tests of his incipient manhood before his departure for France at the young age of eleven or twelve, coupled with his probable attitude of horrified distaste for such practices when he returned as a sixteen- or seventeen-year-old Catholic convert, make it likely that he was now seen by his society, at the age of twenty or twenty-one, as an anomalous creature: a liminal being who was physically adult but religiously and culturally still a child. Pastedechouan's ritual initiation into cultural adulthood would have been beset with any number of problems, yet, equally, his continued status as an uncategorizable "boy-man" would have proved conceptually disturbing to his Innu community.

Pastedechouan's initiation into adulthood through the twin tests of vision quest and battle would have been problematic because of his advanced age. Young boys typically went on their vision quest relatively early in adolescence, optimally before their engagement in sexual activity, which was seen as being incompatible with the physical demands and deprivation of the visionary experience. Pastedechouan's full physical maturity, despite his initially unmarried status, would thus have been somewhat problematic.

A more serious issue, however, was his utterly unbecoming religious mentality and disturbing lack of basic competency. How could a fervent Catholic, taught to regard the aboriginal pantheon as demonic, undertake the ultimate religious experience of the Innu and win the patronage of an animal guardian? How could one who repeatedly failed ritually to entice an animal to die by his arts succeed in the more complex task of persuading an animal benefactor to share with him its unique powers and patronage? Thus, though Pastedechouan's anomalous status as a cultural child would have doubtless been disturbing to those around him, his continued assignment to this role seems more likely than his successful initiation.

Much of the endemic teasing Pastedechouan endured from within his kin group focused upon his apparent chronic inability to succeed in the related ventures of hunting and marriage. As reported by Paul Le Jeune, Pastedechouan's kinswomen would humiliate their young relative by urging their children to approach the luckless young man for food as he invariably returned empty-handed from the hunt. "'Go and see,' they say to their children, 'if he has not killed a Moose;' thus making sport of him for being a poor hunter, a great reproach among the Savages." His brothers, as supportive as they ultimately were, constantly disparaged their youngest sibling's competency, dismissing him as "he who knows nothing" and predicting, presciently, as it turns out, that "he would die of hunger unless we feed him." Even Pastedechouan's last wife, who would leave him with the melting of the spring snows in 1634, openly mocked him, complaining to her sympathetic female peers of his inadequate provision. Le Jeune, overhearing their conversation, reports that they "spoke aloud and freely, tearing this poor Apostate [Pastedechouan] to pieces," and lamented, "If he could only kill something!"[22] Pastedechouan's status as a boy-man unwilling or unable to traverse Innu initiation rituals, then, satisfyingly explained his consistent failures in hunting and in marriage.[23] One did not, after all, expect success in these manly endeavors from one who, all appearances aside, was yet a young and untried child. The group's mockery of Pastedechouan was its attempt to goad him into fullfilling their rigid age and gender expectations. His inability to do so and his consequent public shaming reinforced the very social roles his behavior thwarted.

The man who would have stood silently on the sandy shores of the St. Lawrence, calmly watching the approaching ships, had thus changed considerably from the young lad forcibly accosted on its banks four years earlier. The interlude had probably had a chastening effect upon Pastedechouan. His decisive rejection of service to the English, his desertion by his defeated French mentors, and his consequent reliance upon the provision of his own people had precipitated lasting changes to his allegiances and, ultimately, to his identity. Though his loyalty to the French who had so decisively transformed his sense of self never wavered, motivating his fateful choice to defraud the Kirkes, their long absence had necessitated his hesitant, partial reimmersion into Innu community and culture. For the remainder of his life Pastedechouan's attitude toward the French, particularly Gallic missionaries, would be one of marked, embittered ambivalence.

Paul Le Jeune and the 1632 Reestablishment of the Jesuit Mission

Standing on the salt-stained bow and gazing westward across the glinting water toward the undulating, forested hills, Father Paul Le Jeune silently uttered a prayer of thanks for his company's safe passage across the stormy Atlantic. Departing from Honfleur in April, his eyes had not glimpsed solid land for some six weeks.[24] But though the shore was nigh, still only the ship's ubiquitous creaking would have broken the unearthly stillness. The vast and brooding silence of this beautiful yet forbidding land opening up before him was probably unnerving to this academic accustomed only to the relative quiet of classroom and cloister, the studious peace of which were continually punctuated by the omnipresent bustle of the city life outside their walls.

Gazing over the land that was to be his new home, Le Jeune must have been aware that nothing in his forty-one years had truly prepared him for the nature and scope of the task he was now assigned to undertake. Pressed into service as the Superior of the renewed Jesuit mission to Canada, Le Jeune found himself ultimately responsible for the grandiose ambition of winning a continent's worth of souls for Christ, a challenge for which he had little preparation and even less personal inclination. While Le Jeune's response to word of his challenging new post expressed a dutiful enthusiasm, he initially saw it chiefly as representing a valuable chance to exhibit laudatory obedience to his superiors. Notably lacking was any expression of passionate regard for or identification with the people of this benighted land whose souls, "thousands of years plunged in darkness," he had been sent to enlighten. Explaining his reaction to his new responsibilities, Le Jeune stoically wrote: "I thought nothing of coming to Canada when I was sent here; I felt no particular affections for the savages, but the duty of obedience was binding, even if I had been sent a thousand times further away."[25]

The arrival of Le Jeune's Jesuit entourage replicated, in the religious arena, the actions of the French colonial authorities with whom they traveled. Just as Emery De Cäen, the French commandant, came to claim French rights to governance from the English invaders, so Le Jeune came to take over what had until that point been a predominantly Recollet mission field, commandeering as Jesuit possessions their damaged but still standing buildings.[26]

Like the Recollet missionaries he replaced, Le Jeune perceived indigenous cultural and religious practices as fundamentally incompatible with French Catholicism: "To be a Barbarian and a good Christian, to live as a Savage and as a child of God are two very different things." Emulating his gray-robed predecessors, the Jesuit Superior eagerly envisioned the stationary settlement of migratory native groups and, as an educator, applauded the Recollets' contention that the careful molding of aboriginal children would result, ultimately, in the conversion of entire communities. During his seven-year tenure as Superior, Le Jeune would reimplement the Recollet program of isolating, converting, and reeducating young aboriginal children both in domestic seminaries and abroad in France, in order that the "fathers will be taught through the children."[27] While the damaged Recollet-era buildings were still under reconstruction, Le Jeune then began to resuscitate the educational system that had so decisively formed Pastedechouan's own distinctive religious mentality.

Though Le Jeune, before his arrival at Tadoussac, had never laid eyes upon an aboriginal person, specifically stating, "it was here [at Tadoussac] that I saw Savages for the first time," his image of them—constructed from a pastiche of highly colored popular representations, the writings of his own Jesuit order and the personal memories of his teacher Enemond Massé, an ex-missionary to Acadia—was as fundamentally alien beings, connected with himself by the mere formality of shared humanity.[28] Yet the ship-bound missionary, gazing landward, shared more with the young aboriginal, squinting seaward, than either man could ever have imagined. Neither the ambivalent young Innu nor the fervent Jesuit Superior had been born Catholic. Both were converts: both, in their teens, had undergone a transformation of their most fundamental religious assumptions and allegiances. While Pastedechouan was an early casualty of a missionary experiment that effectively severed his links with his cradle culture, Le Jeune was the product of decades of internecine religious conflict that had divided a country and splintered families along confessional lines. Born in 1591 to wealthy Protestant parents in Châlons-sur-Marne, Le Jeune had converted at the age of sixteen over

Pastedechouan's nemesis, Paul Le Jeune, Jesuit Superior of Canada from 1632 to 1639 and the first author of the *Jesuit Relations*. The intense relationship between these two men, both of whom were converts to Catholicism, profoundly affected Pastedechouan's final years. (Courtesy of the National Archives of Canada.)

their strident objections. Apparently unsatisfied with this divisive demonstration of commitment to the holy mother church, he took his initial vows in the Society of Jesus, that vanguard of the Catholic Reformation (and a suitable replacement "family"), some six years later and spent seven additional years as an educator, forging a generation of young French boys into uncompromising defenders of the true faith. Following their respective conversions, both Le Jeune and Pastedechouan came to regard their previous beliefs—and the families who still held them—with considerable hostility and contempt. Just as the young Pastedechouan characterized his unconverted family as "beasts who know not God," Le Jeune in his voluminous writings caustically described the beliefs of his Calvinist childhood as "poison," and Protestants as "miserable heretics," the "enemies of the truth, of real virtue and their country."[29]

The two, then, shared not simply the distinction of being converts to Catholicism: both the young aboriginal and the older ex-Calvinist were the products of a French culture that understood religious identity in radically exclusivistic and agonistic terms. In early seventeenth-century France, religious identity brooked no middle ground: it was an all-or-nothing, zero-sum proposition. Given the confessional nature of Gallican warfare in the sixteenth and seventeenth centuries, an individual's self-identification as Protestant or Roman Catholic had immediate life-or-death implications and often brought with it a total commitment to the theological and political defeat of one's former religious affines, even family, who became, with conversion, one's intimate enemies.[30]

This radical totalism of French religious identity, experienced by Le Jeune in its most acute form, arguably created the template for how he and his fellow missionaries to Canada envisioned aboriginal conversion to Catholicism. The absolutism which characterized the either-or decision between Protestantism and Catholicism in France was transposed, in colonial North America, to an envisioned either-or choice for its native inhabitants between Catholic Christianity and traditional aboriginal beliefs. In unconsciously replicating their own experiences, Catholics preserved the symmetry of this terrible and final choice by excluding other religious options for aboriginal people, such as Protestantism. The ferocity with which first Recollet and then Jesuit missionaries sought to expunge the religious and cultural beliefs of aboriginal cultures cannot be seen, then, merely as an expression of a limited ethnocentrism. Rather, it expressed in a new

cultural setting the same sense of definitive choice between mutually exclusive religious options that characterized French confessional conflict in
the mid to late sixteenth and early seventeenth centuries.

The fact that Le Jeune and Pastedechouan were each products of the
exacting process Goddard has termed "metanoia" lent a strange degree
of mutual understanding and a subtle intensity to their prolonged encounter.[31] Though in their dealings with one another the two converts
were often antagonists, their shared experiences inculcated in each man
similar assumptions regarding religious identity, which one man would
seek to enforce and the other to evade.

Contested Encounter: The Relationship between Le Jeune and Pastedechouan

The relationship of Pierre-Anthoine Pastedechouan and Paul Le Jeune,
which lasted four years, would have a decisive impact upon the lives and
religious imaginations of both men. The irascible Le Jeune's tempestuous association with the young man—whom he initially idealized,
later detested, and, after Pastedechouan's untimely death, fervently
mourned—was by far the most important and intense liaison that he established with any single aboriginal person during his seven-year tenure
as the Jesuit Superior of New France. His personal relationships with
Pastedechouan and the members of his family would shape Le Jeune's
understanding of aboriginal personality, culture, and propensity for
Christianization, influencing a missionization strategy that would dramatically impact the lives of successive generations of aboriginal peoples
and, through the medium of the *Jesuit Relations,* influence the perceptions of a popular audience in Europe. Pastedechouan's encounter with
the forceful, charismatic Jesuit Superior would trigger a painful reevaluation of his difficult past, ambiguous present, and unclear future. His
agonistic relationship with the dominant older man and his continual
struggle to retain control of his religious and cultural identity during
their association would shape both his interior sensibilities and the dynamics of his key familial relationships during the last several years of
his life.

As teacher and student, penitent and confessor, the two men were
bound together by a complex relationship of mutual dependency, which
neither wished to acknowledge, against which both struggled, and

which each sought to manipulate to his own advantage. Pastedechouan's dependency resulted from a complex admixture of economic, psychological, and religious factors. His inability to master the relational religious ethos and practical skills necessary for adult self-sufficiency in Innu society made his recurrent dependency upon Europeans almost inevitable. But his reliance was more than simply economic. Pastedechouan's childhood religious reeducation, which emphasized the unique spiritual prerogatives of his missionary mentors, predisposed him to acknowledge Jesuit assertions of religious authority even as he sought to evade its implications.

But Le Jeune was also dependent upon Pastedechouan. With few other opportunities for satisfactory language acquisition, the missionary needed the young man's continual pedagogical cooperation to ensure his own linguistic progress, which he saw as a critical factor in the mission's success. Moreover, though Le Jeune would have preferred it otherwise, he was ultimately dependent upon Pastedechouan's cooperation in a more intimate arena: his attempts to effect the young Innu's spiritual rehabilitation. Pastedechouan, however, attenuated his participation in pedagogical and devotional duties pointedly to demonstrate to the older man the reality of his personal religious agency.

The two men, then, from the onset of their relationship, were locked in a struggle to define and control Pastedechouan's religious identity and the degree of his participation in the linguistic, cultural, and religious goals of the newly arrived Jesuit missionaries. Le Jeune sought to reshape Pastedechouan into an active, fervent Catholic by wielding the weapons of guilt, intimidation, friendship, praise, mockery, and occasionally outright coercion. Pastedechouan sought to defend his prerogative to define his own religious and cultural identity by engaging the missionary with passive resistance, boundary marking, active defiance, flight, and overt challenges to Le Jeune's Christian claims.

This chapter and the next will trace the contours of the pair's relationship throughout the two successive winters spent in each other's company—the first of which they passed in the dark, crowded Jesuit residence of Notre Dame des Anges, near the provisional European center at Quebec, and the second amidst the windswept hills and snowy woods of what is today southern Quebec and northern Maine. While keeping their dyadic relationship as its central focus, the successive chapters will also examine how the two men's contentious struggle for dominance impacted Pastedechouan's aboriginal relationships both within and outside the residence, as both Pastedechouan and his would-be mentor sought to interpret and leverage the presence and religious behavior of other native peoples in their ongoing struggle with one another. Examination of each man's relationship with Manitougatche, an Innu elder and Pastedechouan's former father-in-law; Fortune and Bienvenue, two of the young aboriginal borders at the Jesuit residence, whose childhood circumstances closely mirrored Pastedechouan's own; and the young Innu's three older brothers, Carigonan, Mestigoit, and Sasousmat, with whom the pair spent the winter of 1633–1634, will deepen our understanding of the dyad's relational dynamics, even as it allows us to gauge differences in aboriginal reactions to Jesuit claims of Christian exclusivism and authority. Analysis of the perspectives and behavior of these aboriginal actors will allow us to speculate about the obvious differences between Pastedechouan's religious mentality and that of the rest of his family, converts and nonconverts alike. Unlike Pastedechouan, who experienced a childhood inculcation into Roman Catholicism in a French-majority context, his family encountered Christianity within the security of their own cultural milieu and with the greater maturity of adulthood.

Pastedechouan's Arrival at Notre Dame des Anges

From the onset of their relationship, Le Jeune and Pastedechouan were respectively pursuer and pursued. While the two men may have crossed paths upon the missionary's festive disembarkation at Tadoussac that bright June morning, their agonistic engagement truly began only with the onset of Le Jeune's campaign, several months later, to acquire for his order Pastedechouan's linguistic services, which the young man had pledged instead to the service of the returning colonial authorities.

To the newly arrived Jesuit Superior, Pastedechouan's multilinguistic competency and apparent status as one fallen from the faith proved an irresistible double opportunity to acquire linguistic competency and to express appropriate missionary zeal. Le Jeune was convinced that the Jesuit goal of converting aboriginal populations was dependent upon missionaries' ability to communicate eloquently in native North American languages, at least until the aboriginal use of French became more prevalent. His own linguistic progress during his initial summer in New France, however, had proved frustratingly difficult. The majority of

French-aboriginal interactions took place using what Le Jeune describes as "a certain jargon": "[Which] is neither French nor Savage; and yet when the French use it, they think they are speaking the Savage Tongue, and the Savages, in using it, think they are speaking good French."[32] After months of attempting to glean the local lingo through visits to neighboring Innu homes, study of the incomprehensible scratchings of his Je-suit and Recollet predecessors, and interrogation of the often surly and uncooperative professional translators stationed at the fort, the ecstatic Le Jeune perceived the presence of a trilingual aboriginal convert as nothing less than "the admirable kindness and providence of God" on the Jesuits' behalf:

> I desired to obtain a greater knowledge of the language; and seeing that I made no progress, for want of a teacher, I had been thinking for some time of asking God, hoping that we should have this young man with us for a while. We all began to pray for this favor at the throne of our Lord; I felt so strong a desire, combined with so great confidence, that it seemed to me we had him already, all human appearances to the contrary.[33]

In addition to his primary goal of seeking to extract from Pastedechouan the mysteries of his language, Le Jeune cherished confident aspirations of quickly effecting the young man's religious reformation. Just as he had taken title to the still-smoldering Recollet possessions, seeking to reclaim and utilize what the English occupiers had destroyed, so Le Jeune sought to rehabilitate and redeem Pastedechouan, another Recollet "product," whom he saw as having been similarly "spoiled" by the English presence. Initially, then, Le Jeune saw Pastedechouan's ambivalent religious posture not as evidence of hardened apostasy but as the legacy of the young Innu's involuntary suffering at the hands of the hated, heretical invaders: "This young man had been taken to France in his childhood by the Reverend Recollet Fathers . . . Having been brought back to this country, he was again placed in the hands of his brothers, to recover the use of his own language, which he had almost forgotten. This poor wretch has become a barbarian like the others, and persistently followed barbaric customs while the English were here."[34]

Pastedechouan's civic employers at the fort, several miles from the Jesuit residence, quickly acceded to Le Jeune's determined campaign to acquire the young man's services.[35] Their courteous offers to relinquish him were likely made with considerable relief. Pastedechouan had proven himself, over the course of the summer and early fall, to be a difficult, unpredictable employee. "He displeased Sieur de Caën; once and twice, he was disgraced and restored to favor." Though the delicacy of the wording used to describe Pastedechouan's situation makes it difficult to determine with certainty the precise nature of his lapses in judgment while he worked at the fort, his erratic behavior was probably prompted by overindulgence in alcohol.[36] Le Jeune's machinations provided Emery De Caën, the colonial commandant, with a welcome opportunity to part with a troublesome employee while simultaneously accruing the favor of the influential Jesuit Superior. De Caën politely agreed with Le Jeune that the inscrutable workings of divine providence had indeed delivered this talented but corrupted sot to the Jesuits' very door, that they might win from his "infected lips" facility in the Innu language and regain his imperiled soul for Christ. De Caën and his deputy, Charles Duplessis-Bochart, unceremoniously released Pastedechouan from his obligations, urging him to redeem himself in the service of the Jesuits.[37]

Their pleas initially fell upon deaf ears. Pastedechouan proved highly resistant to the courtship of Le Jeune and immune to the infectious enthusiasm of his would-be barterers. He apparently regarded the proposal that he live with and work for the Jesuits with marked, even fearful reluctance. Serving the colonial authorities as a translator and liaison had allowed Pastedechouan to exploit his Innu linguistic talents in a way that did not greatly disrupt his hard-won connections to his community. By contrast, affiliation with the Jesuits—with its attendant reimmersion into disciplined religious observance, obedience to religious superiors, and curtailment of his migratory Innu lifestyle—would limit his freedom and imperil his nascent Innu identity. Such factors were readily appreciated by the canny Le Jeune: "While breathing only liberty, he rather abhorred our house than loved it."[38] Moreover, in taking a position which ensconced him in the Jesuit residence, Pastedechouan would have been effectively abandoning his wife. Women were forbidden entry to the Jesuit house, even under dire circumstances. Indeed, on the same day Pastedechouan crossed the threshold of Notre Dame des Anges, his male and female relatives, fearful of an imminent Mohawk attack, sought shelter in the convent. The Jesuits accepted young children and adult male Innu into their quarters, but refused entry to their wives, sisters, and daughters, insisting that they take shelter at the fort, a considerable distance away.[39]

Just as Pastedechouan had feared in 1626 that return to Tadoussac would erode his identity as a "naturalized Frenchman," he now likely worried that entering the Jesuit milieu would thwart his hard-won re-identification with the culture of his childhood, which had been slowly, painfully, and partially effected during the English interlude.[40] For the previous three years he had labored, with the assistance of his brothers, to make a place for himself in the Innu community. The timing of the negotiations, around the end of October, would have made his decision even more difficult, as circumstances once again conspired to reinforce Pastedechouan's perception of religious affiliation as a mutually exclusive choice. During these fall weeks, his familial band would have been preparing to leave on their six-month-long winter hunt, deep into the Canadian wilderness. Should he be unhappy with the Jesuits, Pastedechouan would be stranded for the winter in a hostile Catholic enclave, unable to locate or reach his faraway kin.

It is likely that Pastedechouan's brothers Carigonan and Mestigoit saw his decision to rejoin European missionaries, even if taken solely for economic reasons, as undoing much of their three years of hard work reaffiliating Pastedechouan with his natal Innu community. Moreover, his brothers' negative perception of his chosen stationary lifestyle seems to have been shared by the wider community. Le Jeune would later bitingly remark, of Pastedechouan, "He gave up Christians and Christianity, because he could not suffer the taunts of the savages, who jeered at him occasionally because he was sedentary and not wandering, as they were: and now he is their butt and their laughingstock."[41] His family likely opposed his reentanglement with missionaries not because they objected to the contents of Catholicism but rather because, by rendering him sedentary, such involvement would preclude his participation in the migratory rhythms of Innu traditional life.

However, despite his correct intimation that his decision to enter Notre Dame des Anges would meet with his family's disapproval and suspicion, Pastedechouan nevertheless, of his own volition, chose to winter at the Jesuit's "little home." Neither the black robes nor his former employers could have compelled him to take this step: the young Innu was a free agent, not a slave or indentured servant. On November 13 of 1632 he crossed the threshold of the Jesuit residence, inaugurating an intermittent liaison with the Society of Jesus that would endure until his death four years later.[42]

Pastedechouan's motivations for this momentous decision, then, are unclear, particularly in light of his reported intransigence before and during negotiations and his decidedly ambivalent behavior afterward. Certainly, economic considerations could have played a role. Perhaps the prospect of working for the Jesuits eventually came to seem more attractive to Pastedechouan than his continued humiliating dependency upon his own people. Or, somewhat ironically, Pastedechouan may have seen employment by Europeans as being his best option to gain a modicum of Innu social status. Working as a translator or language teacher would have allowed Pastedechouan to barter his skills to gain commodities that he could then redistribute to his community. Though this form of provision would have been wholly devoid of the religious valences of hunting, the contribution of valuable supplies would probably still have significantly raised Pastedechouan's social status.

Psychological factors may also have played a role. Pastedechouan's equilibrium may have been affected by the reappearance of the French and the insistent courtship of Le Jeune, which once again placed him between the French Catholic world of his youth and the Innu community of his distant childhood, into which he had been provisionally readopted. Pastedechouan may also have been disconsolate due to the final collapse of his troubled marriage, long plagued by complaints of insufficient provision, which even his position with the civic authorities had apparently failed to ameliorate. Alternatively, he may have had a falling out with his older brothers, perhaps occasioned by his earlier decision to reengage with the returning secular French colonial administration.

Finally, Pastedechouan's decision to join the Jesuits was likely influenced by the chorus of religious arguments to which he was continually subjected by both his would-be hosts and his former employers. After his termination by De Cäen, Pastedechouan implored Duplessis-Bochart, the commandant's deputy and a devout Catholic, to reinstate him.[43] The older man gently refused him, arguing that Pastedechouan's recent troubles were God's punishment for his long inattention to his religious duties and suggesting that he would find temporal and spiritual solace under Jesuit care:

He [Duplessis-Bochart] told him [Pastedechouan] to think carefully and he would see that God was against him and was angry with him for his carelessness about religion; having become a Christian his character ought to conform to Christian principles; matters would never have reached this pass if he had kept his pledge to live a good life; and a good life would be both pleasant and easy if he would live with Le Jeune and teach him the language. Le Jeune would provide for his physical needs and supply him with spiritual counsel as well.[44]

This simple explanation of his present circumstances, coupled with a comprehensive plan to ameliorate his difficulties, may have been attractive to Pastedechouan, who apparently once confessed his lifelong vulnerability to religious persuasion.[45]

Had Pastedechouan fully rejected Catholicism as the result of his youthful experiences in France or his disillusionment with his abrupt abandonment by his Recollet mentors in 1629, it is likely that he would have held to his initial, adamant refusal of the Jesuit invitation. Pastedechouan's intermittent participation in prayer and confession while under their roof, as well as his apparently vivid fears of hell, suggest his continuing, if troubled, engagement with post-Tridentine Catholicism. Though such small clues are less obvious than the young man's covert, continual resistance to Le Jeune's religious authority and demands, the continuing magnetism of the Catholic worldview may be apparent in this initial decision, as well as in its aftermath.[46]

Pastedechouan was welcomed to Notre Dame des Anges with a deeply symbolic gift that epitomized the transformation that the Jesuits hoped to effect upon their wary young teacher. Echoing the visual language of stripping and reclothing that had been a prominent motif in his Recollet baptism eleven years before, Pastedechouan was presented with a rich suit of clothing in the French style, in the hopes that he would "lay aside the inner savage with the outer."[47] The suit, imbued as it was with inescapable overtones of cultural and religious reincorporation, may have stimulated the young man's already heightened fears of an imminent attack on his identity and perhaps deepened his resolve to make minimal concessions to his new environment. The attenuated, ambivalent nature of his religious participation during his five months at Notre Dame des Anges suggests that Pastedechouan was determined to contest the zealous Le Jeune to retain control of his religious identity during this, his second prolonged encounter with post-Tridentine Catholicism.

Reserve and Resistance: Pastedechouan's Boundary-Marking Strategies

From the moment he crossed the threshold of the cramped Jesuit residence, still badly damaged from the indignities of its English occupation, Pastedechouan engaged a number of strategies that were designed to blunt Le Jeune's pointed religious demands and to demarcate the extent of Pastedechouan's willingness to commit himself to the religious life of the Jesuit institution and the linguistic education of its Superior.[48] Throughout his tenure at Notre Dame des Anges, the young aboriginal deliberately controlled the tempo and method of Le Jeune's linguistic instruction and erected and defended clear ritual boundaries between himself and the house's numerous other residents, both European and aboriginal. Pastedechouan's deliberate minimalism in the performance of his pedagogical and religious duties made the cleavage between his initial trumpeted status as divine instrument and the reality of his considerable resistance to reembracing Catholicism increasingly and embarrassingly clear to his would-be mentors.[49]

Pastedechouan's main duty, to teach Le Jeune the basics of Innu grammar and vocabulary, would have commenced from the moment he was greeted by the excited missionary at the residence's threshold, probably with a barrage of questions regarding Innu syntax. In a partnering that replicated even as it contrasted to his education of Recollet lay brother Gabriel Sagard in France a decade previously, Pastedechouan imparted over the course of the subsequent five months enough linguistic information that the missionary was able to compile "our Dictionary," an Innu-French grammar. This tool allowed Le Jeune, following Pastedechouan's abrupt Easter departure, to compose a series of catechistic songs and poems, for his newly established day school and to communicate, albeit in a halting way, with his students and their parents.[50]

From the beginning, Pastedechouan appears to have utilized his position as Le Jeune's private tutor as an opportunity to assert some control in his relationship with the dominant older man. While it was Le Jeune who oversaw Pastedechouan's daily routine, approved his periodic absences from the residence, and instigated the reform of his devotional life, his Innu tutor was quick to take advantage of the powerful Superior's profound dependency upon him for linguistic aid.

As previously noted, Le Jeune, like his Recollet and Jesuit predecessors, was fully committed to missionary competence in aboriginal languages. Though he shared the Recollet vision of an integrated colonial society that was culturally, religiously, and linguistically French, the Superior recognized that this ideal society lay in the future. Until French became the dominant aboriginal lingua franca, the ability to communicate in a sophisticated and nuanced way in native languages, while a difficult challenge, was absolutely necessary to the sacred task of aboriginal conversion. Confidently taking as his own the biblical maxim *fides ex auditu,* Le Jeune defended the paltry results heretofore gained by the Jesuits. Referring to their inadequate linguistic preparation for missionary work, he rhetorically asked, "How can a mute preach the Gospel?"[51] The Superior asserted that if aboriginal peoples could hear the Word eloquently conveyed in their own tongues, their conversion would be all but inevitable, both because of the self-evident truth of Christianity to any reasonable mind and because of the elevated place accorded persuasive rhetoric in aboriginal cultures. By virtually equating missionary linguistic and rhetorical skills with aboriginal conversion, Le Jeune gave Pastedechouan, as his language teacher, a powerful weapon in their ongoing struggle.

Pastedechouan's advantage was heightened because of the unattractiveness of Le Jeune's other linguistic options. The grammars penned by his predecessors the frustrated Jesuit described as confusing and almost useless. Professional European translators, who were conversant in aboriginal languages due to their long years within aboriginal communities, were often openly hostile to missionary overtures. Nicholas Marsolet, a hardened veteran of many winters in Canada, openly declared that he would "never teach the Savage tongue to any one whomsoever," defiantly resisting missionary overtures to tap his accumulated knowledge of both Algonkian and Iroquoian languages.[52] Many such *trouchemens* resented missionary attempts to sedentify and "agriculturalize" aboriginal societies, arguing that such unwelcome interference in traditional aboriginal ways of life foolishly imperiled the fur trade. Confessional tensions also played a role. Protestant coureurs de bois, in the country illegally, resented Jesuit ascendancy and machinations to displace them from a land that they had come to regard as home.

In an environment with few pedagogical options, then, Pastedechouan held over Le Jeune the tantalizing prospect of linguistic competency as well as the more personal prize of his own religious rehabilitation, both of which were deeply attractive to the newly-arrived

Jesuit Superior. Pastedechouan clearly seized on this modicum of power. Le Jeune related in his letters back to France that, in order to learn anything, he was forced adapt himself to his teacher's deliberately haphazard manner of instruction: "Now, having gained this advantage [Pastedechouan], I begin the work incessantly. I make conjugations, declensions and some little syntax, and a dictionary, with incredible trouble, for I was compelled sometimes to ask twenty questions to understand one word, so changeable was my master's way of teaching." Furthermore, Le Jeune was frequently forced to sweeten the deal by offering Pastedechouan inducements in exchange for linguistic information, usually with bribes of tobacco.[53] Such glimpses into their teacher-student relationship make it apparent that though the two often clashed over the extent, duration, and remuneration of Le Jeune's lessons, it was one field from which Pastedechouan consistently emerged the victor.

But the extent of Pastedechouan's involvement in the devotional life of Notre Dame des Anges was an even more hotly contested issue between the two men, for it was in this arena that Pastedechouan was most determined to exercise control of his religious identity and destiny. Le Jeune's uncomfortable dependency upon Pastedechouan for linguistic instruction, however, appears only to have deepened the Jesuit's commitment to asserting his priestly authority by actively reimpressing his wayward teacher with the Catholic stamp. The Superior's increasingly frustrated attempts to coerce Pastedechouan into the performance of his religious duties were to be as fruitless as they were theologically suspect.

Though Le Jeune in his *Relations* reveals few details regarding Pastedechouan's daily religious routine (probably because they would have clashed so incongruously with the missionary's preferred representation of the young man as the "admirable kindness and providence of God in our behalf") it is apparent that his participation in the spiritual life of the residence was tenuous and often reluctant.[54] Pastedechouan's personal devotional schedule would, most likely, have mirrored that of the residence's Catholic laborers, who attended morning mass and evening prayers, observed grace before meals, and obeyed the distant pealing of the Angelus at Quebec. While Pastedechouan apparently participated "from time to time" in the frequent self-examination and confession that characterized the Ignatian program, he reportedly expressed considerable fear of the privations of Lent and "would not take communion, whatever might be said to him," leading to a series of increasingly disruptive confrontations over ritual, identity, and authority between the young man and his would-be spiritual guide.[55]

Pastedechouan's anticipation of the Lenten fasting to come, an observance that appears to have been solemnly marked in the small French colony, apparently led to his first, abortive flight from the residence in late January, only three months after his arrival. Le Jeune confided to his *Relations* that for weeks the young man had been asking "a number of questions, the full tendency of which we did not comprehend; namely, at what age it was necessary to fast; if one should not eat meat at all during Lent, and similar things."[56] Despite these clear indications of the young man's apprehension, Le Jeune was taken by surprise to find, after a cursory survey of Pastedechouan's attic sleeping quarters one winter morning, that his teacher had abruptly bolted, joining his ex-father-in-law, Manitougatche, for an ill-fated hunting trip.[57] Though Le Jeune, characteristically, interpreted Pastedechouan's actions within a providentialist framework, narratively presenting the episode as a drama about whether the Jesuits would be able to recover their "signal favor," the Superior could not resist the temptation to highlight the ironic humor in the situation:

> La Nasse [Manitougatche] having eaten all his game, and finding no more in the woods, was so pressed with hunger that he knew not on which side to turn. Our Pierre [Pastedechouan] found himself fasting before the beginning of Lent; having nearly lost his life upon the ice, which slipped from under him, he passed four days with scarcely anything to eat and returned to us completely exhausted, after 15 days of absence. He did not tell us that hunger had brought him back, therefore I attributed his return to Him who gave him to us for a second time.[58]

Pastedechouan's apparently strong association of deprivation with Catholicism would resurface the following winter, when he would draw upon his own experiences of Lenten fasting to craft, for a rapt Innu audience, an influential anti-Christian polemic, which suggested the antipathy of the Jesuits' God toward those who ate well.[59]

If Lent was the dress rehearsal, Easter was the final curtain. Pastedechouan's actions had demonstrated the lengths to which he was prepared to go to avoid some aspects of Catholic practice, adding flight to his repertoire of defensive maneuvers. It was Pastedechouan's refusal to crown his reluctant Lenten observance with confession and Easter communion that precipitated his climactic confrontation with Le Jeune and his final departure from the Jesuit residence during Holy Week of 1633.

Pastedechouan's refusal to receive Eucharist was apparently long standing: he stated that he had "never taken communion in his country, though he had in France." While this claim of total abstention was probably an exaggeration, in light of his continued association (and probable coresidence) with the Recollets until their forced repatriation in 1629, Pastedechouan's simple explanation of his reluctance—"I was disposed to it more there than here"—nevertheless draws an intriguing experiential, environmental, and temporal boundary which conceptually divides his time in France from all that followed it.[60] In Pastedechouan's own perception, his ritual participation in the Eucharist seemed to belong to a distant land and an irretrievable past.

As frequent communion was a prominent feature of Jesuit worship at Notre Dame des Anges, Le Jeune would have had ample time, during their five months together, to observe the young man's obduracy with regard to this key sacrament. While persuading Pastedechouan to seal his apparently regular confessions with equally habitual communion would have been, for Le Jeune, a gratifying sign of Pastedechouan's spiritual health, such laudatory devotional exercises were not, strictly speaking, obligatory. The Council of Trent had reiterated that annual Eucharist on or before Easter was required for every baptized Catholic, to culminate Lent's somber self-examination and ritual penance, to reconcile the sinner with his suffering Lord, and to facilitate community cohesion. As the long, cold days of a Canadian Lent dwindled and Holy Week loomed, Jesuit interpretations of Pastedechouan's steadfast refusal to communicate would have shifted dramatically. Earlier in the sacred calendar his balking had been tolerated as an unfortunate personal idiosyncrasy. Now it was read as a disturbing symptom of his growing alienation from and defiance of the Catholic community.

By threatening to break the uniformity of mandated Catholic ritual observance at Notre Dame des Anges, Pastedechouan became as much of a conceptual anomaly in the Jesuit residence as he had been in his Innu community. In both contexts, Pastedechouan's reluctance to participate in key community-affirming rituals deprived those around him of the satisfaction of clearly ascertaining his definitive identity. Pastedechouan's unwillingness or unsuitability to undertake a vision quest confounded his Innu categorization, stranding him in the liminal space between child and adult. His equal determination to evade his Easter obligation led to his similarly ambiguous standing at Notre Dame des Anges. On the one hand, the inescapable fact of his baptism, coupled with his linguistic facilitation of the work of God, made him appear a real if errant member of the body of Christ. On the other, his unwillingness to engage Catholicism's central mystery, the consumption of Christ's transubstantiated body, seemed to mark him as a deliberate outsider.

Pastedechouan's obstinacy placed Le Jeune in a difficult position. While the youth's apparent immunity to his Superior's evangelical courtship was merely embarrassing, his outright defiance of a universal Catholic obligation would have put his continued employment in jeopardy. Even in a setting where they had few options for learning aboriginal languages, the Jesuits were choosy about their instructors, perceiving as "tainted instruments" those who professed animosity toward their sacred mission. The mutual hostility between Jesuits and professional translators contributed to Pastedechouan's incredible value in Jesuit eyes—a value which his intransigence now seemed to threaten. Faced with the prospect of Pastedechouan publicly discrediting the worth of his critical linguistic services, Le Jeune finally snapped. Utterly frustrated, the Superior resorted to the theologically questionable tactic of effectively coercing the participation of his recalcitrant teacher. With the complicity of one of Pastedechouan's relatives, Le Jeune made the young man's much-desired temporary release from the residence conditional upon the performance of his religious obligations.

> On Good Friday, he wanted to go hunting with our Savage [Manitougatche], who had returned; but I told him that he should not go until he had rendered to God the devotion that all Christians owed to him at that time. I charged our Savage [Manitougatche] not to receive him in his company, and he did not. Then he confessed and received his Easter communion. The next day, our Savage returning . . . our man [Pastedechouan] accosted him, and said that we had only detained him that he might pray to God on the preceding day; and that, having done so, we were willing that he should go with him. It is true that, in order to please him, we told him that, if he performed his devotions, he might go hunting upon the first opportunity; which he did with the promise to return, but we have not seen him since.[61]

While, from Le Jeune's perspective, Pastedechouan's grudging participation in this coerced communion was a satisfactory ending to the standoff, it would prove to be a Pyrrhic victory. Though the Superior's actions may have resolved, for his Jesuit community, the issue of Pastedechouan's formal religious identity, Le Jeune's resort to such measures critically alienated the subject of his ritual attention. By overstepping the clear boundaries that the young man had so painstakingly erected, Le Jeune left him little choice but to flee. Scheduled to take only a short hunting trip, Pastedechouan permanently departed Notre Dame des Anges on March 26, Holy Saturday, 1633. Though repeatedly prevailed upon by Le Jeune to return, Pastedechouan consistently refused. He would darken the Jesuits' door only once more in his lifetime, shortly before his death.[62]

The Man in the Middle: Manitougatche

It is doubtful whether Le Jeune's gamble to force Pastedechouan to comply with his Easter obligations would have been possible without the complicity of his older relative, Manitougatche. There is a certain delicious irony in the fact that the Jesuit Superior, having exhausted his persuasive repertoire, was dependent upon the assistance of the unbaptized Innu elder in attempting to coerce the Catholic obligations of an aboriginal convert. The three-way relationship that existed between the venerable Innu elder, the middle-aged Jesuit priest, and the youth who was the failed son-in-law of the former and the runaway teacher of the latter, was complex. Both Le Jeune and Pastedechouan attempted to leverage their association with Manitougatche in their ongoing power struggle with one another. That each was able to do so relatively successfully indicates the multivalence of the elder's behavior, identity, and allegiances. Manitougatche's complex personal religiosity, which seems to have interwoven traditional Innu life ways with French Catholicism, made him sympathetic both to the young aboriginal man, eager for some tenuous connection to his absent family, and to the Jesuit Superior who sought to edify his difficult protégé with the example of the as-yet unbaptized Innu elder.

A close relationship existed between Pastedechouan and the father of his former wife, whose apparent desertion of their marriage the previous fall may have influenced the young man's decision to enter the Jesuit enclave.[63] To Pastedechouan, Manitougatche may have represented a treasured link with his Innu community and past. The elder and his family appear to have adopted an atypical lifestyle based at Quebec, close to the

Jesuit residence, a decision likely prompted by a combination of military, religious, and economic factors. Pastedechouan's continued association with his former father-in-law and his affines provided him with an inclusive if somewhat unusual Innu family during his long winter separation from his brothers, who, in accordance with more traditional patterns, were hunting in the Canadian hinterlands. During his winter at Notre Dame des Anges, Pastedechouan, with Le Jeune's blessing, often accompanied the Manitougatche on short hunting forays. Manitougatche's apparent acceptance of his ex-son-in-law's incompetence in the arts of Innu manhood must have come as a welcome relief from the constant ribbing of Pastedechouan's other family members. The elder's greater patience with Pastedechouan's ineptitude may have devolved from Manitougatche's evident respect for the young man's position as a teacher at Notre Dame des Anges, the prestige of which may have offset the young man's pronounced failure in more traditional areas.

Both of Pastedechouan's unauthorized absences from the residence—his penultimate Lenten and ultimate Easter flight—were made in the company of the older Innu. These two contrasting episodes compellingly demonstrate the ambiguity of his elderly relative's religious influence. Manitougatche's facilitation of Pastedechouan's abortive pre-Lenten escapade demonstrated to the young man that their association could provide not only an authorized release from the pressures of life with the Jesuits but also an escape hatch from the tight corners of Catholic ritual obligation. However, as the later, Holy Week confrontation illustrates, Manitougatche's influence cut both ways, providing a means to enforce as well as elude these dreaded responsibilities. The fact that Le Jeune was able to appeal to the Innu elder to modify his own plans so as to manipulate his former son-in-law into the performance of his Easter duties is compelling evidence of the depth of Manitougatche's sympathy for the missionary's agenda as he understood it.

Nor was Manitougatche's advocacy for the embattled missionary an isolated incident. The elderly man often echoed or amplified the Jesuit Superior's sentiments when speaking to Pastedechouan. Manitougatche apparently expressed to his former son-in-law a deep interest in the missionary's novel doctrines, as Le Jeune noted: "the Savage Le Nasse [Manitougatche] being with us, I [Le Jeune] instructed him about the Creation of the world, the Incarnation, and the Passion of the Son of God. We talked well into the night, everyone being asleep except him. Returning to his cabin, he said to Pierre that he was much pleased to listen to such talk." The elder also apparently urged his young relative to be more diligent in his education of Le Jeune: "Teach that man as soon as you can . . . in order that we may be able to understand what he says."[64]

Manitougatche's status as a Catholic neophyte and French ally long predated his association with the newly arrived Superior. Prior to the 1629 surrender of French forces, Manitougatche had lived on cleared land provided by the Jesuits, absorbing both their farming techniques and the strictures of Catholicism. As a staunch French ally, he was harassed by the English during their three-year tenure at Quebec, eventually necessitating his escape beyond their influence. The elderly man was quick to reestablish relations with the Jesuits upon their 1632 return to Quebec. He rebuilt his small, European-style cabin, burnt to the ground by the English on its original site just feet from Notre Dame des Anges, and decorated it with "the name of Jesus, on a paper."[65] While retaining something of the seasonal rhythms of traditional Innu life and likely his religious understanding of the relationship between hunter and prey, Manitougatche was also apparently open to Catholic influences. Le Jeune reports that the Innu elder forswore work on Sundays, learned and kept the Ten Commandments, took an evangelical role both within and outside his familial band, and frequently attended Mass and catechism at the residence, often staying overnight after evening prayers, probably in Pastedechouan's sleeping loft. Manitougatche, moreover, was instrumental in the provision of Le Jeune's unofficial seminary with its first five students, traveling considerable distances to bring the Jesuits orphaned children and volunteering his own grandson for instruction at the residence.[66]

The unbaptized elder's apparent evangelical enthusiasm was in stark contrast with his baptized son-in-law's attenuated restraint. The contrasting religious attitudes and behaviors of these two men, each of whom had been profoundly affected by their encounter with the agents of French Catholicism, help us to understand how the critical factors of age and mission context affected converts' religious susceptibility. In their broadest outlines, the contrasting Christianization of Pastedechouan and Manitougatche represented respectively the legacy and the future of Jesuit missionization; rehearsing the shift from a child-focused, individual, orthodoxic approach until approximately 1640, to an adult-centered, communal, and orthopraxic strategy in successive decades.[67] The two men's differing levels of maturity and the contrasting contexts in which they first encountered Catholic agents demonstrably influenced the degree to which they participated as active agents in this religious encounter, and decisively shaped their perceptions of the relationship between Christian and Innu identity.

As a tiny minority dwarfed by a dominant aboriginal population accustomed to negotiation rather than imposition in their relationship with their European allies, missionaries in 1620s Canada were unable simply to force their exclusivist views onto their independently minded aboriginal audience. Unlike Pastedechouan, whose childhood immersion in French Catholicism took place an ocean away from his family and culture, Manitougatche was a mature middle-aged man when he first encountered the gray- and black-robed representatives of post-Tridentine Catholicism on his own shores. As well as having the experience, self-confidence, and social prestige of aboriginal maturity, Manitougatche also retained control of the extent and duration of his experimentation with the social and religious practices introduced by the missionaries.

The divergence between Pastedechouan's and Manitougatche's religious ethos is strikingly encapsulated in an incident related by Le Jeune. "In the evenings when he [Manitougatche] sleeps with us, he attends the Litanies in our Chapel; and as he was answering with us *ora pro nobis*, Pierre [Pastedechouan], laughing at this, asked him if he had thoroughly understood what he had said. 'No' says he, 'but I believe it is good, since those Fathers say it in praying to God.'"[68] In deriding Manitougatche's enthusiastic participation in the Latin prayers, Pastedechouan demonstrated his own Recollet-derived assumption that being Christian demanded a high level of linguistic and theological knowledge. The rigorous training both Jesuit and Recollet missionaries bequeathed to seventeenth-century aboriginal children was predicated upon their assumption that acquisition of doctrinal knowledge should precede and inform their ritual practice.

Manitougatche's riposte suggested, however, that the pious desire to engage holy mysteries through the imitation of religious authorities was more important than a detailed understanding of each term or gesture used, as these were merely the means of expressing an already present attitude of devotion. Later Jesuits agreed wholeheartedly with Manitougatche's central premise. Abandoning their predecessors' faith in the ability of children to serve as leaders in the conversion of their own people, Jesuits in the 1640s and 1650s, posited that the collective performance of Catholic ritual would stimulate and facilitate aboriginal receptivity to the doctrinal truths of Christianity. In this model, collective participation in Catholicism's rich ritual life was seen as properly preceding and precipitating broad doctrinal knowledge as the all-important first step in Christian formation. Through both his own example and his articulate arguments, Manitougatche thus presaged a future missionization approach, which stressed the ritual participation of aboriginal adults rather than the theological education of native children. Indeed, though the Innu elder was critical in the procurement of young aboriginal students, for the Jesuits, he challenged as well as facilitated the Superior's pedagogical focus upon children, as Le Jeune himself noted: "As I [Le Jeune] was instructing his grandson, he [Manitougatche] said to me: 'Teach me, I shall retain it better than he;' and, joining his hands, he pronounced the blessing at the table."[69]

At the time it was uttered, however, Manitougatche's protest fell upon deaf ears. Children rather than adults would continue to be the preferred targets of missionary activity during and beyond Le Jeune's tenure as Superior. Jesuit fears that the baptismal sacrament might be profaned by the subsequent apostasy of mature converts are well illustrated by the extraordinary caution with which they treated Manitougatche, for whom their trust and affection was evident. Le Jeune's almost hagiographic depiction of the Innu elder (which may have overstated considerably the degree of his interest in and commitment to Catholicism), merely highlights the conservatism of the Jesuit response.[70] Though the Superior confided in the *Relations* his fervent wish that Manitougatche's family burdens were lighter so that he could reside continuously with the Jesuits, he envisioned Manitougatche's position as that of a domestic rather than a student, donné, or Jesuit postulate. Moreover, though Le Jeune adjudged the elder sufficiently well instructed to receive baptism, he cautioned that Manitougatche's formal admission to the church should be made only "should he be in danger of death . . . we shall not make haste until we know how to speak the language well." This conservative Jesuit response was modeled on the policy of their Recollet predecessors which targeted the dying and children for ritual incorporation into the church. Le Jeune wrote, "We dare not yet trust baptism to any except those whom we see in danger of death, or to children who are assured to us; for, not yet being able to fully instruct these Barbarians, they would soon show a contempt for our holy Mysteries, if they had only a slight knowledge of them."[71] Language barriers and lingering concerns regarding aboriginal apostasy precluded Manitougatche's official recognition as a Christian while he was still in robust health, thus thwarting his potential establishment of a nascent diocese of Innu adults.

In addition to explicitly challenging the Jesuit focus upon the theological education of children, Manitougatche's admonition to Le Jeune to redirect his catechistic efforts from grandson to grandfather also illustrated his clear sense of himself as an active theological agent. While Pastedechouan's condescending mockery of the older man's willingness to utilize a language he did not comprehend implicitly suggested the older man's forfeiture of his intellectual independence, such a presentation grossly distorts Manitougatche's high degree of theological autonomy. Though the elder's appreciative imitation of the Jesuits' ritual words and actions is in apparent contrast with Pastedechouan's seemingly defiant campaign of boundary setting, the older man, unlike his young relative, took for granted both his prerogative and his ability to dispute with the Jesuits regarding both their methods and their message. Not content simply to question his mentor's focus upon the indoctrination of children, Manitougatche also challenged the missionary's religious exclusivism and repeatedly rebuked Le Jeune for his denigration of aboriginal cultural and religious practices:

> Our Savage [Manitougatche] came to see us, and said that one of his sons-in-law had dreamed that we would give him a piece of *petun,* or tobacco, as long as his hand. I refused him, saying that I did not give anything on account of dreams; that they were only folly, and that, when I knew his language, I would explain to him how they originated. He [Manitougatche] replied to me that all nations had something especially their own; that, if our dreams were not true, theirs were; and that they would die if they did not execute them . . . He replied that his son-in-law's dream was not bad; and just as he believed us when we told him something, or when we showed him a picture, so likewise we ought to believe him when he told us something that was accepted by his people. More than that, he was astonished that we, who did not use tobacco, liked it so much. Finally, we found it necessary to give him some, taking good care to make him understand that it was not in consideration of his dream, and that we would refuse him whatever he asked under that pretext. He said he would no longer believe in such fancies, but that his son-in-law could do as he liked.[72]

In his engagements with the Superior, then, Manitougatche forcefully articulated his desire that missionary-aboriginal dialogue become a true exchange characterized by mutual comprehension, tolerance, and respect. Pastedechouan lacked Manitougatche's sense of confident entitlement to engage the missionary as an equal. His religious participation was much less enthusiastic than that of his elderly relative, and he was far more reticent in explicitly or directly questioning Christian teachings or Jesuit prerogatives.[73] Pastedechouan's continual recourse to evasion, delay, and passive resistance at Notre Dame des Anges seem to indicate that he had retained a great deal of his conditioned respect for religious authority (as well, perhaps, as some traditional Innu politesse). His skirting, thwarting, or blunting of Le Jeune's requests for linguistic assistance or ritual participation did not overtly challenge the missionary's spiritual authority, the basis upon which the Superior demanded Pastedechouan's willing obedience.

In addition to their dissimilar understandings of the nature of religious participation, their different degrees of religious autonomy, and their contrasting evaluations of Jesuit authority, Pastedechouan and Manitougatche experienced and expressed opposing perspectives as to how Christian commitments interfaced with traditional Innu beliefs and practices. The differing degrees to which each man accepted the exclusivism of his Christian mentors greatly impacted his sense of personal identity and community allegiance.

As a young child under Recollet supervision, Pastedechouan was taught that Christian doctrine and aboriginal belief systems were essentially incompatible. This exclusivism arguably underlay all of his subsequent struggles with his variegated personal identity. Isolated in an exclusively Catholic milieu for five years, Pastedechouan experienced a revolution in his religious consciousness and personal sense of identity, and a concomitant rejection of his cradle culture, a rejection which his subsequent forced reimmersion in it during the English episode could only partially abrogate.[74]

Manitougatche's experience of the relationship between Christian commitments and Innu priorities contrasted sharply with that of his young relative. As indicated by the tenor of his chiding remarks to Le Jeune, Manitougatche's interpretive stance remained characteristically relativistic. As well as defending the religious perspective of his son-in-law and suggesting that the Jesuits should listen as well as talk, Manitougatche also championed the right of each person to come to their own religious conclusions. In drawing upon his considerable religious knowledge and personal prestige as an Innu elder in his dealings with Le Jeune, Manitougatche tried to alert the Superior to the necessity of respecting Innu beliefs to which he himself still adhered.

Unlike Pastedechouan, Manitougatche felt entirely free to envision the relationship between Innu traditional beliefs and Christianity syncretically. In participating in French religious observances, Manitougatche was in no way forsaking his own culture's spiritual realities or abandoning its social priorities.

Manitougatche's cultural and religious relativism was typical of the mind-set of many aboriginal people in early to mid-seventeenth-century Canada. In his successive relationships with the other members of Pastedechouan's family, Le Jeune would repeatedly encounter a stance of genuine openness to his religious perspective coupled with a simultaneous demand that he reciprocally acknowledge the validity and wisdom of aboriginal perspectives and practices.[75]

Recognition of the contrasting experiences of Manitougatche and Pastedechouan with the missionary agents of post-Tridentine Catholicism is critical to our understanding of how evolving missionization models definitively affected the religious experiences, perspectives, and commitments of individual aboriginals in seventeenth-century Canada. The Jesuits' initial commitment to an uncompromisingly exclusivist adoption of French Catholicism by native peoples forced them to focus solely upon those sectors of the population whom they could completely control. To this end they isolated children from their families and communities and carefully taught them that their adoption of this new religion entailed the forfeiture of their spiritual and cultural heritage. Later generations of Jesuits, while retaining their predecessors' commitment to the ultimacy of Christian truth, would come to define a broad range of aboriginal traditional beliefs and practices as religiously "neutral." In so doing, these blackrobed missionaries belatedly recognized the validity of Manitougatche's argument that one could simultaneously hold to traditional ways and adopt the religious culture of the French.

Echoes of his Past: Pastedechouan and Fortune

Manitougatche was not the sole Innu who ventured inside the walls of Notre Dame des Anges only to become caught up in the ongoing struggle between the Superior and his Innu language teacher. Another aboriginal actor inexorably swept into the two men's turbulent relational dynamics was a nine- or ten-year-old Innu orphan adopted by the Jesuits in December 1632. As Le Jeune recorded, the boy was named "Fortune" by the Jesuits, to commemorate his luck in narrowly escaping the fate of his younger brother following their late mother's demise:

> We have named him Fortune, until he can be baptized. Oh, what good fortune he has met with! Being at Tadoussac, forsaken by everyone, a Savage gave an arquebus to our Pierre [Pastedechouan], telling him to kill this miserable child, because, having no parents, he would be abandoned by everyone during his lifetime. Our Savage [Manitougatche], on hearing that, had pity on the little one, took him, and fed him up to the time when he gave him to us . . . He [Fortune] one day showed me the place where his mother died, and told me that, as soon as she expired, the Savages killed a little brother of his, perhaps to save him from the suffering he would have to endure after the death of his mother; they would have done the same to him if he had not already been quite large.[76]

Fresh from the trauma of witnessing his mother's death and his brother's slaying, Fortune was to endure the vociferous and contrary urgings of two potential mentors at the Jesuit house, Le Jeune, the ardent missionary, and Pastedechouan, his fellow tribesman. Sequestered within the walls of Notre Dame des Anges, the young boy functioned as an emotionally potent symbol for both men—regarded as a beacon of hope for the future of his benighted people by the Superior, he appears to have been seen by Pastedechouan as a tragic replication of his own damaging past.

For Le Jeune, Fortune, along with the rest of the tiny cadre of young boys residing that winter within the residence's walls, was a brand plucked from the burning, who represented the fragile hope of a perverse and hell-bound people. The Superior's characteristically Augustinian outlook led him to evaluate negatively the propensities of aboriginal adults, whom he regarded as steeped in sin and "imbued with error." Though he described with considerable eloquence the openhearted generosity of many Innu social practices, Le Jeune was nevertheless quick to state that as they were motivated by a desire for social harmony and cohesion rather a desire to imitate Christ, such acts fell far short of "real moral virtue."[77] The bleak darkness of Le Jeune's interior palette was relieved, however, by his affectionate idealization of the innocence, tractability, and harmless playfulness of his growing "family" of young charges. Fortune's advent five weeks after Pastedechouan's arrival provided considerable comfort to the Superior, as he regarded the intelligent and amenable boy as the potential leader of a spiritual revolution among his people and the seedbed of a future aboriginal church.[78]

Le Jeune sought to enhance his young students' nascent goodness by winning their confidence and affection and transforming them into learned and devout Catholics. Fortune and his compatriots were taught to read, write, and "pray to God, in Latin and in their own language," and coached in suitable deportment toward their religious superiors.[79] Like Pastedechouan's Recollet mentors, the Jesuit Superior sought to instill in his cadre of boys the salutary virtues of discipline, obedience, and humility. Preferring to motivate his students by utilizing the children's growing affection for their missionary mentors, Le Jeune was nevertheless not adverse to the use of corporal punishment to discourage idleness or assertiveness.[80] Writing in 1636, Le Jeune reflected upon the marked differences in Fortune's behavior and allegiances following several years of Jesuit coaching in both Canada and France:

> Our little Fortune, who has been sent back [from France] because he was sick, and who cannot return to his parents, for he has none, is quite different from what he was, although he has lived only a little while in France; so far from mingling with the Savages, he runs away from them, and is becoming very obedient. In truth he astonishes me, for he used to begin to run to the cabins of the barbarians as soon as we said a word to him; he could not suffer anyone to command him, whoever he might be; now he is prompt in whatever he does.[81]

The young boy's conduct upon repatriation, particularly his apparent fear of association with native visitors, was strikingly similar to that of the young Recollet-influenced Pastedechouan following his own return to Canada eleven years earlier.

The Superior's evident delight in observing these tangible shifts in Fortune's deportment was apparently not shared by Pastedechouan, who witnessed at close range the boy's transformation during the winter of 1632–1633. Pastedechouan's observation of his ten-year-old bunkmate's naïve interactions with the Jesuits probably triggered vivid memories of his own childhood experiences of isolation and religious reeducation under Recollet tutelage. In response, he covertly urged the younger boy to flee the Jesuits and return to his people, advice that he apparently punctuated with threats and outright physical abuse. Writing retrospectively after the premature deaths of both his secretive teacher and his beloved young student in 1636, Le Jeune related his horror upon discovering Pastedechouan's violent confrontations with the young boy during their coresidence at Notre Dame des Anges: "We have learned that the wicked Apostate [Pastedechouan], seeing that we loved him [Fortune] for his docility, very often urged him to leave us, even going so far as to strike and whip him two or three times on this account; but this good little fellow would not obey him."[82]

Pastedechouan's apparently vehement reaction to witnessing Fortune's linguistic, theological, and behavioral molding by the Jesuits reveals his probable discomfort both with the memories of his own missionary-influenced childhood and his current, ambivalent association with Le Jeune and his compatriots. His secret haranguing of Fortune, whose circumstances so perfectly mirrored his own at the same age, was probably inspired by a well-meant desire to prevent the young boy's life from following the same disastrous trajectory as his own. His violent insistence that Fortune forsake the residence and return to his community, made with the full awareness of the privation and possible dangers that awaited him there, surely reflected his evaluation that the boy's youthful alliance with the Jesuits was ultimately more threatening to his long-term well-being. Devoid of the Innu imprimatur—earned through teenaged mastery of survival skills, endurance of grueling rites of passage, and the winning of an other-than-human mentor—Fortune would be destined for a life of dependency, either upon European provision (which Pastedechouan from his own experience knew to be ultimately unreliable), or upon the community from which he was being systematically alienated. Long-term residence with the Jesuits would facilitate Fortune's estrangement from native culture, deepen his sense of moral superiority as a Christian neophyte, and establish his total reliance upon the economic provision and spiritual authority of the Jesuits, attitudes that Pastedechouan knew would negatively impact Fortune's vital relationship with his Innu community. Rather than being simply the opportunistic, vicious abuse of one younger and weaker than himself, Pastedechouan's actions demonstrate the degree to which he had internalized European norms regarding pedagogical violence in attempting to use French methods to drive Fortune from a French enclave.

With these actions, Pastedechouan effectively telegraphed his negative evaluation of his own childhood experiences with European missionaries and, ineffectually, sought to prevent their recurrence in the experiences of the younger generation.

Its benevolent motivations aside, there is little doubt that Pastedechouan probably enjoyed the experience of directly challenging and contravening the powerful Superior's behavioral prescriptions, if only in his clandestine bullying of Fortune. In making Fortune's "docility" the especial focus of his secret rage, Pastedechouan communicated to the boy how unbecoming such behavior was in an Innu man, while simultaneously demonstrating how thoroughly he himself had been indoctrinated by similar behavioral proscriptions. Though he urged the younger boy to resist servility toward his missionary mentors, the covert nature of Pastedechouan's angry defiance was itself evidence of how deeply this conditioned respect for missionary spiritual authority had been impressed upon him during his own childhood encounter with the agents of post-Tridentine Catholicism. Throughout his five-month tenure at the Jesuit residence, Pastedechouan was unable himself to take the twin steps he repeatedly urged upon the reluctant Fortune. His own behavior remained subservient: the evident resentment and anguish he so readily expressed to the younger boy remained, outside this context, firmly hidden behind a mask of sullen capitulation. Until Holy Week, when the zealous missionary finally pushed him beyond endurance, Pastedechouan was unable to model for the boy he had taken as his unwilling protégé the second step he had long advocated. Only on Holy Saturday, 1633, did Pastedechouan forever desert Notre Dame des Anges.[83]

The years 1627–1633 were critical in Pastedechouan's development, inaugurating a characteristic ambivalence toward French Catholicism that was to linger until his early death, by starvation, three years later. While the young man, following his Recollet-initiated reinsertion into Innu society in 1626, remained identified with French colonial society, the abrupt repatriation of his missionary mentors in 1629 signaled the beginning of his forced rapprochement with the culture of his childhood. Such incorporation could never be complete, given the troubling, liminal nature of Pastedechouan's personal identity, which resisted easy categorization and ritual remediation. His lingering commitments to Catholicism and French culture, his relatively advanced age, and his seeming inability to master either the technological or the relational aspects of Innu survival made him an unsuitable candidate for initiation into Innu manhood. Perhaps seeking to enhance his Innu social status, Pastedechouan sought employment from returning colonial officials in 1632, but his unpredictable behavior soon made this arrangement untenable. Faced with the prospect of casting his lot with the Jesuits, Pastedechouan initially quailed but ultimately entered their walls, bringing with him a repertoire of defensive, boundary-marking behaviors aimed at the preservation of his religious autonomy and hard-won if mitigated Innu cultural identity.

His advent at Notre Dame des Anges initiated his chronic struggle with the residence's Superior, Paul Le Jeune. The two men shared a common experience of religious conversion, defined in early modern France as an exclusivistic choice entailing a simultaneous rejection of one's previous self and former familial bonds. This shared experience intensified their subsequent encounters, in which Le Jeune attempted to lure Pastedechouan into a wholehearted reassertion of his formerly devout Catholicism, while the young man sought to evade or deflect the older man's religious demands and to avoid participation in key, identity-asserting Catholic rituals.

Pastedechouan's apparently reluctant participation in the devotional life of Notre Dame des Anges, coupled with his lackluster performance as Le Jeune's personal language instructor, might lead us to conclude that the young man was merely attempting to do the bare minimum to prevent himself from once again being fired. Such an evaluation would doubtless have an element of truth. My feeling is, however, that Pastedechouan's pattern of behavior during his winter at the Jesuit residence is more significant than this. Had Pastedechouan merely been interested in the easiest path, he would have found full compliance with Jesuit demands far less demanding psychologically and emotionally than his own carefully charted course of conditional, mitigated involvement. Pastedechouan's behavior is best understood as illustrating his deep religious ambivalence, because his actions represent a deliberately chosen compromise between the extremes of utterly avoiding intercourse with newly returned missionary agents and an unqualified embrace of post-Tridentine Catholicism. The very fact of Pastedechouan's uncoerced presence at the residence, his apparently willing participation in some aspects of the Catholic ritual repertoire, and his continued if reluctant acknowledgement of Jesuit spiritual authority suggest that, at some level, Pastedechouan continued to be intellectually and emotionally engaged with the Catholicism of his childhood. These evident propensities toward a partial embrace of his Catholic past, however, were countered by his constant, wary defensiveness; his secret indulgence of a violent distaste for the missionary education of his young compatriot; his repeated escapes from Notre Dame des Anges; and, most importantly, his definitive rejection of both the deprivations of Lent and the ultimate Catholic ritual of individual and collective incorporation, the Eucharist. Avoidance of these ritual commitments made the definition of his religious identity as problematic in the Jesuit context as it had been in the Innu milieu. Our assessment of the fundamentally ambivalent nature of Pastedechouan's religious mentality is affirmed by Le Jeune's own reflection upon his teacher's religious propensities, made just after Pastedechouan's final escape from the residence: "For my part I think he has faith; I have seen strong indications of it; but as it is a faith born of fear and slavishness, and as, moreover, he is enchained by a multitude of bad habits, as he has great difficulty in abandoning the wicked liberty of the Savages and submitting to the yoke of the law of God."[84]

Examination of Pastedechouan's aboriginal liaisons while at Notre Dame des Anges allows us to assess the idiosyncratic features of his religious mentality and provides us with clues as to how he himself perceived the process that had molded this characteristic outlook. His relationship with Manitougatche discloses key differences between Pastedechouan's religious outlook engendered a world away from his family and culture, and that of the older man, who encountered French Catholicism from within the security of a familiar cultural context and with the accumulated wisdom and confidence of maturity. Pastedechouan's tempestuous association with Fortune appears to indicate his fundamentally negative assessment of his formative religious experiences and his attempt to prevent their effective replication. Comparative examination of the religious attitudes of these three actors permits us to appreciate the momentous impact of missionary strategies upon the self-perceptions, religious identity, and social allegiances of targeted aboriginals. The child-focused missionary strategy encountered by the two boys, roughly a decade apart, utilized cultural isolation to nip in the bud prevalent aboriginal tendencies toward religious relativism and confident theological agency, replacing these propensities with an acceptance of an essentially foreign

religious exclusivism and a deep respect for and dependency upon missionary spiritual authority. Only after Manitougatche, Pastedechouan,
and Fortune had met their respective deaths would Le Jeune gradually
come to perceive the curiosity of influential aboriginal adults as an inviting opportunity rather than a dangerous risk, reflecting: "When we first
came into these countries, as we hoped for scarcely anything from the
old trees, we employed all our forces in cultivating the young plants; but,
as the Lord gave us the adults, we are turning the great outlay we made
for the children to the succor of their fathers and mothers."[85] The
earnest Superior's belated recognition of Manitougatche's earnest argument, however, would do little to rehabilitate the children whose interior lives and social relationships Catholic missionary orders had so
intrusively affected.

4

"God Has Let His Thunderbolts Fall"

Apostasy and Death in the Canadian Woods

It was a defeat snatched from the jaws of victory. For some nine weeks Jesuit Superior, Paul Le Jeune, had struggled to impose a modicum of Christian belief and practice upon the small Innu hunting band he was accompanying on its six-month-long winter journey. Enduring both the unaccustomed rigors of a Canadian winter and the ubiquitous teasing that met his defiance of Innu behavioural norms, the beleaguered missionary finally appeared to have reached a dramatic breakthrough. Several continuous weeks of disastrous hunting had left the group shaken and near starvation. His Christmas dinner, Le Jeune bleakly recorded, consisted of "the little ends of the trees, which I ate with delight." Desperate, Pastedechouan and his older brother Mestigoit appealed to the Jesuit for his ritual intercession as the band's plight steadily worsened:

> The Renegade [Pastedechouan] came to tell me that the Savages were greatly terrified; and my host [Mestigoit], addressing me seriously, asked if I did not know some remedy for their misfortune. There is not," said he, "enough snow to kill Moose, Beaver, and Porcupines; we find almost no game; what shall we do? Don't you know what will happen to us? Don't you see within yourself what should be done?[1]

Seizing upon the opportunity afforded by the escalating crisis to press home his Christian message, Le Jeune "composed two little prayers, which he [Pastedechouan] turned into savage." Menaced by the specter of starvation, the entire band—men, women, and children—assembled in a provisional "oratory" that Le Jeune had hastily erected out of pine boughs and decorated with a crucifix, reliquary, and pictures torn from

165

his breviary.[2] With Pastedechouan translating, the Superior made an emotional appeal to the assembly, arguing that his God had the power to save them from the jaws of death and from hell itself, if only they would believe wholeheartedly in him. Kneeling in the snow alongside the ambivalent Pastedechouan and anxious Mestigoit was their eldest brother Carigonan, the band's shaman, whom Le Jeune saw as his archrival for the group's religious loyalties. Along with the assembly of twenty-six other Innu, the fraternal trio bowed their heads and repeated aloud the prayer Le Jeune had composed, pledging themselves body and soul to the eternal service of the Christian God as they begged his deliverance from starvation:

> Great Lord, you who have made heaven and earth, you know all, you can do all. I promise you with all my heart (I could not lie to you) I promise you wholly that, if it pleases you to give us food, I will obey you cheerfully, that I will surely believe in you. I promise you without deceit that I will do all that I shall be told ought to be done for love of you. Help us, for you can do it, I will certainly do what they shall teach me ought to be done for your sake. I promise it without pretence, I am not lying, I could not lie to you, help us to believe in you perfectly, for you have died for us. Amen.[3]

The solemnity with which this improvised rite was celebrated, the participation of Carigonan, its influential shaman, and the spectacular hunting success that immediately followed the band's self-dedication to Le Jeune's God would seem to signal the Jesuit's growing influence upon the religious imagination and loyalties of Pastedechouan's clan. But, in fact, the opposite was the case. Christmas 1633 *did* mark a turning point in the missionary's tenuous relations with the Innu group, but rather than ushering in their adoption of Christian beliefs and practices, its dramatic events augured the imminent collapse of the fragile mutual regard that had briefly come to exist between the Superior and his hosts. The very ritual acts that Le Jeune fleetingly believed to have prefigured the reception of the small group into the body of Christ he would later identity as those that had indelibly branded Pastedechouan and his kin with the mark of apostasy—destining the family, root and branch, for a future of eternal punishment.

At the apex of Le Jeune's apparent victory, the cumulative legacy of his previous months of interaction with the trio of brothers and his deliberate ritual infractions would estrange him from his hosts and decisively thwart his attempts to consolidate this brief triumph into more lasting gains. Le Jeune's conceptual framing of the Christmas hunt did succeed in resolving Pastedechouan's intensifying religious ambivalence. But far from precipitating the young man's passionate reembrace of his Catholic past, as Le Jeune intended, the missionary's ritual intervention and its results would provoke Pastedechouan into an unprecedented campaign of active and articulate resistance to the Superior and his message, moving him from oblique to overt rebellion. The pattern of Le Jeune's past encounters with Carigonan, which had combined inadvertent insult with deliberate religious provocation, would lead the shaman defiantly to assert his own religious authority within the group, and enthusiastically to back his youngest sibling's determined efforts to contest the missionary's theological message. Between them, the brothers would effectively thwart Le Jeune's evangelical efforts for the remainder of their shared journey, leading the isolated missionary to spiral steadily downward into a spiritual anomie of illness, depression, and despair.

This chapter will chart the evolving, triangular relationship between the two older religious authorities, Le Jeune and Carigonan, and the younger man, Pastedechouan, who was the spiritual son of the former and the blood brother of the latter. It will explore the complex relational dynamics that preceded and precipitated Le Jeune's fleeting Christmas victory, outlining the Jesuit Superior's reengagement of his recalcitrant language teacher and exploring how his advent within the heart of Pastedechouan's family intensified the characteristic patterns of insistence and resistance, pursuit and flight which the pair had established at Notre Dame des Anges the previous winter. As a French Catholic missionary, Le Jeune was an anomaly within the culturally, religiously, and linguistically homogeneous Innu band.[4] His destabilizing presence alone would doubtless have affected Pastedechouan's pronounced religious ambivalence and tenuous social position. But the missionary's constant and frequently insensitive demands upon the young man—coupled with his highly provocative missionization strategy, which sought, through contestation with Carigonan, to replace the shaman's religious authority with his own—escalated what was an inevitable impact into an outright crisis, precipitating Pastedechouan's dramatic Christmas confrontation with Le Jeune. Postulating that the Superior's plummeting evangelical fortunes were the result of his relational insensitivities, which pushed Pastedechouan from ambivalence to apostasy, and his exclusivistic and confrontational missionary strategy, which estranged the initially receptive Carigonan, this chapter will directly challenge Le Jeune's own assertions that his meagre gains resulted from the three brothers' unholy plot against his sacred mission, hatched before their journey even commenced.[5]

Autumn Rapprochement

Le Jeune and Pastedechouan had reestablished their tempestuous relationship five months previously, during August 1633, following the young man's abrupt Easter departure from Notre Dame des Anges and a long summer spent apart: Le Jeune at Quebec and the Pastedechouan at Tadoussac, which was once again overrun by English forces. Both the Jesuit Superior's tempered response to Pastedechouan's abrupt departure and his relatively optimistic evaluation of the young man's spiritual proclivities had altered dramatically when the Superior learned of Pastedechouan's apparent drunken association with English Protestants:

> On the 8th of June, Father Massé arrived from Tadoussac . . . He told us that Pierre Pastedechouan was more wicked than ever; that the English who were at Tadoussac had ruined him by drunkenness. Oh, how guilty before God will he be who has introduced heresy into this country! If this Savage were intelligent, corrupted as he is by these miserable heretics, he would be a powerful obstacle to the spread of the faith; even now, he will cause only too much injury to it, if God does not touch his heart. To judge from his conduct, it would seem that he was given to us to draw from him the principles of his language, and not for the welfare of his soul, as he now leagues against his God and against the truth.[6]

Despite this scathing indictment of Pastedechouan, Le Jeune, who avidly wished to resume his interrupted instruction in the Innu language, redoubled his pursuit of the young man, "allured by my hopes, if not of bringing the Renegade to a sense of his duty, at least of drawing from him some knowledge of the language." When Pastedechouan, accompanied by his brothers and his new wife, frequented the fishing grounds around Quebec in early August, Le Jeune commenced a series of diplomatic visits to his former teacher, repeatedly inviting him to return to Notre Dame des Anges for the coming winter.[7] Though Pastedechouan, whom Le Jeune now consistently referred to as "the Renegade" or "the Apostate," apparently expressed a desire to "return to God," he was nevertheless unwilling to abandon his spouse, whom he had married over the summer, for his cold cot in the all-male Jesuit residence.[8] Having failed to entice Pastedechouan to reenter the institution, Le Jeune was himself forced to leave it and to follow Pastedechouan and his familial band on their winter hunting journey deep into the woods of present-day southern Quebec and northern Maine.[9]

The resumption of the two men's agonistic relationship was thus inaugurated with an apparent reversal. Whereas the previous autumn it had been the young Innu who reluctantly left his family to enter the orbit of the Jesuit Superior, regulating each day in accordance with the tolling of the Angelus bells, this fall it was Le Jeune who left behind the familiar company of his European brothers in Christ to become what he called "a Savage with the Savages."[10] Adopting the rigorous migratory lifestyle of his hosts in the hopes of mastering the Innu language and winning the small band for Christ, Le Jeune endured long, snow-shoe clad treks from camp to camp, fighting the cutting wind and struggling through the drifting snow. He exchanged the quiet isolation of his tiny cell for the shared shelter of his Innu hosts (replete with numerous exuberant dogs and a fire that seared the flesh of one's chest while leaving one's back covered in ice), and days regulated with the collective observance of Catholic prayer for nights punctuated by the ubiquitous drumbeat of Innu religious ritual.[11]

Adding to the apparent symmetry of this reversal was the Superior's utter isolation from the tiny enclaves of French colonial society and his total dependence upon his hosts, circumstances that more closely approximated Pastedechouan's childhood experience in France than his attenuated freedom at the Jesuit residence the previous winter. The previous winter, Pastedechouan left Notre Dame des Anges when his patience with Le Jeune's manipulative demands was finally exhausted. As a child, however, he had had no such luxury. Even if he managed to escape La Baumette, the boy would still have been embedded in the heart of Europe, an ocean away from his home and family. Similarly, Le Jeune's life was in the hands of his Innu hosts. Had they, at any time, decided to stop providing for him or to abandon him, Le Jeune would have been incapable of meeting his own needs or of navigating alone the hundreds of miles that separated him from the Jesuit outpost near Quebec. Enfolded within the Innu band, Le Jeune was as effectively isolated as if he had the

Atlantic, instead of merely the frozen St. Lawrence, between him and the familiar comfort of Notre Dame des Anges.

Though the dynamics of reversal are arresting, the dramatic symmetry of the two men's successive experiences of displacement, isolation, and dependency should not be presented (in either context) as the straight-forward dominance of a privileged "insider" over an alienated "outsider." While, as we have seen, Le Jeune enjoyed considerable authority over his young teacher at the Jesuit residence, Pastedechouan's canny campaign of ritual boundary setting severely hampered Le Jeune's attempts at his re-Christianization. In fact, Pastedechouan's constant, low-grade resistance to his efforts gradually eroded Le Jeune's militant optimism. Similarly, Pastedechouan's advantage over the Jesuit within his own kin group could easily be overstated. Though the black robe was highly dependent upon Pastedechouan to achieve his linguistic and missionary goals, to portray the younger man as ascendant would be to overlook the implications of Le Jeune's presence on Pastedechouan's psychological equilibrium, fraternal relations, and status within the group.

The Destabilizing Impact of Le Jeune's Presence upon Pastedechouan

Le Jeune's anomalous presence within his family shattered any remaining conceptual, temporal or spatial barriers that Pastedechouan had managed to erect between his two disparate communities, each of which had a claim upon his religious loyalties. With the missionary's intrusion into his family unit, what Pastedechouan had been taught to view as the mutually exclusive worlds of French Catholicism and Innu traditional lifeways abruptly collided. The Superior's exclusivistic message, re-soundingly declaimed within the citadel of Pastedechouan's Innu identity, would reignite the young man's religious ambivalence even as Le Jeune's contentious encounters with his older siblings would prompt them to seek new indications of their youngest brother's fraternal fidelity. Moreover, the missionary's presence would accentuate the aspects of Pastedechouan's cultural and religious identity that he was trying to hide or deny, for in addition to their confessional and linguistic ties, both men confounded Innu expectations for adult male behavior in similar ways. Excoriated throughout the winter for their inability to provide for themselves and others, both were deemed "parasites" in a situation where the margin for survival was thin indeed.[12]

The destabilizing effects of Le Jeune's presence upon Pastedechouan were apparent from the journey's commencement on October 18, 1633, when the small group, amid considerable fanfare, left Quebec. As the lingering warmth of the auspiciously sunny day cooled with the lengthening shadows of evening, the band pulled ashore for the night on a small, pleasant island in the St. Lawrence. The rest of the group being busily occupied in preparing the evening meal and the night's shelter, Pastedechouan, unnoticed, stole away to the abandoned canoes, where he had seen Le Jeune's cask of sacramental wine.

> Screaming and howling like a demon, he [Pastedechouan] snatched away the poles and beat upon the bark of the cabin to break everything to pieces. The women, seeing him in this frenzy, fled into the woods, some here, some there. My Savage [Mestigoit] . . . was boiling in a kettle some birds he had killed, when this drunken fellow, coming into the scene, broke the crane and upset everything into the ashes. No one seemed to get angry at all this, but then it is foolish to fight with a madman. My host gathered up his little birds and went to wash them in the river, drew some water and placed the kettle over the fire again. The women, seeing that this madman was running hither and thither on the shores of the Island, foaming like one possessed, ran quickly to get their bark and take it to a place of security, lest he tear it to pieces, as he had begun to do. They had scarcely time to roll it up, when he appeared near them completely infuriated, and not knowing upon what to vent his fury, for they had suddenly disappeared, thanks to the darkness which had begun to conceal us.[13]

His kin responded to Pastedechouan's frenzied behavior with considerable restraint, apparently believing, as did Le Jeune, that his inebriation had sparked a kind of madness. But Pastedechouan's drunken persistence in despoiling the meal, thus dishonoring the sacrifice of the other-than-human persons who had so generously given of themselves, led to his eventual chastening at the hands of his older brother:

> He [Pastedechouan] approached the fire, which could be seen on account of its bright light, and was about to take hold of the kettle to overturn it again; when my host [Mestigoit], his brother, quicker than he, seized it and threw the water into his face, boiling as it was. I leave you to imagine how this poor man looked, finding himself thus deluged with hot water. He was never so well washed. The skin of his face and whole chest changed. Would to God that his soul had changed as well as his body.[14]

Pastedechouan's furious assault upon the group's collective food and shelter can be read as an attack on the physical and relational mechanisms of Innu survival and as a symbolic protest of the inferior status to which his lack of skill in hunting (the result of his truncated Innu education) had relegated him. But his drunken outburst also encoded his fundamentally ambivalent reaction to Le Jeune's intrusion into his familial group, which appears to have undermined the strategies by which the young man habitually dealt with both his social marginality and his religious confusion. His destructive behavior thwarted by his brother's decisive intervention, Pastedechouan, undeterred, turned to an alternate target, the Jesuit Superior himself.

> My host [Mestigoit] has told me since that he asked for an ax with which to kill me [Le Jeune]; I do not know whether he really asked for one, as I did not understand his language; but I know very well that, when I went up to him and tried to stop him, he said to me in French, "Go away, it is not you I am after; let me alone"; then, pulling my gown, "Come, said he, let us embark in a canoe, let us return to your house; you do not know these people here; all they do is for the belly, they do not care for you, but for your food." To this I answered in an undertone and to myself, *in vino veritas*.[15]

Though Mestigoit confided Pastedechouan's apparent threats to Le Jeune only after the fact, the missionary had some intimation of danger at the time. Having withdrawn alone to perform his evening devotions, Le Jeune was followed by Mestigoit's wife, who threw him some boughs and signaled for him to remain apart, hidden under them. Unnerved, Le Jeune readily complied, spending the first night of his nascent mission to the tiny Innu group condemned to silence and solitude by the unstable, violent behavior of the translator he had fully expected to assist him.[16]

Pastedechouan, during his drinking binge, utilized his unique linguistic skills to impart in two different languages, to two different audiences, two disparate solutions to the evident emotional crisis that Le Jeune's presence had precipitated within him. To his kin, in Innu, he apparently expressed his desire to murder the missionary. To the Superior, in French, he explicitly disavowed any violent intentions toward him, pleaded for their immediate retreat to Notre Dame des Anges, and deprecated what he presented as his family's cynical, grasping attitude toward the missionary. The fire wall of mutually incomprehensible languages ensured that each of his small audiences remained unaware of the contrary comments he had so forcefully communicated to the other. Even as Pastedechouan's drunken rage arguably expressed his frustration with having simultaneously to negotiate the very different cultural and religious expectations of the missionary and his kin group, it inaugurated a strategy of independent conciliation by suggesting two discrete solutions to the missionary's problematic presence and couching each in terms appropriate to the audience.[17] Only the surreptitious gestures of Mestigoit's wife breached the linguistic barrier, correcting Le Jeune's mistaken impression that he was not in any immediate danger from his incensed teacher.

Pastedechouan's twin fantasies of killing Le Jeune and returning with him to Notre Dame des Anges, though contradictory and mutually exclusive, would each have performed a similar psychological function. Either option would have clarified his religious identity and allegiances and rendered his external environment religiously and culturally homogeneous. Slaying the Jesuit would serve as a violent repudiation of his Catholic past and restore the religious uniformity of his family group. Accompanying Le Jeune back to Quebec, conversely, would signal Pastedechouan's reembrace of French Catholicism and effect his immersion into a confessionally homogeneous setting. The fact that Pastedechouan expressed both of these fantasies but acted upon neither suggests that his long-standing ambivalence about the religious aspects of his own identity was dramatically heightened by the missionary's penetration of his kin group. The fact that he saw his options in such stark, dramatic terms would seem to indicate that Pastedechouan still conceived of religious identity in the either-or terms bequeathed to him by the Recollets. Had his childhood mentality not been so profoundly impressed with their exclusivistic stamp, Pastedechouan's religious anxieties would have been neither so pronounced nor so easily recognized and exploited by his Jesuit guest.

But we are not dependent upon Pastedechouan's actions alone to posit his intensifying religious confusion amidst the rubble of his collided worlds. His own purported words eloquently express it. In an intimate, late-night conversation the two men conducted across the glowing embers of a dying fire, only days after his drunken melee, Pastedechouan confided to Le Jeune his porous sense of personal identity and his lifelong vulnerability to alternate religious and cultural influences. Responding to the Superior's impassioned assertions that by neglecting the duties of a baptized Christian, he was courting eternal torment, Pastedechouan, according to Le Jeune, replied,

> I see clearly that I am not doing right; but my misfortune is that I have not a mind strong enough to remain firm in my determination; I believe all they tell me. When I was with the English, I allowed myself to be influenced by their talk; when I am with the Savages, I do as they do; when I am with you, it seems to me your belief is the true one. Would to God I had died when I was sick in France, and I would now be saved. As long as I have any relations, I will never do anything of any account; for when I want to stay with you, my brothers tell me I will rot, always staying in one place, and that is the reason I leave you to follow them.[18]

Pastedechouan's candid confession, which disclosed the overwhelming impact of external forces on his eroded personal identity, intimated the turmoil he faced now that these competing influences had become simultaneous rather than successive. In a few sentences the young man sketched the competing pressures to which he saw himself as being subject, revealing both his continued vulnerability to the missionary's threats of eternal damnation and his counterbalancing fear of his elder brothers' contempt or condemnation. By disclosing his past experiences of the tensions between Le Jeune's religious demands and his family's cultural priorities, Pastedechouan vividly communicated his increasingly tenuous position simultaneously negotiating their competing expectations. The young man's words eloquently foreshadowed how his ongoing association with the Jesuit Superior would affect the dynamics of his fraternal relationships, particularly after the missionary's fateful decision to initiate an all-out war for religious dominance with Pastedechouan's influential eldest brother, Carigonan.

The "Sorcerer" and the Superior

Whereas Pastedechouan and Le Jeune, despite their frequent conflict, were influenced by a similarly exclusivistic set of religious preconceptions, Le Jeune and Carigonan had no such basis of shared assumptions with which to mediate their relationship. Rather, the two men, from the beginning of their association, perceived one another in the radically different terms dictated by their characteristic religious approaches to the world.

Their relationship was formally initiated when Carigonan, as his family leader, visited Notre Dame des Anges in the early fall of 1633 to extend to Le Jeune an invitation to accompany his band on their winter hunting trip. Because the shaman apparently apprehended the Superior as a religious specialist very much like himself, his offer was framed in terms that encoded his sense of similarity to and affinity with the missionary. Expecting to establish a collaborative and mutually beneficial relationship, Carigonan explicitly expressed his hope that Le Jeune would utilize his relational expertise with the powerful beings of the Christian pantheon to aid him in his ongoing illness, which repeated recourse to his own arts had proven unable to ameliorate:

> The sorcerer, having learned from the Renegade that I wished to pass the winter with the Savages, came so see me . . . and invited me to share his cabin,—giving me as his reason that he loved good men, because he himself was good, and had always been so from his early youth . . . He asked me if Jesus had not spoken to me about the disease which tormented him. "Come," said he, "with me, and thou wilt make me live now, for I am in danger of dying."

The exclusivistic Le Jeune, however, perceiving Carigonan as his moral and spiritual antithesis, immediately rejected both his offer of hospitality and his request for healing:

> But as I knew him [Carigonan] for a very impudent fellow, I refused him as gently as I could; and taking the Apostate aside . . . I told him that I would be glad to winter with him and with his brother Mestigoit, on condition that we should not go across the great river, that the sorcerer should not be of our party, and that he, who understood the French language well, would teach me. They both agreed to these three conditions, but they did not fulfill one of them.[19]

Le Jeune's unfavorable response to Carigonan's friendly overtures is initially puzzling, since the selective targeting of a society's religious leaders for intensive catechistic attention was a time-honored Jesuit conversion technique, with a history of great success in their Asian missions. Even Le Jeune himself belatedly admitted that had the influential shaman "come to know God . . . all the Savages, influenced by his example, would [have] like[d] to know him also." The missionary's unwillingness to engage "the most famous sorcerer or *manitousiou* . . . of all the country" suggests that Le Jeune was influenced by Jesuit apprehensions of shaman as the darkest manifestations of aboriginal depravity, demonism, and ignorance.[20]

Whether the Superior employed the preconceptions of Augustinian moralism, Jesuit diabolism, or Renaissance humanism to analyze Carigonan's character and social role, his diagnosis of the shaman's spiritual propensities remained bleak. Viewed through the somber Augustinian lens, Carigonan's complaint (which according to Le Jeune was venereal in nature), took on the darkest tincture of rapacious lust: "His disease . . . was a pain in the loins, or rather an infirmity resulting from his licentiousness and excesses . . . He is vile to the last degree."[21] The shaman's undeniable ritual powers, examined in the light of Jesuit assumptions of prevalent aboriginal diabolism, suggested Carigonan's personal congress with Satan. Couched in more humanistic terms, the religious leader's considerable social status resulted from his cynical manipulation of his community's abject and pitiable religious ignorance. What Le Jeune's contrasting frames of analysis lacked in intellectual coherency they made up for in their uniform negativity. Informed by these contradictory understandings of the shamanic role as immoral, demonic or fraudulent and exploitative, the missionary regarded "the wretched Magician" as the epitome of all that was wrong with Innu society. By attempting to exclude the shaman from his own familial band, Le Jeune hoped to create a religious vacuum within the group that his own presence could effectively fill.[22]

But the Superior's fateful decision to snub Carigonan's invitation merely postponed his encounter with the "Demon," who ignored the missionary's stipulations and rejoined his kin two weeks into their journey, still smarting from his insult. His arrival precipitated the religious engagement of the two men that Le Jeune had so ardently hoped to avoid. Forced by Carigonan's presence to formulate an alternate method by which to claim as his own the mantle of religious leadership within the group, Le Jeune abruptly launched an all-out campaign of religious contestation with the surprised manitousiou, attacking his intellectual credibility and ritual efficacy as part of a wider assault upon the underlying structure of Innu traditional beliefs and practices: "Seeing that he acted the Prophet, amusing these people by a thousand absurdities, which he invented . . . I did not lose any opportunity of convincing him of their nonsense and childishness, exposing the senselessness of his superstitions."[23]

During the months they spent together, the two religious specialists would hotly debate their contrasting epistemic standards for religious "facts," dispute the relative attractions of this life and the next, and discuss the nature and identity of the beings that constituted each tradition's pantheon. But as their animosity deepened, Le Jeune abandoned these relatively civil debates, opting instead to desecrate Innu ceremonies in an attempt to prove their inefficacy. When, in mid-November, Carigonan held a shaking tent ritual to discern the fate of his seriously ill wife and to court animals who were already proving to be distressingly elusive, Le Jeune peppered the ceremony with his acerbic comments: "I was seated like the others, looking on this wonderful mystery, forbidden to speak; but as I had not vowed obedience to them, I did not fail to intrude a little word into the proceedings. Sometimes I begged them to have pity on this poor juggler, who was killing himself in this tent; at other times I told them they should cry louder, for the Genii had gone to sleep."[24] Over time, the missionary's manifest disrespect of Innu religious personages became more pronounced and explicit. To the horror of his hosts, Le Jeune deliberately invoked and insulted Innu other-than-human persons, triumphantly citing his apparent immunity from their wrath as proof of their illusory or impotent nature.[25]

Le Jeune's aggressive policy of proselytization through contestation flew in the face of established Innu wisdom as to how best to preserve intragroup relations. Traditionally, as we have seen, the Innu abhorred direct confrontation, whether verbal or physical. Innu relational protocol, aimed at the maintenance of group cohesion, called upon individuals to suppress their antisocial feelings of anger, frustration, or jealousy and to avoid provoking such emotions in others. To this end, the Innu generally utilized oblique forms of correction or challenge, avoided or mitigated direct demands, and seasoned their requests or rebukes with a leavening humor. Indeed, the Innu's first subtle and then increasingly intense teasing of Le Jeune was a prime example of the way in which they attempted to utilize humor to mitigate objectionable behavior.[26] Le Jeune's strongly worded denunciations of Innu traditional belief and practice, then, would have been seen by his hosts as almost unbearably rude and disruptive. His techniques of deliberate provocation and ritual desecration, the vehicles by which he had chosen to impart Christianity to the group, were to overshadow, obscure, and discredit his substantive evangelical message. In his determination to safeguard Catholicism from the group's relativistic appropriation, the Superior successfully communicated his faith's trenchant exclusivism, but little else.

Though debate, contestive display, and ritual provocation all characterized the two religious leaders' increasingly intense engagement, it was their ongoing attempts to explain and ritually respond to the misfortunes that stalked the band throughout the dying fall and interminable winter that formed the true crux of their struggle for religious authority. Central mysteries crying out for interpretation were illness, death, and dearth. The two men vied with one another to present emotionally and intellectually credible explanations as to why such calamities were repeatedly visited upon the group and, perhaps more importantly, how they could be successfully averted. Each man attempted to depict his own changing fortunes, as well as those of the group, in a way that confirmed his own religious authority. Each attempted to use his rival's experiences of illness or bereavement to contest the other's apprehension of religious reality and claims to ritual efficacy.

Shortly after he rejoined the group, Carigonan's lingering physical ailment once again became the focus of intense negotiation between the two men. Previously, it had been the shaman who unselfconsciously requested Le Jeune to speak to Jesus regarding his healing. Now it was the missionary who guardedly offered his conditional assistance. Le Jeune's offer was not made out of simple compassion for his rival's suffering. Rather, the Superior sought to transform the shaman's distress into his own missionary gains by seeking to persuade Carigonan that his illness was evidence of his gross moral turpitude, ritual impotence, and religious ignorance and by suggesting that all these maladies could be cured by submission to Le Jeune's spiritual direction. The Jesuit envisioned this intervention not as a private arrangement between the two men, however, but as a public contest that would definitively determine the truth of each religious tradition by subjecting their ritual approaches to careful testing over a period of weeks. Accordingly, Le Jeune demanded that, prior to his own religious intervention, Carigonan publicly exhaust the corpus of his own traditional rituals, telling the shaman,

> Beat thy drum for ten days, sing and make all the other sing as much as thou wilt, do all thou canst to recover they health, and if thou art not cured in that time confess that thy din, howls and songs cannot restore thee to health. Now abstain ten more days from all these superstitions,

and . . . I will withdraw for three days to pray in a little cabin that shall be
made farther back in the woods. There I will pray to my God to give thee
health of body and of soul . . . Thou shalt say with all thy heart the
prayers I will teach thee, promising God that, if it pleases him to restore
thee thy health, thou wilt call together all the Savages of the place, and in
their presence thou wilt burn thy drum and all the other silly stuff that
thou usest to bring them together, saying to them that the God of the
Christians is the true God, and they must believe in him and obey him.[27]

The Superior clearly hoped that his daring experiment would lead Carigonan to experience and publicly confess the truth of Christianity and
repudiate his obnoxious claims to shamanistic authority through the
symbolic destruction of his precious ritual objects.

Carigonan responded enthusiastically to the missionary's proposal
and requested that Le Jeune immediately commence his own phase of
active ritual intervention, stating that he was already ready to admit his
own ritual impotence:

I shall not think that it [my healing] has come from my drum; I have
sung and have done all could, yet I have not been able to save the life
of one man; I myself am sick, and to cure myself have made use of all
the resources of my art; and behold I am worse than ever. I have used
all my inventions to save the lives of my children, especially of the last
one who died only a short time ago, and to save my wife, who has just
passed away, yet all this has not succeeded; so if you cure me I shall not
attribute my health to my drum nor to songs.[28]

As surprised as Le Jeune doubtless was at this artless confidence, he continued to refuse Carigonan's request solely on the grounds that to grant
it might endanger the shaman's recognition of God's hand in his prospective miraculous healing. In reality, Carigonan's private admission of despair was not enough for Le Jeune: he wanted a public drama in which
the medicine man's shamanistic arts, like those of the ancient Canaan-
ites, would be thoroughly tested and wholly defeated by the triumph of
the Elijah-like Le Jeune and his God. Though he saw Carigonan as a
modern-day priest of Baal, the Jesuit Superior sought merely his public
humiliation rather than his physical death.[29]

The contrasting religious orientations of each ritual specialist were
starkly revealed in this encounter. For Le Jeune, the proposed intervention was less an occasion for healing than it was a holy contest pitting

the specious powers of Innu traditional religion against the efficacious benevolence of the Christian God. For the Superior, the conclusive victory of Christianity was predicated upon the ignominious defeat of aboriginal beliefs. The intervention represented to the missionary a risky opportunity to transform his perceived rival into a powerful advocate for the group's adoption of Catholicism.

For the suffering shaman, however, the aim of the exercise was clearly relief from his painful physical symptoms. While Carigonan clearly hoped that his healing would be effected through the intervention of nontraditional ritual actors and foreign deities, he apparently did not perceive this possibility as vitiating his own religious reality, authority, or allegiance. Seeing no reason why the ritual interventions of Innu traditional religion and post-Tridentine Catholicism could not work in tandem rather than sequentially, he failed to apprehend the contest in the exclusivist terms demanded by Le Jeune leading the Superior to scuttle the healing contest.[30]

By failing to intercede ritually for Carigonan when the shaman perceived himself as bereaved, vulnerable, and impotent, the missionary lost a precious chance to recover the medicine man's bruised confidence. Moreover, Le Jeune's own rhetorical position of health and strength proved fleeting. In the aftermath of the Christmas debacle, Carigonan was quick to turn the tables on the demoralized missionary, triumphantly subjecting the blackrobe's own prolonged illness to his own unflattering analysis.

Le Jeune's initial rejection of Carigonan's invitation of hospitality, his refusal to engage the ameliorative rituals of Christianity on the shaman's behalf, and his disruption and ridicule of Innu rituals eventually motivated Carigonan to defend his religious leadership in the face of the missionary's constant provocation. Gradually intimating the exclusivistic nature of Le Jeune's claims and discerning that the Superior sought, not a mutually beneficial exchange of religious information, but merely to impose his own views, the shaman's attitude toward Le Jeune began to harden. Entering into the spirit of Le Jeune's competitive engagement, Carigonan sought to demonstrate his influence over the group, particularly his brothers. The Superior's consistently challenging behavior had aroused an opponent worthy of his mettle, who met the missionary's theological onslaught with trenchant intelligence, psychological acuity, and an often biting humor.[31]

Le Jeune's antagonistic response to Carigonan's religious authority would have placed Pastedechouan in an untenable position as the two leader's struggle for dominance escalated. Obedience to the missionary's frequent demands for linguistic assistance would have forced Pastedechouan to contravene the norms of Innu etiquette and familial respect, as many of the Superior's requests combined deliberate provocation with unconscious cultural insensitivity. Le Jeune unsuccessfully petitioned Pastedechouan's help in his fruitless attempts to convert Carigonan's wife, directly contesting both her husband's religious authority and his demands that he leave his dying spouse in peace. Pastedechouan's continuing dependency upon his brothers for his survival and for the modicum of social acceptance he enjoyed made him reluctant to risk Carigonan's perception of his involvement with the missionary as signaling his own oblique rebellion, as even Le Jeune recognized: "This miserable Renegade, fearing to displease his brother, would not even open his mouth."[32] But Pastedechouan's conformity to Innu social and religious norms was not solely the result of external pressure. Though Le Jeune paints the young man's participation in the rites of his people as coerced by his powerful eldest brother, counter indications within Le Jeune's own writing reveal Pastedechouan's strong preoccupation with dreams, one of the pillars of Innu religious life.[33] His refusal of Le Jeune's repeated requests for aid, however, sentenced Pastedechouan to constant harassment by the missionary, who played upon his inchoate, residual attachment to Catholicism and his lingering fears of hell in an attempt to force the young man's facilitation of the Superior's ambitious missionization agenda.

From the group's departure from Quebec on October 18 until December 25, 1633, when poor hunting made starvation appear imminent, Pastedechouan's religious ambivalence, though arguably heightened, remained unresolved. Subjected to the contrary demands of Carigonan and Le Jeune, he was commanded by the former to dance, and by the latter, to pray.[34] As a participant in many traditional Innu rituals, sometimes serving as his brother's acolyte, Pastedechouan was also the facilitator of Christian worship. Within the same week that he aided Carigonan in his unsuccessful attempts to kill, through magical means, a distant, rival shaman, Pastedechouan helped Le Jeune explain the concept of intercessory prayer to a group of Innu women.

Though Pastedechouan's intermittent refusals to help Le Jeune during this period can be read as his vain attempt to dramatize his religious and social distance from the missionary, whose anomalous cultural features so closely mirrored his own, the young interpreter was still willing to do so when such aid did not exact too high a price in terms of family peace. Though his services were rendered intermittently and often grudgingly, on numerous occasions during the initial three months of their shared journey Pastedechouan provided cursory linguistic instruction to the missionary, voluntarily translating his prayers and eager explanations of Christian beliefs and practices to the larger group. Moreover, it was Pastedechouan, along with his older brother Mestigoit, who precipitated Le Jeune's attempts ritually to ameliorate the group's steadily worsening plight in late December. The resultant Christmas prayer service would not have been possible without his linguistic aid. But the very events that Pastedechouan's urging had unleashed and that his own expertise facilitated would have the altogether unforeseen result of transforming the young man's passive ambivalence into active, outspoken, and articulate criticism of Christianity and of forging between him and his eldest brother a shared antipathy to the missionary and his message.

The Christmas Hunt Revisited

The collective repetition by the group, crowded in the provisional chapel of boughs, of the prayers hastily written by Le Jeune during the desolate Christmas of 1633 preceded a dramatic hunting breakthrough that precipitated a frisson of receptive interest in the Christian God and Le Jeune, his human representative. The missionary excitedly related that upon returning to camp with three large beavers, Mestigoit "approached joyfully, recognizing the help of God, and asked what he should do. I said to him, 'Nicanis, my well beloved, we must thank God who has helped us.'" But just as Le Jeune was poised to promulgate a Christian interpretation of the hunt's successful outcome, he was forced to confront the fury of its sole exception: Pastedechouan himself. Returning "empty-handed" from the chase, Pastedechouan, overhearing the exchange between his older brother and the missionary and "angry at being the only one who had not taken something," interjected, "What for indeed? We could not have failed to find them [the game] even without the aid of God," prompting the stricken missionary to lament, "At these words I cannot tell what emotions surged in my heart; but if this traitor had given me a sword-thrust, he could not have saddened me more; these words alone were needed that all might be lost."[35]

Le Jeune's remarks regarding the devastating impact of this attack proved prescient. With this initial "sword thrust," Pastedechouan inaugurated an effective campaign to counter Le Jeune's linkage of the hunt's success with the Innu's bands propitiation of a beneficent Christian God. Effectively questioning both God's power and his mercy, Pastedechouan argued that He was unable to affect Innu hunting outcomes either because of His essential impotence or because, as one who "neither sees nor hears anything," He was unresponsive to human anguish. The young Innu then contradicted these related premises by suggesting that while divine mediation of hunting outcomes was possible, it was biased and unreliable, indicating only God's inscrutable and unfair favoritism rather than His reliable succoring of true Christians. In a heated discussion with Le Jeune, the young man exclaimed, "That's all very well for you others whom God helps: but he has no interest in us, for, whatever he may do, we still die of hunger unless we find game."[36] Depending on our interpretation of the "us" and "you others" of this passage, it would appear that Pastedechouan was making a distinction between French and Innu relations with the Christian deity. His suggestion that God's supposedly generous provision extended only to Europeans may have reflected his and his family's experiences during the English interlude, when they were abruptly abandoned by their French allies, as well as, perhaps, by their God.

Pastedechouan also expressed profound skepticism regarding the missionary's presentation of the divine nature as beneficent, merciful, and loving, postulating instead that He was punishing, miserly, and, "angry because they [the Innu] had something to eat." Continuing his commentary with each new hunt, Pastedechouan speculated as to the Christian God's reaction to its results. When a wily young moose successfully eluded his Innu pursuers, Pastedechouan, warming to his theme, remarked, "The God who is sorry when we eat, is now very glad that we have not anything to dine upon." Observing butchered porcupines being brought back to fill the camp's waiting kettles, he warned, "God will be angry because we are going to fill ourselves up."[37]

From the fragmentary evidence available, it is difficult to determine definitively why Pastedechouan so strongly associated the Christian God with physical and emotional privation. Perhaps the reasons were as various as his theological arguments themselves. As already noted, his apparent fears of fasting the year before at Notre Dame des Anges had been strong enough to prompt his first abortive escape from the Jesuit residence. His strong anxiety regarding the rigors of Lent may have reflected the austerity of its Gallic celebration at La Baumette or simply his Innu estimation of the foolhardiness and blasphemy of rejecting freely offered flesh for what seemed to be a dangerously long period of time.

Whatever his motivation, Pastedechouan's decision to impugn Le Jeune's God on the basis of His supposed aversion to feasting was a shrewd manipulation the very real cultural and religious differences between the two societies regarding the consumption of food. Simply put, Innu ethics (as well as the realities of migratory life on the north shore of the St. Lawrence) demanded the immediate communal sharing and consumption of available food resources, often to what seemed to be excess to European onlookers. One "ate well" when food was available, in light of the ever-present uncertainty as to future hunting outcomes. Innu ritual feasting cemented a strong sense of interdependence both within the human community and between it and the other-than-human beings upon which it ultimately depended.[38] Unlike Catholic Christians—who could "feast" and "fast" at the same time, by ritually ingesting their holy sustenance, the Eucharist, even as they ritually abstained from temporal, profane food—for the Innu everyday food *was* sacred food. It was in gratefully consuming one's "daily meat" that one acknowledged the intercession and sacrifice of other-than-human persons on one's behalf. Catholic Christians sought, during the forty-day period of fasting leading up to Holy Week, to display ritually their sincere repentance for their sins of the previous year, in anticipation of the annual commemoration of Christ's suffering and sacrifice. Lenten rejection of meat would have been problematic in Innu terms because of the spiritual significance of flesh and its privileged place in the nonagricultural Innu diet.

This is not to say, however, that religiously motivated deprivation was unknown in Innu culture: on the contrary, it was a prominent feature of Innu ritual life. Both before war excursions and during vision quests, it was customary for the Innu to abstain from both food and sex—that is, temporarily to withdraw themselves from the web of social relations characterized by the exchange of these social "currencies." Generally, however, these periods of voluntary abnegation were relatively short, and were motivated by fundamentally different considerations than the Christian concept of sin. During a vision quest, an Innu youth's abstinence from food and water signaled to potential animal guardians his helplessness and the necessity of their immediate intervention on his behalf. Only shaman and the bereaved were expected substantially to modify their diets for extended periods, the former to showcase their exceptionalism or to prepare for particularly demanding ceremonies, and the latter ritually to demonstrate the depths of their mourning.

Aboriginal individuals who embraced Christianity often found that their refusal to share in Innu feasts or to eat meat on Fridays resulted in a backlash against their new beliefs, which were deemed antisocial, as they seemed to impugn the importance of communal ties within the human community and their collective bond with the other-than-human world. Moreover, universal abstention for protracted periods, such as the forty days of Catholic Lent, may have seemed to Innu sensibilities too closely to mimic environmentally induced deprivation, which, though it was an endemic reality, was nevertheless feared as a powerful threat to Innu communal bonds and values. The grisly specter of the windigo, the ghastly man-eater, was the Innu personification of widespread aboriginal fears that the cold logic of starvation might prompt the hard-pressed to do the unthinkable—kill and eat their own. Thus, while an abundance of food affirmed the smooth functioning of the Innu socioreligious universe, dearth signaled its breakdown.

Pastedechouan's post-Christmas characterization of the divine nature as miserly and austere would have been particularly effective and damaging because his allegations against God appeared to be observably true of Le Jeune, his human representative. Always at pains to demonstrate that his prerogatives and character mirrored those of the God he strived to serve, Le Jeune ill appreciated how, conversely, his own faults and transgressions were imaginatively transposed by the Innu group onto the deity in whose image he presented himself. The Superior's repeatedly stated concerns that Innu feasts were the occasion of sinful gluttony would have been deeply unwelcome in a culture in which the ritual detection, ceremonial capture, and celebratory sharing of animals reinforced social and religious ties and obligations. Moreover, the missionary's frequent deprecation of Innu concerns regarding their collective survival would have unwittingly reinforced Pastedechouan's allegations in the minds of his Innu audience:

They cannot understand what we ask from God in our prayers. "Ask him," they say to me, "for Moose, Bears, and Beavers; tell him that you want them to eat," and when I tell them that those are only trifling

things, that there are still greater riches to demand, they laughingly reply, "What could you wish better than to eat your fill of these good
dishes?" In short they have nothing but life; yet they are not always
sure of that, since they often die of hunger.[39]

Such exchanges indicate the Innu's relativistic propensity to absorb the
Christian pantheon by extending to it the traditional functions of their
own other-than-human persons. Le Jeune's pedantic and dismissive objections, however, would have disrupted this process of conceptual affiliation and quite possibly sent an unintended message of divine hostility
toward treasured Innu social and religious goals.[40]

Pastedechouan's contestive campaign had defensive as well as offensive
capabilities. His success in preventing the missionary from offering
prayers of thanksgiving at the celebratory feast immediately following the
Christmas hunt effectively denied Le Jeune a public platform from which
to solidify his gains. Where previously Pastedechouan's opposition would
likely have been limited to a refusal to translate for the missionary, the
young man now coupled this standard interjection with a terse warning
to Le Jeune, who, astonished, wrote: "Not only would he not help me, but
even imposed silence upon me, abruptly commanding me to keep still."[41]
The young Innu's muzzling of the loquacious Superior in the immediate
aftermath of the successful hunt, prevented Le Jeune's dissemination of
his Christian message when the group's memory of their recent brush
with death was still fresh. Coupled with Pastedechouan's continuous conceptual assaults on the missionary's key theological assertions, this maneuver appears to have prevented the Jesuit from cementing his modest
success in winning the confidence of the group.

But why did the events of Christmas 1633 turn Pastedechouan from an
inconsistent, passive thwarter of Le Jeune's evangelism into an active
theological agent with a consistently anti-Christian message? Perhaps
because the equation that Le Jeune so neatly set up in his original prayers—
that the believing Christian will be a successful hunter—so thoroughly and
brutally contradicted Pastedechouan's own experience. The young man's
inability to resume a respected place in his society was largely due to the
fact that he had spent five crucial years away from it learning to be a good
Catholic. The lost years of his Innu education and his consequent ineptitude in the arts of Innu manhood led directly to his social ostracism, marital failures, and humiliating dependency upon his older brothers. Le Jeune's

well-intentioned Christmas prayers had inadvertently painted his young translator as doubly inadequate, as Pastedechouan's empty-handed return to camp branded him a failure in Christian as well as Innu terms. Moreover, any secret sense of residual pride or distinctiveness that Pastedechouan may have felt being the sole Innu Catholic of the group was dashed as those victorious in the hunt now enjoyed the visible blessing of the God to whom he alone was officially consecrated. Just as the climactic confrontation between the two men regarding Pastedechouan's Easter obligations had prompted the young man's abrupt departure from Notre Dame des Anges, the events of Christmas 1633 provided a similar catalyst, propelling Pastedechouan from undecided ambivalence about Le Jeune and the faith he represented to determined and forthright opposition to the missionary and his evangelical designs upon the small kin-group.

"Contaminating their Feast": Le Jeune's Profanation of an Innu Ritual

Pastedechouan's persuasive articulation of the fundamentally antisocial nature of the Christian God was resoundingly reinforced by Le Jeune's deliberate ritual profanation only three days after the Christmas hunt. Preoccupied, as always, with what he perceived as the gluttony and "excess" of Innu eat-all feasts, Le Jeune first objected to the size of his apparently hearty portion and then invited another man to eat some of his serving. Finally, unwilling to consume the meat which yet remained, the missionary "threw another piece of it, secretly, to the dogs."[42]

Le Jeune's actions cannot be interpreted as anything other than deliberate provocation, probably triggered as much by his mounting anger and frustration regarding his effective silencing by Pastedechouan and Carigonan as by his evident religious scrupulosity. Writing the previous year, well before he embarked upon the winter hunt, Le Jeune had enumerated for his religious superiors in France the key taboos of Innu ritual. He carefully noted the Innu belief that profanation of animal remains (negligent spilling of their blood, wasting of their meat, or giving their bones to the camp's dogs), when witnessed by the animal's lingering, watchful soul, resulted in the unwillingness of others of their species to surrender themselves for slaughter. Thus, in committing such an outrage, Le Jeune would have been fully aware of the meaning and consequences of his actions in Innu terms.[43]

Even with this foreknowledge, the missionary was taken aback by the level of horror, fear, and contempt that greeted his thoughtless violation of Innu feasting practices. In the days that followed, the Superior was repeatedly asked why he wished to endanger the group's survival. The band clearly perceived such impious behavior, particularly during this difficult winter, as tantamount to attempted murder:

> The Savages began to suspect something, from the fight that afterwards took place among these animals [the dogs]; and commenced to cry out against me, saying that I was contaminating their feast, that they would capture nothing more, and that we would die of hunger. When the women and children heard of this . . . they looked upon me as a very bad man, reproaching me disdainfully, and saying that I would be the cause of their death.[44]

With this single rash act, Le Jeune had inadvertently relinquished the credibility he had so dazzlingly attained only days before, transforming himself from the group's savior to its nemesis. His profanation of their feast precipitated the Innu band's wholesale reevaluation of the missionary's character. Their initial tolerant curiosity of his odd appearance, language, beliefs, and behavior abruptly gave way to increasing suspicion and derision, as his critical infraction cast his earlier actions in a new, sinister light.[45]

The Superior had long confounded the group with his European appearance; celibacy; unwillingness to share his goods; refusal to shoulder his own load on the long, cold marches between camps; hostility to Innu traditional religion; and puzzling lack of responsiveness both to oblique and overt attempts to change his objectionable behavior. While Le Jeune, in the *Relations,* casts himself in martyr-like terms as one nobly bearing the senseless insults of his hosts.[46] It is apparent that the Innu band were vainly attempting to goad the recalcitrant Jesuit into adjusting his conduct to approximate their social norms:

> They continually heaped upon me a thousand taunts and a thousand insults; and I was reduced to such a state, that, in order not to irritate them or give them any occasion to get angry, I passed whole days without opening my mouth. Believe me, if I have brought back no other fruits from the Savages, I have at least learned many of the insulting words of their language. They were saying to me at every turn, *eca titou,*

eca titou nama khitirinisin, "Shut up, shut up, you have no sense," *Achineou,* "He is proud;" *Moucachtechiou;* "He plays the parasite;" *sasegau,* "He is haughty;" *cou attimou,* "He looks like a Dog;" *cou mascoua,* "he looks like a bear;" *cou ouabouchou ouichtoui,* "He is captain of the Dogs;" *cou oucousimas ouchtigoanan,* "He had a head like a pumpkin;" *matchiriniou,* "He is deformed, he is ugly;" *khichcouebeon,* "He is drunk." So there are the colours in which they paint me, and a multitude of others, which I omit.[47]

After Le Jeune's unfortunate act of impiety, what had heretofore been perceived as his unfortunate social awkwardness now appeared to be something at once more fundamental and more dangerous.

Le Jeune's antisocial actions would have dovetailed in the minds of the Innu band with Pastedechouan's depictions of a harsh, punishing Christian God displeased by feasting. Had the missionary deliberately decided to estrange his potential converts or to reinforce Pastedechouan's already persuasive arguments, he could not have done so more effectively. Though the young Innu's theological assertions and the Superior's ritual profanation were unrelated, each intimated that the Christian God and his followers were sources of antisocial danger which threatened both the group's cohesion and its larger web of interdependence with other-than-human beings. Le Jeune's willingness to imperil future hunting outcomes by deliberately angering the powerful souls of slain animals would have reinforced Pastedechouan's assertions of his God's fundamental hostility to Innu health and happiness. In two disastrous missteps, Le Jeune had, by the very terms in which he couched the Christmas hunt, inadvertently alienated the person upon whom his mission's success was most dependent and, with his deliberate profanation, demonstrated his apparent hostility to the sources of Innu succor, horrifying the band as a whole.

But the estrangement, it appears, was mutual. While Christmas 1633 and its aftermath triggered profound changes in Pastedechouan's religious perspective and prompted the entire band's reappraisal of the Jesuit Superior, it also precipitated a new pessimism in Le Jeune's evaluation of the group's readiness to embrace Christianity. Sadly, ruminating upon his prevention from leading them in prayers of thanksgiving following the Christmas hunt's success, Le Jeune compared the family's joyful feasting upon their God-given bounty to swines eating of wind-fallen nuts: "Then behold my pigs devouring the acorns, regardless of Him who shook them down. They vied with each other in their happiness; they were filled with joy, and I with sadness; we must yield to the will of God, for the hour of this people is not yet come."[48]

Though Le Jeune was to spend an additional three months with the group, the Christmas hunt marked the apex of his missionary success. Having effectively lost Pastedechouan's cooperation, Carigonan's interest, and his own sense of missionary fervor and optimism, the Jesuit Superior was unable to institute any other Christian observances between December 26, 1633, and his departure from the band on April 5, 1634. His waning evangelical fortunes and profound disaffection with the Innu group in which he was embedded appears to have triggered his long downward spiral into self-doubt, illness, and spiritual despair, which culminated in his early return to Quebec.

A Sickness unto Death

In the aftermath of the Christmas debacle, Le Jeune first began to experience the symptoms of the illness and profound ennui that would torment and weaken him for the remainder of the journey, distracting him from his missionary goals and precipitating his preparation for what he saw as his imminent death and judgment. While it would be easy to dismiss the physical aspects of his ailment—which included fever, cramping, fatigue, and weakness—as simply the result of physical exertion, an unpredictable diet, and unremitting exposure to the unforgiving cold of a Canadian winter, to do so would be to ignore the significance that both Le Jeune and his principal Innu antagonists imputed to his experience and to overlook the critical role his sickness played in his ongoing relationship with the larger kin group.[49]

Le Jeune himself entertained two competing explanations for his woes, one that emphasized physical causes and another that postulated a strong spiritual dimension to his suffering. Pragmatically, Le Jeune connected the onset of his illness with the establishment of a more reliable food supply. Noting this apparent irony, he explained that while initially the availability of large quantities of fresh meat was a boon to his health, its subsequent smoking and drying, which rendered it, he said, "as hard as wood and as dirty as the street," caused his new diet to disagree with him, often violently.[50]

But Le Jeune also discussed the spiritual aspects of his illness, contrasting his intimacy with God, who had sustained him during the fall's prolonged famine, with his spiritual abandonment during the days of his hibernal affliction, which he presented, alternatively, as the physical manifestation of and the punishment for his declining spiritual health. In a series of scattered, cryptic passages, Le Jeune sketched the faith and ardor of his God-supported momentum in the lean, hungry weeks of the long autumn, during which he enjoyed excellent health, modest progress in his mission, and mystical, divine consolations. By forcing his utter reliance upon God, who "glories in helping a soul when it is no longer aided by his creatures," the chronic dearth of the fall, he explained, had turned the famine into a memorable spiritual "time of abundance." The new plenty of January and February, by confounding his salutary reliance upon the Creator, led inevitably to Le Jeune's punishing illness and pervasive despair. "This is what I am: as soon as we were assisted by creatures, I became sick in body and in soul, God causing me to see what he is and what I am . . . I tried to put an end to this condition of misery; but, as my passions are altogether depraved, I stumbled at every step, bringing back nothing from this journey except my faults."[51] Using the same notions of sweet privation and poisonous satiation that had so unnerved his Innu audience, Le Jeune signaled his awareness that the relative plenty had precipitated a new dynamic in his relationship with God and the small Innu group he had been sent to "save." His words eloquently express his sense of rejection by both Creator and creatures and his impotent sorrow over his apparent inability substantially to ameliorate the physical ailment, spiritual debility, and interpersonal tensions that were to make his last three months amidst the Innu group a veritable hell.

Le Jeune was not alone in seeing a hidden significance in his debilitating condition during the deep winter and dawning spring. Mestigoit and Carigonan each saw their guest's illness as a sign of the Jesuit's emotional incompetence and religious foolhardiness. Mestigoit drew upon traditional Innu understandings of the relationship between ill health and antisocial emotions to pronounce Le Jeune's complaint psychosomatic, whereas Carigonan, the former recipient of Le Jeune's pitiless spiritual diagnosis of his own ills, gleefully turned the missionary's own analysis against him.[52] Each unflattering interpretation of the missionary's condition emphasized Le Jeune's inability to approximate Innu religious and social norms, thus stressing his utter marginality. Their influential pronouncements on the nature and meaning of the Superior's suffering, coupled with Pastedechouan's campaign against him, and the missionary's own relational missteps, would strengthen Innu resistance to his Christian message and sap the missionary's sense of purpose and resolve throughout the waning months of the journey.

Mestigoit repeatedly suggested to the distressed Superior that his illness was the inevitable result of his unwillingness to follow Innu practices of affective hygiene. After witnessing Le Jeune's antagonism of his two brothers, which often discernibly raised the emotional temperature of the familial group, even in the cold heart of winter, Mestigoit would warn the irascible missionary that his inability stoically to master his anger, frustration, and despair would lead to his sickness and death. Following an incident early in the journey, in which Pastedechouan's sullen refusal to help his brother had resulted in the loss of one of the group's canoes, Le Jeune related the following exchange between himself and Mestigoit, beginning with a rhetorical question to his European reader:

> Who would not have been vexed at that Renegade [Pastedechouan], whose negligence caused us untold trials, considering that we had a number of packages among our baggage, and several children to carry? Yet my host, barbarian and savage that he is, was not at all troubled at this accident; but, fearing it might discourage me, he said to me, "*Nicanis,* my well-beloved, are you angry at this loss, which will cause us many difficulties?" "I am not very happy over it," I answered. "Do not be cast down," he replied, "for anger brings on sadness, and sadness brings sickness. *Petrichtich* [Pastedechouan] does not know anything; if he had tried to help me, this misfortune would not have happened." And these were all the reproaches he made. Truly, it humiliates me that considerations of health should check the anger and vexation of a Barbarian; and that the law of God, his good pleasure, the hope of his great rewards, the fear of his chastisements, our own peace and comfort, cannot check the impatience and anger of a Christian.[53]

In the Innu context, the stalwart repression of emotions that could fracture the smooth functioning of the group was conditioned from childhood. The Innu belief that affective infractions would be punished with an individual's physical illness facilitated the dispersal of these antisocial emotions before they precipitated behavior that could threaten the health of the social body. Disregard of these strong emotive and behavioral taboos signaled either the individual's contemptible lack of self-mastery, or their indulgence in behavior-modifying substances such as alcohol. This may be why, amidst the torrent of insults Le Jeune received, he was accused of being "drunk."[54] In Innu terms, inebriation would satisfactorily explain the missionary's unwillingness to follow Innu behavioral cues.

Mestigoit followed his diagnosis of Le Jeune's irascible emotionality with a prescription, explicitly warning the ill Superior that unless he immediately exerted some control over his turbulent feelings, his condition could only deteriorate: "Do not be sad; if you are sad, you will become still worse; if your sickness increases, you will die. See what a beautiful country this is; love it; if you love it; you will take pleasure in it, and if you take pleasure in it you will become cheerful, and if you are cheerful you will recover."[55]

While Mestigoit postulated that the Superior's inability to practice Innu emotional discipline was responsible for his debilitation, Carigonan enthusiastically subjected the stricken Jesuit to a dose of his own interpretive medicine. Just as Le Jeune had suggested that Carigonan's chronic venereal disease represented the divine punishment of his moral turpitude, Carigonan postulated that the Superior's prideful refusal to change his behavior and his repeated infractions of Innu ritual had caused his affliction. Referring to Le Jeune's repeated attempts to demonstrate publicly his imperviousness to the attacks of Innu religious personages by actively challenging them to punish his flagrant insults, Carigonan suggested that, contrary to Le Jeune's claims, these provocations had not gone unnoticed. The missionary's illness, he suggested to his Innu audience, was the just deserts of his ill-considered impiety:

> He continually reproached me with being proud, saying that the Manitou had made me sick . . . "It is not," I said to him, "the Manitou or devil that has caused this sickness, but bad food, which has injured the stomach, and other hardships that have weakened me." All this did not satisfy him; he did not cease to attack me, especially in the presence of the Savages, saying I had mocked the Manitou, and that he had revenged himself upon me for my pride.

Faced with this interpretation of his illness, Le Jeune escalated rather than attenuated his provocative behavior:

> One day, when he was casting these slurs upon me, I sat upright, and said, "That you might know it is not your Manitou who causes sickness and kills people, hear how I shall speak to him." I cried out in their language, in a loud voice: "Come, Manitou; come, demon; murder me if you have the power, I defy you, I mock you, and do not fear you; you

have no power over those who believe and love God; come and kill me if your hands are free."[56]

As Le Jeune's understanding of the nature of Innu religious life wavered between a humanistic emphasis upon its utter ignorance of the divine and an alternate hypothesis that Innu religious personages corresponded to the darker side of the Christian pantheon, his deliberate antagonism of other-than-human persons had several contradictory aims. By provoking such beings and actively petitioning them to punish him, Le Jeune was trying to illustrate that, as they did not really exist, they could not harm him. But he also wished to demonstrate his salutatory courage in provoking their wrath and his protection by a yet more powerful deity. All of these somewhat confused aims, however, backfired spectacularly. The missionary's very willingness to engage in such risky behavior, particularly following his critical ceremonial infraction, was seen as indicating his foolhardy disregard for the health and safety of the rest of the group. For the Innu, ritual infractions, whether inadvertent or deliberate, were dangerous because they had collective as well as individual ramifications. In the unpredictable world of amoral personal power, one could never be sure as to how wide the net of inevitable revenge would be cast. As putting one's own needs or desires before the welfare of the rest of the group constituted the most unpardonable Innu sin, Le Jeune's ostentatious defiance of other-than-human persons was probably perceived by his incredulous Innu audience not as admirable courage but as the ultimate in selfish, rash arrogance.[57]

Though the brothers' explanations for Le Jeune's ailments differed considerably, each stressed that the missionary was suffering the consequences of his stubborn refusal to respect the web of intra- and extrahuman relationships that sustained Innu communal life. By choosing to treat the Superior's illness as symptomatic of his disdain for Innu psychological, social, and religious imperatives—painting him either as the unwitting victim of his own disturbing lack of emotional self-control or as the target of the retributive justice of the Innu pantheon—Mestigoit and Carigonan succeeded in using the missionary's own behavior and circumstances to illustrate his fundamental alterity. Le Jeune's stubborn unwillingness to modify his behavior in any way or to engage in a truly mutual dialogue with his hosts had finally, fatefully, cast him as a recalcitrant "other" incapable of being subsumed into the Innu family.[58]

As the Superior's health continued to deteriorate over the late winter and into the spring, Mestigoit, who had assumed responsibility for Le Jeune's safety during his sojourn with the Innu band, decided that the missionary's lingering ailment necessitated his evacuation to Quebec. Alarmed that the influential Jesuit might die whilst in Innu custody, the able hunter and woodsman, accompanied by Pastedechouan and the ill Superior, set off on a dangerous five-day journey, during which the trio repeatedly cheated death on the treacherous, ice-filled St. Lawrence. On the first day, the sharp spring ice gouged a hole that, in Le Jeune's words, "let water into our canoe and fear into our hearts," necessitating the men's immediate retreat to a nearby island for repairs. Subsequently, larger floes threatened to crush and break the diminutive craft "like a grain of wheat between two millstones," prompting Mestigoit and Pastedechouan to jump nimbly from one floe to the other, pushing the ice away with their paddles, and causing Le Jeune drily to remark that he was "nearer dying from water than from disease." After further dramatic struggles with ice and wind in their "calendar of wretched days and nights," the three safely reached Quebec on Palm Sunday, April 9, 1634.[59]

Joyfully reunited with his brothers in Christ, Le Jeune's physical condition stabilized within a month. His spiritual health and mental stability remained tenuous for considerably longer. Incapacitated by what appears to have been an emotional breakdown, the Superior, "seeking a retreat in our little house took to his bed, unable to so much as write for some six weeks following his return.[60] The spiritual anguish that Le Jeune had endured during the waning months of his Innu sojourn persisted in the isolation of his solitary cell, where it appears that the troubled Superior struggled with an ongoing nightmare of self-recrimination for his missionary ineptitude, linguistic incompetence, and personal faults. When he finally became strong enough to commit his thoughts to paper, Le Jeune immediately wrote to France, asking to be relieved of his post as Superior and contrasting his spiritual lassitude, tempestuous character, and lack of patient humility with the talents of his companions in Christ:

> Just here I have two humble requests to make of Your Reverence. I make them in the name of Jesus Christ from the very depths of my heart. My Reverend Father, I beg your Reverence to discharge me. I sometimes say to the little crosses which come to me, "And this also and as many as you wish, O my God." But those which Father Lallemant has brought me in Your Reverence's letters, which continue me in

my charge, I have said this more than three times, but with a shrinking of the heart which could not drink this cup. In truth, my Reverend Father, I have not the talents, nor the qualities, nor the mildness, necessary to be superior.[61]

Having penned this startling admission of his personal weaknesses in a private letter to his immediate superior, Le Jeune went on to draft a caustic, bitter, and biased account of his winter with Pastedechouan's family group, in which he blamed the three Innu brothers' diabolical collusion against his nascent mission for its resounding failure. Immediately published upon its reception in France, his diatribe has become immortalized as famous the *Relation* of 1634.[62]

A Trio of Deaths

Le Jeune's bedridden recovery from the physical ailments and spiritual malaise that had dogged him in the preceding months also inaugurated his protracted hiatus from contact with his former Innu hosts: he wrestled with them now only as characters in his voluminous retrospective description of their prolonged encounter. Apparently estranged from Pastedechouan, probably as the result of the young man's spiritual truculence, Le Jeune next mentions the exploits of the trio of brothers only as, with the passing months and years, they took a turn for the tragic. Preceded in death by their second-youngest brother, Sasousmat, who had succumbed to illness during their winter absence and died, in January 1634, as a baptized Catholic convert, Carigonan, Mestigoit, and Pastedechouan would successively meet their fates between 1634 and 1636, dying respectively of fire, water, and exposure to the frigid air of a Canadian winter.[63] In a series of reflections meditating upon their collective fate, Le Jeune would rhetorically link their unrelated deaths both with one another and with the climactic events of Christmas 1633, presenting the three brothers as an unholy trinity whose gruesome deaths presaged their shared future of eternal torment.

Carigonan, the eldest, was the first of the three to die. Embroiled in an ongoing dispute with a Gaspé medicine man whom he had repeatedly tried to kill by means of shamanic arts, Carigonan was burned alive in his shelter sometime before the end of 1634, in a fire that may have been deliberately set by his rival.[64] Mestigoit only briefly outlasted his elder brother. Having survived his harrowing journey delivering Le Jeune back to Quebec in early April of 1634, when the first thaw had rendered the St. Lawrence a formidable obstacle course of giant, deadly chunks of ice, Mestigoit was to drown when summer had rendered the river tranquil and sunlit. Deprived of his sanity by a raging fever, Mestigoit somehow fell or jumped into the river's glassy depths and failed to reemerge.[65]

Only Pastedechouan remained. The successive deaths of his three older brothers would have left him devastatingly bereft. He owed his very life to his siblings, who, despite his evident cultural alienation and crippling dependency, had taken him under their collective wing following his abandonment by his French mentors in 1629. Though they, like the rest of his kin group, had caustically denounced Pastedechouan's ineptness and ridiculed his dependency, they nevertheless displayed deep concern for their youngest brother's welfare, faithfully providing him with food and shelter and facilitating each of his marriages, even though this meant assuming the extra burden of providing for his successive wives and, quite possibly, his offspring.[66] While they lived, they had used their social prestige to shelter their youngest sibling from rejection precipitated by his disturbingly liminal status, the result of his inability, despite his physical maturity, to assume the religious and social responsibilities of Innu manhood. Bereft of his brothers' generous psychological, social, and physical succor, Pastedechouan faced an uncertain future.

Confused and grieving, the young Innu journeyed back to Notre Dame des Anges. In his anxiety to see his onetime student Le Jeune, he broke, for the first time, their characteristic relational dynamic of flight and pursuit. At the residence's threshold, Pastedechouan earnestly expressed to the suspicious Superior his desire to reembrace the church and to resume his former teaching role.

In light of Pastedechouan's protracted campaign against Le Jeune during the waning months of their shared hibernal journal and his shift from religious ambivalence into apparent apostasy, his pleas are somewhat surprising and initially seem to offer a stark interpretive choice between religious sincerity and economic opportunism. Faced with Pastedechouan's presence on his doorstep, Le Jeune was unmoved. Discounting his ex-teacher's possible spiritual motivations, the Superior acidly commented that Pastedechouan was merely "pretending that he wished to be reconciled to the Church," perceiving the young man's change of heart as dictated by his stomach rather than his soul. Coolly rebuffing Pastedechouan, Le Jeune told him to prove his religious sincerity by returning during a time of plenty. "We demanded some proof of his good will; namely, that he should come to see us, not when the Savages were having a famine, which forced him to seek the French, but in the time of their abundance; if he returns then, we will receive him, and keep him several months before giving him permission to enter the Church."[67]

Le Jeune's dismissive evaluation of Pastedechouan's behavior as crassly self-interested, however, assumed that the contours of the young man's religious and economic dependency could easily be separated, either cognitively or practically. But Pastedechouan's successive periods of economic reliance upon both his brothers and European missionaries had been accompanied by his acceptance, whether mitigated or wholehearted, of their religious authority. The young man's apparent inability to be self-sufficient was matched by his self-confessed difficulty in resisting the religious and cultural influence of those upon whom he successively relied.[68] With the death of his brothers, it is perhaps not surprising that Pastedechouan once again sought out the ministrations of Catholic missionaries, the only other reliable providers he had ever known. Indeed, given the abrupt cessation of his brother's countervailing influence, it is not unthinkable that Catholicism might once again have exerted its subtle pull upon the deeply ambivalent young man. As vociferous as Pastedechouan's theological diatribes had sometimes been, none of his comments had questioned the existence of a God whose ritual demands and threatened punishments seemed to have an inexorable hold upon his religious imagination, such that they decisively shaped even his most impious outbursts.[69]

After the fact, Le Jeune came to regret his cavalier dismissal of Pastedechouan, his fellow Catholic. Aware of the young man's precarious social position and perhaps perceiving his own response as lacking in Christian charity, Le Jeune belatedly besieged Tadoussac, Pastedechouan's probable destination, with a blizzard of letters proposing the young man's immediate return to the Jesuit enclave. But his missives went unanswered, and his tardy invitation, ignored. Having spurned his ex-teacher, Le Jeune never saw him alive again. The Superior commented that, of the four Canadian winters he had personally witnessed, that of 1636 was by far the most bountiful, blessed as it was by a deep, killing snow that engulfed the long legs of struggling moose and caribou while providing hunters with a thick crust easily navigated by snowshoe. Nevertheless, it was this plenteous season that would witness the young

Innu's lonely death. Apparently "abandoned in the woods like a dog," Pastedechouan succumbed to starvation and exposure, proving his eldest brother's prediction that he would "die of hunger, unless we feed him" eerily prescient.[70] His solitary demise in the frozen forest is eloquent testimony to his ultimate rejection by both the band whose approval he had so assiduously courted and by the church that had instilled within him such fatal ambivalence.

"Manifest Chastisements": Le Jeune's Analysis of the Brothers' Deaths

No longer contradicted by the unwelcome disputation of his now-deceased antagonists, the surviving Superior took advantage of the rhetorical opportunity provided by their deaths to press home his own interpretation of their previous interactions deep in the Canadian hinterlands. In death the three brothers proved considerably more pliable than they had been in life, when their vigorous debate with the missionary as to the meaning of the dearth and illness that plagued their shared sojourn had proven both challenging and heated. Though Pastedechouan's demise occurred some three years after the events of Christmas 1633, Le Jeune connected it, along with his brothers' earlier deaths, to their fateful encounter with his God in the improvised oratory he had constructed on that now-distant festival. Painting the trio of horrifying deaths as a remorseless drama of divine "vengeance," Le Jeune attributed their successive punishments to the brothers' collective failure to honor their solemn promises to believe exclusively in his God should He deliver them from their desperate privation:

> Some one has said that God has feet of wool and hands of lead. It seems to me that he has had the feet of a Deer and arms of iron or bronze, in the punishment of certain Savages . . . I have often been astonished in thinking it over, how God has let his thunderbolts fall, so to speak, upon the three brothers with whom I passed the winter, for having wickedly violated the promise they had made to acknowledge him as their sovereign, to love and to obey him as their Lord. They had had recourse to his goodness in their extreme famine; he had succored them, giving them food in abundance . . . They had not yet swallowed the morsel when God took them by the throat. Before the year had expired, the eldest, that wretched Sorcerer, who had given me a great deal of

trouble, was burned alive in his own house. The second, who was my host, a man who had naturally a good disposition, but who, to please his brother, was willing to displease God, was drowned, having lost his mind . . . There remained the Apostate, the youngest of the three. I believe that the stamp of the Christian for a little while arrested divine justice. But, as he would not acknowledge it, the same thunderbolt that struck his brothers, reduced him to ashes.[71]

Forming a diptych with Le Jeune's euphoric presentation of the "happy deaths" of Manitougatche and Sasousmat, who had died as converts in the ritual embrace of the church, the three condemned brothers' chilling fates illustrated for Le Jeune's European audience the dangers of denying or mocking the prerogatives of the Christian God.[72]

In presenting their successive deaths as the dramatic unfolding of divine retributive justice for their "having wickedly violated the promise they had made to acknowledge him as their sovereign," Le Jeune ignored the conceptual gulf that separated the baptized Pastedechouan's actions from those of his brothers—confusing the characteristic religious relativism of the unbaptized aboriginal majority with the determined and conscious contestation of Christian theology "from within" by an aboriginal convert.[73] Indeed, to suggest that Carigonan and Mestigoit were in any sense blaspheming apostates is to charge them with vandalizing a sanctuary that, by definition, they never truly entered. Unbaptized, the two, by participating in Le Jeune's improvised Christmas prayer service, were merely experimenting with a novel ritual form during a profound subsistence crisis, not abrogating the validity of their traditional beliefs. As they seemed to have viewed Christianity relativistically, the brothers were doubtless attempting to align the purported powers of the Christian pantheon with the familiar aims of Innu religious ritual: the provision of direly needed sustenance from other-than-human persons. By painting their conceptual appropriation of Catholicism as an act of apostasy, Le Jeune condemned as the ultimate sin their earnest attempts to understand and ritually experience his missionary message. While the Recollets had similarly censured the relativistic usurpation of Christianity by aboriginal peoples some twenty years earlier, they at least had the decency to wait until their converts had, through baptism, crossed the church's threshold before consigning them to hell for their attempts to conceptually assimilate Christianity.[74] In presenting the two brothers' repetition of his hastily written Christmas prayer as the culmination of the catechistic process, rather than its mere inception, Le Jeune effectively blamed the two deceased brothers for his own inability to compellingly articulate the contours of his faith.

Le Jeune consigned his perceived nemesis Carigonan to hell's eternal flames with eager dispatch and not a small note of triumph. He condemned Mestigoit only with considerable reluctance, writing, "I have been particularly grieved about my host, for he had good inclinations, but having sneered . . . at the prayers which I made them say in the time of our great need, he was involved in the same vengeance."[75] But it was in his judgment of Pastedechouan's fate that the missionary's narrative juggernaut ultimately faltered. The length and intimacy of the two men's volatile relationship, as well as Pastedechouan's recent petitionary visit to Notre Dame des Anges, precluded Le Jeune's unequivocal assertion of his ex-teacher's damnation. Rather, Le Jeune's epitaph for Pastedechouan reveals both the depth and ambivalence of his feelings for his fallen ex-teacher. Echoing the missionary's equivocal actions just prior to Pastedechouan's death, which encompassed his forthright rejection of the young man on the threshold of the Jesuit residence and his frantic attempts to contact him at Tadoussac, Le Jeune's post-mortem reflections yoked definitive condemnation with more hopeful assertions of Pastedechouan's possible deliverance.

Perhaps conscious of the myriad ways in which he himself had failed the dead youth, Le Jeune's meditation on Pastedechouan's passing was, by turns, an agonized admission of his own culpable behavior, an emotionally distanced summary of a condemned savage's distasteful end, and the heartfelt grieving of a bereaved friend.[76] If the young man had provoked in life the Jesuit's intense frustration, anger, and even hatred, in death Pastedechouan wrung from Le Jeune a reluctant compassion. In his epitaph for his teacher, the Superior defiantly defended his multiple attempts to contact Pastedechouan from those who openly celebrated the "wicked man's" demise:

> Some one assuring me, not long ago, that he was pleased to hear of his death, reproached me for having this year again invited him to come and see me, knowing well that he was a wicked man. I admit that he was a wicked man. I confess that last year, and again this year, I wrote to Tadoussac to have him come to me.

Le Jeune rhetorically placed himself with Pastedechouan in his probable torment, imaginatively extending to him the last chance for confession and spiritual comfort that his own abrupt dismissal of the young man at Notre Dame des Anges had precluded:

I say even more; that, if it were in my power to free him from the irons and chains in which perhaps he now is, I would release him, that I might procure for him, in exchange for the wrongs he has done me, the greatest blessing that can be obtained for a reasonable creature, eternal salvation. Alas! is it then so small a thing that a soul be damned? All the great affairs of Conclaves, of the Courts of sovereigns, of Palaces, and of Cabinets, are only child's play, in comparison with saving or losing a soul.

Finally, Le Jeune comforted himself with the thought that, even in Pastedechouan's final moments, when he lay abandoned by both his Innu kin and his missionary mentors, the young man was in the company of one who had infinite power to bring this wayward convert back to Himself: "In a word, the Apostate is dead. Whether he died an Apostate or not, I do not know, at least he died without any earthly help; I do not know whether he received any from Heaven; I would be very glad if it were so."[77]

The Jesuit's ultimate recognition of the essential mystery of Pastedechouan's spiritual disposition and ultimate fate was in sharp contrast to his generally terse, definite, and negative evaluations of the young man's religious propensities. The missionary had long encoded his essentially pessimistic judgment of Pastedechouan's spiritual fitness in his ubiquitous nicknames for the young man: "the Renegade" and "the Apostate." Le Jeune's final and reluctant relinquishment of Pastedechouan to the ministrations of God represented his belated acknowledgment that the young man had a full, inner, and private relationship with the divine, akin to his own and beyond the assertions of his missionary authority. In death Le Jeune finally granted his ex-teacher the spiritual independence and maturity he had refused to allot him in life, abjuring his own centrality in Pastedechouan's religious drama. In memorializing the man with whom he had had such an intense relationship, Le Jeune belatedly displayed the humility and respect that might have substantially changed the tenor of their interactions during Pastedechouan's life. But just as Le Jeune's letters came too late to prevent Pastedechouan's lonely death, the missionary's posthumous acknowledgment of his spiritual independence and dignity could not affect the young man's already entrenched religious sensibilities nor color Pastedechouan's own, likely pessimistic, interpretation of his ultimate fate.

"Abandoned in the Woods Like a Dog": Pastedechouan's Final Days

Little is known of the precise circumstances of Pastedechouan's death. Le Jeune tersely relates, "I do not know the particulars of this accident; the Savages merely told us that they had found him starved to death in the woods."[78] In his long days and nights alone, before the end finally came, it is likely that mounting anxiety drove Pastedechouan to seek a range of solutions to his isolation and privation. Perhaps he walked for miles through the woods, seeking his kin, startling when the ice-laden trees cracked like gunshots, shattering the unearthly stillness. Likely, he would have tried to stalk game, silently pleading with the Innu and Christian pantheons to guide his aim, but with failure and the howling wind as his only answers. Weakening, he would have struggled to maintain his fire and to build a rude shelter from the indomitable cold. As starvation and exhaustion took their toll, Pastedechouan's vision would have dimmed, cutting the snow's harsh glare. The unbearable numbness and pain in his extremities would have given way, in his last hours, to an illusion of comforting warmth.

But the rigid theology that had long held him in its inflexible grip afforded him not even the meager illusion of comfort. Unaware of and unaffected by Le Jeune's belated softening, Pastedechouan's final days would probably have been haunted by his knowledge that even his looming death was not the worst that awaited him and that his probable fate would escalate rather than relieve his physical and mental suffering. Plucked from his family as a child, Pastedechouan, despite his increasingly active and articulate opposition to Christianity, may well have been dogged to his death by its frightening intimations of future punishment for the wayward. His always lively fear of hell, first inculcated in a Recollet classroom at La Baumette and cannily manipulated by Le Jeune throughout their association, would likely have only intensified as his physical strength ebbed.[79] Possibly Pastedechouan, in his final days and hours, would have performed a sort of mental scapulimancy: attempting to read in the patterns of his own past actions some indication of his approaching fate, just as his people ritually examined the burned vertebrae of animals for clues as to approaching storms and the future whereabouts of game.[80] It is unlikely, however, that his possible ruminations about his relationship with God, his missionary representatives, or his own past of fervent devotion would have brought him any measure of comfort.

Though Le Jeune, in his epitaph, tenderly bequeathed Pastedechouan to the mercies of a loving, ever-present God, it is unlikely that Pastedechouan himself found contemplation of or communication with the Almighty a source of significant consolation. If he thought of the Christian deity at all in his final days, it was probably with the grim belief that his present predicament pleased Him. As we have seen, during his latter years Pastedechouan seems to have strongly associated the French God with frightening privation. Running from this inexorable equation during his tenure at Notre Dame des Anges, Pastedechouan had unsuccessfully attempted to avoid the rigors of Lent. Perceiving his lack of success during the Christmas hunt as indicating his personal rejection by the Almighty, Pastedechouan had drawn upon his experiences to articulate a theology that presented God as being fundamentally opposed to Innu health and happiness. Characterizing the Christian deity as "he who neither saw nor heard anything," Pastedechouan hinted at a personal history of unanswered prayer.[81] For the young Innu, his adopted God was like the dazzling winter sun that blinded without warming: he was remote, merely witnessing rather than relieving human suffering. Pastedechouan's alienated vision of the Almighty would have made Him as cold a comfort as the frozen streams and icy, wind-rocked woods that surrounded him.

But even if Pastedechouan's personal ontology had not been so bleak, it is unlikely that he would have felt able to engage the Christian deity in his solitude. The young man had not been encouraged by either of the successive missionary orders who attempted to regulate his religious life to experience a personal, unmediated relationship with God. The hierarchical, authoritarian, and highly ritualized nature of post-Tridentine Catholicism would, rather, have facilitated his dependency upon God's representatives on earth and their ritual mediation of salvation through the sacraments. From his childhood incarceration at the distant La Baumette, Pastedechouan had been taught that his salvation lay in a formula of cultural relinquishment and salutary dependency upon missionary authority. Whether encoded in the language of aboriginal cultural inferiority, dramatized in priest-centered ritual, or promulgated in the classroom, where the teacher's authority was absolute, the Innu child would quickly have absorbed the Recollet message that his avoidance of hell depended upon his total and willing obedience to his religious superiors and his submission to their ongoing ritual remediation of his sins. Indeed, though Le Jeune suggested that Pastedechouan's was a "faith born of fear and slavishness," his own interactions with the young man had nurtured rather than challenged this objectionable ethos.[82] The Jesuit Superior, like his Recollet predecessors, made the young man's submissive obedience to his own authority central to his intermittent evaluations of Pastedechouan's spiritual health, painting Pastedechouan's defiance as an unholy rebellion against God himself and repeatedly playing upon the young man's fears of damnation to wrest his reluctant cooperation with the Jesuit agenda.

Pastedechouan's likely perception that his salvation was dependent upon his unwavering obedience to his religious superiors would not have consoled him as he sat shivering and isolated in the Canadian woods. Even the most optimistic reading could not have intuited a happy posthumous fate in the recent history of his encounters with the Jesuit Superior. First there had been Pastedechouan's active theological campaign against Le Jeune's interpretation of the Christmas hunt, then the two men's long estrangement, and finally the Jesuit's decisive rejection of his pleas to return to the Church at the threshold of Notre Dame des Anges. Probably unaware of Le Jeune's subsequent missives, Pastedechouan may well have perceived the Superior's intransigence as sealing his ultimate as well as his immediate fate.

The young man's inculcated dependency upon the mediation of Catholic ritual would also have deepened his loneliness and sense of impending doom. Having likely lingered beside Christian and aboriginal deathbeds, Pastedechouan well knew that both were generally crowded with friends, family, and ritual specialists gathered to assist the dying and witness the death, comforts that his present physical isolation denied him.[83] Pastedechouan's long association with the Jesuits precluded the possibility that his baptism alone would have provided him with any assurance of his impending salvation. The demanding nature of Ignatian spirituality demanded a continuous confession and absolution of sins as they occurred, like chalk being wiped off of a slate.[84] Infrequent recourse to the sacrament meant that one's lurid, unabsolved sins of thought, word, and deed remained indelibly written upon one's soul, exposed to the eyes of a condemning God. The hellfire preaching that dominated missionary rhetoric continually goaded aboriginal converts into a constant, active scrupulosity.[85] Pastedechouan would have known, then, that his baptism alone was powerless to rescue him from his looming fate. Denied recourse to final confession and the last rites, Pastedechouan likely would have felt abandoned to certain damnation, as he probably lacked Le Jeune's confidence in God's presence and consolations. The dying Innu's consideration of his relationship with the Christian God and his representatives on earth would thus, if anything, have only increased his apprehension.

Any pleas Pastedechouan might have made to the other-than-human persons of Innu traditional religion were met with only the harsh reality of his continued privation. Though the isolation and fasting of Pastedechouan's last days ironically mimicked those of a youth seeking, through vision quest, the lifelong guidance of an animal, his presence alone in the woods signaled his ejection from rather than his entry into the interdependent web of Innu social relationships. His abandonment had marked his rejection by his human kin. His starvation marked his final desertion by the Innu pantheon, from whom he had been alienated since his adolescence.

During Pastedechouan's last hours, the dying sun would have turned the snow outside his shelter into a vivid carpet of pale gold, striped with the deep blue shadows of the high trees. With the sheltering dimness of evening, the dark branches high above him might have seemed to mimic the steep, vaulted ceiling of the Angers cathedral. As he lay tightly hugging his legs on the floor of his makeshift shelter, the illusory warmth of his final hours might have made Pastedechouan feel that he was once again being carried in a soft moss bag by his long-dead mother. Perhaps comforted, he would have slept.

5

Pastedechouan's Legacy

Concluding his extended reflection upon Pastedechouan's death and probable fate, Le Jeune exclaimed, "Alas! is it then so small a thing that a soul be damned? All the great affairs of Conclaves, of the Courts of sovereigns, of Palaces, and of Cabinets are only child's play, in comparison with saving or losing a soul. But let us pass on."[1]

In our capacity as the witnesses of Pastedechouan's short life and tragic death, albeit from the remove of almost four hundred years, we too are faced with the somewhat anticlimactic duty of "passing on" from dramatic narrative and detailed analysis to more general reflection and assessment. Having traversed with Pastedechouan his full score of twenty-eight years, we must now confront the central question of his life's ongoing significance. Having pursued, in all of its intimate contours, the personal history of this young Innu man, what have we found to challenge or illuminate? What is Pastedechouan's legacy to us, as scholars and as human beings?

Pastedechouan's contributions to our understanding of life in seventeenth-century North America are several. His story, in its nuanced complexity, allows us to challenge the entrenched historiographic stereotypes of which we are so often unaware, inviting us to work toward subtler insights which more deftly capture the living realities of aboriginal people facing a maelstrom of political, military, cultural, and religious change. Pastedechouan's experiences demonstrate the necessity of recognizing rather than dismissing religious factors in our attempts to understand the difficult conceptual challenges aboriginal peoples faced as the result of a second European advent—the arrival of the missionaries. The story of Pastedechouan and his family, moreover, affirms not simply the possibility of interreligious communication in seventeenth-century Canada but also its variety. While Pastedechouan's childhood immersion in France epitomizes missionary preference for the one-way imposition of their religious commitments onto vulnerable children, Le Jeune's experiences in the midst of the young man's familial group disclose Innu propensities toward relativistic incorporation of foreign religious ideas and practices. By providing us with intimate access to the mentality of a young convert subject to the extraordinary demands of the prevailing missionization models of his time, Pastedechouan's story thus poses a range of significant new theoretical challenges to the study of European-aboriginal interaction.

This young aboriginal man's narrative of religious reeducation and cultural disenfranchisement is also of enduring value, however, because of its contemporary relevance to both native and nonnative people. His experiences vividly speak to those of his Innu descendents who have collectively endured a dispiritingly similar process of assimilative education and comparable reactions of cultural anomie, religious ambivalence, and inward- and outward-turned violence. Pastedechouan's people, though they were one of the first aboriginal groups to encounter Europeans in mid-sixteenth century North America, managed to postpone, due to their strategic withdrawal from densely populated areas, the systematic reduction, reeducation, and assimilation that was the fate of so many of their aboriginal contemporaries in the nineteenth century. It has only been since the 1940s and 1950s, well within the living memory of many in the contemporary community, that the Innu have faced a renewed assault upon their traditional, nomadic lifeways. Pastedechouan's experiences with Europeans during the cultural, religious, and economic negotiations that accompanied early seventeenth-century contact, then, have more than an anecdotal or historical interest for his people: rather, they correspond in often startling ways to their contemporary realities.

Finally, Pastedechouan's struggles have a human appeal which transcends his historiographic importance, temporal specificity, and ethnic identity. The attempts of this young Innu to discern and assert his personal identity in the face of powerful, contradictory pressures to conform to the expectations of his community and missionary mentors engender the empathic engagement of a wide nonnative audience, many of whom are struggling with their own issues of cultural and religious identity in our own time of similarly profound change.

Ambiguity and Liminality:
The Historiographic Legacies of Pastedechouan's Story

From an academic perspective, Pastedechouan's story is valuable because of its ability to shatter historiographic stereotypes and to destabilize entrenched scholarly definitions and assumptions. Following its narrative thread, we initially appear to have fallen down a rabbit hole into a strange new world, in which nothing is as it appears and in which everything confounds our preconceived expectations. A netherworld of gray shades, it refuses to respect our analytic preference for the crisp starkness of black and white. In this early Canadian "wonderland," we search in vain for exemplary aboriginal converts and adamant traditionalists, encountering instead "converts" who fail to remain converted and "apostates" who, inconveniently, don't ever quite seem to apostatize. We encounter Innu shaman who seek Christian healing and unbaptized neophytes who collude with missionaries to effect the religious rehabilitation of their sanctified peers. We fail utterly to recognize the Jesuits, who appear to have abandoned their familiar historiographic garb as benevolent cultural relativists for the dour gray gowns of their exclusivistic Recollet colleagues. Even as Jesuit accommodationism in Asia was raising papal eyebrows, black robes in early modern Canada dramatically highlighted the differences rather than the similarities between their faith and the beliefs of the native groups they encountered, presenting conversion as requiring the utter repudiation of the convert's former way of life. This exclusivistic pattern, so evident in Pastedechouan's dealings with both religious orders, suggests that our understanding of the Society of Jesus needs to be nuanced considerably to reflect the fact that the Jesuits' celebrated relativism was dependent upon their perception of the level of cultural sophistication of the groups they targeted for missionization. In early modern North America, Jesuit appreciation of the complexity and sophistication of aboriginal religions and cultures, and its resultant accommodationism, came only after decades of encounter.

Continuing our confusing historiographic journey, we meet the much-maligned fur traders of late sixteenth- and early seventeenth-century Canada, who appear, in fact, to have established a more tenable, mutually productive with Pastedechouan's people than did the more celebrated missionaries who followed them some fifty years later. Though European traders pursued an individualistic agenda that contrasted sharply with the collectivism of their aboriginal hosts, their presence before and during Pastedechouan's childhood affirmed rather than eroded Innu collective identity, as Innu exposure to these outsiders' codes of conduct only reaffirmed their attachment to their own collectivist social contract. Moreover, because fur merchants benefited from the maintenance of traditional aboriginal lifeways, they were often forthright in their opposition to missionary attempts to sedentify and agriculturalize nomadic indigenous groups.

Scholars have sometimes presented merchants and missionaries as being, like Tweedledum and Tweedledee, the near-identical purveyors of disastrous social change amongst early modern aboriginal cultures. However, the distinctiveness of their agendas and the results of their presence were so different that it behooves us to demarcate what were, effectively, two different eras of contact and to revise substantially our ideas regarding how relational "middle grounds," in Richard White's terms, are created between cultures. White suggests, based on his study of eighteenth-century European-aboriginal interactions in the Great Lakes region, that as long as two groups maintain positions of equal power, each will seek to sustain and expand this safety zone of mutually acceptable conduct and shared practices. This liminal world, he theorizes, will disappear only when one group achieves significantly more economic, political, and military clout than the other, allowing the more powerful group to repudiate negotiation for coercion.[2]

While the conduct of sixteenth- and seventeenth-century traders along the St. Lawrence generally conforms to White's theory, however, that of the missionaries defiantly contradicts it. Even when numbering less than the fingers of one hand, the Recollets audaciously sought nothing less than the total cultural and religious capitulation of native societies to their priestly authority, resisting rather than facilitating the development of a shared conceptual or behavioral world with the aboriginal populations who dwarfed the Recollets' tiny cadre. For seventeenth-century missionaries relating the Gospel was thought to be possible only after the systemic cultural and linguistic reformation of aboriginal peoples, who had to be "humanized" before they could be Christianized.

Differences between the intentions and results of merchant and missionary contact can be seen in miniature when we examine Pastedechouan's journey to France. Innu consent to this venture was predicated upon his people's previous experiences with such overseas diplomacy: the visits of other Innu to France in the late sixteenth and early seventeenth century, which had established stronger economic, military, and political ties between the French and Innu. Apprehended in Innu terms as a symbolic, human gift and as a trade ambassador, young Pastedechouan was one of the instruments his people used to gauge the intentions and capabilities of their Gallic allies. It was the Recollets who reshaped what had been an institution of the Innu-trader middle ground—the economic and military delegation—into an instrument of individual religious transformation. Frustrated by their inability to transform native cultures, the Recollets resorted to the reproduction of their exclusivistic mentalities on the few children they were able to wrest from their communities. Upon his reluctant return from Angers, Pastedechouan, like the proverbial canary in the coal mine, signaled to his people through his immaturity and truncated ability to comport himself in a way reflective of Innu norms, the incompatibility of missionary-sponsored education with their values.

At the outer limits of our exploration of this disconcerting new historiographic world, we glimpse the Innu. At least we think it is the Innu. Contrary to our entrenched expectations, they do not passively sit, awaiting the stamp of Christian missionization. Nor do they lie supine, intimating their cultural death as the victims of European colonization, as we would anticipate from the often frankly elegiac note of much aboriginal history.[3] Nor are they inanimate, frozen in time, condemned to a spurious precontact cultural "purity." Rather, in this strange netherworld, the Innu are cultural actors seeking to maintain their social and religious values whilst creatively adapting foreign technology, material culture, and religious ideations to their own needs and priorities in a time of systemic change.

Eventual acclimatization to Pastedechouan's initially unnerving historiographic world brings with it the awareness that its surprises and apparent distortions are the result not of any inherent strangeness but of our own scholarly conditioning, which trails in its wake more than a century of blithe overgeneralizations, distorted definitions, and a continuing penchant for the facile moral and spiritual judgment of historical actors. The fact that denizens of this strange world fail to meet our preconceptions speaks to the urgent need to pioneer better models, which can more closely approximate the ambiguous complexity of their historical experiences.

Between the Extremes:
Rethinking "Conversion" and "Apostasy"

Our encounter with Pastedechouan, a figure who eludes easy categorization into the religious pigeonholes of "convert" or "apostate," suggests the necessity of a new understanding of early modern aboriginal Christianization. The young man's childhood association with the Recollets appears to have been successful in definitively stamping Pastedechouan's religious consciousness with their exclusivist assumptions, such that, even after his 1629 abandonment by his missionary mentors, their influence is demonstrably evident in his subsequent behavior. Ensconced at La Baumette, Pastedechouan was taught to see conversion as a stark, either-or choice between heaven and hell, God and Satan, the followers of Christ and the worshippers of the false Beast: a choice that necessitated his derisive rejection of his cradle culture. Had this exclusivistic element been absent from his encounter with European missionaries, there is every likelihood that Pastedechouan could have braided his religious and cultural identities and loyalties in the relativistic manner of his own family, who met Catholic missionaries on their own soil and from firmly within their own preconceptions. Though many of Pastedechouan's actions obliquely questioned Catholic ritual even as his words directly challenged a theology grounded upon God's benevolent intervention, the young Innu's transactions with his Recollet mentors, Jesuit interlocutors, and the members of his own family vividly dramatize his lifelong retention of seventeenth-century Catholic exclusivism. In the final analysis, then, it was Pastedechouan's perception of the Innu traditional religion of his childhood and the post-Tridentine Catholicism of his youth in inimical terms and his ambivalent, back-and-forth movement between what he had been taught to see as mutually exclusive religious options which were responsible for engendering much of his evident suffering and confusion. Rather than approximating either of the categories of "convert" or "apostate," Pastedechouan, in his characteristic religious ambivalence, was crucified between their extremes.

Pastedechouan's agonistic experiences with early modern Catholicism stand as a mute rebuke to the ongoing scholarly propensity to isolate exemplary native converts for intensive study and to the self-perpetuating assumptions that such a selection invariably brings to our understanding of the aboriginal confrontation with Christianity. Despite the professed delight of postmodernists in the ambiguous and the liminal, aboriginal individuals, such as Pas-tedechouan, who defy easy cultural or religious categorization have long languished unstudied. Failure to pay adequate attention to such individuals has resulted in a falsely dichotomized picture of aboriginal religious affiliation as a zero-sum proposition instead of what Pastedechouan's story reveals it to be, a shifting, ambiguous, and highly variable association. Though he was a "convert" to Christianity, the complex variability of Pastedechouan's self-identification as such throughout his short life should complicate our understanding of the conversion process, which, despite changes in nomenclature, continues to revert reflexively to missionary assumptions and conceptualizations, inevitably characterized by their exceptionalism and exclusivism.[4]

In short, the ambiguity of Pastedechouan's religious identity challenges us as scholars of aboriginal-European interaction to make missionary perceptions of aboriginal "conversion" the *subject* of our study, rather than allowing them to continue to influence *our own* apprehensions of indigenous religious responses to Christianity. To continue to utilize, however unconsciously, early modern missionary definitions of conversion and apostasy is uncritically to accept the utopian dreams of a small cadre of seventeenth-century Europeans as normative in exploring the postcontact religious lives of aboriginal peoples. By accepting the notion that Christianity was the prerogative of Europeans ritually to award, withhold, or revoke at their whim, we effectively truncate our exploration of how aboriginal people explored, claimed, rejected, and appropriated aspects of post-Tridentine Catholicism.

To turn to aboriginal perceptions of "conversion," on the other hand, recognizes the rhetorical power that such classifications afford the judger, resists the seduction of definitive external judgment, and repositions aboriginal religious and cultural self-definition as authoritative. Such a shift changes the very nature of the questions we ask, from "Was this person a convert or a traditionalist?" and "Was he a faithful Catholic or an apostate?" to questions like: "How did this person understand Christianity?" "Did this person regard himself or herself as a Christian?" "How did (s)he express, mitigate, or complicate this affiliation?" "What were the social, cultural, political, and economic results of this new sense of identity?" "How did (s)he understand, transform, evade, or oppose Christian beliefs and practices?" Such questions will be a powerful tool for scholars of encounter who aspire to "face east from Indian country."[5]

In this study, I have attempted to refrain from pigeonholing Pastedechouan's behavior into the exclusivist extremes so common in my missionary-authored sources, choosing to regard Le Jeune's choleric characterizations of the young man as "an apostate, renegade, excommunicate, atheist, and servant to a Sorcerer who is his brother" as evidence as much of the high emotional temperature of the two men's complex, interdependent relationship and of the Jesuit Superior's disappointed expectations in his spiritual son as they were of Pastedechouan's supposed religious status.[6] I have tried, rather, to ascertain how this young Innu man himself understood and responded to the multiple pressures he faced and to explore his complex negotiations with the competing cultural and religious communities in which he was simultaneously embedded, each of which sought to define him and have him define himself in a particular manner.

The Importance of Religion in Pastedechouan's Story

Pastedechouan's story is inescapably a religious one. Though political, military, and economic factors also affected the course of his life, religion was critical in formulating the intimate recesses of Pastedechouan's individual identity. Religious relationship with the human and other-than-human members of his community lay at the heart of the childhood identity bequeathed to him through the careful yet diffuse process of Innu traditional education. Religion, moreover, was at the crux of the changes made to the young Innu's identity in the shaded recesses of the Recollet sanctuary at La Baumette, changes which directly affected his fateful inability to fit back into the cradle culture from which he had been plucked so young. Both the traditional beliefs of his Innu childhood and the post-Tridentine Catholicism that Pastedechouan appropriated during his five years in France had the power to mold the way in which this young Innu perceived himself and to shape how he was apprehended by others. Throughout his short life, Pastedechouan's religiously based self-perceptions and the contrasting religious expectations of his two communities, Innu and Catholic, decisively impacted his mental health, social standing, and material well-being, illustrating the power of religious ideas and identity definitively to shape both worldview and concrete circumstances.

In addition to providing unique insight into the human cost of the seventeenth-century missionaries child-focused approach to Christianization, Pastedechouan's story also discloses critical information as to how those of his people who never experienced such a radical cultural and religious disjuncture perceived the gray- and black-robed missionaries who lived amongst them. Almost all of Pastedechouan's people, unlike their young kinsman, met the messengers of post-Tridentine Catholicism from a position of solid majority dominance, upon their own soil and from firmly within their enduring framework of cultural and religious values, practices, and priorities. Missionaries' impositionist model of religious engagement, epitomized by Pastedechouan's experiences, was not the only form of interreligious communication inaugurated with the 1615 landing of the Recollets, nor was it the most dominant. In the woods and valleys of early modern Canada, aboriginal peoples utilized their own preferred methods of assessing the claims and ideas of missionaries, deflecting Catholic ambitions of religious hegemony with their own distinctive imperative of religious dialogue and incorporation.

Carefully read against its hagiographic grain, Le Jeune's account of the winter he spent embedded within Pastedechouan's familial band provides intriguing clues as to how the Innu typically apprehended and assessed the novel religious claims of European missionaries. Eager to engage the missionary in their midst, the individual members of Pastedechouan's family appear to have enjoyed their opportunities to spar with Le Jeune on questions of morality, ontology, and epistemology, subjecting his self-presentation as the messenger of an authoritative, exclusive truth to pointed criticism, generally on an evidential or relativistic basis. In defiance of Le Jeune's characterization of Christian commitment as entailing an either-or choice that had immediate repercussions for their traditional way of life, the Innu appear to have seen Catholicism as presenting them with a potential means of augmenting traditional Innu sources of power, healing, wisdom, and nurturance. The Jesuit Superior's Christianization campaign was at its most effective when he engaged his hosts' central concerns, demonstrating the superiority of his rituals in alleviating the dearth and death which stalked the small group. Ultimately, however, Le Jeune's insistence upon the incomparability and incompatibility of the two religious systems, his contemptuous rejection of Innu attempts to understand his Christian message, and his utter lack of respect for their own treasured beliefs and practices led Pastedechouan's band derisively to dismiss the missionary. It is important to note that, in so doing, the Innu were signaling their rejection not of Christianity but of the religious exclusivism to which, in the seventeenth century, it was inextricably linked.

Despite their evident dissimilarities, the impositionist model of religious indoctrination that Pastedechouan experienced within the quiet cloisters of an Angers convent and Le Jeune's encounter with the incorporationist proclivities of Pastedechouan's familial band in the jaws of a Canadian winter both suggest that, contrary to Bruce Trigger's arguments, religious communication was possible—indeed, it was critical—in the encounter between European missionaries and aboriginal peoples in early modern Canada.[7] Moreover, Catholic exclusivism was central in both of these scenarios, sculpting Pastedechouan's distinctive religious mentality and thwarting his family's tendencies selectively to appropriate the novel promises and practices introduced by the black-robed stranger amongst them.

Powerlessness and Agency in Pastedechouan's Story

As well as affirming the importance of religious factors in aboriginal-European encounters and questioning sharply drawn binaries of "conversion" and "apostasy," Pastedechouan's short life also challenges us imaginatively to straddle another interpretive dichotomy in the historiographic presentation of aboriginal peoples: agency and powerlessness. In 2001 Natalie Zemon Davis rhetorically asked, "Should we see Pastedechouan, as has one commentator, as merely 'an early victim of French-Indian cultural conflict . . . a tragic example of one aspect of the European impact on Indian culture'? Or should we view him rather as a seventeenth-century man with multiple and contradictory resources, striving to find his way of being in the world in a coercive setting.?"[8] In answer to Davis' challenge, I have attempted to navigate between the Scylla of according Pastedechouan insufficient agency, presenting him merely as a tragic figure whose cultural and religious integrity was crushed beneath the oppressive weight of European missionary strategies, and the Charybdis of artificially overemphasizing his opportunities for self-assertion.

Indisputably, Pastedechouan while yet a young boy was put in a situation in which his opportunities for volitional action and self-assertion were systematically and deliberately truncated. While yet twelve or thirteen years old, Pastedechouan was separated from his family and immersed in a wholly unfamiliar cultural and religious context, where his immaturity and isolation placed him at a decisive disadvantage in his interactions with missionaries who sought to control every aspect of his behavior and beliefs. The Recollet education Pastedechouan received dramatically emphasized the necessity of embracing the disciplinary yoke of Christ and respecting His representatives on earth, in order to avoid the fearful punishment of God in this life and the next. The silken threats of the Tapestry of the Apocalypse, with its flamboyant presentation of the lugubrious fate reserved for Christ's enemies, was merely a stark visual representation of a more diffuse early modern theology of fear, which stimulated laypeople's terror of hell to ensure their respect for priestly authority and their embrace of ritual obligations.[9] Le Jeune's evaluation of Pastedechouan's adult religious mentality as one "born of fear and slavishness" and the Jesuit's apparent ability to manipulate the young man's unease concerning his ultimate fate demonstrate the decisive role that psychological intimidation likely played both in the formation of the young man's religious consciousness and in his subsequent relations with the human representatives of post-Tridentine Catholicism.[10]

In addition to the intended effects of Pastedechouan's Recollet education, which encouraged his disdainful rejection of his cradle culture and placed him in what was perceived by his Innu community as an inappropriately servile, childlike relationship with his missionary mentors, we must also consider the unintended consequences of his five-year French indoctrination, which also dramatically narrowed Pastedechouan's future options. The boy's lengthy absence from his culture during a critical period of his development affected his future relations with his people in ways which were anticipated by neither his Recollet hosts nor by the community that had voluntarily surrendered him to their tutelage. Bereft of both the technical and relational skills necessary for hunting and ill disposed upon his return to attempt the twin rituals of Innu manhood, Pastedechouan throughout his remaining life was classified as a liminal "boy-man." His inability to provide for himself provoked the withering ridicule of his kin and necessitated his ongoing economic relationship with European groups, both civic and religious.

To stress only the aspects of Pastedechouan's life which were outside of his control, however, is to run the risk of portraying him merely as a passive victim and thus failing to acknowledge the reality of his diminished yet extant agency. Though the events of his early teen years did have repercussions that continued to effect his social, religious, and economic status, Pastedechouan was continually faced with a range of options as to how, given his past, to cope creatively with his present and future. It is in our witnessing of Pastedechouan's responses to each of these unfolding opportunities—from his decision to retain his proxy identity as a Frenchman upon his reluctant return to Canada, to his rejection of an alliance with the invading Kirke brothers, to his hesitant courtship of his natal culture after his abandonment by the French, to his attempts to negotiate his divided religious loyalties—that we get the fullest sense of his agency and his humanity. This study demonstrates how Pastedechouan was able creatively to engage in a number of boundary-setting behaviors with his own people and with French missionaries, which allowed him to negotiate a tenuous, liminal identity at the fringes of either community by both participating in and refraining from key markers of ritually instituted collective identity. In presenting Pastedechouan's life I have tried consistently to imagine what exposure to such an intense form of religious reeducation would have felt like as a living reality, and how it would have influenced this young man's fateful actions and decisions. I have attempted to attain a difficult interpretive balance—acknowledging the limitations of this young man's agency in his own life, yet insisting upon the reality of his continued, if diminished ability to make his own choices.

Pastedechouan Now

Pastedechouan's experience of cultural and religious disjunction, though it took place nearly four hundred years ago, casts a lingering shadow even today. As we have seen, seventeenth-century missionaries' minority status in an aboriginal-dominated context made their dreams of transforming such societies unrealistic, even laughable. Their tiny numbers initially forced early Recollet and Jesuit missionaries to miniaturize their aspirations in the persons of individual children, whom they removed to a European setting in which they could enjoy an artificial cultural dominance over their aboriginal charges. Though the Jesuits eventually acknowledged the failure of this child-focused approach, their discredited pedagogical model of extraction, isolation, and reeducation was to prove fatefully influential in subsequent centuries.

As disease-decimated and geographically displaced aboriginal populations gradually became a minority in their own land, ascendant Europeans were quick to label them, in the verbiage of the day, a social, economic, and religious "problem" or "question."[11] Like their seventeenth-century predecessors, North America's political and religious elites looked to educational institutions that, though they took numerous denominational incarnations, collectively promised to assimilate aboriginal cultures into the European mainstream by removing the education of their children from the hands of native parents. By disrupting the inter-generational replication of cultural and religious lifeways, educational leaders boasted that they could "have the Indian educated out of them," rendering their young charges productive, loyal citizens and devout Christians.[12] Just as Champlain and his Recollet allies had argued that the native inhabitants of North America could become, through the softening influences of Christianity and agriculture, proxy Frenchmen, nineteenth-century promoters of residential schools for aboriginal youth promised that the troubling "wildness" of these scattered, "uncivilized" bands could be effectively tamed and their distinctive cultures discretely extinguished, through a gradual process of assimilative education. The dream of a widespread imposition of Old World religious ideas upon New World native groups, cherished but unrealized by figures such as Le Caron and Le Jeune, would gradually make European-influenced aboriginal figures like Pastedechouan the norm rather than the exception.

Sedentary, agricultural groups whose traditional lands abutted or were taken over by the incoming tide of European settlement, such as the Iroquois and the Ojibwa, were the first to bear the brunt of nineteenth-century attempts at assimilative education. Commencing with the Mohawk Institute, founded in 1829, large educational institutions increasingly separated aboriginal children from their families and communities.[13] As Europeans explored and colonized the West, they took this assimilative model of aboriginal education with them, dramatically affecting the contours of religious and cultural encounters throughout the Plains.

Remote, migratory groups such as the Innu, who had gradually been displaced from their southerly summering places along the St. Lawrence and now resided year-round in their former hibernal hunting grounds, initially managed to avoid the brunt of these renewed attempts at assimilation. Following the failure of the Jesuits' first attempt at Innu sedentification at Sillery in the 1640s, the Innu retained for another three hundred years their traditional nomadic, hunting-based way of life in Nitassinan, on the rugged Canadian Shield. Europeans' sporadic attempts at mission-ization and assimilative education of the Innu, notably the efforts of the Missionary Oblates of Mary Immaculate, were, like Le Jeune's winter journey with Pastedechouan's family in 1633–1634, generally adapted to the migratory ways of their Innu hosts.[14]

In the 1940s and 1950s, however, a number of military, political, and economic factors prompted Euro-Canadian reevaluation of the potential of Innu traditional lands. During the Second World War, the establish-ment of a military base in Goose Bay, Labrador, brought an influx of out-siders into this Innu fastness. Discovery of the mineral riches under the barren tundra of the Labrador interior precipitated increased mining ac-tivity. The 1949 entry of the province of Newfoundland and Labrador into the Canadian union brought with it pressure to accelerate the economic development of this youngest daughter of confederation. All but ignored for centuries, due to their perceived geographic and cultural marginality, the Innu, one of the first aboriginal groups in Canada to encounter Euro-peans, found themselves "rediscovered" in the mid-twentieth century, as first their land and then their people were targeted for reassessment and attempted "development."[15]

Once again Innu religion and traditional lifeways became, as they had been in Pastedechouan's time, subject to the increasingly invasive scrutiny and criticism of outsiders. Intruding into Innu strongholds, Euro-Canadians became, like the Pygmalion Recollets and Jesuits who had preceded them, preoccupied with how to remake the Innu into their own image.[16] The ancient trio of Christianization, sedentification, and as-similation to European norms was once again seen as the key to making these "children of Cain" a "functioning" and "viable" part of "modern" society.[17] This ambitious agenda would rest once more on the fragile shoulders of the young.[18] Unconsciously parroting the black- and gray-robed missionaries of three hundred years earlier, twentieth-century edu-cators stated that the Innu would be rescued from "backwardness" and "barbarism" through the education of their most junior members.

The system of modern assimilative education which arose in the nine-teenth century and continued through the twentieth bore a number of striking similarities to the original child-centered system pioneered by seventeenth-century Recollets and Jesuits. There is thus a stunning congruency between Pastedechouan's isolated reeducation in France, which made him fear, disdain, and avoid his own family and culture, and the experiences of modern native peoples subjected to a comparable educational regimen on their own soil. While the intervening centuries had brought new pedagogical developments and vocational priorities, the overall premise of these educational institutions remained unchanged.[19] Educators took as their touchstone the notion that aboriginal traditional religions and cultures represented the perverse continuation of a sinful, savage way of life, whose very existence belied the social "progress" in which they so ardently believed. They thus sought utterly to transform the cultural, social, and religious identities of their aboriginal students, stripping children of their native ontology, epistemology, and ethics and substituting for their traditional sense of personal identity an adherence to the theological and behavioral dictates of an essentially foreign ideology. Despite the passage of centuries, the damaging psychological and sociological effects of prolonged immersion in such assimilationist institutions, referred to by many survivors as "cultural" or "emotional genocide," have remained horrifyingly consistent.[20]

The renewed European assaults on aboriginal lifeways witnessed by the nineteenth and twentieth centuries were more ferocious than the seventeenth-century experiments which preceded them for several reasons. First, the sheer scope of the unfolding educational project dwarfed even the wildest dreams of its missionary progenitors.[21] Second, the mandate of later schools considerably expanded the earlier emphasis upon children's cultural and religious reformation, seeking in addition to quash student facility in and usage of their native tongues. Third, nineteenth- and twentieth-century standards for aboriginal conformation to European religious norms differed considerably from the "exceptionalist" agenda of earlier French missionaries, an agenda that had envisioned the possibility of individual aboriginal children spiritually surpassing their European mentors. Fourth, the nineteenth-century overlay of cultural and religious variations with new conceptualizations of inherent, "natural," and inalterable racial differences profoundly affected perceptions of the appropriate social position of such institutions' young graduates. Finally, nineteenth- and twentieth-century aboriginal residential schools appear to have exceeded their seventeenth-century predecessors in the degree of the violent coercion of young residents.

Though its impact upon those individuals whom it targeted was profound, seventeenth-century reeducation of aboriginal children had been, by virtue of the tiny number of missionaries involved and the chronic funding problems which plagued their efforts, a very modest enterprise numerically. The Recollets and Jesuits, between them, probably sent less than fifty children to France in the first half of the seventeenth century and educated maybe seventy-five more in domestic residential seminaries, which housed perhaps ten or twelve students simultaneously. By contrast, each of the more than one hundred aboriginal residential schools operating in Canada by 1930 brought together hundreds of students. While the identification of suitable students in the seventeenth century depended largely upon the vagaries of fate—as missionaries often isolated for educational attention those whose ties to their communities were already attenuated by parental death—later aboriginal participation in the residential school system, because it was legally mandated and zealously enforced, was more universal. Parents who refused to surrender their children to authorities for incarceration in the residential school system were often subject to police intimidation, including the threatened loss of crucial trapping lines. They could also face significant legal repercussions, including arrest.[22]

Unlike Pastedechouan's total isolation in France, separated even from other aboriginal children who had likewise made the dangerous overseas journey, native students in modern residential schools entered a diverse community of their fellows, encountering both traditional allies and enemies. The historical animosity between students of rival aboriginal nations often prompted considerable friction. Factions could also develop according to the degree of student identification with the assimilationist aims of the institutions, or simply according to ancient demarcations of age and strength. Finally, reflecting the emergent racialism of nineteenth-century thought, students often grouped themselves or were grouped by their teachers along a spectrum of their "whiteness."[23]

The sheer number of incarcerated students dramatically amplified the sociological impact of modern residential schools on aboriginal communities. The size of these institutions, however, spared students the loneliness that had characterized Pastedechouan's experiences. Large and diverse student populations fermented both factionalism and fellowship and could foster the development of multiple forms of covert resistance to institutional authority. It is clear both from the models of discipline unselfconsciously embraced by school administrators and from aboriginal-authored memoirs that violence and coercion were virtually synonymous with the modern aboriginal educational experience, which was designed to be physically and psychologically invasive. Because students at aboriginal residential schools, some as young as four, faced a regimented, depersonalized existence; were often the victims of emotional, physical and sexual abuse; and visited their families only infrequently, they needed all the potential venues for comfort and collusion that such childhood alliances could afford.[24]

Nineteenth- and twentieth-century assimilative education also significantly expanded the mandate of its seventeenth-century progenitors. Native linguistic proficiency—deliberately fostered by Recollets and Jesuits, who, in an oblique acknowledgment of their minority position in aboriginal-dominated New France, were eager to master aboriginal languages—was specifically targeted for elimination in modern institutions. Met at the school's threshold, incoming students were separated by gender, stripped of their traditional clothing, shorn of their long hair, and informed that to speak what was for many the only language they knew was to invite swift and immediate punishment.[25] Educators' correct perception that a culture's language encoded a powerful sense of autonomy and identity in its speaker motivated such harsh measures.

Modern assimilative education, moreover, used significantly different standards than had early modern missionaries to evaluate aboriginal Christianization. Seeking to hold new aboriginal converts to standards exceeding those of their European flocks, Recollets and Jesuits rewarded with baptism and the perception of sanctity those individuals who, respectively, met or exceeded their grueling expectations. Though exacting, this model of aboriginal conversion at least recognized the possibility that these new souls in Christ might eventually outstrip their mentors in sanctity. In modern schools, piety, rather than being envisioned as a contest in which aboriginal converts could best their European tutors, was now seen merely as the religious dimension of the aboriginal capitulation to the self-evident superiority of Euro-Canadian culture. Christianization appears to have been perceived by the architects of such schools less as an interior transformation than as a key element of students' conformation to institutional expectations, signaled by their docile involvement in the daily and weekly religious routine of Christian prayer and religious services.[26]

Furthermore, nineteenth and early twentieth century residential

schools were more damaging than their seventeenth-century predecessors because they linked what were shared assumptions of aboriginal cultural inferiority with the new specter of racial difference. Pastedechouan's
mentors were optimistic Pygmalions. Having altered the young man's
identity, allegiances and behavior, they triumphantly asserted that they
had created "a naturalized Frenchman, and very devout."[27] Seventeenth-
century notions of aboriginal plasticity and amenability to religious influence, while predicated upon a condescending assessment of native
religion and culture, did not perceive aboriginal populations as ethnically or racially different from Europeans. Rather, early Canadian Recollets and Jesuits perceived aboriginal physiognomy and intellectual
capabilities as, variously, indistinguishable from or superior to those of
the general French population.[28] Seventeenth-century Recollets attempted
to transform the religious and cultural ethos of aboriginal peoples to prepare them to assume a dominant role in the Catholic métis culture they
envisioned as the future of New France. Conscious that France could
not populate Canada's vast expanses without fatal enervation of the
homeland, early colonial and religious authorities saw Gallic intermarriage with aboriginal allies as critical to the firm establishment of a thriv-
ing colony.

In nineteenth-century North America, on the other hand, deprecations
of indigenous culture and religion were grounded in a new critique of
aboriginal peoples as ethnically different and racially inferior. In the intervening centuries, aboriginal "otherness" had taken on a new, "physiological" dimension. Nineteenth-century educators of aboriginal youth
suggested that their racial inferiority would preclude their making genuine contributions to the dominant culture into which they were simultaneously attempting to assimilate them.[29] In contrast with Champlain
and the Recollets' vision of a métis Canada made up of Frenchmen, aboriginal people, and their mixed-blood descendents, nineteenth-century
Canadians, from their new position of majority dominance, generally
looked askance at miscegenation. Escalating female immigration from
Europe led the powerful Hudson's Bay Company to bar its bush employ-
ees from sexual congress with aboriginal women, despite the fact that
such liaisons had played a significant role in the company's past success.
By educating Europeans new to life in Canada's challenging climate and
by transforming them into welcome members of the community, aboriginal women had traditionally facilitated European greenhorns' eventual

economic success. As in the American context detailed by Richard White, with European ascendancy over aboriginal peoples came their systematic repudiation of the intimate shared culture to which they owed their ancestors' survival and much of their own accumulated power and wealth.[30]

Finally, modern aboriginal residential schools differed from their seventeenth-century predecessors in the amount of violence that they promoted, tolerated, or discreetly ignored. In both eras, coercion and abuse can be divided into two categories. The first was disciplinary violence, which, because it was seen as aiding in the accomplishment of educational and behavioral objectives, was openly condoned by the pedagogical mores of each period. The second form of mistreatment was covert abuse, either physical or sexual in nature which, though it may have been tacitly tolerated by the institution's authorities, was not publicly acknowledged or admitted. Any comparison of early modern and modern aboriginal experiences of abuse in educational settings, however, can only consider the question of licit violence, as the one-sided nature of missionary-generated documents and the absence of aboriginal-authored descriptions of student experiences in missionary-run institutions do not permit the reconstruction of illicit violence in the seventeenth-century context. This makes it impossible definitively to determine whether the epidemic levels of sexual and physical maltreatment in nineteenth- and twentieth-century aboriginal schools were a novel departure or merely an escalation of already present tendencies within such totalist institutions.

As already explored, seventeenth-century missionaries relied upon physical punishment as an essential part of their educational program. In letters to his superiors in France, Paul Le Jeune emphasized that aboriginal children receiving a Jesuit education had to first be isolated from their families and communities. Their seclusion, he explained, was undertaken because of the unbridgeable gap between European and aboriginal perceptions of the appropriateness of violence toward children in the service of their education: "The reason why I would not like to take the children of one locality [and teach them] in that locality itself, but rather in some other place, is because these Barbarians cannot bear to have their children punished, nor even scolded, not being able to refuse anything to a crying child. They carry this to such an extent that upon the slightest pretext they would take them away from us, before they were educated." Denied their traditional recourse to coercive tactics,

Le Jeune stated, the Jesuits would not be able to succeed in their educational objectives, an admission which highlights the centrality of corporeal discipline in early modern education generally.[31]

If pedagogical violence had been a requirement for the success of the famed early modern Jesuit educational model, in later centuries the use of humiliation and physical punishment seems dramatically to have escalated. In the mid-twentieth century, Innu children who arrived late, spoke their own language, or otherwise "misbehaved" faced a range of humiliating punishments. Such rebels might be beaten on their exposed buttocks in front of their fellow students or be denied permission to leave the classroom, forcing them to soil themselves. One Innu boy whom his teacher adjudged to be questioning the benevolence of the Christian God was soundly beaten with a Bible. Justified as being "for their own good," such abusive tactics were seen as facilitating administrators' "control" over their young charges.[32]

A number of factors played a role in the escalation of violence in residential schools. Missionaries' scrutiny of their aboriginal pupils through the newly ground lens of race likely facilitated educators' perception of students in the depersonalized terms that often facilitate violence against or degradation of those so perceived. The changed demographic and legal situation, moreover, encouraged rather than thwarted coercion. While seventeenth-century residential schools existed at the whim of numerically dominant aboriginal nations, in the twentieth century native willingness was no longer a precondition for such institutions' viability. After the Canadian federal government, in 1920, made attendance of assimilative schools compulsory, threatening aboriginal families who resisted with economic and legal retaliation, coercion became the very foundation upon which the system rested. Teachers and administrators who utilized violence and degradation within such institutions were simply taking their coercive cue directly from federal authorities.

Finally, the ambiguous mixture of paternalistic benevolence, fear, and anger that aboriginal people unfailingly aroused in the Christian bosoms of nineteenth-century whites, when coupled with their positions of absolute power over the lives and persons of young aboriginal children, seemed a sure recipe for abuse and neglect. Euro-Canadians during this period appear to have oscillated between their sense of obligation to fulfill "the white man's burden" by converting the "heathen"; a wish to protect their jobs and communities from aboriginal graduates seeking entry into white economic and social circles, and the desire to teach what was perceived to be a troublesome segment of the population "a lesson."[33] This fundamental ambivalence expressed itself administratively as the simultaneous desire to run assimilative schools and an unwillingness to allocate appropriate resources to do so. Chronic underfunding and the systematic withholding of the choicest resources for the use of administrators and staff was responsible for much of the everyday suffering experienced by native students at these schools. In concert with overcrowding and unsanitary conditions, malnutrition of students made residential schools a perfect breeding ground for diseases such as tuberculosis.[34]

In contrast to seventeenth-century youngsters—who apparently informed their families of any physical "correction" they experienced—a novel feature of the modern residential school was its rigidly maintained code of silence around violence and sexual abuse. A near-impenetrable wall of secrecy only now being breached was created by censorship of outgoing student communications, overt threats against student disclosure of their abuse by abusers, and the self-censorship of aboriginal young people due to self-blame, fear of parental disbelief or condemnation, or reluctance to reengage the powerful feelings of rage and hurt that the memory of such experiences engenders. Today, thousands of aboriginal people throughout Canada and the United States are seeking to bring their individual abusers to justice and pursuing recognition of and compensation for their suffering in schools which, like those of their seventeenth-century predecessors, had as their fundamental mandate the cultural, linguistic, and religious refashioning of aboriginal children.[35]

Contemporary Fallout from Aboriginal Assimilative Education

Pastedechouan's seventeenth-century subjection, far from his family, to an ambitious program of Christian reeducation designed to extinguish his existing cultural and religious identity thus presaged aboriginal peoples' endurance of centuries of strikingly similar indoctrination even into the present day—for although Canada has either closed or transformed all of its aboriginal residential schools, such institutions continue to operate in the United States. Pastedechouan's reactions to his attempted assimilation varied from compliance and apparent identification with European norms, to flight, boundary marking, and violent, self-destructive behavior. His equivocal pattern of conformity and rebellion, despair and lashing out also characterizes the experiences of subsequent generations of aboriginal peoples exposed to the assimilative efforts of modern educational institutions.

Abruptly abandoned by his European mentors in 1629, Pastedechouan attempted to reintegrate back into the community of his childhood, only to discover that his experiences had unfitted him, both conceptually and practically, from approximating their exacting social and religious expectations. Suspended between two cultures, and an anomaly in each, Pastedechouan spent the remainder of his short life searching for personal identity and societal acceptance, each of which proved painfully elusive. Like Pastedechouan, contemporary survivors of assimilative schooling often express a sense of cultural and religious anomie. Having received an education that precluded their formation of a coherent native identity, traumatized them by abuse both experienced and witnessed, and engendered their physical and psychological distance from family and community, residential school graduates were linguistically and conceptually estranged from their natal communities, even as racism often precluded their acceptance into the white world they had been groomed to join.[36]

The endemic presentation of Christianity and aboriginal traditional religions as inimical opposites in many modern assimilative schools has also fostered in many contemporary native people a painful religious ambivalence strikingly similar to Pastedechouan's own.[37] While angrily grieving the open wounds of their residential school experiences, many still self-identify as members of the very religious institutions that inflicted these gross injuries. Mike DeGagne, the Executive Director of the Aboriginal Healing Foundation, a Canadian organization dedicated to the assuagement of the effects of generations of residential schooling, still holds to his Catholic identity, despite his bitterness that the church has adamantly refused to apologize for its role in the abuse and cultural dislocation of generations of aboriginal children.[38]

These feelings of religious ambivalence are experienced at the collective as well as the individual level. By the mid-seventeenth century, struggles between Christian and traditionalist factions fragmented previously cohesive aboriginal communities. Today, one of the lingering effects of assimilative education is the continuing identification of many native elders with an exclusivist Christianity that often leads them to perceive the younger generation's growing interest in their traditional cultural and religious identity with alarm and distrust.[39] In a recent ceremony marking the reopening of a former residential school under new native auspices, a dispute erupted between participants over just such an issue of collective religious identity. A group of young "traditional" drummers wished to stage a demonstration of their prowess as part of the festivities. This proposal was opposed by the older generation, who condemned such drumming as anti-Christian and insisted that the school opening should be graced with the chanting, in Cree, of the Lord's Prayer. Eventually a compromise was reached in which both elements were incorporated into a composite ceremony, suggesting the happy reconciliation of the frank traditionalism of the young drummers and the Cree-inflected Christianity of the older generation. The peaceful coexistence of these two prototypes for contemporary Cree religious identity, however, was more apparent than real: when the "pagan" drums were brought out onto the stage, the Christian elders of the group collectively turned their backs upon both the traditional instruments and their young players. Reminiscent of Pastedechouan's intolerance of his own people's ways upon his return from France, such incidents demonstrate the power of totalist institutions decisively to affect their graduates' lifelong sense of identity and allegiance and the impact that this has both upon relations between generations and upon the ability of elders to pass on traditional religious knowledge to their descendents.[40]

Return of the Acten: Alcoholism, Self-Destruction, and Violence

Experiencing the confusion and anguish that comes from cultural anomie and religious ambivalence, Pastedechouan, during his adulthood, repeatedly sought the false solace of alcohol, which provided temporary, though doubtless welcome escape from his probable feelings of inadequacy and confusion. Consumption of alcohol dampened Pastedechouan's inhibitions enough to allow him to freely express his rage, hurt, and frustration through the angry violence normally frowned upon by his culture. On one such occasion recorded by Le Jeune, Pastedechouan drank so much that he nearly drowned. Rallying, he then lashed out, vociferously expressing his grievances against his own people and his violent impulses toward Le Jeune himself. This pattern of serious, if intermittent, drinking continued until (and may, indeed, have facilitated) his death at the age of twenty-eight.

The multiple roles played by alcohol in Pastedechouan's life—as a goad to confrontation, instrument of rebellion, purveyor of false bonhomie, and source of blessed release—were complex, as were his motivations for consuming it: feelings of powerlessness and anger, perceptions of social rejection or persecution, and a strong desire to escape from a seemingly untenable self or situation. One of the key challenges currently facing Pastedechouan's descendants (and the wider aboriginal community) is the issue of pervasive and debilitating substance abuse, which is wreaking havoc with individual lives and family relationships, as well as collective identity and community coherence. Alcohol and drug addiction have fueled aboriginal suicide and domestic violence rates, which soar above those of the majority Euro-Canadian population.[41]

Whilst living in the Jesuit convent during the winter of 1632–1633, Pastedechouan on several occasions allegedly violently confronted a much younger student, Fortune. He beat the boy, who may have reminded him of his own childhood self, when young Fortune failed to heed his warnings regarding the dangers of dependency upon Europeans. In attempting to contravene European influence on the lad and prompt his return to the Innu culture, Pastedechouan, ironically, utilized French disciplinary methods, contravening his own society's strongly asserted taboos on abuse of the young. But for human products of assimilative education (such as Pastedechouan and more recent generations of residential school graduates), violence against younger, weaker members of the community was no longer necessarily seen as taboo. By institutionalizing children from a young age and tacitly condoning their violent abuse at the hands of Euro-Canadian staff, modern aboriginal residential schools effectively taught children to take out their frustrations on their younger, weaker peers. While many children formed close, protective friendships and alliances in such institutions, the bitter lessons learned there also meant that those students fortunate enough to evade abuse at the hands of teachers or administrators might experience it from other children.

Endemic in the now largely defunct residential school system, intra-aboriginal violence and abuse has transferred its insidious, intergenerational grip to the families established by the schools' graduates. Placed in an institutional setting in which their ability to form normal affective ties was severely compromised, graduates, like Pastedechouan, often experience successive marital failures and blighted family relationships. As a result, many contemporary aboriginal peoples seek healing not just for their own wounds but for those that they, in their hurt and rage, inflicted upon others.

In 1993, six Innu children of Davis Inlet, Labrador, attempted suicide by sniffing gas, prompting the Canadian federal government unilaterally to move the entire community further south, in hopes of ameliorating the evident despair of its youth by improving access to health care, counseling services, and employment opportunities.[42] These emergency measures, however, were unsuccessful in addressing self-destructive patterns of behavior in the Innu community. Indeed, the move itself renewed Innu complaints that, by acting in such a unilateral manner, the government's interference merely exacerbated the negative collective self-perception which had led to the substance abuse in the first place. Such disturbing incidents were, the Innu argued, motivated by pervasive feelings of powerless due to their historical exclusion from the decision-making process, and the despair and loss of identity caused by government-sponsored sedentification.[43]

Since the beginning of Innu sedentification in the 1950s and 1960s—undertaken by the Canadian government, which wanted to facilitate Innu access to what it sees as the benefits of modern society—many Innu have expressed their concern that because sedentary living ill suits traditional Innu lifeways, it has been responsible for the outbreak of a number of social problems that can be collectively summarized as inward- and outward-turned violence. Sequestered in artificial communities that, ironically, are often devoid of the very social services in whose name they were established, Innu critics have contended that their people, deprived of their traditional nomadic way of life and denied recourse to their traditional means of providing for themselves and their families, have, atcen-like, turned their rage and pain on the members of their own community.

Just as Pastedechouan's individual inability to actively participate in his people's dynamic and reciprocal relationship with animals led to his fatal estrangement from them, contemporary economic, political, and judicial threats to traditional Innu lifeways threaten the Innu's strong relationship with the land, its beings, and one another. Innu elders repeatedly state that, with sedentification, their traditional values of respect for the natural world and reciprocity between human and nonhuman persons are being eroded, resulting in the spiritual dispossession of their people. Pointing to the increased community cohesion and the amelioration of social problems when the Innu follow traditional patterns of migratory hunting in *nutshimit,* or the bush, elders have suggested that the solution to social dissolution is not continued acculturation but the reassertion of ancient norms and patterns.

Contemporary Innu who do seek to live on their traditional lands in their traditional manner, however, face a number of barriers, from the development of their land, Nitassinan, by provincial governments and private companies, to land usage (such as low-level flight testing) that makes hunting in nutshimit very difficult to their prosecution under laws designed to monitor Euro-Canadian sport hunting. Just as the Innu once faced fines or imprisonment for their failure to surrender their children for compulsory assimilative education, contemporary Innu who wish to follow the way of their ancestors risk similar incomprehension and punishment by provincial authorities.[44]

Pastedechouan's experiences, as tragic as they were, had only a peripheral effect upon the family members of his own generation and virtually no repercussion upon his possible descendents. In the Innu-dominant context of his time, his experiences could be dismissed as troubling but ultimately anomalous. Modern assimilative education, however, has had complex intergenerational effects upon every aspect of aboriginal societies. Even though the assimilative school system is largely defunct, it continues to exert its influence, from beyond the grave as it were, upon the prospective religious and cultural identities of the rising generation. Children and grandchildren of those who attended residential schools, though they did not personally experience its rigors, thus remain in its long shadow.

Pastedechouan's Story Is Our Own

Finally, Pastedechouan's story is important and relevant because we recognize aspects of ourselves in his painful experiences of identity formation and disruption. The young man's lifelong struggle to discern and express his variegated cultural and religious identity and his fruitless search for belonging has an immediate human resonance that transcends its particular historical setting.

Being human arguably involves a continuous process of identity crafting. Each of us carries a mental map of our past experiences that tells us where we've been, who we are, and how we relate to those around us.

Uniquely individual yet always informed by the master narratives of our shared cultures, histories, and religions, this ever-changing, fluid sense of self is the result of constant negotiation, both with the intimate others who surround us in our daily lives and with the more distant "them" against which our society collectively articulates itself. Our sense of identity is, then, a relational one: we are who we are in intimate connection with those amongst and against whom we continually redefine ourselves.

This always delicate task of relational self-negotiation becomes more difficult during periods of accelerated social change, when both individual and collective self-definition are at once more tenuous and more defensive. The process of such change—which is often precipitated or accompanied by the increased proximity, in either geographical or conceptual terms, of previously unfamiliar cultures—introduces an array of material, social, economic, and religious variables which can profoundly destabilize individual and collective identity. Early modern North America was one time and place that experienced such a maelstrom of unprecedented social change. Our own shrinking globe, at the dawn of the twenty-first century, is another: the pace, scope, and nature of the change we are currently experiencing evinces striking similarities with Pastedechouan's vanished world. Like the aboriginal peoples and European missionaries of seventeenth-century Canada, whose interrelations forced them to acknowledge that their world was larger and more diverse than they had previously understood, we, as contemporary citizens of an increasingly interconnected planet, experience the exhilaration and disorientation that accompany unprecedented levels of geographic mobility; intercultural contact; and the economic, religious, and technological changes triggered by them. As we attempt in our own time to weave an increasingly complex tapestry of religious, cultural, ethnic, ideological, and class affiliations into our individual and collective identities, we recognize that, as often as not, these diverse ideations and expectations clash as well as cohere. We fear that, like Pastedechouan, we might face the negative judgments of the various cultural and religious audiences in front of whom we publicly and privately enact our most intimate selves. Our often tenuous attempts personally to connect apparently disparate worlds of experience and meaning with the fragile bridges of our own lives means that, for many of us, Pastedechouan's story resonates with both our continued experiences and our deepest anxieties.

In particular, Pastedechouan's conundrum as a man caught between two cultures, who, unable to fit into either, was ultimately rejected by both, draws the sympathetic recognition of many who feel a similarly variegated sense of cultural, religious, or ethnic identity. Many of the central issues of this work, such as the interplay between religious and cultural commitments and self-perception, are universal, illuminating not just a small corner of the early modern Catholic world but the relationship between religion and cultural identity more broadly. A stranger to whom I confided Pastedechouan's story met it with tears of recognition and the confession that, as the daughter of immigrants, she felt culturally inauthentic in both the United States and her parents' native Taiwan. A young immigrant born and raised in the Dominican Republic, upon hearing of Pastedechouan's negative reception by his Innu community, expressed her own profound fears that, upon her return to her homeland, her cultural assimilation to Canadian gender norms would subject her to a similar fate of uncomprehending condemnation.

It is such expressions of genuine engagement with Pastedechouan's story that suggest to me both its enduring value and the scholarly necessity of empathically connecting with the experiences of other human beings across the vagaries of time and ethnicity. While fully appreciating the necessity of remaining aware that seventeenth-century historical actors, both indigenous and European, moved within different interior universes than our own, I would contend that such salutary awareness of distance and difference should not preclude us from taking advantage of what is perhaps our most important and most underrated methodological tool as historians and religionists: our capacity for empathetic, imaginative human engagement with the individual actors we study. The historical specificity of the events under consideration and the ethnic identities of its key participants, while important, must not detract from our appreciation of Pastedechouan's story in more general terms: indeed, it is the ability of this story to demand our personal engagement that is part of its power. Though I have tried, in this work, intimately to understand the religious journey of an early seventeenth-century Innu man, I believe that the interplay between his devotional commitments and self-perception have universal human resonance and thus the power to illuminate not simply his world but our own.

Finding Pastedechouan:
A Note on Sources and Methodology

As Pastedechouan belonged to an oral Innu culture which kept no written records of its history or conceptual universe, to reconstruct the outer shell of his life and plumb the depths of his inner world we are limited to three basic sources of information: that contained in the European historical record, that postulated through ethnohistorical techniques such as "backstreaming," and that intuited through creative interpretation of oral and visual rather than textual sources. Though Pastedechouan himself was literate, coproducing two French-Innu dictionaries—one in France with Gabriel Sagard, a Recollet lay brother, and a second in Canada with Paul Le Jeune, the Jesuit Superior of New France—both of these, along with other materials written in his "clear hand" appear to have been lost to history.[1]

Though Pastedechouan's story in many ways typifies the experiences of the small cadre of aboriginal children who made the perilous journey across the Atlantic to France in the seventeenth century, the level of European documentation for his particular case appears to be highly unusual. Unlike many of his fellow reluctant ambassadors, who appear as mere pious footnotes in devotional histories, reveal little of their distinctive individuality which the variety and depth of the documentary sources in Pastedechouan's case allow for a rich reconstruction of this young man's outer world and inner life. His lifetime of encounter with a variety of European actors—spanning the advent of Recollet engagement with Innu culture in 1615, the interruption of French colonial progress in 1629 by the ascendant English, and the consolidation of Jesuit power after 1632—resulted in a surprisingly loquacious record of his actions and words in the formal and informal writings of the many Europeans, both religious and secular, who encountered him. The manuscript and printed sources of the European record fall naturally into two categories: those that detail Pastedechouan's childhood instruction under Recollet supervision in 1620s

France, and those that chronicle his agonistic adult relationship with their Jesuit successors at home in the St. Lawrence River valley.

The principal published Recollet sources for Pastedechouan's childhood experiences in France (1620–1625) and his reimmersion back into Innu society (1626–1628) are Recollet historian Christian Le Clercq's *First Establishment of the Faith in New France* and the four-volume work written by Pastedechouan's one-time student, Gabriel Sagard, his *Histoire du Canada*.[2] The first work provides the reader with an excellent idea of the probable circumstances of Pastedechouan's early encounter with the newly arrived Recollet missionaries and his recruitment to go to France. It outlines the curriculum of his five years of theological and linguistic education and details both his reluctance to return to Canada and the circumstances of his reimmersion into Innu society at Tadoussac. Sagard's four volumes are the single best source for Pastedechouan's critical encounter with the invading Kirke brothers in 1628 and afford telling glimpses of his relationships, both with the religiously factionalized Innu community and with the overconfident French colonial hierarchy in the period shortly before its temporary eclipse by the English.

Manuscript sources for this period of Pastedechouan's life include his baptismal record; a detailed, hauntingly evocative description of his Angers baptism by layman Jean Louvet, a French barrister's assistant who witnessed it; and the letters and vita of Father Jean Dolbeau, the Recollet missionary who accompanied the twelve-year-old Pastedechouan to France and served as an important mentor to him during his time at La Baumette, the Recollets' convent near Angers.[3]

The Jesuit record of Pastedechouan's life, while less varied, is no less rich. Penned almost entirely by one man, Pastedechouan's nemesis, Paul Le Jeune, who was the Jesuit Superior of New France from 1632 to 1639, these documents give intimate insights into the young man's words, behavior, and possible motivations with a detail, richness, and psychological acuity unrivaled by many of the earlier Recollet materials.[4] Le Jeune's association with Pastedechouan, which began shortly after his arrival in Canada in June 1632, ended only with the young Innu's death during the winter of 1636. The Superior's descriptions of his frequently fractious interactions with the young Innu during the intervening four-year period, recorded in both private letters and in the official reports, or "Relations," which Le Jeune carefully penned and sent to his superiors in France annually, contain an extraordinarily detailed, emotionally col-

ored description of the Jesuit's evolving relationship with both Pastedechouan and the other members of his family, whom the missionary accompanied on their six-month-long winter hunting expedition during
the winter of 1633–1634.

Le Jeune's *Relations* for the last years of Pastedechouan's short life (and
beyond) pioneered the beginning of a new literary form, preserved key
ethnographic information about seventeenth-century aboriginal life, and
unleashed a powerful propaganda and fund-raising tool.[5] The *Relation of
1634*, which describes Le Jeune's winter with Pastedechouan's kin group
deep in the Canadian woods, due to its invaluable ethnographic information, the narrative pull of its dramatic plotline, and its unforgettable characters, has been singled out for a number of critical editions, besides
being reproduced in the two standard collections, Thwaites's *Jesuit Relations and Allied Documents* and Campeau's *Monumenta Novae Franciae*.[6]
While utilizing all the available versions, I have consistently referenced
the Thwaites edition, because it is easily available and features an English
translation and the text in its original language (usually archaic French
but occasionally Latin) on facing pages.

In addition to its obvious interest from a strictly narrative perspective,
the analytical and historiographic challenges it presents, and the contemporary resonances it never fails to evoke, Pastedechouan's story provides
its investigator with the opportunity to confront one of the thorniest
methodological conundrums in the study of early modern native peoples.
A fierce controversy continues to rage as to whether European-authored
sources can reward their careful reader with intimations of aboriginal perspectives. The key question in this debate is "Can we get 'through' European authors 'to' the aboriginal people they discuss, or must we content
ourselves merely with analyzing European perceptions of aboriginal
peoples?" Such a question is obviously critical for the current study,
which relies heavily upon such sources in its quest to uncover critical aspects of Pastedechouan's religious identity from his own perspective.

Some scholars have answered this question in the negative. Emphasizing the flawed, "partial" (in both senses of the word), and propagandistic
nature of missionary accounts, such scholars present them as so occluded
with European prejudice as to be almost entirely unhelpful in the uncov-
ering the beliefs, practices, and perceptions of aboriginal peoples. Jesuits
and Recollets alike, they argue, interpreted aboriginal behavior through
the lens of their own Christian proclivities and included descriptions of

aboriginal lifeways in reports intended to glorify their own missionary activities in order to attract funding, political support, and manpower. Such scholars perceive the subjectivity of missionaries as inescapable and present as fruitless, naïve, and misguided claims to be able "sift through" Europeans' biases to discern aboriginal perspectives.[7]

Other scholars, however, defend missionary-authored texts as an invaluable resource for discerning aboriginal voices from the past. Such scholars have pioneered a number of techniques designed to help contextualize and "read through" their prevalent authorial bias. They advocate the thorough interrogation of a text's intent, audience, and genre to help determine the value of the information it contains. They distinguish between missionary description and missionary analysis, arguing that while Jesuit characterizations of aboriginal religion as either a laughable illusion or a demonic reality vitiates their interpretation of Innu ritual, it does not necessarily damage the factuality of their descriptions of such ceremonies. Finally, such scholars rely upon discourse analysis to help them interpret the multiple, complex meanings of key signifiers in European texts. Approached cautiously and with the proper techniques, they argue, missionary-authored narratives, despite their biases, can provide an invaluable if distorted window into the lifeworld of early modern aboriginal peoples.[8]

My own experience with missionary-authored documents has deeply impressed me with their complexity and firmly convinced me of their irreplaceable worth as a source for both missionary and aboriginal perspectives in seventeenth-century North America. Though their authors' narrative strategies and inescapable subjectivity do pose daunting challenges for contemporary interpreters, these are not insurmountable. By systematically probing these writings for their narrative tensions and overt contradictions, we can intuit, almost four hundred years later, echoes of the perspectives of Pastedechouan and his family.

For example, in plumbing the depths of Paul Le Jeune's *Relations* for 1633 and 1634, my richest, most layered sources, I encountered both the past as its Jesuit author wanted it to appear and ample, tangible evidence of what he tried to ignore, deny, or suppress. For example, in the *Relation of 1633*, Pastedechouan is presented as a God-given boon to Jesuit missionary success, as Le Jeune, delightedly recording Pastedechouan's arrival at the small Jesuit residence, was determined to squeeze the young Innu's ungainly and reluctant foot into the glass slipper of his optimistic providentialism. Having cast Pastedechouan in his narrative as a God-given linguistic font who would single-handedly solve the Jesuits' paramount missionization challenge—their ignorance of aboriginal languages—the Superior was loath to blur or taint this image with a forthright account of Pastedechouan's evident religious ambivalence. But despite Le Jeune's desire to excise Pastedechouan's evident anomie from his master narrative of God's beneficent provision, the young man's spiritual ambivalence was ultimately undeniable and, for the alert reader, continuously challenges the Superior's idealized presentation of his young teacher. Similarly, a surface reading of Le Jeune's *Relation of 1634* leaves the reader with the notion that both Pastedechouan and his eldest brother Carigonan were implacably opposed from the outset to the Superior's one-man mission within their small familial band, dooming it to failure. But substantial contradictions within Le Jeune's own text, such as his admission that Carigonan approached him to request his prayers for healing, allow the reader to ascertain that both brothers were initially receptive to the missionary's presence and message but gradually became alienated because of Le Jeune's insensitivity and rigidity. Le Jeune's numerous narrative contradictions and anomalies, then, allow his reader to disrupt the missionary's self-serving rhetorical strategies, reveal new strata of meaning, and discern hidden aboriginal perspectives.

In addition to the challenges posed by the missionary bias of extant European historical sources, this study, as the religious biography of a relatively unknown seventeenth-century aboriginal man, also confronts the ubiquitous problem of gaps in the historical record. While, as mentioned, the European record of Pastedechouan's life is unusually full, there nevertheless remain significant regrettable yet inevitable lacunae. As noted by Dorris, investigators who yearn for "historian's heaven," where we can "truly, utterly, absolutely, completely, finally know" what occurred in the past, are, unfortunately, offered "hardly even purgatory" in their work on seventeenth-century aboriginal subjects.[9] Such gaps, however, can be creatively addressed through the use of ethnohistorical techniques such as "backstreaming" and the trenchant interrogation of nontextual sources, such as mythology, artifacts, and imagery.

For example, though we know very few details of Pastedechouan's particular childhood, embedded in a small, migratory Innu band living on the north shore of the St. Lawrence River, we have a wealth of information on the contours of everyday Innu life obtained from both early seventeenth-century sources and from more recent anthropological lit-erature. The careful application of information regarding aboriginal be-liefs and practices observed and recorded at a later period in history to an earlier era in which records are either scarce or slanted—a process known as "backstreaming"—allows us creatively to address some of these lacunae. In the case of Pastedechouan's childhood, our examina-tion of Innu child-rearing practices, pedagogical techniques, conceptu-alizations of gender and age, and rites of passage—if sensitively evoked within the distinctive sociohistorical context of the early seventeenth century—allows us to create an accurate picture of what it may have been like to be a young boy in such a culture, at such a time.

Moreover, our understanding of Pastedechouan's experiences and per-ceptions can be invaluably supplemented through the careful inspection and analysis of the visual artifacts with which he would have been fa-miliar. Careful perusal of historical Innu artifacts, such as hunting ap-parel and pack straps, with their elaborate tracings of images revealed in dreams, can help us, because of their Janus-faced ability both to com-memorate and to precipitate religious actions, to better comprehend the imaginative religious world of Pastedechouan's people. Our evocation of the boy's experiences in France can also be enhanced through the sys-tematic, disciplined use of visual clues. Lacking detailed information on Pastedechouan's precise curriculum during his French sojourn, I trav-eled to Angers to reconstruct as much as possible his "classroom of the eyes," postulating that the messages silently contained in the devotional art he confronted there, be they ornate frescos, wonder-working statues, or the nightmarish panels of the Tapestry of the Apocalypse, helped to shape his characteristically exclusivistic religious mentality as much or more than what he read or was explicitly taught.

In contrast with the inevitable reality of historical gaps, there are in-stances where the sources seem almost suspiciously generous, as when we confront what are purportedly direct quotations from aboriginal ac-tors. These too require careful handling. For example, in both the Rec-ollet and Jesuit sources, there are (relatively rare) instances when Pastedechouan seems to speak to us directly out of the text. Though cau-tion is advisable in approaching the purported quotations of aboriginal peoples in missionary writings, I feel that we are justified in accepting such utterances as basically accurate when they coincide with what we know about the broad contours of an individual's behavior. Thus, while we cannot definitively know whether Pastedechouan uttered the exact words he is credited with—"My father, how could your reverence want to send me back to the beasts who know not God?"—we are justified in accepting this exclamation as a likely approximation of his sentiments because Pastedechouan's marked reluctance to return to Canada and his attempts to avoid contact with his own people even after his repatriation are well attested in multiple sources.[10]

While the opaque, flawed, and frustratingly incomplete nature of the available sources do pose daunting interpretive challenges, to exaggerate them runs the greater risk that we might fail in our obligation imaginatively to use the existing historical data to reconstruct, however provisionally and incompletely, the lives of Pastedechouan and his family. By choosing to regard the complexity of the primary material as a positive feature to be embraced rather than as a daunting hurdle foreclosing further exploration and by creatively engaging a range of analytical and interpretive tools, we can throw light on the motivations and experiences of the young Innu, his community, and the various Europeans who encountered them.

Notes

1. "Thy God Has Not Come to Our Country"

1. Aboriginal stoicism in childbirth: Bruce Trigger, *The Children of Aatahaensic: A History of the Huron People to 1660* (Cambridge, 1976), 1: 47; James Axtell, *The Indian Peoples of Eastern North America: A Documentary History of the Sexes* (Oxford, 1981), 3. Innu births as an exclusively female event, then and now: Diamond Jenness, *Indians of Canada* (Ottawa, 1932), 273; M. Pritzker, *A Native American Encyclopedia* (Oxford, 2000), 508; Serge Jauvin, *Aitnanu: The Lives of Helene and William Mathieu Marks,* ed. Daniel Clement (Hull, 1993), 32; John T. McGee, *Cultural Stability and Change Among the Montagnais Indians of the Lake Melville Region of Labrador* (Washington, 1961), 44. I have used the spelling of Pastedechouan's name given by Paul Le Jeune in the *Jesuit Relations* (Rueben Gold Thwaites, ed., *Jesuit Relations and Allied Documents, 1610–1791* [Cleveland, 1898], 5: 107) and adopted by G. W. Brown et al., *Canadian Dictionary of Biography* (Toronto, 1966), 533, and Lucien Campeau, *Monumenta Nova Franciae* (Quebec; Rome, 1987), 2: 847–848. Contemporary accounts vary the spelling of Pastedechouan's name somewhat: his baptismal notice (MS GG 100, folio 223, Archives Municipal d'Angers refers to him as "Pastre-Chouen"; Gabriel Sagard calls him "Patetchouenon": Gabriel Sagard, *Histoire du Canada* (Paris, 1866), 504. The names of Pastedechouan's parents are not noted in the European historical record. For his status as the youngest in a family of four sons, see Thwaites, *Jesuit Relations,* 6: 109 and 7: 69.

2. Serge Bouchard, *Caribou Hunter: A Song of a Vanished Innu Life* (Vancouver, 1989), 3.

3. Jenness, *Indians,* 272; Pritzker, *Native American,* 509. The religious ideations and social practices described in this chapter represent a living social reality rather than a relic of the past. Though the Innu as a people have been deeply affected by geographic displacement, the changes of modernity, and European cultural imperialism, contemporary Innu nevertheless mirror many of the beliefs and practices of their early modern ancestors, particularly in their ethic of reciprocity, their educational practices, and their beliefs about the proper means of relating to animals.

The contemporary persistence of or variations upon early modern Innu beliefs and practices will be noted throughout this chapter.

4. Thwaites, *Jesuit Relations,* 6: 161, 175–177, 215, 7: 27; Joseph Le Caron, in Christian Le Clercq, *First Establishment of the Faith in New France* (New York, 1881), 1: 216; Alain Beaulieu, *Convertir le Fils de Cain: Jesuits et Amerindiens Nomades en Nouvelle France, 1632–1642* (Saint-Jean, PQ, 1990), 32–33; Kenneth Morrison, "Baptism and Alliance: The Symbolic Meditations of Religious Syncretism," *Ethnohistory* 33 (1990): 416–437; and Kenneth Morrison, *The Solidarity of Kin: Ethnohistory, Religious Studies, and the Algonkian-French Religious Encounter* (Albany, 2002), 1–39. The sun, in particular, appears to have been an important member of the Innu pantheon (Le Caron, in Le Clercq, *First Establishment,* 1: 216). Scholars have speculated that Innu torture practices, like those of the Iroquois, were timed to coincide with the rising of the sun, so that the captive's last breath might be seen as a sacrifice to its rising: Jose Brandão, *"Your Fyre Shall Burn No More": Iroquois Policy toward New France and Its Native Allies to 1701* (Lincoln, Neb., 1997), 40. Innu who converted to Christianity appear often to have associated Jesus with the sun: Thwaites, *Jesuit Relations,,* 4: 201–203; see also Alfred Goldsworthy Bailey, *The Conflict of European and Eastern Algonkian Cultures, 1504–1700: A Study in Canadian Civilization* (Toronto, 1969), 134–135.

5. Irving Hallowell originated this phraseology, preferring it to the "spirits" or "beings" often used by commentators, because it better conveys a sense of the individual personalities of the aboriginal pantheon: they are non-human people rather than abstract concepts. For that same reason I will be using *personal* pronouns (he, she his, her) to refer to other-than-human actors, rather than the personal non-aboriginal "it/its," which implies animals are more like objects than persons. A. Irving Hallowell, "Ojibwa Ontology, Behavior, and World View," in *Contributions to Anthropology: Selected Papers of A. Irving Hallowell* (Chicago, 1976), 54; see also Morrison, *Solidarity,* 37–58.

6. The Innu propensity to construct community in ways that traversed species was and is a common aboriginal cultural trait. On the Ojibwa, see Hallowell, "Ojibwa"; on the Cree, see Naomi Adelson, *"Being Alive Well": Health and the Politics of Cree Well-Being* (Toronto, 2000); on the Dene Tha, see Jean-Guy Goulet, *Ways of Knowing: Experience, Knowledge, and Power among the Dene Tha* (Vancouver, 1998), 60–87; on various Plains cultures, see Howard Harrod, *Renewing the World: Plains Indians Religion and Morality* (Tuscon, 1987), 157–172.

7. Thwaites, *Jesuit Relations,* 5: 155, 6: 157–159; Le Caron, in Le Clercq, *First Establishment,* 1: 217. Variants of this "earth-diver" myth are widespread

in northeastern North America: see Trigger, *Children,* 1: 77–78: Dean R. Snow et al., *In Mohawk Country: Early Narratives about a Native People* (Syracuse, 1996), 45: Daniel Richter, *The Ordeal of the Longhouse: The Peoples of Iroquois League in the Era of European Colonization* (Chapel Hill, N.C.; Williamsburg, Va., 1992; 10–11).

8. Seventeenth-century descriptions of animal masters: Thwaites, *Jesuit Relations,* 7: 159–161. Modern Innu descriptions: Frank Speck, *Naskapi: The Savage Hunters of the Labrador Peninsula* (Norman, Okla, 1935), 86–80, 110–113, 117–123; Marie Wadden, *Nitassinan: The Innu Struggle to Reclaim Their Homeland* (Vancouver, 1991), vii, 22–23. Cree descriptions: Adelson, *Being Alive,* 70–71; Peter Armitage, "Religious Ideology among the Innu of Eastern Quebec and Labrador," Religiologiques, vol. 6, 1992, 68–72.

9. Thwaites, *Jesuit Relations,* 7: 175–177; Speck, *Naskapi,* 77; Antonia Mills and Richard Slobodin, *Amerindian Rebirth: Reincarnation Belief among North American Indians and Inuit* (Toronto, 1994), 22.

10. Thwaites, *Jesuit Relations,* 7: 161. Such seasonal gatherings could be large, numbering in the hundreds or even, according to Champlain, writing in the summer of 1603, topping one thousand. H. P. Biggar, *The Works of Samuel de Champlain* (Toronto, 1971), 1: 105; Pritzker, *Native Amerians,* 508.

11. My estimate of Pastedechouan's birth date is based upon the impressions of Europeans who encountered him. Jean Dolbeau, the Recollet father who brought Pastedechouan to France describes him, in 1620, as "un petit sauvage de douze ou treize ans.": MS 509, folio 171, Bibliothèque Municipal d'Orleans, reproduced in Odoric Jouve, *Dictionnaire biographique des Récollets missionaires en Nouvelle-France, 1615–1645, 1670–1849: province franciscaine Saint-Joseph du Canada.* Odoric Jouve avec la collaboration de Archange Godbout, Hervé Blais et René Bacon [Saint-Laurent, Québec]: Bellarmin, 1996 (Montreal, 1996, 371–372). This gives us a birth date of 1607 or 1608. Even if we take Dolbeau's estimate of Pastedechouan's age in 1620 as accurate, it is possible that he looked younger than his years. Jean Louvet, an eyewitness to Pastedechouan's baptism at Angers in 1621 who, unlike Dolbeau, did not know Pastedechouan personally, describes him as "a young boy aged ten or eleven years" ("Journal de Jean Louvet," MSS 862, Bibliothèque d'Angers), which would put his birthday around 1609 or 1610.

12. Trigger, *Children,* 1: 362.

13. Biggar, *Works of Champlain,* 5: 3.

14. Innu clothing: Thwaites, *Jesuit Relations,* 6: 9–19, 5: 23–25. Religious meaning of: Jenness, *Indians,* 274; Speck, *Naskapi,* 190–191; Wadden, *Nitassinan,* 22–23. The association of hunting with decorative finery can still be observed in contemporary Innu communities. Though the material uti-

lized has changed from caribou hide to lightweight, factory-made cloth, the Innu still often decorate hunting clothing with elaborate needlework, as do the Cree, another Algonkian group (Adelson, *Being Alive*). Makeup and tattoos: Thwaites, *Jesuit Relations,* 5: 23, 105–107; Le Clercq, *First Establishment,* 1: 89. Distaste for facial hair: Thwaites, *Jesuit Relations,* 7: 63.

15. Appearance and construction of Innu homes: Thwaites, *Jesuit Relations,* 5: 27, 7: 35–37, 113–115. Northerly Innu or "Naskapi" utilized caribou hides (Jenness, *Indians,* 271). Use of boughs on the floor: Thwaites, *Jesuit Relations,* 5: 27, 163–165. Spruce or fir boughs are still the preferred Innu mattresses today, and gathering them is still the women's responsibility (Jauvin, *Aitnanu,* 15; Wadden, *Nitassinan,* 13; Armitage, "Religious Ideology," 94).

16. Thwaites, *Jesuit Relations,* 6: 255. Modern Innu sex roles: Bouchard, *Caribou Hunter,* 136. In fact, Innu culture was quite patriarchal. Although Innu women enjoyed far more personal and sexual freedom than did their French counterparts and performed roles which were respected within their culture, they appear not to have approximated the level of religious and political leadership exhibited by aboriginal women in more agricultural societies, who often played a key role in the practical and ritual aspects of the cultivation of the earth, which was often understood in feminine terms: Theda Perdue, *Cherokee Women: Gender and Culture Change, 1700–1835* (Lincoln, Neb., 1998), 17–40. It is possible that Innu women, as part of a society which depended upon and glorified the relationship between the male hunter and his prey, were more marginalized than their agriculturalist counterparts because of their apparent exclusion from prestigious hunting roles.

17. Jenness, *Indians,* 273.

18. Pastedechouan himself married, during one of his four or possibly five ill-fated unions, a "foreign" woman from another tribe (Thwaites, *Jesuit Relations,* 7: 69, 173–175).

19. Repeatedly urged by French missionaries to give up polygamy on the basis of its carnal "immorality," the Innu countered that it was compassionate provision for rather than ruthless sexual exploitation of the vulnerable. Beaulieu, *Convertir,* 28–30; Colin Samson, *A Way of Life That Does Not Exist: Canada and the Extinguishment of the Innu* (London, 2003), 159.

20. J. R. Miller, *Shingwauk's Vision: A History of Native Residential Schools* (Toronto, 1996), 20.

21. Thwaites, *Jesuit Relations,* 7: 127; see also 5: 131–133. Sometimes the stoicism necessary to withstand periods of privation would have coalesced with the competitive nature of Innu education. Young children, particularly boys, probably emulated their elders' games, designed to both competitively exhibit and expand the range of physical punishment they could tolerate.

22. Thwaites, *Jesuit Relations,* 7: 111.
23. Ibid., 5: 153–155, 7: 175, 279, 295; Miller, *Shingwauk's Vision,* 18.
24. Thwaites, *Jesuit Relations,* 5: 221; see also 6: 153–155. Horror at French abuse in the service of education was not limited to the Innu but was a widespread aboriginal reaction. See Olive Dickason, "Campaigns to Capture Young Minds: A Look at Early Attempts in Colonial Mexico and New France to Remold Amerindians," *Historical Papers* 61 (1987), 44–66; Trigger, *Children,* 1: 263; Miller, *Shingwauk's Vision,* 18.
25. McGee, *Cultural Stability,* 45–49. This strong emphasis upon children's responsibility for themselves is a pan-aboriginal phenomenon (Miller, *Shingwauk's Vision,* 15–38). For both an excellent overview of the theoretical basis for anthropological presentation of such pedagogical propensities and their appearance in the contemporary Dene Tha context, see Goulet, *Ways,* 36–47.
26. Thwaites, *Jesuit Relations,* 5: 133, 6: 233–235; Beaulieu, *Convertir,* 28–30. Such sharp articulations of age and gender roles were typical of many other precontact aboriginal groups. See Trigger, *Children,* 1: 34–45, for the Wendat; and Perdue, *Cherokee,* 17–40, for the Cherokee.
27. Importance of strict gender roles in aboriginal education: Dickason, "Campaigns," 61–62; Miller, *Shingwauk's Vision,* 15–38. Hunting as a male prerogative, then and now: Jauvin, *Aitnanu,* 69–70; Wadden, *Nitassinan,* 17–18. Hunting shifting to a female job: Speck, *Naskapi,* 77; Kim Cheena, personal communication with the author, 2004. Bouchard states that the ancient division of labor still holds, in that women hunt and trap small animals, leaving the larger game for the men (*Caribou Hunter,* 26–27). Transportation: The women carried their heavy burdens on their backs, holding them in place with cords passed across their foreheads (Thwaites, *Jesuit Relations,* 6: 111; 7: 85, 109). Maintenance of fire, then and now: Thwaites, *Jesuit Relations,* vol. 5: 133; 6: 233–235; Jenness, *Indians,* 156–157; Wadden, *Nitassinan,* 17.
28. Thwaites, *Jesuit Relations,* 5: 133; see also Beaulieu, *Convertir,* 28.
29. Axtell, *Indian Peoples,* 3, 12; Trigger, *Children,* 1: 47. Breast-feeding until toddlerhood helped to reduce aboriginal family size. It was also practical, in that children needed some teeth to be able to eat the meat-heavy Innu winter diet, even when meat was prechewed for them by their mothers (Jenness, *Indians,* 149). Contemporary Innu practices are roughly similar, though breast-feeding periods are shorter, around a year. Innu mothers still grind or prechew young children's meat or feed children meat broth thickened with flour (Jauvin, *Aitnanu,* 32–35).
30. Thwaites, *Jesuit Relations,* 7: 95–97.
31. Ibid., 4: 295–317.

248   *Notes to Pages 24–28*

32. Ibid., 6: 175.
33. Speck, *Naskapi*, 41.
34. Seventeenth-century descriptions of Innu soul concepts: Thwaites, *Jesuit Relations*, 6: 175–177; Le Caron in Le Clercq, *First Establishment*, 1: 217–219. Contemporary descriptions: Speck, *Naskapi*, 41–51. Speck's study of early twentieth-century Innu reveals that modern Innu refer to their soul as *Mista'peo* or the "Great Man," powerfully evoking this sense of an inner, powerful stranger who guides an individual's actions. Modern Innu generally refer to their soul in indirect terms as "my friend" (Speck, *Naskapi*, 42).
35. Le Caron in Le Clercq, *First Establishment*, 1: 216–218, Thwaites, *Jesuit Relations*, 6: 181–183. Dreams are still related and interpreted in the contemporary community, and it is still believed that to ignore their messages leads to unfortunate consequences: Lawrence Millman, *Wolverine Creates the World: Labrador Indian Tales* (Santa Barbara, 1993), 18–19.
36. Thwaites, *Jesuit Relations*, 6: 161.
37. Speck, *Naskapi*, 186–188.
38. Thwaites, *Jesuit Relations*, 5: 161; see also 6: 183.
39. Ibid., 6: 183.
40. Ibid., 6: 175; Speck, *Naskapi*, 41.
41. Souls as threat to children: Thwaites, *Jesuit Relations*, 6: 211. Use of different door for dead: Ibid., 5: 129; 6: 209. Innu burial practices: Jenness, *Indians*, 273; Thwaites, *Jesuit Relations*, 6: 211.
42. Thwaites, *Jesuit Relations*, 6: 179. Afterlife as a physical place: Ibid., 6: 177. Association of souls with light: Speck, *Naskapi*, 50–51, 65. Path of souls: Thwaites, *Jesuit Relations*, 6: 179–181; Le Caron, in Le Clercq, *First Establishment*, 1: 218; Speck, *Naskapi,* 50–51. The Innu believed that it was only the *souls* of these implements that would leave with the deceased, leaving their material forms in the grave with the deceased's body. The Innu were thus understandably less than impressed with Europeans who sought to "prove" to them the falsity of their beliefs by pointing out that the donated articles remained in the grave.
43. Speck, *Naskapi*, 47–50. The failure to recognize Innu reincarnation concepts is part of a larger analytical phenomenon in which the preeminent place of reincarnation in aboriginal belief and practice has been systematically misunderstood or ignored (Mills and Slobodin, *Amerindian*). It is also possible that the Innu reconciled this duality by positing that the animating soul went to the afterlife, while the journeying soul reincarnated back into the land of the living, in a sort of spirit form of bilocation. Goulet (*Ways*, 186–192) states that while he initially found simultaneous the belief of contemporary Dene Tha people in a (Christian-influenced) after-

world and reincarnation intellectually incoherent, this concern was denigrated by his informants as an insensitive misunderstanding of their beliefs.

44. While the Innu idea that a deceased soul can return in a new body is relatively straightforward, it is unclear how the Innu conceptually dealt with instances in which the same individual might be inhabited simultaneously by both their own and another soul, like a child given the name of a deceased relative. The fact that Innu treated adopted prisoners of war as if they had actually become the souls whom they socially replaced suggests an Innu belief that the invading soul completely suppressed or extinguished the individual's existing identity.

45. Speck, *Naskapi*, 20.

46. Thwaites, *Jesuit Relations*, 6: 203.

47. Jenness, *Indians*, 273; Thwaites, *Jesuit Relations*, v6: 215; Speck, *Naskapi*, 140–163. Scrying was until recently used by contemporary Innu people to forecast hunting fortunes (Millman, *Wolverine*, 12–13; Wadden, *Nitassinan*, vii; Armitage, "Religious Ideology," 64, 79–81 Denise Robertson, personal communication, 2007).

48. For seventeenth-century European description of this ceremony, see Thwaites, *Jesuit Relations*, 6: 163–169; Le Caron in Le Clercq, *First Establishment*, 1: 135–136. For a contemporary description of the practice, including photographs of a shaking tent being constructed, see Jean-René Proulx, "Acquisition de pouvoirs et tente tremblant chez les Montagnais," *Recherches Amérindiennes au Québec*, vol. 28, no. 2–3 (1988), 51–59. The identities and roles of the ceremonies' other-than-human participants are complex. The Innu appear to have conceived of a role of intermediary beings interceding between the ritual specialist and the animal spirits both historically and in the recent past. Jesuit Superior, Paul Le Jeune, writing of a shaking tent ritual he had personally experienced, suggested that the ritual specialist communed with *Khichicourai*, which he translated as "genies of light," who acted as intermediaries between the specialist and animal beings (Thwaites, *Jesuit Relations*, 5: 170–171). Le Jeune's presentation of the shaking tent ritual as a mediated event is supported by Peter Armitage's research among contemporary Innu people. He suggests that contemporary Innu people believe that their ritual specialist is aided in his dialogue with other-than-human persons by a *Mishtapeu*, a benevolent giant figure who acts as an interpreter for animal spirits: "thus . . . there are two mediators in the shaking tent: the *katushapatak* (ritual specialist) and his *Mistapeu*. In a sense, each is delegated by his group to facilitate communication between the two worlds: the *kakushapatak* interpreting for the Innu, and the interpreting for the animal masters" (Armitage, "Religious *Mistapeu* Ideol-

ogy," 75). For more on the Innu shaking tent ritual in the twentieth century, see Sylvie Vincent, "Structure du rituel: la tente tremblante et le concept de la mista pe.w," *Recherches Amérindiennes au Québec*, vol. 3, no. 1, 69–83; Wadden, *Nitassinan,* 3; Jauvin, *Aitnanu,* 99–101; Millman, *Wolverine,* 124, 149; Samson, *A Way,* 167. Though the ritual has been a feature of Innu religious life in the recent past, it has not been documented by researchers since 1973 (Armitage, "Religious Ideology," 84). The shaking tent ritual was not used exclusively by the Innu, but was also used in the Algonkian, Cree, and Ojibwa communities. For the Cree, see Adelson, *Being Alive,* 71–75. For the Ojibwa, see Christopher Vecsey, *Traditional Ojibwa Religions and its Historical Changes* (Philadelphia, 1983), 103–106.

49. Construction of the shaking tent: Thwaites, *Jesuit Relations,* 5: 157; Jenness, *Indians,* 273. Behavior of the ritual specialist: Thwaites, *Jesuit Relations,* 6: 163.

50. Thwaites, *Jesuit Relations,* 6: 163.

51. Ibid., 5: 159.

52. Speck, *Naskapi,* 57, 100–101; Armitage, "Religious Ideology," 76–79. Tobacco may have been given to the animals in the form of a birchbark pipe, which could be lit. There is one such pipe on display at the Musée Amérindien de Mashteuiatsh. Such pipes were still in use until recently (Denise Robertson, personal communication, 2007).

53. Speck, *Naskapi,* 92.

54. Soul's observation of its treatment: Le Caron, in Le Clercq, *First Establishment,* 1: 220. Gender and age cohorts in feasting: Thwaites, *Jesuit Relations,* 6: 219; Jauvin, *Aitnanu,* 101. Beavers: Thwaites, *Jesuit Relations,* 6: 211; Armitage, "Religious Ideology," 77. Bears: Speck, *Naskapi,* 102; Armitage, 77. Caribou: Jauvin, *Aitnanu,* 101. Transporting caribou antlers is a contemporary practice and may or may not have been done in the seventeenth century.

55. Thwaites, *Jesuit Relations,* 6: 223.

56. Thwaites, *Jesuit Relations,* 6: 211–213; 7: 163. See also Le Clercq, *First Establishment,* vol. 1: 220.

57. Thwaites, *Jesuit Relations,* 6: 211–213.

58. See also Le Caron, in Le Clercq, *First Establishment,* 1: 220; Thwaites, *Jesuit Relations,* 6: 211–213, 7: 163.

58. Thwaites, *Jesuit Relations,* 6: 219, 7: 89.

59. Bailey, *Conflict,* 136; Jenness, *Indians,* 273; Pritzker, *Native American,* 508. The Jesuit missionary Paul Le Jeune does not mention the vision quest in his survey of Innu beliefs and practices in 1634. This can mean one of several things: that he failed to recognize or observe what was a common practice; that he simply subsumed his observations regarding Innu visionary experiences into a more general discourse on dreams; that the vision

quest, like many aspects of Innu religion, was successfully hidden from his prying eyes (for Innu attempts to safeguard the secrecy of their religious practices see Thwaites, *Jesuit Relations,* 6: 171); or that vision quests were a later development in Innu religious history, perhaps the result of intra-aboriginal diffusion from neighboring groups, in which the vision quest was common. If this last possibility is the case, vision quests would not have been a part of Pastedechouan's religious world. For information on Ojibwa vision quests, see Vecsey, *Traditional Ojibwa,* 121–143; for the phenomenon in various Plains cultures, see Harrod, *Renewing,* 22–37; for contemporary Dene Tha experiences, see Goulet, *Ways,* 60–87.

60. Beaulieu, *Convertir,* 30; Daniel Richter, "War and Culture: The Iroquois Experience," *William and Mary Quarterly* 40 (1983): 528–559; Richter, *Ordeal,* 32–38.

61. The triad is Morrison's. See Kenneth Morrison, "The Cosmos as Intersubjective: Native American Other-Than-Human Persons," in *Indigenous Religions: A Companion,* ed. Graham Harvey (London, 2000), 13–15, 23–36. Such personalistic conceptualizations of the natural world were not exclusive to the Innu but were a common part of the mental and cultural map of many early modern aboriginal cultures. See also Morrison, *Solidarity,* 15, 25–30, 37–58, on the concept of "persons" in Innu and Algonkian cultures; Hallowell, "Ojibwa," 359–378, on Ojibwa conceptualizations of person and power; and Harrod, *Renewing,* 157–172, on similar concepts in Plains cultures.

62. Though I will argue in subsequent chapters that the Innu and the early modern missionaries who encountered them were to find common ground in their similarly "personalistic" attribution of the events of daily life, Innu commitment to the fundamental amorality of personal power and their tendency to judge moral identity on the basis of practical outcomes ran contrary to Catholic attribution of a static moral status for their religious actors. An amoral attribution of power meant that Innu could flexibly attribute both "good" and "bad" behavior to the same agent. European missionaries, on the other hand, were often at a disadvantage in their theological debates with the Innu: committed to the idea of an all-beneficent deity, missionaries were forced to argue that a God who was both benevolent and all-powerful nevertheless allowed unfortunate events to occur. Innu styles of reasoning would lead them to conclude, more logically, that persons who commit antisocial acts (or allow them to occur) are themselves morally suspect.

63. European missionaries were often seen by their aboriginal host communities through a shamanic lens and thus were feared as sources of powerful contamination even as they were courted as potential healers.

64. Thwaites, *Jesuit Relations,* 5: 103; Morrison, *Solidarity,* 59–78. Beliefs

regarding the windigo (wi'tigo) and acten (atce'n or atshen) are still prevalent in the Innu community: Speck, *Naskapi,* 45–47; Millman, *Wolverine,* 66–83; Armitage, "Religious Ideology," 71, 99. Atcen stories and beliefs were not peculiar to the Innu context but formed a part of the cultural backbone of the many northeastern and subarctic tribal groups, including the Algonkian, Iroquois, Penobscot, Maliseet, and Mi'kmaq. For a brief overview of the atcen or windigo in Ojibwa culture, see Vecsey, *Traditional Ojibwa,* 77–78.

65. "Innuification" of strangers: Morrison, *Solidarity,* 63–68, Primal anxieties: Millman, *Wolverine,* 66–83. Taking form of a family member: Morrison, *Solidarity,* 64; Speck, *Naskapi,* 73–75; Millman, *Wolverine,* 76.

66. Quoted in Morrison, *Solidarity,* 64. Shunning of cannibals: Thwaites, *Jesuit Relations,* 8: 31–35. Suicide of cannibals: Morrison, *Solidarity,* 71. Predictably, those who had eaten their own kin, because of the repugnance with which they viewed their own actions, regarded with some skepticism the claims of French missionaries to be able to cleanse them from such sins (Morrison, *Solidarity,* 71).

67. Eating of living victim's heart: Thwaites, *Jesuit Relations,* 5: 29–31, 55.

68. Morrison, *Solidarity,* 68. European missionaries, unlike some more modern commentators (see Speck, *Naskapi,* 44–46) clearly recognized the Innu distinction between ritual cannibalism and the desperate recourse to the eating of one's own family in times of famine. Missionaries' moral evaluation of the two actions, however, reversed those of the Innu. Though both were judged inhuman, "circumstantial" or privation cannibalism (which also occurred in the French context) was evaluated far less harshly, because of the desperate circumstances surrounding the act. The ritual cannibalism of defeated enemies, however, was regarded with greater horror, as an act of unparalleled barbarism.

69. Thwaites, *Jesuit Relations,* 6: 245.

70. For such an instance, see ibid., 9: 225.

71. On "egalitarian" and "flat" descriptions of Innu society, see Jenness, *Indians,* 161, 272; Pritzker, *Native American,* 508.

72. Thwaites, *Jesuit Relations,* 4: 289. In times of famine, of course, this rule was somewhat relaxed (ibid., 291).

73. On European chiding of Innu improvidence, ibid., *Jesuit Relations,* 5: 165, 171–173, 179. Many of the distinctions regarding age and gender norms still hold in the contemporary distribution of Innu hunting spoils (Jauvin, *Aitnanu,* 101; Wadden, *Nitassinan,* 19–20). Similarly, Adelson relates that modern Cree, a linguistically and culturally related aboriginal group, still offer bear or caribou meat to the oldest man of the group first (*Being Alive,* 63) and follow strict conventions as to what parts of the animal can be

eaten by the different age and gender cohorts of Cree society (ibid., 82–83).

74. Thwaites, *Jesuit Relations*, 6: 293.

75. Bewitchment and illness: Thwaites, *Jesuit Relations*, 6: 195–197. Taboo breaking and illness: Bailey, *Conflict*, 80. As caused by an other-than-human person: Thwaites, *Jesuit Relations*, vol. 6: 175. As caused by antisocial emotions: Thwaites, *Jesuit Relations*, 7: 83–85, 105, 191.

76. Appeasement: Thwaites, *Jesuit Relations*, 6: 187. Sweating and purgatives: Ibid., 7: 129.

77. Requests: One could requeset items which one had dreamt about occurred even when one was not ill (Thwaites, *Jesuit Relations*, 5: 183; Speck, *Naskapi*, p. 183). Within the Innu context, such requests were generally obeyed, as to refuse them meant courting accusations that one was ungenerous, a serious allegation. Dancing: Thwaites, *Jesuit Relations*, 6: 189.

78. Though the designation "Mohawk" derives from an Algonkian word meaning "eaters of human flesh" (Richter, *Ordeal*, 31), I have used it here because it is the preferred self designation of the contemporary community.

79. Trigger, *Children*, 1: 221–224, 209–214; Marcel Trudel, *The Beginnings of New France, 1524–1663* (Toronto, 1973), 140–141; Bruce G. Trigger and Wilcomb E. Washburn, *The Cambridge History of the Native Peoples of the Americas* (Cambridge, 1996), 1: 342, 352–355; Beaulieu, *Convertir*, 40; Olive Dickason, *The Myth of the Savage and the Beginnings of French Colonialism in the Americas* (Edmonton, 1997), 178.

80. The Iroquois League was composed of five separate nations: the Mohawk, Oneida, Onondoga, Cayuga, and Senaca (later joined by the Tuscarora). Formation and purpose of the league: Richter, *Ordeal*, 7, 15, 30–31; Jose Brandão, *Your Fyre*, 1–3, 29; Daniel Richter and James Merrell, *Beyond the Covenant Chain: The Iroquois and Their Neighbors in Indian North America, 1600–1800* (University Park, Pa., 1987), 16–19.

81. I use the term "semisedentary" to indicate two things: First, while Mohawk villages were occupied year round, not all members of the society remained stationary. Women, responsible for tending, weeding, and protecting the growing crops, tended to stay home during the summer months, while their menfolk often deserted the towns to engage in hunting or war. This male pattern of migrating in the summer and remaining stationary in the winter perfectly inverts Innu norms. "Semisedentary" also seems an apt term because it captures the fact that these towns were not permanent, but rather were abandoned every ten years, after the soil around them became depleted (Richter, *Ordeal*, 23–24).

82. Mohawk gender roles: Denys Delâge, *Bitter Feast: Amerindians and Europeans in Northeastern North America, 1600–1664* (Vancouver, 1993), 69;

Richter, *Ordeal,* 19–23, 35, 43; Natalie Zemon Davis, "Iroquoian Women, European Women," in *Women, "Race," and Writing in the Early Modern Period,* ed. Margo Hendricks and Patricia Parker (New York, 1994), 243–258. Myth of Atahensic: Le Clercq, *First Establishment,* 1: 216–217; Thwaites, *Jesuit Relations,* 8: 117–119, 10: 127–131.

83. Richter, "War and Culture," 528. See also Richter, *Ordeal,* 32–38.

84. Thwaites, *Jesuit Relations,* 5: 29–31; see also 6: 245.

85. Thwaites, *Jesuit Relations,* 5: 29; see also 5: 30, 31, 6: 245.

86. Ibid., 6: 235–237.

87. Ibid., 5: 29, 6: 245.

88. Le Clercq, *First Establishment,* 1: 222.

89. Thwaites, *Jesuit Relations,* 5: 119–121.

90. Ibid.

91. Richard White, *The Middle Ground: Indians, Empires, and Republics in the Great Lakes Region, 1650–1815* (Cambridge, 1991).

92. Trigger, *Children,* 1: 182–188; Dickason, *Myth,* 165–171, 210–211; Trigger and Washburn, *Cambridge History,* 1: 382–387.

93. Innu pre- and postcontact population numbers are notoriously difficult to determine. However, it would appear that an initial healthy population in the 1550s was largely untouched by European illness until the mid-seventeenth century, when wave after wave of devastating epidemics came to reduce their numbers by as much as one-third. As recently as the early to mid-twentieth century, the Innu were described as having a declining population. The dawn of the twenty-first century brings with it an Innu population which is demographically growing, has successfully laid claim to some of its land base, and seems to exhibiting signs of a new cultural self-confidence, even as it continues to struggle with the aftermath of colonialism. Wadden, *Nitassinan;* Jose Mailhot, *The People of Sheshatshit: In the Land of the Innu* (St. John's, NF, 1997); Millman, *Wolverine;* Samson, *A Way;* Nympha Byrne and Camille Fouillard, *"It's like the Legend:" Innu Women's Voices* (Charlottetown, PE, 2000).

94. William Coverdale, *Tadoussac Then and Now: A History and Narrative of the Kingdom of the Saguenay* (New York, 1942), 11; Trigger, Children, 1: 228–229.

95. Le Clercq, *First Establishment,* 1: 235. Innu delegations overseas: Biggar, *Works of Champlain,* 1: 98–104, Trigger and Washburn, *Cambridge History,* 1: 337–338; Trigger, *Children,* 1: 230–233. Innu ubiquity in areas the French wanted: Trigger, *Children,* 1: 229–230.

96. Natalie Zemon Davis, *The Gift in Sixteenth-Century France* (Madison, Wis. 2000), 81–84.

97. A third type of child gift exists today. Some Innu give one child to his or her

grandparents so that they can educate the child in traditional ways. The child then cares for them in their old age (Wadden, *Nitassinan,* 17).

98. Davis, *Gift,* 81.

99. Le Clercq, *First Establishment,* 1: 136. European missionaries proved more astute than traders at grasping the collective slant of Innu relational ethics. In their descriptions of Innu social relations, missionaries approvingly noted the generosity and kindness which governed Innu collective behavior. Much like modern historians and anthropologists, however, missionaries tended to abstract such behavior from its environmental context. By emphasizing the laudable morality of Innu actions, European missionaries failed to appreciate how Innu social relations appealed both to the self-interest of individuals as well as the larger collective good.

100. Gabriel Sagard, *The Long Journey into the Country of the Huron,* ed. George Wrong (Toronto, 1939), 45–46, 55–56. The aboriginal in question was actually named Erouachy, who was a prominent liaison and negotiator with Europeans in the early seventeenth century (Brown et al., *Canadian Dictionary,* 1: 32).

101. The Wendat were referred to as the "Huron" by sixteenth- and seventeenth-century French. Trigger notes the uncertain origin of the term, pointing out that "Huron" was a slang French term for rube or rustic. He also notes the folk etymology linking "hure" to "boar's head," which possibly referenced the spiky hairstyles affected by the Wendat (Trigger, *Children,* 1: 27; Wrong, in Sagard, *Long Journey,* xvi). On Innu collective values: Trigger, *Children,* 1: 361–364.

102. Thwaites, *Jesuit Relations,* 6: 259–261.

2.   "Do Not Take Me Back to Those Beasts"

1. Born in 1586 near Paris, Claude Le Caron, after entering the priesthood, served as a chaplain and tutor to a noble family before entering the Recollet order in 1610 or 1611, when he took the name Joseph. His career in Canada began in 1615 and was interrupted by the defeat of French forces by the English in 1629. Le Caron punctuated his missionary work amongst the Innu and Wendat peoples with repeated trips back to France, where he passionately presented Recollet complaints against Canadian Huguenot, whom he argued were impiously bent upon obstructing the work of God in this new land. See G. W. Brown et al., *Canadian Dictionary of Biography* (Toronto: 1966), 1: 436–438; Odoric Jouve, *Dictionnaire biographique des Récollets missionaires en Nouvelle-France* (Montreal, 1996), 555–565; Le Caron in Christian Le Clercq, *First Establishment of the Faith in New France, 1645–1645, 1670–1849* (Paris, 1881), 1: 134–137.

2. Le Caron, in Le Clercq, *First Establishment,* 1: 134–137.
3. Ibid., 135. The Monsieur Hoüel Le Caron refers to was likely Sieur Louis Hoüel, the king's secretary and controller of a salt works at Brouage. Hoüel was the original liaison between Champlain, the marine adventurer turned colonizer and the Recollet fathers of the Province of Saint-Denis, from whom he would seek aid (Le Clercq, *First Establishment,* 1: 70–72; Gabriel Sagard, *The Long Journey into the Country of the Huron,* ed. George Wrong (Toronto, 1939), xxiv.
4. Ibid., 135; misspelling of Tadoussac in original.
5. H. P. Biggar, ed., *The Works of Samuel de Champlain* (Toronto, 1971), 25. Conventionally regarded as the "father of New France," (ibid., 1: xv) despite the possible claim others could make to that role (Cartier, de Monts, etc.), Samuel de Champlain was born sometime between 1567 and 1570 in largely Protestant Brouage. He was probably trained as a geographer or draftsman before beginning his military career and traveling in the West Indies. In 1603, when Champlain first embarked for Canada, he went as a private passenger with no rank, probably included in the expedition solely for his cartographic skills. Prior to his 1608 founding of Quebec, Champlain had been a key player in the founding of the Acadian colony (in what is now the Canadian Maritime provinces) from 1604 to 1607 (Brown et al., *Canadian Dictionary,* 1: 186–204; Sagard, *Long Journey,* xxi). In the years following, Champlain would rise to positions of power and authority in the young colony.
6. Champlain's Appeal to Recollet: Le Clercq, *First Establishment,* 1: 72; Jouve, *Dictionnaire,* 555–565. Term "francization": Cornelius Jaenen, "Education for Francization: The Case of New France in the Seventeenth Century," in *Indian Education in Canada* vol. 1: *The Legacy,* ed. Jean Barman, Yvonne Hebert, and Don McCaskill (Vancouver, 1986), 45–47.
7. Sagard, *Long Journey,* xxvi.
8. John Moorman, *A History of the Franciscan Order from Its Origins to the Year 1517* (Oxford, 1968), 506; see also Lázaro Iriarte, *Histoire du Franciscanisme* (Paris, 2004), and David Flood and Thaddée Matura, *The Birth of a Movement: A Study of the First Rule of St. Francis* (Chicago, 1975).
9. Gabriel Sagard, *The Long Journey into the Country of the Hurons* (Toronto, 1939) trans. George M. Wrong, p. 19. Date of departure: Jouve, *Dictionnaire,* 555–556.
10. *Regula Non Bullata,* in Flood and Matura, *Birth,* 85.
11. Sagard, *Long Journey,* xxix; Flood and Matura, *Birth,* 67.
12. Biggar, *Works of Champlain,* 3: 16. Champlain's confessional identity: Marcel Trudel in Brown et al., *Canadian Dictionary* 1: 186–187. Association of agriculture with Christianity: Bigger, *Works of Champlain,* 1: 110, 117,

295–296, 2: 15–16. Though it is clear that Champlain initiated his alliance with the Recollets, commentators have differed as to the direction and degree of influence between the two parties in this union. Bruce Trigger (*The Children of Aatahaensic: A History of the Huron People to 1660* [Montreal, 1976], 1: 377) suggests that Champlain was the driving ideological force, stating that he selected the Recollet friars because of his perception that Franciscan missionary methodology, as previously employed in Mexico and Latin America, was well suited to his own vision for Canadian development. This implies that the Recollets' own policy articulations in 1616 were merely following Champlain's strong lead. By contrast, Marcel Trudel (*The Beginnings of New France, 1524–1663* [Toronto, 1973]), emphasizes Recollet influence on Champlain's initially vague visions of a colonial partnership between settled Frenchmen and converted aboriginals. Champlain's ideas in this early period, though definite in their commitment to aboriginal "civilization," conversion, and sedentification, lacked both detail and a clear strategy for implementation. Nor did Champlain, before his association with the Recollets, call for the banning of Huguenots from Canada, a key Recollet demand. Thus, I would agree with Trudel's contention that Champlain's association with the Recollets and his participation in their key 1616 summit informed the more developed colonization strategy he articulated in 1618 (Trudel, *Beginnings*, 123). This being said, however, the influence was clearly mutual.

13. Rueben Gold Thwaites, ed. *The Jesuit Relations and Allied Documents, 1610–1791* (Cleveland, 1897), 6:213.

14. Biggar, *Works of Champlain,* 3: 22.

15. Jamet's (his surname is sometimes spelled "Jamay") date of birth is not known. He did not long survive his time in Canada, dying in France in 1625, only ten years after he had first set foot on Canadian soil. (Brown et al., *Canadian Dictionary,* 1: 385–386; Jouve, *Dictionnaire,* 524–529; Odoric Jouve, *Les Franciscains et le Canada* vol. 1: *L'établissement de la foi, 1615–1629* (Quebec, 1915), 433–444. Du Plessis's birth date and many of the details of his life are unknown. During his brief tenure as a Canadian missionary, before his death in 1619, Du Plessis, in addition to utilizing his pharmacological skills, taught young aboriginal children the basics of the faith (Brown et al., *Canadian Dictionary,* 1: 305).

16. Dolbeau was born on March 2, 1586, in the duchy of Anjou and died June 9, 1652, in Orléans, where he had spent his latter years. Thanks to a *vita abregé* written after his death by a Benedictine monk named Dom Gilles Jamin and preserved in five slightly different forms at the Bibliothèque Municipal d'Orléans ("Abrège de la vie du Reverend Père Dolbeau," MS 509, folio 171), we know quite a bit about his spiritual insights as well as

the details of his life. See also Brown et al., 265; Jouve, *Dictionnaire*, 368–373.

17. Sagard, *Long Journey*, xviii. Choumin (or "Chomina") was an influential member of the Innu community from 1612 to 1629. See Brown et al., *Canadian Dictionary*, 1: 222; Gabriel Sagard, *Histoire du Canada* (Paris, 1886), 2: 498–513; Campeau, *Monumenta*, 2: 814.

18. It was these two men who would have the strongest and most enduring relationships with Pastedechouan. The young boy probably first encoutered Dolbeau during his initiatory experiences with the Innu people during the winter of 1615–1616. The bond between Pastedechouan and this mystic likely deepened in 1620, when Dolbeau personally escorted Pastedechouan to the Recollet convent of La Baumette to instruct him in preparation for his baptism. As already intimated, Pastedechouan was likely Le Caron's student during his day-school experiment at Tadoussac. He was also a key influence in Pastedechouan's life after his return to Canada in 1625, when he ineptly attempted to defend the young man from the criticism and distrust he faced from his Innu community (unfortunately in terms that further estranged them). By contrast, Du Plessis was never stationed at Tadoussac, and died in 1619, a year before the young Pastedechouan went to France (Brown et al., *Canadian Dictionary*, 1: 305). Jamet, due to his responsibilities as Superior, spent much of his time either at the administrative center of Quebec or in France itself, facilitating the Recollet mission. He was thus absent from Canada for much of the period before Pastedechouan left for France. Jamet's return to Canada was occasioned by the establishment of the aboriginal seminary, which Pastedechouan's overseas trip of the same year would help to fund (ibid., 386).

19. Wendat life: Trigger, *Children*.

20. Le Clercq, *First Establishment*, 1: 110, 94. See also Bigger, *Works of Champlain*, 1: 110, 117, 295–296, 3: 15–16.

21. Le Clercq, *First Establishment*, 1: 142.

22. Sagard, *Histoire*, 3: 628–629. Franciscan use of art in worldwide missions: Gauvin Alexander Bailey, *Art on the Jesuit Missions in Asia and Latin America, 1542–1773* (Toronto, 1999), 35–38. Art in Canadian Franciscan missions: François-Marc Gagnon, *La Conversion part l'image: Un aspect de la mission des Jésuites auprès des Indiens du Canada au XVIIe siècle* (Montreal, 1975), 17–19.

23. Le Clercq, *First Establishment*, 1: 141. The association of baptism with the establishment of a trade or military alliance was common to many aboriginal groups among the St. Lawrence (Trigger, *Children*, 1: 193).

24. Le Caron, in Le Clercq, *First Establishment*, 1: 217.

25. Ibid.

26. Ibid., 109–113.
27. Ibid., 110, 214; see also Trigger, *Children,* 1: 377, 380–381.
28. Campeau, *Monumenta,* 2: 105.
29. Le Clercq, *First Establishment,* 1: 141, 143.
30. Olive Dickason, "Campaigns to Capture Young Minds: A Look at Early Attempts in Colonial Mexico and New France to Remold Amerindians," *Historical Papers* 61 (1987): 44–66; Thwaites, *Jesuit Relations,* 6: 83–85, 87–89, 153–155.
31. Inga Clendinnen, "Disciplining the Indians: Franciscan Ideology and Missionary Violence in Sixteenth Century Yucatan," *Past and Present* 94, no. 1 (1982): 27–48.
32. Le Clercq, *First Establishment,* 1: 121–128; Trudel, *Beginnings,* 127.
33. Thwaites, *Jesuit Relations,* 9: 9, 61, 10: 67, 11: 107, 119, 163, 195, 16: 155, 17: 97.
34. Le Clercq, *First Establishment,* 1: 144, 176.
35. Charles Des Boves (alternate spellings Des Boüis, Des Boües) was a generous donor the Recollet cause in Canada, providing funds (as did Sieur Louis Hoüel and Henri de Bourbon, the latter's arms were emblazoned on the Recollets' Quebec convent), for the Recollets' convent and aboriginal seminary, the latter of which was named after Des Boves's name saint, Charles (Le Clercq, *First Establishment,* 1: 145–149). On Jamet's sending Pastedechouan to France: Sagard, *Histoire,* 1: 72; Jouve, *Dictionnaire,* 92.
36. Antagonism between merchants and missionaries: Trigger, *Children,* 1: 380–382. Tiny number of missionaries: Trudel, *Beginnings,* 118. Protestant background of many merchants: Marc-André Bédard, *Les Protestants en Nouvelle France* (Quebec, 1978), 11–14.
37. Trudel, *Beginnings,* 135; date of foundation: Brown et al., *Canadian Dictionary,* 1: 265, and Jouve, *Dictionnaire,* 526–527.
38. Children as cementing native alliances: Trigger, *Children,* 1: 64, 173, 182–183. *Trouchemens:* until the 1660s, the French used this term, originating from their colony in Brazil, instead of the more familiar "coureur de bois." (Cornelius Jaenen, personal communication with the author, 2004; see also Philippe Jacquin, *Les Indiens blancs: Français et Indiens en Amerique de Nord (XVI–XVIII siècle)* (Montreal, 1996), 35–61. Aboriginal children in France: Trigger, *Children,* 1: 183, 204, 233, 261–264. Nigamon and Tebachi as reparations: Le Clercq, *First Establishment,* 1: 127; Sagard, *Histoire,* 56–57; Trudel, *Beginnings,* 127; Trigger, *Children,* 1: 363. Nigamon sent to France: Le Clercq, *First Establishment,* 1: 127; Marcel Trudel, *Histoire de la Nouvelle-France* (Montreal, 1966), 2: 259, 324, 327, 351); Guy LaFlèche, *Relation de 1634 de Paul Le Jeune: Le Missionaire, l'apostat, le sorcier* (Montreal, 1973), 259–260.

39. Innu journey in 1602: Biggar, *Works of Champlain,* 1: 98–104; see also 188. Bruce G. Trigger and Wilcomb E. Washburn, eds., *The Cambridge History of the Native Peoples of the Americas* (Cambridge, 1996), 1: 337–338; Trigger, *Children,* 1: 232; Olive Dickason, *The Myth of the Savage and the Beginnings of French Colonialism in the Americas* (Edmonton, 1997), 212. This may not have been the first time that an Innu contingent went to France. The traders of Saint-Malo had long been instigators in bringing aboriginals to France (Dickason, *Myth,* 206). Cartier brought Donnacona, his sons, and several in his entourage there in 1538. Saint-Malo merchants also transported a number of coastal peoples, probably Beothuk, in the 1550s, 1570s, and 1580s. At the turn of the century these traders once again set their sights on the St. Lawrence, bringing home several aboriginals from the river valley. Though the records are vague as to their precise tribal affiliation, they were probably Innu, as Tadoussac was the preeminent center of European-aboriginal trade during the period (Trigger, *Children,* 1: 212).

40. Biggar, *Works of Champlain,* 1: 188. Innu with the dauphin: Trigger and Washburn, *Cambridge History,* 1: 338.

41. Erosion of Innu-French trading relationship: Trigger, *Children,* 1: 337, 342; Trudel, *Beginnings,* 99, Alain Beaulieu, *Convertir le fils de Cain: Jesuits et Amerindiens nomades en Nouvelle France* (Saint-Jean, PQ, 55–56). Refusal of French requests to go north: Trudel, *Beginnings,* 98. Trade motivated murders: Trigger, *Children,* 1: 213. Tarriffs: Trigger, *Children,* 1: 342. Rumor campaigns: Trigger, *Children,* 1: 214, 273.

42. Le Clercq, *First Establishment,* 1: 142.

43. *Uzureau,* "Le Couvent," 15; John McManners, *French Ecclesiastical Society under the Ancien Regime: A Study of Angers in the Eighteenth Century* (Manchester, 1960), 83. The quote is attributed to P. Gonzague in his 1587 "De Regime: A Study of Angers in the Eighteenth Century* (Manchester, 1960), origine seaphicae religionis franciscanoe." Pastedechouan's age, journey: Bibliothèque Municipal d'Orléans ("Vie Abrège de Père Dolbeau," MS 509, folio 171). Brown et al., *Canadian Dictionary,* 1: 1966, 265; Jouve, *Dictionnaire,* 368–373. René of Anjou: colloquially called "Roi René," he was king not of France but of Provençe, Jerusalem, and Sicily. Dedication of La Baumette to the Magdalene: F. Uzureau, "Le Couvent de la Baumette-lès-Angers, 1456–1791," *Andegaviana* 32 (1938): 59–60.

44. Cordeliers: Jouve, *Dictionnaire,* 842; *Uzureau,* "Le Couvent" 13; F. Uzureau, "Le Sacre d'Angers' avant la Revolution," *Andegaviana* 17 (1915), 113; D. B. Lewis, *Doctor Rabelais* (New York, 1968), 43; McManners, *French Ecclesiastical,* 3. La Baumette as one of the first convents to adopt the stricter rule: A. J. Krailsheimer, *Rabelais and the Franciscans* (Oxford, 1963), 8–9; Uzureau, "Couvent," 52, 60. As previously noted, it was Father Garnier de

Chapoüin who in 1614 had been approached by Samuel de Champlain, who would seek an expeditionary force of missionaries to accompany him to Canada the following year (F. Uzureau, "Un Recollet de la Baumette, missionaire au Canada," *Andegaviana* 22 (1921): 101–106).

45. Lewis, *Doctor,* 42. The establishment of Observant "Houses of Study" was yet another legacy of the ongoing internal factionalism that plagued the Franciscan order. While, as previously noted, Observant Franciscan groups such as the Recollets enjoyed berating their Coventual counterparts for their supposed lack of rigor, the Conventual counterretort usually targeted the Observants' lack of education, linking their fidelity to the Primitive Rule of St. Francis with his ambivalence toward higher education (Krailsheimer, *Rabelais,* 11). It was a mark of the Recollets' desire to combat these Conventual slurs that, in 1447, Franciscan Observant groups established an educational center for each of their provinces, "that we might not be accused of ignorance" (Moorman, *History,* 507). Though the life of scholarship may have originally been assumed as a defensive reaction to their Conventual colleagues and appears initially to have been regarded as a potential threat to devotional life, it soon became an established part of Observant practice. At Angers, the connection between La Baumette and the local university allowed the convent's friars to read for a degree.

46. University founding: Francois LeBrun, *Histoire d'Angers* (Toulouse, 1975), 328. Sacre: MácManners, *French Ecclesiastical,* 12–25; Uzureau, "Sacre d' Augers"; F. Uzureau, "Le Chapitre de la Cathédral d' Angers avant la Révolution: Processions," *Andegaviana* 24 (1925): 64–70.

47. Krailsheimer, *Rabelais,* 8.

48. F. Uzureau, "L'Assemblée de la Baumette-lès-Angers, 22 juillet," *Andegaviana* 33 (1939): 276–277.

49. The Recollets at La Baumette collectively observed the Divine Office, celebrating Matins, Lauds, Prime, Tierce, Sext, None, Vespers, and Compline, as laid out in the 1221 *Regula Non Bullata* or First Rule of St. Francis (Flood and Matura, *Birth,* 67–69). Until a papal bull in 1517 exempted them from it, Franciscans at La Baumette were obliged to say rather than sing the office in deference to the wishes of their founder, René of Anjou, who was concerned that the longer sung offices would cut into their time for personal prayer and meditation (Krailsheimer, *Rabelais,* 9; Uzureau, 15). It is possible that Pastedechouan, perhaps during the latter years of his stay, would have served as an altar boy during these religious observances, as he, like other young aboriginal boys in France, was probably "trained to piety and the service of the altar" (Le Clercq, *First Establishment,* 1: 235).

50. Quoted in *Uzureau,* "Le Couvent" 16.

51. Rabelais's presence at La Baumette is "an old, but quite unconfirmed, tradition" (Krailsheimer, *Rabelais*, 8). Long-standing attestations as well as references in Rabelais' writing make it very likely. Though Rabelais himself mentions La Baumette only once, describing its stables, which he probably had mucked out as a young student (*Pantagruel*, Book II) scholars have also found his work replete with other Anjou references: Donald Frame, *François Rabelais: A Study* (New York, 1977): paper 8; Lewis, *Doctor*, 41–49; Uzureau, "Couvent," 50.

52. Uzureau, "Couvent," 50.

53. Le Clercq, *First Establishment*, 1: 145–149.

54. Sagard, *Histoire*, 3: 785. Rohan's careful provision in his will for the continuation of Pastedechouan's education allowed it to continue even after Rohan's untimely 1622 death (F. Uzureau, "Baptême d'un Montagnais a la Cathedrale d'Angers, le 27 Avril 1621," *Le Canada Français* 4 (1922): 390–393; Le Clercq, *First Establishment*, 1: 235). Des Boves's death the following year, in contrast, was a devastating blow to the St. Charles Seminary, as the vicar general had failed to make similar provisions for his seminary. It is possible that, whilst in France, Pastedechouan met with two other generous donors to the Recollet cause, Henri de Bourbon, who was Prince of Condé, and Sieur Louis Hoüel, who had been instrumental in linking Champlain with the Recollets originally. Both these men were donors to Recollet building projects in Quebec (Brown et al., *Canadian Dictionary*, 1: 385–386; Jouve, *Dictionnaire*, 596–529).

55. Uzureau, "Baptême," 392 (my translation).

56. Algeirdas Julien Greimas and Teresa Mary Keane, eds., *Dictionnaire du moyen Français: La Renaissance* (Paris, 1992), 162–163.

57. Uzureau, "Baptême," 392–293 (my translation).

58. Dickason, *Myth*, 205–229; Christian Feest, ed., *Indians and Europe: An Interdisciplinary Collection of Essays* (Lincoln: University of Nebraska Press, 1999), 61–140. Though the baptism of Pastedechouan and other child converts in the seventeenth century would arguably provide a powerful new model of incorporation rather than exoticization, European collective curiosity about aboriginal alterity continued into the late nineteenth century and, some would argue, into our own times. For example, an ill-fated expedition of an 1880 contingent of fur-clad Labrador Inuit were exhibited to curious German crowds in much the same way as their ancestors had been in 1566 Antwerp (ibid. 61–68). Despite the fact that some of these Moravian-educated Innu shared the common Protestant worldview of their spectators, they were presented in a way that denied their confessional commonalities with their audiences while maximizing their alterity.

See Hartmut Lutz, *The Diary of Abraham Ulrikab: Text and Context.* (Ottawa, 2005).

59. Trudel, *Beginnings,* 37.
60. Feest, *Indians,* 131.
61. Uzureau, "Baptême," 393 (my translation).
62. French citizenship: Trigger, *Children,* 2: 456.
63. Cornelius Jaenen, personal communication with the author, 2004.
64. Le Caron, in Le Clercq, *First Establishment,* 1: 215.
65. Ibid., 216–222.
66. Ibid., 235.
67. Leon Pilatte, ed., *Edits, Déclarations et Arrests,* concernans la Réligion p. réformée 1662–1751. Paris: Librairie Fischbache and Co. 1885. 1885, p. 639.
68. Importance of observation in aboriginal education: Dickason, "Campaigns," 61–62; J. R. Miller, *Shinguak's Vision: A History of Native Residential Schools* (Toronto, 1996), 15–38. Rejection of physical punishments: Thwaites, *Jesuit Relations,* 1897, 6: 153–155. Horror at French abuse in the service of education was a widespread aboriginal reaction. See Dickason, "Campaigns," 61; Trigger, *Children,* 1: 263. Emphasis upon stoicism: Thwaites, *Jesuit Relations,* 6: 241.
69. Though the general contours of Pastedechouan's education are clear—"he had made much progress in Christianity, in the usages of the world and the French mode of life . . . [and] he had made great progress in Latin and in many natural and civil acquirements" (Le Clercq, *First Establishment,* 1: 235)—it is difficult to determine his precise program of studies or the texts he might have encountered. In keeping with Franciscan norms for what should be taught to lay people, Pastedechouan's theological education would likely have included his familiarization with the articles of faith, the Ten Commandments, the evangelical precepts, the works of mercy, the seven deadly sins, the seven virtues, and the sacraments: Bert Roest, *Franciscan Literature of Religious Instruction before the Council of Trent* (Leiden, 2004), 232. In terms of the actual textbooks that he used, it is possible that Pastedechouan encountered the Observant classic *Oratorio de religiosos* by Antonio de Guevara, which was published throughout Europe, undergoing at least seven editions between 1542 and 1605, and which discussed the internalization of religious virtues, the necessity of corporal mortification, and the nature of prayer (Roest, *Franciscan Literature,* 225–226).
70. "Abrège de la vie du Reverend Père Dolbeau." For a more general discussion on the evolution of the role of the novice master or guardian in Franciscan convents, see Roest, *Franciscan Literature,* 208, and Lewis, *Doctor,* 41–42.

71. Roest, *Franciscan Literature*, 209–211, 222–223; Krailsheimer, *Rabelais*, 9; Moorman, *History*, 508.
72. Roest, *Franciscan Literature*, 209.
73. McManners, *French Ecclesiastical*, 18. In all likelihood a similar pattern would have been observable for the previous century.
74. Bailey suggests that, as imposing church architecture took time to build, paintings and statues were even more critical at the beginning of encounters with aboriginal peoples (Bailey, *Art*, 35).
75. Sagard, *Histoire*, 3: 628–9; Gagnon, *Conversion*, 17–19. In addition to the public religious imagery of the convent and chapels, there are indications that missionaries also used the pictures in their personal breviaries to instruct potential converts. Paul Le Jeune, in a fit of missionary fervor, actually tore etchings from his breviary to decorate the provisional chapel he created while accompanying Pastedechouan's family band on their winter hunt (Thwaites, *Jesuit Relations*, 7: 149).
76. Francis Muel, *Front and Back: the Tapestry of the Apocalypse at Angers* (Nantes, 1996), 3–9.
77. The only real way to experience the impact of these massive, masterful works of art is to see them "in person," as it were. Though still officially the "treasure" of cathédral Saint-Maurice, they have, in a sense, come home, in that they are now safely displayed in René's magnificent Chateau d'Angers. However, books such as Muel's (*Front and Back*) give some idea of their detail and splendor.
78. Muel, *Front and Back*.
79. Sagard, *Histoire*, 3: 865. Fear of hell: Thwaites, *Jesuit Relations*, 7: 103
80. Rabelais probably experienced the 1518 plague at Angers, as reflected in the second book of Pantagruel (Lewis, *Doctor*, 48). Angers intermittently experienced outbreaks of the plague (in 1487–1497, 1518, 1552, 1565, 1582, 1584, 1586, 1598, 1600, 1602–1603, 1605, 1606, and 1626).
81. Thwaites, *Jesuit Relations*, 7: 89–91.
82. Louvet, Sagard, *Histoire*, 3: 785.
83. Sagard, *Histoire*, 2: 340; Trigger, *Children*, 1: 389.
84. Not much is known about Gabriel Sagard's early life. What is clear is that by 1604 he had joined the Recollets as a lay brother. In 1614 he was employed as a private secretary by Father Jacques Chapoüin, who had assisted Champlain with the provision of missionaries for Canada. Sagard himself was not selected for duty overseas until 1623. The future author of several multivolume works detailing the Recollets' Canadian escapades, Sagard would later chronicle Pastedechouan's 1625 return to Canada, his abortive missionary career, and his 1628 capture by the English. Sagard's writings reveal him to be a curious and observant man with a particularly

keen interest in the natural world; he tamed a pet muskrat while in Canada (Sagard, *Long Journey,* xv). Sagard remained a lay brother throughout his career, and in 1636, the year of his former teacher's death, he left the Recollets to join the rival Franciscan group, the Cordeliers. The date of his death is unknown.

85. Sagard, *Histoire,* 2: 334 (my translation). As discussed previously, the Innu at Tadoussac were often referred to simply as "the Canadians." Sagard's departure date: Brown et al., *Canadian Dictionary,* 1: 1966, 590; Sagard, *Long Journey,* xxxiv.

86. Le Clercq, *First Establishment,* 1: 235; Sagard, *Histoire,* 3: 785, 936; Thwaites, *Jesuit Relations,* 5: 109: François Du Creux, *The History of Canada or New France* (Toronto, 1951), 140.

87. Le Clercq, *First Establishment,* 1: 236.

88. Recollet father Joseph de la Roche-Daillon, of noble birth, had only a short career in New France. The date of his birth is unknown. After having arrived with Pastedechouan at Quebec in June of 1625, he became a missionary to the Neutral peoples (so called because they were allied with neither the Algonkian-Huron alliance nor the Iroquois confederacy). Following the fall of Quebec to the Kirke brothers in 1629, Roche-Daillon returned permanently to France, dying in Paris in 1656 (Le Clercq, *First Establishment,* 1: 234).

89. From 1625 to 1629, with the fall of Quebec to English forces, the Recollets and Jesuits would work peaceably together (Sagard, *Long Journey,* xxxvi). Following Recollet exclusion from New World missionization, however, they would blame the wealthier, more politically connected Jesuits for their snub (Sagard, *Histoire;* Le Clercq, *First Establishment*). Some modern historians have disputed this characterization, arguing, variously, that it was Recollet incompetence that was responsible or that the mechinations of other Franciscan factions were at fault.

90. Le Clercq, *First Establishment,* 1: 273.

91. Sagard, *Histoire,* 3: 785–786 (my translation); see also Le Clercq, *First Establishment,* 1: 273.

92. Le Clercq, *First Establishment,* 1: 274; Sagard, *Histoire,* 3: 786.

93. Thwaites, *Jesuit Relations,* 7: 287.

94. K. Tsianina Lomawaima, in *They Called It Prairie Light: The Story of the Chilocco Indian School* (Lincoln, Neb., 1994), xiv, postulates that similar factors were operative in late nineteenth- and early twentieth-century American residential schools for aboriginal students.

95. Thwaites, *Jesuit Relations,* 6: 85.

96. It was this second model that had characterized all Innu-French overseas encounters before that of Pastedechouan, which is one of the reasons his

changed mentality came as such a shock to his people. Both Savignon (see Biggar, *Works of Champlain*, 2: 142, 187; Trigger, *Children*, 1: 261–264), a Wendat youth who went to France ten years before Pastedechouan, and Amantacha (Louis de Sainte-Foi), another Wendat, who followed six years after him, are excellent examples of the drastic difference a few additional years of maturity can make in holding to a strong sense of self and in promoting reacceptance back into aboriginal society. Savignon was probably around eighteen years of age when traders took him to France in 1610. He appears to have proved resistant to religious education and was described by the Recollets as being too old to be an ideal student (Sagard, *Histoire*, 2: 330–322). Not only did Savignon hold to his own identity, but he was apparently trenchant in his criticisms of French society, though he may have been used as a literary mouthpiece for liberal French discontent. See Marc Lescarbot, *The History of New France* (Toronto, 1907), 3: 22. Amantacha (see Le Clercq, *First Establishment*, 1: 275–276; Thwaites, *Jesuit Relations*, 5: 239–245, 6: 21–23) was sent over to France in 1626, a year after Pastedechouan's return to Canada, at the age of sixteen. Regarded as a prize by both the Recollets and the Jesuits, after a protracted dispute he was educated under Jesuit rather than Recollet tutelage, following a magnificent baptismal ceremony in Rouen. Captured upon his attempted return to Canada, Amantacha was captured by British invaders in 1628. Prior to his 1629 return to Canada, he became a something of a celebrity in England, being featured in a local broadside verse (which J. Stevens Cox in Michael Harrison, ed., *Canada's Huguenot Heritage* Toronto, 1987, 149–163) reproduces without an awareness that the verses discussing the "Prince of Canaday" refer to Amantacha). Both Savignon and Amantacha appear to have reintegrated fairly smoothly into Huron society following their respective European soujourns. Certainly, both were accepted as legitimate hunters and warriors in a way denied Pastedechouan. The contrasting experiences of the three could suggest that Savignon's and Amatacha's completion of the religious and cultural rites of passage into aboriginal adulthood prior to their overseas journeys may have facilitated both a less psychologically destructive soujourn and an easier cultural reimmersion upon its conclusion. However, cultural differences between the Wendat and Innu cultures also have to be taken into account. While hunting was still critical to the definition of the Wendat male role, the provision of meat was not as critical in the Wendat context as it was in the Innu mileau because the Wendat relied upon agriculture for their main dietary staples, whereas the Innu did not.

97. Le Clercq, *First Establishment*, 1: 236, 184.
98. Trigger, *Children*, 1: 329, 363; Trudel, *Beginnings*, 98.
99. Bédard, *Protestants*, 14–15.

100. Laws against Protestants: Ibid., 9; Leslie Choquette, "A Colony of "Native French Catholics? The Protestants of New France in the Seventeenth and Eighteenth Centuries," in *Memory and Identity: The Huguenots in France and the Atlantic Diaspora,* ed. Bernard Van Ruymbeke and Randy Sparks (Columbia, S.C., 2003), 255. Singing of hymns: Robert Larin, *Brève histoire des protestants de Nouvelle France et au Quebec:* xvle–xixe siècles (St. Alphone du Granby, PG, 1998), 97.

101. Le Clercq, *First Establishment,* 1: 111.

102. Biggar, *Works of Champlain,* 5: 3–4. For more on the perceived link between Protestantism and potential political disloyalty to the throne, see Bédard, *Protestants,* 21.

103. Biggar, *Works of Champlain,* 6: 50–51.

104. Confessional tensions: Ibid., 5: 4, 50–51, Trigger, *Children,* 1: 362–363. Jesuit controversy: Bédard, *Protestants,* 73.

105. Sagard, *Histoire* 2: 498–515.

106. Small European population: Bédard, *Protestants,* 74. Innu seen as a threat: Biggar, *Works of Champlain,* 5: 124–125; Trigger, *Children,* 1: 363. Murders of Europeans by Innu: Trigger, *Children,* 363. Champlain's severity: Trigger, *Children,* 94–100, 363. Though Champlain's early career was characterized by its cultural accommodation to aboriginal groups, with his increasing power he quickly became more intolerant. Trigger sees the souring of Champlain's relations with the Innu as being the result of his emphasis upon sedentification and his high-handed attempts to render them subjects rather than partners (Trigger, *Children,* 274, 366, 380).

107. Le Clercq, *First Establishment,* 1: 274.

108. Ceremonial torture: Thwaites, *Jesuit Relations,* 5: 29–31, 55; Kenneth Morrison, *The Solidarity of Kin: Ethnohistory, Religious Studies, and the Algonkian-French Religious Encounter* (Albany, 2002), 68. Integration of war captives: Daniel Richter, *The Ordeal of the Longhouse: The Peoples of the Iroquois League in the Era of European Colonization* (Chapel Hill, N.C.; Williamsburg, Va., 1992), 32–58; Daniel Richter, "War and Culture: The Iroquois Experience," *William and Mary Quarterly* 40 (1983): 528–559.

109. Sagard, *Histoire,* 3: 628–9; Gagnon, *Conversion,* 17–19.

110. Sagard, *Histoire,* 2: 498–513; Jouve, *Franciscains,* 370–388. Splintering effects of Christianity on other aboriginal groups: Daniel Richter, "Iroquois versus Iroquois: Jesuit Missions and Christianity in Village Politics," *Ethnohistory* 32, no. 1 (1985): 1–16.

111. Sagard, *Histoire,* 2: 515 (my translation). Mathican Atic had several names, with several variant spellings. This is the version of his name used by Sagard, so I have reproduced it here. He was born Miristou (which is how he is listed in Brown et al., *Canadian Dictionary,* 508–509), the son of

Anadabijou, but assumed the name Mathican Atic (Sagard) or Mathigan Aticq Ouche (Champlain) upon his elevation to a position of some political power in 1622, with Champlain's aid.

112. Trigger, *Children,* 1: 193; Biggar, *Works of Champlain,* 1: 98–101.

113. Biggar, *Works of Champlain,* 1: 101–102.

114. Trigger, *Children,* 1: 562.

115. Sagard, *Histoire,* 2: 515–516.

116. Mathican Atic's position: Brown et al. *Canandian Dictionary,* 508–509;Trudel, *Beginnings,* 143. Naming child after missionary: Sagard, *Histoire,* 1: 64; Jouve, *Franciscans,* 371; Brown et al., *Canadian Dictionary,* 222.

3. **"I Have Not a Mind Strong Enough to Remain Firm"**

1. Pastedechouan captured: Gabriel Sagard, *Histoire du Canada* (Paris, 1866), vol. 4: 850–852. Tadoussac as the center of illegal trade: H. P. Biggar, *The Works of Samuel de Champlain* (Toronto, 1925), 5: 4, 50–51; Bruce Trigger, *The Children of Aatahaensic: A History of the Huron People to 1660* (Montreal, 1976), 1: 362–363. Exile of French after defeat: G. W. Brown et al., *Canadian Dictionary of Biography* (Toronto: 1966), 404–408; H. P. Biggar, *The Early Trading Companies of New France* (New York, 1965), 139–149; Marcel Trudel, *The Beginnings of New France, 1524–1663* (Toronto, 1973), 171–176; Marcel Trudel, *Histoire de la Nouvelle-France* (Montreal, 1963), 3: 32–34.

2. Rueben Gold Thwaites, ed. *The Jesuit Relations and Allied Documents* (Cleveland, 1898), 5: 41. See also Biggar, *Early Trading Companies,* 139, and Trudel, *Beginnings,* 171–173. For a fuller discussion of the Kirkes' parentage and nationality, see Biggar, *Early Trading Companies,* 139, and Leon Pouliot, "Que penser des frères Kirke?" *Le Bulletin des recherches historiques* 44, no. 11 (1938): 321–335. For reference to their birthplace, see Thwaites, *Jesuit Relations,* 5: 41. Jesuit Superior Paul Le Jeune describes the Kirkes as "Huguenots" of a Calvinist stripe, who imprisoned a Lutheran minister during their period in Quebec (Thwaites, *Jesuit Relations,* 5: 41, 49).

3. Pouliot, "Que Penser," 325; see also Brown et al., *Canadian Dictionary,* 405; Trudel, *Beginnings,* 172; and Lucien Campeau, *Monumenta Novae Franciae* (Quebec; Rome, 1987), 2: 831.

4. J. Stevens Cox in Michael Harrison, *Canada's Huguenot Heritage, 1685–1985* (Toronto: 1987), 149–163 (all spelling irregularities in the original). Cox reprints both the original woodcuts, as well as his own transcription of the broadsheet poem, which celebrates not the final victory of the Kirke brothers with Quebec's surrender of 1629 but their earlier victories further east at Tadoussac, which Pastedechouan personally experienced. It was written sometime between David Kirke's return to

England at the end of September 1628 and news of the fall of La Rochelle only weeks later. This is the same broadsheet ballad, referred to earlier, that celebrated the presence in London of Amantacha, the Rouen-educated young Wendat who was captured by English forces during his voyage home from France and brought to London. For more on Amantacha's experiences, see Brown et al., *Canadian Dictionary*, 1: 32; Christian Le Clercq, *First Establishment of the Faith in New France* (New York, 1881), 1: 275–276; Sagard, *Histoire*, vol. 5; Thwaites, *Jesuit Relations*, 6: 21–23; and Campeau, *Monumenta*, 2: 177–182, 203, 214, 799–800.

5. George M. Wrong, *The Rise and Fall of New France* (Toronto, 1928), 41–45, 50–61, 102–107, 144–145.

6. Banishment of Henrietta's entourage: Biggar, *Early Trading Companies*, 138; Wrong, *Rise*, 256–257. Seizure of English goods: Biggar, *Early Trading Companies*, 138–139. English support for Protestants at La Rochelle: Trudel, *Beginnings*, 172. Seventeenth-century spelling of Canada: Cox, *News from Canada*, 1628, 149–163. Exile of Protestants: Biggar, *Early Trading Companies*, 136–137. Strategy of the king: Biggar, *Early Trading Companies;* 139, Trudel, *Beginnings*, 172.

7. Sagard, *Histoire*, 4: 850–852.

8. Ibid. (my translation).

9. Trade jargon: Thwaites, *Jesuit Relations*, 5: 113–115, 151. French difficulties in learning native languages: Trudel, *Beginnings*, 155–159. Anti-Catholic allegations and their influence: Sagard, *Histoire*, 2: 498–515; Odoric Jouve, *Les Franciscains et le Canada* vol. 1: *L' Éstablissement de la foi* (Quebec, 1915), 370–388; Biggar, *Works of Champlain*, 5: 4, 50–51, 124–125; Trigger, *Children*, 1: 362–363.

10. Forced departure of Recollets: Trudel, *Beginnings*, 177.

11. As Pastedechouan's parents are almost entirely absent from the European historical record, a definitive statement as to when they died is impossible. However, the fact that they are nowhere mentioned in the Recollet and Jesuit accounts of Pastedechouan's relationship with his family suggests that they had predeceased their four sons, likely before Pastedechouan's 1625 return from France. If Pastedechouan had sisters, they are nowhere mentioned in the extant European record.

12. Thwaites, *Jesuit Relations*, 7: 69. Much of our evidence as to the characters, propensities, occupations, and approximate ages of Pastedechouan's three brothers comes from the writings of Jesuit Superior Paul Le Jeune, Pastedechouan's erstwhile biographer, who became intimately acquainted with the two eldest members of the family, Carigonan and Mestigoit, between his arrival in 1632 and the brothers' successive deaths in, respectively, 1634 and 1635. As Recollet writings contain far fewer references to Pastedechouan's family, the brief sketches of the brothers provided here are

drawn retrospectively from this Jesuit's slightly later writings of 1632–1636 (Thwaites, *Jesuit Relations*, vols. 5–7).

13. Ibid., 7: 109. Sasousmat's relative obscurity is largely due to the fact that he, unlike his three brothers, did not go on the 1633–1634 winter hunt, which Le Jeune, also a participant, would later immortalize in his *Relation of 1634*. It is this single, rich source which gives us the best insight into the character and actions of the rest of the family, including Pastedechouan. See Thwaites, *Jesuit Relations*, 7: Alain Beaulieu, *Convertir le fils de Cain: Jesuits et Amerindiens nomades en Nouvelle France, 1632–1642* (Saint Jean, PQ, 1999); Guy LaFlèche, *Relation de 1634 de Paul Le Jeune: Le Missionaire, l'apostat, le sorcier* (Montreal, 1973). Almost all of the little that we know of Sasousmat was recorded by Jean de Brebeuf, the acting Superior in Le Jeune's stead, who converted and ministered to the ill young man in the months preceding his death at the Jesuit residence (Thwaites, *Jesuit Relations*, 7: 109–113; see also 6: 119–121).

14. Because Pastedechouan was not viewed as much of a marital "catch," it is likely that it was Sasousmat who initiated intermarriage with Manitougatche's family and who then introduced one of the headman's daughters to his younger brother. The fact that Sasousmat was associated with Manitougatche, who appears to have played an informal evangelical role among his large extended family and to have had an exceptionally close relationship with European missionaries both before the fall of Quebec and after the return of the French (Thwaites, *Jesuit Relations*, 5: 57, 117, 119, 137–139, 161–163, 167, 6: 109–115, 117–121, 137) makes it difficult to determine whether Sasousmat's interest in Christianity was triggered by the influence of his father-in-law, his younger brother, or both.

15. In more easterly Acadian colony, which had a chronic shortage of priests, colonial Catholics survived by improvising their own forms of collective ritual engagement, such as the "messe blanche" or "dry mass," which laypeople could perform in the absence of clerics. It is interesting to speculate whether, had the historical case been reversed and Pastedechouan had been a Protestant convert isolated from his Huguenot mentors, his ability to retain his adopted faith amid the counterpull of traditional Innu religion would have been any different.

16. Thwaites, *Jesuit Relations*, 5: 39, 45, 57.

17. Le Clercq, *First Establishment*, 1: 216; Thwaites, *Jesuit Relations*, 6: 175–177; Beaulieu, *Convertir*, 32–33; Kenneth Morrison, "Baptism and Alliance: The Symbolic Mediations of Religious Syncretism," *Ethnohistory* 37 (1990): 418–419; Kenneth Morrison, *The Solidarity of Kin: Ethnohistory, Religious Studies, and the Algonkian-French Religious Encounter* (Albany, 2002), 1–39.

18. Thwaites, *Jesuit Relations*, 5: 175, 7: 71, 171–175; Peter Armitage, "Reli-

gious Ideology Among the Innu of Eastern Quebec and Labrador," *Religiologiques,* vol. 6 (1992): 78.

19. Ibid., 7: 105, 171.

20. Naomi Adelson, *"Being Alive Well": Health and the Politics of Cree Wellbeing* (Toronto, 2000), 89. The Innu, however, had very similar stories: Frank Speck, *Naskapi: The Savage Hunters of the Labrador Penninsula* (Norman, Okla., 1935), 90; Armitage, "Religious Ideology," 93.

21. Alfred Goldsworthy Bailey, *The Conflict of European and Eastern Algonkian Cultures: A Study in Canadian Civilization* (Toronto, 1969), 136; Diamond Jenness, *Indians of Canada* (Ottawa, 1932), 273; K. Pritzker, *A Native American Encyclopedia* (Oxford, 2000), 508; Beaulieu, *Convertir,* 30; Daniel K. Richter, "War and Culture," *William and Mary Quarterly* 40 (1983): 528–530.

22. Thwaites, *Jesuit Relations,* 7: 173–175.

23. Pastedechouan was married, according to Jesuit missionary Paul Le Jeune, as many as four or five times. Each successive marriage failed, as each wife in turn deserted him. (Thwaites, *Jesuit Relations,* 7: 173).

24. Ibid., 5: 11.

25. Ibid., 267, 5: 31.

26. Ibid., 5: 45. With the exceptions of the Jesuit incursions into Acadia in 1611–1613 and the Jesuits' joint foray with the Recollets between 1625 and 1629, the Canadian mission field had been dominated by the Recollets, though even at its height it encompassed only a handful of scattered missionaries. Le Jeune's arrival signaled the beginning of the forty-year exclusion of Pastedechouan's erstwhile Recollet hosts, as Cardinal Richelieu, impatient with their paltry results and chronic funding issues, in 1632 offered the conversion of Canada exclusively to the Jesuits, whom he perceived as better funded and organized.

27. Ibid., 5: 33. Sedentification: Ibid., 5: 33–35, 7: 145–151. Jesuit commitment to focus on children: Ibid., 7: 83–89.

28. On Le Jeune's first encounter with aboriginal peoples: Ibid., 5: 23. On Massé: Born with the first name Nesmes in 1575 Lyons, Massé entered the Society of Jesuit as a novice in 1595, taking the name Enenmond. He was selected as a missionary to Acadia in 1611, earning the nickname "Père Utile" for his levelheadedness and practical skills. Upon his return to France, he was posted at the University of Clermont, which is where he would have encountered the young Le Jeune. For the next eleven years, Massé reportedly practiced austerities to render himself worthy of returning to the New World. In the spring of 1625 he got his wish, decamping for Canada with Pastedechouan, his Recollet mentors, and two other Jesuits, Charles Lallement and Jean de Brebeuf (Le Clercq, *First Establish-*

ment, 1: 234). Between 1625 and the French exile in September 1629, Massé was responsible for directing the building of the Jesuit quarters at Quebec. Massé remained as a missionary until his death in 1646 at Sillery, the settlement near Quebec that the French had established with the hope of rendering the Innu sedentary. A master of the Innu language, in his latter years Massé would teach it to his fellow missionaries.

29. Thwaites, *Jesuit Relations,* 7: 239, vol. 5: 215, 43–45. Le Jeune's conversion: LaFlèche, *Relation,* xvi. Le Jeune's early life: Brown et al., *Canadian Dictionary,* 1: 453–457; Campeau, *Monumenta,* 2: 837–838; Beaulieu, *Convertir,* 13–34; Dominique Deffain, *Un voyageur français en Nouvelle France au XVII siècle: étude littéraire des Relations du Père Paul Le Jeune (1632–1641)* (Tubingen, 1995), 22–29; Réal Ouellet, *Rhétorique de conquete missionaire: le Jésuite Paul Lejeune* (Sillery, PQ: 1993), 2–20. LaFlèche, *Relation,* provides a bibliography of the manuscript sources for Le Jeune's life (i–xix).

30. Allan Greer, "Colonial Saints: Gender, Race, and Hagiography in New France," *William and Mary Quarterly,* 3rd ser., 57 (2000): 17; Barbara Diefendorf, *Beneath the Cross: Catholics and Huguenots in Sixteenth-Century Paris* (Oxford, 1991), 49–63; Barbara Diefendorf, "Houses Divided: Religious Schism in Sixteenth-Century Parisian Families," in *Urban Life and the Renaissance,* ed. Susan Zimmerman and Ronald Weissman, Newark, Del., 1989), 80–99; Phillip Benedict, "The Catholic Response to Protestantism: Church Activity and Popular Piety in Roeun, 1580–1600," in *Religion and the People,* ed. J. Obelkevich (Chapel Hill, N.C., 1979), 27.

31. Peter A. Goddard, "Converting the Sauvage: Jesuit and Montagnais in Seventeenth-Century New France," *Catholic Historical Review* 84, no. 2. (1998): 225.

32. Thwaites, *Jesuit Relations,* 5: 113–115, 151.

33. Ibid., 5: 107. Professional translators: Ibid., 5: 113–115; see also Kenneth Morrison, "Discourse and the Accomodation of Values: Toward a Revision of Mission History," *Journal of the American Academy of Religion* 103, no. 3 (1985): 368.

34. Thwaites, *Jesuit Relations,* 5: 109.

35. Ibid., 5: 109–111.

36. Ibid.; see also François Du Creux, *The History of Canada or New France* (Toronto, 1951), 1: 140–141.

37. Thwaites, *Jesuit Relations,* 6: 119; see also ibid., 5: 109–111; Du Creux, *History,* 1: 140–141.

38. Thwaites, *Jesuit Relations,* 5: 109.

39. Ibid., 5: 107.

40. Le Clercq, *First Establishment,* 1: 273.

41. Thwaites, *Jesuit Relations,* 7: 173, 91.

42. Ibid., 5: 45, 107.

43. Duplessis-Bochart was Emery de Cäen's lieutenant (ibid., 5: 283). Le Jeune often turned to Duplessie-Bochart when he needed assistance with the practical implementation of pious good works. The two collaborated on an ultimately unsuccessful attempt to send Iroquois prisoners of war who were to be executed by the Innu to France (ibid., 5: 45–47). Duplessis-Bochart was also helpful in providing free passage for young aboriginal children being sent to France for Jesuit education (ibid., 6: 89).

44. Du Creux, *History,* 1: 141. See also Thwaites, *Jesuit Relations,* 5: 111.

45. Thwaites, *Jesuit Relations,* 7: 89.

46. Prayer and confession: Ibid., 5: 117, 173. Fears of hell: Ibid., 7: 89–91, 165–167.

47. Du Creux, *History,* 1: 141; see also Thwaites, *Jesuit Relations,* 5: 111. Seventeenth-century aboriginal peoples frequently utilized elements of French dress. However (in a move reminiscent of their religious relativism), they did so without abandoning their own clothing, using French articles as a supplement rather than as a replacement. Thus, while many aboriginals wore hats, shirts, or other pieces of French clothing (ibid., 5: 27), the sporting of an entire suit would have been highly unusual and would have visually signaled its wearer's incorporation into French society.

48. On damaged Jesuit residence: Thwaites, *Jesuit Relations,* 5: 39, 45, 57, 6: 71–73. On Pastedechouan's strategies: There is no indication that the young man ever taught other members of the Society of Jesus. Le Jeune's apparent plan was to coax the rudiments of the language from Pastedechouan, deduce its grammar and syntax, and then have his fellow missionaries systematically study the resultant work (ibid., 5: 111–113). This system, though likely instituted as a time-saving measure, might also, when less charitably read, be accounted a mark of Le Jeune's arrogance in presuming that he could teach his European colleagues better than could a trilingual native speaker.

49. Ibid., 5: 107–113, 173–177.

50. Ibid., 5: 111, 175, 187–189. Education of Sagard: Sagard, *Histoire,* 2: 334.

51. Thwaites, *Jesuit Relations,* 5: 191. Jesuit commitment to learning native languages: Ibid., 5: 33–35, 111–115. Perceived inevitability of conversions: Ibid., 5: 33–35, 191–195.

52. Ibid., 5: 113, 283–285. Marsolet likely came to Canada with Champlain and quickly learned a range of aboriginal languages. He deserted to the English following the Kirkes' successful takeover of Quebec in 1629. Though Marsolet later was to protest that his assistance to the English was coerced, his repeatedly refusals to teach aboriginal languages to either French administrative or religious agents is suggestive. Charles Lallemant, Le Jeune's predecessor, was successful in prevailing upon Marsolet to share

some of his knowledge, which he wrote down, but Le Jeune states that, as Marsolet's nowhere explained the grammar of native languages, these scribbles were of only limited use (ibid., 5: 113). For a thumbnail sketch on the linguistic difficulties facing the newly arrived Jesuits, see Margaret Leahey, "'Comment peut un muet prescher l'evangile?' Jesuit Missionaries and the Native Languagues of New France," *French Historical Studies* 19, no. 1, (1995): 101–131; Olive Dickason, *The Myth of the Savage and the Beginnings of French Colonialism in the Americas* (Edmonton, 1997), 254–257; Morrison, "Discourse," 368–370; and Trudel, *Beginnings,* 156–159.

53. Thwaites, *Jesuit Relations,* 5: 111, 187. Tobacco inducements: Ibid., 5: 113.

54. Ibid., 5: 107.

55. On infrequency of Pastedechouan's participation: 5: 173. On schedule of lay Catholic devotion: Ibid., 6: 103.

56. Ibid., 6: 173. In addition to the general observance of abstension from eating meat, Le Jeune recounts the pentitential feats of several of the colony's laypeople, including a young man who, in fullfillment of a vow to Jesus, walked the entire distance from the fort at Quebec to the Jesuit residence several miles inland, traveling through the snow in his bare feet "to offset the licentiousness which is carried on in other placed during the Carnival" (ibid., 6: 103–105).

57. Ibid., 6: 69. The Jesuit residence was a small four-roomed building that had to accommodate priests, donnés, workers, and aboriginal students. The Jesuits themselves shared small cells, the working men had a room in which they cohabitated, and guests and resident aboriginals were likely consigned to sleeping in a "garret" described as being "so low that no one can dwell there."

58. Ibid., 5: 173–175.

59. Ibid., 7: 159–167.

60. Ibid., 7: 173.

61. Ibid., 5: 175.

62. Pastedechouan's date of departure: Ibid., 5: 175. Attempts to prompt his return: Ibid., 7: 67.

63. Ibid., 5: 111; Du Creux, *History,* 1: 141.

64. Thwaites, *Jesuit Relations,* 5: 117.

65. Ibid., 5: 121. Manitougatche's adoption of agriculture: Ibid., 5: 57, 6: 117–121.

66. Ibid., 5: 57, 117, 119, 137–139, 161–163, 167, 6: 109–115, 137.

67. Ibid., 18: 79; Olive P. Dickason, "Campaigns to Capture Young Maids: A Look at Early Attempts in Colonial Mexico and New France to Remold Amerindians," *Historical Papers* (1987): 63–65; Greer, "Colonial," 13; Allan Greer, "Conversion and Identity: Iroquois Christianity in Seventeenth-

Century New France," in *Conversion: Old Worlds and New,* ed. A. Grafton and K. Mills (Rochester, 2003), 181–187; Allan Greer, *Mohawk Saint: Catherine Tekakwitha and the Jesuits* (Oxford, 2005), 100–105; Goddard, *Converting,* 237–238; Cornelius Jaenen, "Education for Francization: The Case of New France in the Seventeenth Century" in *Indian Education in Canada,* vol. 1: *The Legacy,* ed. Jean Barman, Yvonne Hebert, and Don Mc-Caskill (Vancouver, 1986), 48–50; McCaskill Beaulieu, *Convertir,* 73–76, 144–150; John Webster Grant, *Moon of Wintertime: Missionaries and the Indians of Canada in Encounter since 1534* (Toronto, 1984), 16–24; Carole Blackburn, *Harvest of Souls: The Jesuit Missions and Colonialism in North America, 1632–1650* (Montreal, 2000), 3–15; James Axtell, *Beyond 1492: Encounters in Colonial North America* (New York, 1992), 34–40.

68. Thwaites, *Jesuit Relations,* 5: 117. Inability to force views: Ibid., 5: 191–195; see also Morrison, "Discourse," 369–370; Dickason, "Campaigns," 44–66; Cornelius Jaenen, *Friend and Foe: Aspects of Amerindian Cultural Contact in the Sixteenth and Seventeenth Centuries* (New York, 1976), 70–71; Greer, "Colonial," 10–13; Greer, *Conversion,* 179.

69. Thwaites, *Jesuit Relations,* 5: 119. Initial emphasis on doctrinal knowledge: Le Clercq, *First Establishment,* 1: 235–236. Introduction of collective ritual practice: Greer, Mohawk, 89–100; Greer, "Conversion," 175–198. New focus on adults: Thwaites, *Jesuit Relations,* 18: 79; Jaenen, "Education," 48–50; Beaulieu, *Convertir,* 73–76, 144–150.

70. Propensity to focus upon children: Thwaites, *Jesuit Relations,* 5: 151, 6: 83–89, 151–155, 7: 227, 265, 9: 103, 109; see also Dickason, *Myth,* 258–260. Le Jeune's descriptions of Manitougatche: Thwaites, *Jesuit Relations,* 5: 107, 117–121, 6: 117–125. Hypothetical place of Manitougatche: Thwaites, *Jesuit Relations,* 5: 117; see also Dickason, Myth, 263–264.

71. Thwaites, *Jesuit Relations,* 5: 117, 7:00 275.

72. Ibid., 5: 159–161.

73. Le Jeune records only two incidents in which Pastedechouan overtly questioned Catholic theology or ritual practice. In late January of 1633 Pastedechouan expressed concerns regarding Lenten fasting (Thwaites, *Jesuit Relations,* 5: 173). The following winter he launched a far more trenchant anti-Christian campaign that utilized themes of deprivation to challenge Le Jeune's presentation of God's benevolence (Ibid., 7: 159–167). While precient and passionately argued, Pastedechouan's comments challenged neither God's existence (merely his nature) nor the authority of his missionary representatives (in fact, he conflated God's presumed perspectives with those of Le Jeune, his instrument).

74. Le Clercq, *First Establishment,* 1: 235; Sagard, *Histoire,* 3: 785, 936; Thwaites, *Jesuit Relations,* 5: 109; Du Creux, History, 1: 140.

75. Le Clercq, *First Establishment,* 1: 141–142, 217, 221; Thwaites, *Jesuit Relations,* 5: 159–161, 7: 69–71, 85–87, 99–103, 129–135, 145–147, 153–154, 165–167; Axtell, *Beyond 1492,* 78–83.
76. Thwaites, *Jesuit Relations,* 5: 137; ibid., 9: 225. Biography of Fortune: Campeau, *Monumenta,* 2: 803.
77. Thwaites, *Jesuit Relations,* 7: 125, 239, 18: 79. Other aboriginal residents at Notre Dame des Anges: Ibid., 5: 137, 167. During the five months that Pastedechouan was in residence, the Jesuits' provisional boarding school lodged, in addition to Fortune, Bienvenue, a seven-year-old Innu boy; an unnamed black slave brought by the English and subsequently given by his pious French owners to the Jesuits; and a sickly three-year-old whom Le Jeune had promised to nurse until the child's inevitable death. At least two other aboriginal children briefly stayed at the residence on their way to France in accordance with the Superior's plan to send at least one student a year abroad. Le Jeune's Augustinianism: Ibid., 7: 231–233; Charles Principe, "A Moral Portrait of the Indian of the St. Lawrence in One Relation of New France," *Historical Studies* 57 (1990): 32–47; Charles Principe, "Trois Relations de la Nouvelle France écrites par le Père Paul Le Jeune," *Cahiers de l'Association internationale des études françaises* 27 (1975): 87–95; Peter Goddard, "Augustine and the Amerindian in Seventeenth Century New France," *Church History* 67, no. 4 (1998): 665–681, particularly 673–679; Goddard, "Converting," 224–225. Le Jeune's perceptions of aboriginal morality: Thwaites, *Jesuit Relations,* 6: 69, 231–239; Principe, "A Moral," 40–44.
78. Thwaites, *Jesuit Relations,* 5: 137–139, 163, 171.
79. Ibid., 5: 139; see also 5: 57.
80. Ibid., 5: 197, 221, 6: 153–155.
81. Ibid., 6: 85.
82. Ibid., 9: 223; see also ibid., 9: 71–73, 221–222. Though we cannot establish definitively when these incidents took place, it is likely that they occurred sometime between December 21, 1632, when Fortune entered Notre Dame des Anges, and March 27, 1633, when Pastedechouan left it, as Pastedechouan never again lived at the Jesuit residence and was absent from Quebec from October 1633 to April 1634. Fortune himself was sent to France sometime between 1633 and 1635, and both young men died in 1636, Pastedechouan sometime during the winter and Fortune in May. Thus, while it is possible that these episodes occurred while Pastedechouan was visiting the residence sometime between the spring of 1634 and his death in 1636, he would have had more ample opportunity and likely greater motive while the two were cohabitating at Notre Dame des Anges during the winter of 1632–1633.

83. Ibid., 5: 175, 215.
84. Ibid., 5: 177.
85. Ibid., 18: 79.

4.   "God Has Let His Thunderbolts Fall"

1. Rueben Gold Thwaites, ed., *Jesuit Relations and Allied Documents,*
   1610–1791 (Cleveland, 1898), 7: 145, 147.
2. Ibid., 7: 149.
3. Ibid., 7: 153. Makeup of the Innu group: Ibid., 7: 73. The original group
   that left Quebec on October 18, 1633, was composed of twenty Innu men,
   women, and children. When their band merged with another in mid-
   November, their numbers temporarily reached forty-four (ibid., 107). As was
   typical of winter hunting bands, the group's numbers fluctuated, as it amal-
   gamated, when necessary, with other hunting bands, combining forces and
   then separating once again when there wasn't enough food to support a larger
   group. Le Jeune's perception of Carigonan: Ibid., 7: 153.
4. Le Jeune was the sole European in the band. All the rest were aboriginal.
   With the exception of a young Iroquois prisoner of war (ibid., 7: 159, 171)
   and Pastedechouan's wife, described as "of another nation" (ibid., 7: 69,
   175), the group was exclusively Innu.
5. Ibid., 7: 31, 55, 71, 6: 187; see also Kenneth Morrison, "Discourse and the
   Acommodation of Values: Toward a Revision of Mission History," *Journal*
   of the American Academy of Religion 10, no. 3 (1985): 372–373, 376.
6. Thwaites, *Jesuit Relations,* 1898, 5: 215. Le Jeune's evaluation of spiritual
   proclivities: Ibid., 5: 175–177.
7. Ibid., 7: 67–69.
8. Ibid., 7: 71; see also François Du Creux, *The History of Canada or New*
   France (Toronto, 1951), 1: 140.
9. Retracing of their journey: Adrien Caron, "La Mission de Père Paul Le
   Jeune, S. J., sur la Côte-du-Sud, 1633–1634," *Revue d'histoire de l'Amérique*
   française 17, no. 3 (1963): 371–395.
10. Thwaites, *Jesuit Relations,* 7: 169.
11. Ibid., 7: 35–45, 55, 117–121, 129–131, 6: 187, 227. Circumstances did not
    permit Le Jeune's erection of a separate shelter, which Jesuits generally in-
    sisted upon, in order to have more peace and privacy for devotional activ-
    ities, and to protect "religious eyes" from "the sight of so much lewdness,
    carried on openly" (ibid., 4: 197), as Charles Lallement had written in
    1626.
12. Thwaites, *Jesuit Relations,* 7: 63, 173.
13. Ibid., 7: 73–75. Alcohol was seen by the Innu as a captivating force that

undermined the rational thought of those who imbibed it. The Innu generally attributed rash or violent acts committed under the influence as the wishes of the invasive force itself, rather than of its "host" (Ibid., 5: 51); Cornelius Jaenen, *Friend and Foe: Aspects of Amerindian Cultural Contact in the Sixteen and Seventeenth Centuries* (New York, 1976), 116–118.

14. Thwaites, *Jesuit Relations* 7: 73–75.

15. Thwaites, *Jesuit Relations,* 7: 75–77.

16. Ibid., 7: 77. The name of Mestigoit's wife is not recorded, nor is that of Pastedechouan's. This is unfortunately typical of the male-oriented focus of the Jesuit *Relations* as a genre.

17. It is unlikely that Pastedechouan's threats to kill the missionary would have been welcomed by the Innu group. His elder brother Mestigoit had taken responsibility for the Superior's safety, earnestly promising his own life as forfeit should the Jesuit die while in his custody (ibid., 7: 71–73). The deliberate murder of Le Jeune would have guaranteed that the wrath of the civic administration would fall very hard upon the tiny band.

18. Ibid., 7: 89–91.

19. Ibid., 7: 69–71. Carigonan's initial invitation: Ibid., vol. VII, 69–71. Carigonan's attitude of religious relativism and his desire to incorporate Christianity into his Innu belief system is also prevalent among his contemporary descendants. See Peter Armitage, "Religious Ideology Among the Innu of Eastern Quebec and Labrador," *Religiologiques,* vol. 6 (1992); 66–67.

20. Ibid., 7: 131, 69. Jesuit diabolism and Jesuit-shaman relations in seventeenth-century Canada: Peter A. Goddard, "The Devil in New France: Jesuit Demonology," *Canadian Historical Review* 78, no. 1 (1997): 40–62; Guy LaFlèche, *Relation de 1634 de Paul Le Jeune: le missionaire, l'apostat, le sorcier* (Montreal, 1973), 137–160. Pierre Berthiaume, "Paul Lejeune ou le missionaire possédé" Voix et Images, vol. 23, no. 3 (1998): 529–543.

21. Thwaites, *Jesuit Relations,* 6: 169.

22. Jesuit analysis of shaman's roles: Ibid., 5: 57, 65, 159, 6: 199–201, 7: 89, 93; Peter A. Goddard, "Augustine and the Amerindian in Seventeenth-Century New France," *Church History* 64, no. 4 (1998): 55–59.

23. Thwaites, *Jesuit Relations,*7: 57; see also 7: 59–65, 117.

24. Ibid., 6: 165–167. Discussions of epistomology: Ibid., 7: 101–103, 123–125, 165, 6: 181. Discussions of the afterlife: Ibid., 7: 135, 6: 179–181. Discussions of supernatural beings: Ibid., 7: 101–103, 6: 171–173. Such extensive and imaginative engagement contradicts the arguments of Bruce Trigger in *Natives and Newcomers: Canada's "Heroic Age" Reconsidered* (Kingston, ON, 1985), 294; Trigger has suggested that because the mental universes of aboriginal people and early modern missionaries were so different, their ability

to engage in mutually comprehensible dialogue regarding religion was highly limited, if not impossible. The encounter between Le Jeune and Past-edechouan's family suggests, to the contrary, that they were able to challenge one another by probing and interpreting the meaning of everyday events, in a manner that confirmed their own religious preconceptions.

25. Thwaites, *Jesuit Relations,* 7: 61, 181–183, 299–301. But Carigonan, in turn, exploited this technique, blaspheming the Christian God and triumphantly noting how the punishments threatened by an affronted Le Jeune failed to materialize.

26. Ibid., 7: 61–63. Avoidance of antisocial emotions: Ibid., 6: 231; Morrison, "Discourse," 371–375.

27. Thwaites, *Jesuit Relations,* 7: 131–133.

28. Ibid.

29. I Kings 18: 21–40.

30. Christian Le Clercq, *First Establishment of the Faith in New France* (New York, 1881), 1: 141–142, 217, 221; Trigger, *The Children of Aataentsic: A History of the Huron People to 1660* (Montreal, 1976), 1: 193.

31. Thwaites, *Jesuit Relations,* 7: 165, 179.

32. Ibid., 7: 103. Le Jeune's attempts to convert Carigonan's wife: Ibid., 7: 103, 123–125.

33. Ibid., 7: 167. Pastedechouan's fears of hell: Ibid., 7: 103.

34. Ibid., 6: 167.

35. Ibid., 7: 159.

36. Ibid., 7: 167, 185.

37. Ibid., 7: 163, 165.

38. Ibid., 6: 283; Morrison, "Discourse," 375.

39. Thwaites, *Jesuit Relations,* 7: 9. Jesuit perceptions of Innu feasting as "gluttony": Ibid., 7: 163, 6: 283–285.

40. Le Clercq, First Establishment, 1: 141–142, 217, 221; Trigger, Children, 1: 193, Thomas L. Altherr, "Flesh Is Paradise of the Man of Flesh: Cultural Conflict over Indian Hunting Beliefs and Rituals in New France as Recorded in the "Jesuit Relations," *Canadian Historical Review* 64, no. 2 (1983): 274–275.

41. Thwaites, *Jesuit Relations,* 7: 185.

42. Ibid., 7: 161–163. Ironically, Le Jeune's own name closely approximates the French word for a fast (le jeûne).

43. Ibid., 5: 165, 179, 6: 211, 221, 283, 5: 165–167.

44. Ibid., 7: 163.

45. Ibid., 7: 61–63.

46. Le Jeune's attitude is evident in his choice of the chapter title "What One Must Suffer in Wintering with the Savages" (ibid., 7: 35), which seems to

suggest that their behavior has nothing to do with his own chosen course of conduct.

47. Ibid., 7: 63. Le Jeune's refusal to share items: Ibid., 7: 55–57, 137, 237–239, 5: 171. His refusal to transport his belongings: Ibid., 7: 115.

48. Ibid., 7: 161.

49. Ibid., 7: 33, 51–53.

50. Ibid., 7: 51, 179–181.

51. Ibid., 6: 39–41, 7: 51.

52. Mestigoit's analysis has been seconded by contemporary commentators. Morrison also describes Le Jeune's illness as "the psychosomatic reactions to culture shock" ("Discourse," 376). (Pierre Berthiaume, "Paul Lejeune ou le missionnaire possédé," Voix et Images, vol. 23, no. 3 (1998) suggests that Le Jeune's position within the hostile group and his belief that Carigonan did have dark powers negatively affected his health.

53. Thwaites, *Jesuit Relations,* 7: 83; see also 7: 85, 105, 191.

54. Ibid., 5: 63.

55. Ibid., 7: 191.

56. Ibid., 7: 181.

57. Le Jeune's contradictory aims: Ibid., 7: 85–87, 183. I postulated earlier that Le Jeune may have taken as his model the Hebrew Bible figure of Elijah in his energetic (and henothetic) contests with the priests of Baal, in which there is a similar ambivalence regarding the ontological status of figures: are they nonexistent or simply inferior? Le Jeune's actions perceived as foolhardy: Ibid., 7: 183.

58. Morrison, "Discourse," 374.

59. Thwaites, *Jesuit Relations,* 7: 195, 197. Mestigoit's responsibility for Le Jeune: Thwaites, *Jesuit Relations,* 7: 195. Motivated by the promise of two payments of supplies for the group, Mestigoit willingly assumed responsibility for the Superior, apparently reassuring the governor by saying, "If the Father dies, I will die with him, and you will never see me in this country again" (ibid., 73).

60. Ibid., 6: 39–41. Stabilizing health: Ibid., 7: 179. Inability to write: Ibid., 7: 211.

61. Ibid., 6: 61. Le Jeune's self-blame: Ibid., 6: 39–41.

62. Le Jeune wrote his first two *Relations* (for 1632 and 1633) without knowing that they would be published by his superiors. However, in preparing his manuscript of the 1634 *Relation,* he was well aware of his audience and, accordingly, expanded and more clearly categorized the information in his report, utilizing chapter divisions for the first time. See Morrison, "Discourse," 367; LaFlèche, *Relation,* 3–5; LaBras et al., *L'Amerindien dans*

les Relations du père Paul Le Jeune: Études sur la relation de voyage en Nouvelle France (Sainte-Foy, PQ: 1994), 1–10); Beaulieu, *Convertir,* 2–5.

63. Thwaites, *Jesuit Relations,* 6: 109–115.
64. Ibid., 6: 195–201; see also 7: 299–301, 9: 69.
65. Ibid., 7: 195–209, 299–301, 9: 69.
66. It is nowhere noted in the European record whether Pastedechouan had any children. The fact that he married four or five times would suggest that he must have fathered offspring, who may have accompanied their mothers as each, successively, left him. However, had Pastedechouan had children, it is almost certain that Le Jeune would have attempted to pressure the young man to have them instructed and baptized, and this is nowhere mentioned in the extant record. Alternatively, it is possible that Pastedechouan's childhood illness in France (ibid., 7: 89–91), which could have been the mumps, may have rendered him sterile.
67. Ibid., 7: 303.
68. Ibid., 7: 89–91.
69. Ibid., 7: 103, 113–115.
70. Ibid., 9: 71 7: 173.
71. Ibid., 9: 69–71; see also 7: 299–301.
72. Ibid., 6: 109–127.
73. Ibid., 9: 69.
74. Le Clercq, *First Establishment,* 1: 142.
75. Thwaites, *Jesuit Relations,*7: 301; see also 7: 299–300, 9: 69.
76. Ibid., 9: 69–73.
77. Ibid., 9: 71.
78. Ibid.
79. Ibid., 7: 113–115; see also 7: 103.
80. Ibid., 6: 215; Diamond Jenness, *Indians of Canada* (Ottawa, 1932), 273; Thwaites, *Jesuit Relations,* 6: 215; Frank Speck, *Naskapi: Savage Hunters of the Labrador Penninsula* (Normon, Okla., 1935), 140–163.
81. Thwaites, *Jesuit Relations,* 7: 185.
82. Ibid., 5: 177.
83. Ibid., 6: 109–135.
84. Ibid., 5: 173. A. Lynn Martin, Jesuits and Confession: *The Jesuit Mind: The Mentality of an Elite in Early Modern France* (Ithaca, NY), 1988, 120–124; John O'Malley, *The First Jesuits* (Cambridge, Mass., 1993), 175–179.
85. Goddard, "Devil," 56–57, Jean Delameau, *La péché et la peur* (Paris, 1983), 369–400; François-Marc Gagnon, *La Conversion par l'image: un aspect de la mission des jésuites auprès des Indiens du Canada au XVIIe siècle* (Montreal, 1975), 47–60.

5.   Pastedechouan's Legacy

1. Rueben Gold Thwaites, ed. *Jesuit Relations and Allied Documents, 1610–1791* (Cleveland, 1898), 9: 71–73.

2. Richard White, *The Middle Ground: Indians, Empires, and Republics in the Great Lakes Region, 1650–1815* (Cambridge, 1991).

3. See, for example, the title of Serge Bouchard's recent book, *Caribou Hunter: A Song of a Vanished Innu Life* (Vancouver, 2004), in which Bouchard described his main respondent, Mathieu Mestokosho, as a "powerless witness" (23) to social change, or Colin Samson's title, *A Way of Life that Does Not Exist: Canada and the Extinguishment of the Innu* (London, 2003). While the history of the Innu people doubtless has its tragic aspects, to cast Innu collective life as effectively over, seems needlessly pessimistic.

4. Allan Greer, "Conversion and Identity: Iroquois Christianity in Seventeenth-Century New France," in *Conversions: Old Worlds and New,* ed. A. Grafton and K. Mills (Rochester, 2003), 176–177.

5. Daniel Richter, *Facing East from Indian Country: A Native History of Early America* (Cambridge, Mass., 2001).

6. Thwaites, *Jesuit Relations,* 6: 119.

7. Bruce Trigger, *Natives and Newcomers: Canada's "Heroic Age" Reconsidered* (Kingston, ON, 1985), 294–295.

8. Natalie Zemon Davis, "Polarities, Hybridities: What Strategies for Decentering," *Decentering the Renaissance: Canada and Europe in Multidisciplinary Perspective, 1500–1700,* ed. Germaine Warkentin and Carolyn Podruchny (Toronto, 2001), 27.

9. Jean Delameau. *La Péché et la peur* (Paris, 1983).

10. Thwaites, *Jesuit Relations,* 5: 177.

11. "Problem": K. Tsianina Lomawaima, *They Called It Prairie Light: The Story of the Chilocco Indian School* (Lincoln, Neb., 1994), 31. "Question": Celia Haig-Brown, *Resistance and Renewal: Surviving the Indian Residential School* (Vancouver, 1988), 27.

12. A 1918 letter of an anonymous teacher, quoted in J. R. Miller, *Shingwauk's Vision: A History of Native Residential Schools* (Toronto, 1996), 151.

13. Miller, *Shingwauk's Vision,* 72–73. Even earlier schools appeared in New Brunswick and Manitoba.

14. Attempts at conversion and European education of Innu prior to 1940: Samson, *A Way,* 163–165; John McGee, *Cultural Stability and Change among the Montagnais Indians of the Lake Melville Region of Labrador* (Washington, D.C., 1961), 128–134.

15. Mining: Samson, *A Way,* 152–153; Marie Wadden, *Nitassinan: The Innu Struggle to Reclaim their Homeland* (Vancouver, 1991), 34–44. Escalating

change after 1960: Samson, *A Way,* 165–166; Bouchard, *Caribou Hunter,* 22–23.

16. Samson, *A Way,* 165.

17. "Children of Cain": Bouchard, (*Caribou Hunter,* 18) attributes the phrase to Jacques Cartier); Samson (*A Way,* 161) attributes it to Le Jeune.

18. Samson, *A Way,* 173.

19. Basil Johnston, *Indian School Days* (Toronto, 1988), 7, 26–27; Lomawaima, *They Called It,* 1–4, 41, 65–67, 81–99; Haig-Brown, *Resistance,* 64–65; Miller, *Shingwauk's Vision.*

20. Haig-Brown, *Resistance,* 11. Bernard Christmas, speaking of his father's experiences in residential schools, uses the term "emotional genocide" (Steven Frank, "Schools of Shame," July 2003, 31–39).

21. By the 1930s, more than one hundred aboriginal residential schools operated across Canada (Frank, "Schools," 35).

22. A 1920 amendment to the Indian Act made it mandatory for aboriginal parents to send their children to residential schools (Frank, "Schools," 34). Enforcement and resistance: Haig-Brown, *Resistance,* 27; Jean Barman et al., *Indian Education in Canada: The Legacy* (Vancouver, 1986), 11; Johnston, *Indian School Days,* 8; Kim Cheena, personal communication with the author, 2004.

23. Lomawaima, *They Called It,* xi–xiii, 29–30; Johnston, *Indian School Days,* 41–42; Haig-Brown, *Resistance,* 14–15).

24. Young age of incarceration: Johnston, *Indian School Days,* 20; Haig-Brown, *Resistance,* 13. Depersonalization: Johnston, *Indian School Days,* 10, 23, 33–34. In many institutions, students were stripped even of their names and were referred to instead by assigned numbers. Isolation from families: Both Johnston (*Indian School Days,* 9) and Lomawaima (*They Called It,* 3, 24) suggest that this isolation from parents was pedagogically deliberate, as it had been in the seventeenth century. Childhood comfort and collusion: Johnston, *Indian School Days,* 23, 28–30, 44–47; Lomawaima, *They Called It,* xi–xiv, 29, 101–105; Haig-Brown, *Resistance,* 66, 88–103; David Adams, *Education for Extinction: American Indians and the Boarding School Experience, 1875–1928* (Lawrence, Kans., 1995), 209–237.

25. Kim Cheena, personal communication with the author, October 2004; Miller, *Shingwauk's Vision,* 199–220; Johnston, *Indian School Days,* 7, 9–10; Lomawaima, *They Called It,* xiv–xv; Frank, "Schools," 34–35; Haig-Brown, *Resistance,* 11.

26. Thompson Highway—a native writer whose devastating semiautobiographical novel, *The Kiss of the Fur Queen,* recounts the residential school experiences of two brothers—presents the prayer of his young Cree an-

tagonists as the mindless parroting of ill-understood words and phrases in an atmosphere of anticipatory dread. See also Adams, *Education,* 164–173, and Johnston, *Indian School Days,* 28–47.

27. Christian Le Clercq, *First Establishment of the Faith in New France* (Paris, 1881), 1: 273.

28. Thwaites, *Jesuit Relations,* 5: 23, 33–35.

29. Miller, *Shingwauk's Vision,* 183–216; Lomawaima, *They Called It,* xiii, 3–4.

30. White, *Middle Ground,* 62–63.

31. Thwaites, *Jesuit Relations,* 6: 153–155.

32. Samson, *A Way,* 174–180.

33. On "white man's burden": Samson, *A Way,* 135–138, 141, 166, 171.

34. Haig-Brown, *Resistance,* 18; Miller, *Shingwauk's Vision,* 45–46, 130–134, 301–305, 349–350.

35. A compelling example of this silence, even in disclosure, is Basil Johnston's memoir *Indian School Days* (Toronto, 1988). Though in many ways a hard-hitting exposé, the work is completely silent concerning his years of sexual abuse there. Prosecution: Miller, *Shingwauk's Vision,* 439–441; Aboriginal Healing Foundation, *The Healing has Begun,* 2002, 3; Mike De-Gagne, personal communication with the author, 2005.

36. Miller, *Shingwauk's Vision,* 420–438; Aboriginal Healing Foundation, *The Healing has Begun,* 1–10; Barman, et al., *Indian Education,* 1–17; Johnston, *Indian School Days,* 7–9; Frank, "Schools," 38; Haig-Brown, *Resistance,* 16–20, 104–114.

37. Samson, *A Way,* 168.

38. Mike DeGagne, speech to Aboriginal Religions class at Queen's University, Kingston, Ontario, Canada, October 2004.

39. Daniel Richter, "Iroquois versus Iroquois: Jesuit Missions and Christianity in Village Politics," *Ethnohistory* 32, no. 1 (1985): 1–16.

40. Mike DeGagne, presentation to Aboriginal Religions class, Queen's University, Kingston, Ontario, Canada, October 2004; see also Samson, *A Way,* 173, 180.

41. Samson, *A Way,* 177, 269–295; Wadden, *Nitassinan,* 5, 76–80; Haig-Brown, *Resistance,* 23–24.

42. Canadian Broadcasting Corporation, "A Heart-Wrenching Cry for Help," *The National,* January 28, 1993.

43. Bouchard, *Caribou Hunter,* 23–36; Samson, *A Way,* 145–148, 269–299; Wadden, *Nitassinan,* vii, 5, 9, 20, 198–202; Jose Mailhot, *The People of Sheshatshit: In the Land of the Innu* (St. John's, NF, 1997), 165–168; Nympha Byrne and Camille Fouillard, *It's Like the Legend: Innu Women's Voices* (Charlottetown, PE, 2000), 17–22; Lawrence Millman, *Wolverine Creates*

the World: Labrador Indian Tales (Santa Barbara, 1993), 10, 19. Peter Armitage, "Religious Ideology among the Innu of Eastern Quebec and Labrador," *Religiologiques,* vol. 6, 1992, 64, 85.

44. Samson, *A Way,* 148–149; Wadden, *Nitassinan,* 32. The provincial governments in question are those of Newfoundland and Labrador and Quebec.

Finding Pastedechouan

1. Gabriel Sagard, *Histoire du Canada* (Paris, 1866), 2: 334.
2. Christian Le Clercq. *First Establishment of the Faith in New France* (New York, 1881). Le Clercq's work is doubly valuable because it preserves some of the writings of the first Recollet Superior to Canada, Joseph Le Caron, the originals of which have been lost. Sagard, *Histoire.*
3. Pastedechouan's baptismal record: MS GG 100, folio 223, Archives Municipal d'Angers, which is also reproduced in N. E. Dionne, "Le Sauvage Pastedechouan en France," *Recherches Historiques,* 30 (1907): and F. Uzureau, "Baptême d'un Montagnais a la Cathédrale d'Angers, le 27 Avril 1621," *Le Canada Français,* 4 (1922): 390–393. Louvet diary: Jean Louvet, "Journal de Jean Louvet," Dolbeau vita: "Vie Abrège de Père Dolbeau," MS 509, folio 171, Bibliothèque Municipal d'Orleans. MS 862, folio 134, Bibliothèque Municipal d"Angers.
4. The only published source for Pastedechouan's life during this period not written by Le Jeune is François Du Creux's *The History of Canada or New France* (Toronto, 1951), which is a largely derivative, condensed repackaging of Le Jeune's *Relations.*
5. The *Relations* were initially published by Sebastien Cramoisy of Paris (except for the 1637 *Relation,* which was printed by Jean Le Boullenger at Rouen) from 1632 to 1673. Both Université Laval in Quebec City and Brown University in Rhode Island own copies of this edition. The next printing was in 1858 in Quebec and reproduced the exact text of the Cramoisy edition. In the 1890s Reuben Gold Thwaites brought out his *Jesuit Relations and Allied Documents, 1610–1791* (Cleveland, 1897–1898) which for the first time supplemented the actual *Relations* with letters written by pivotal Jesuits at the same time as these public documents; see G. W. Brown et al., *Canadian Dictionary of Biography* (Toronto, 1966), 1: 455–456; Wroth, 1936, 110–149). Finally, there is the work of Lucien Campeau, whose *Monumenta Novae Franciae* (Quebec; Rome, 1987), which recompiled the *Relations,* adding other materials.
6. See, for example, Alain Beaulieu, *Un Français au "Royaume des Bestes Sauvages"* (Montreal, PQ, 1999); Guy LaFlèche, *Relation de 1634 de Paul*

Le Jeune: Le Missionaire, l'apostat, le sorcier (Montreal, 1973); Dominique Deffrain, *Un Voyager Français en Nouvelle-France au XVII siècle: Étude littéraire des Relations du Père Paul Le Jeune (1632–1641)* (Tubingen, 1995).

7. Carole Blackburn, *Harvest of Souls: The Jesuit Missions and Colonialism in North America: 1632–1650* (Montreal, 2000); Bruce G. Trigger, *The Children of Aataentsic: A History of the Huron People to 1660* (Montreal, 1976); Angela Cavender Wilson, "American Indian History or Non-Indian Perceptions of American Indian History," in Devon A. Mihesuah, ed., *Natives and Academics: Researching and Writing about American Indians* (Lincoln, Neb., 1998), 23–40.

8. Ken Morrison, "Discourse and the Accommodation of Values: Towards Revision of Mission History." *Journal of the American Academy of Religion,* vol. 103, no. 3 (1985): 366, 368; Allan Greer, *The Jesuit Relations: Natives and Missionaries in Seventeenth-Century North America* (Boston, 2000), 1–3, 14–19. Methodology is a major focus of Jennifer Brown and Elizabeth Vibert's *Reading Beyond Words: Contexts for Native History* (Peterborough, Ont., 1996); Daniel K. Richter, "Iroquois versus Iroquois: Jesuit Missions and Christianity in Village Politics," *Ethnohistory* 32, no. 1 (1985): 1–1; Cornelius Jaenen, *Friend and Foe: Aspects of Amerindian Cultural Contact in the Sixteenth and Seventeenth Centuries* (New York, 1976), 120–122.

9. Dorris in Calvin Martin, *The American Indian and the Problem of History* (New York, 1987), 107.

10. Sagard, *Histoire,* 865.

Bibliography

Primary Sources

Archives Municipal d'Angers. Pastedechouan's baptismal certificate, MS GG 100, folio 223.

Bibliothèque Municipal d'Angers. "Journal de Jean Louvet," MS 862, folio 134.

Bibliothèque Municipal d'Orléans. "Vie Abrège de Père Dolbeau," MS 509, folio 171.

Biggar, H. P., ed. *The Works of Samuel de Champlain*. 6 vols. Toronto: Champlain Society, 1971.

Campeau, Lucien, ed. *Monumenta Novae Franciae*. Vols. 2 and 3. Quebec: Laval University Press; Rome: Monumenta Historica Societatis Jesu, 1987.

Dionne, N. E. "Le Sauvage Pastedechouan en France." *Recherches Historiques* 30 (1907): 120–124.

Du Creux, François. *The History of Canada or New France*. Toronto: Champlain Society, 1951.

Le Clercq, Christian. *First Establishment of the Faith in New France*. trans. John Gilmary Shea. New York: John G. Shea, 1881.

Lescarbot, Marc. *The History of New France*. Trans. Grant. W. L. Toronto: The Champlain Society, 1907.

Sagard, Gabriel. *Histoire du Canada* Paris: Librarie Tross, 1866.

———. *Long Journey into the Country of the Hurons*. Ed. George Wrong. Toronto: Champlain Society, 1939.

Thwaites, Rueben Gold, ed. *The Jesuit Relations and Allied Documents, 1610–1791*. Cleveland: Burrows Brothers Co., 1897.

Uzureau, F. "Baptême d'un Montagnais a la Cathedrale d'Angers, le 27 Avril 1621." *Le Canada Français* 4 (1922): 390–393.

Secondary Sources

Aboriginal Healing Foundation. *The Healing Has Begun*. 2002.

Adams, David. *Education for Extinction: American Indians and the Boarding School Experience, 1875–1928*. Lawrence: University of Kansas Press, 1995.

Adelson, Naomi. *"Being Alive Well": Health and the Politics of Cree Well-Being.* Toronto: University of Toronto Press, 2000.

Altherr, Thomas L. "'Flesh Is the Paradise of the Man of Flesh': Cultural Conflict over Indian Hunting Beliefs and Rituals in New France as Recorded in the Jesuit Relations." *Canadian Historical Review* 64, no. 2 (1983): 267–276.

Armitage, Peter. "Religious Ideology Among the Innu of Eastern Quebec and Labrador," *Religiologiques,* vol. 6 (1992): 63–105.

Austin, Alvyn and Jamie S. Scott, *Canadian Missionaries: Indigenous Peoples: Representing Religion at Home and Abroad.* Toronto: University of Toronto Press, 2005.

Axtell, James. *Beyond 1492: Encounters in Colonial North America.* New York: Oxford University Press, 1992.

———. *The Indian Peoples of Eastern North America: A Documentary History of the Sexes.* Oxford: Oxford University Press, 1981.

Bailey, Alfred Goldsworthy. *The Conflict of European and Eastern Algonkian Cultures, 1504–1700: A Study in Canadian Civilization.* Toronto: University of Toronto Press, 1969.

Bailey, Gauvin Alexander. *Art on the Jesuit Missions in Asia and Latin America, 1542–1773.* Toronto: University of Toronto Press, 1999.

Barman, Jean, Yvonne Hebert, and Don McCaskill, eds. *Indian Education in Canada.* Vol. 1: *The Legacy.* Vancouver: University of British Columbia Press, 1986.

Beaulieu, Alain. *Convertir le Fils de Cain: Jesuits et Amerindiens Nomades en Nouvelle France, 1632–1642.* Saint-Jean, PQ: Nuit Blanche, 1990.

———. (Le Jeune, Paul.) *Un Français au "Royaume des Bestes Sauvages" (1634).* Montreal, PQ: Comeau and Nadeau, 1999.

Bédard, Marc-André. *Les Protestants en Nouvelle-France.* Québec: La Société Historique de Québec, 1978.

Behiels, Michael, ed. *Aboriginal Peoples in Canada: Futures and Identities.* Montreal: Association for Canadian Studies, 1999.

Benedict, Phillip. "The Catholic Response to Protestantism: Church Activity and Popular Piety in Rouen, 1580–1600." In *Religion and the People,* ed. J. Obelkevich. Chapel Hill: University of North Carolina Press, 1979, 168–190.

Berthiaume, Pierre. "Paul Lejeune ou le missionnaire possédé." Voix et Images, vol. 23, no. 3 (1998): 529–543.

Biggar, H. P. *The Early Trading Companies of New France.* New York: Argonaut Press, 1965.

Blackburn, Carole. *Harvest of Souls: The Jesuit Missions and Colonialism in North America: 1632–1650.* Montreal: McGill–Queen's University Press, 2000.

Bouchard, Serge. *Caribou Hunter: A Song of a Vanished Innu Life.* Vancouver: Douglas and McIntyre Publishing Co., 2004.

Brandão, Jose. *"Your Fyre Shall Burn No More": Iroquois Policy toward New France and Its Native Allies to 1701.* Lincoln: University of Nebraska Press, 1997.

Brown, G. W., M. Trudel, and A. Vachon, *Canadian Dictionary of Biography,* Vol. 1. Toronto: University of Toronto, 1966.

Brown, Jennifer and Elizabeth Vibert, eds. Reading Beyond Words: Contexts for Native History. Peterborough, Ont.: Broadview Press, 1996.

Byrne, Nympha, and Camille Fouillard, *It's like the Legend: Innu Women's Voices.* Charlottetown, PE: Gynergy Books, 2000.

Caron, Adrien. "La Mission de Père Paul Le Jeune, S.J., sur la Cote-du-Sud, 1633–1634." *Revue d'Histoire de l'Amerique Française* 17, no. 3 (1963): 371–395.

Chatellier, Louis. *The Religion of the Poor: Rural Missions in Europe and the Formation of Modern Catholicism, c. 1500–1800.* Cambridge: Cambridge University Press, 1997.

Chausse, Gilles. "Le Père Paul Le Jeune: Missionnaire-colonisateur," *Revue d'histoire d'Amerique Francais* 12 (1959–1960): 56–79.

Choquette, Leslie. "A Colony of Native French Catholics? The Protestants of New France in the Seventeenth and Eighteenth Centuries," In *Memory and Identity: The Huguenots in France and the Atlantic Diaspora,* ed. Bertrand Van Ruymbeke and Randy Sparks. Columbia: University of South Carolina, 2003.

Clendinnen, Inga. "Disciplining the Indians: Franciscan Ideology and Missionary Violence in Sixteenth Century Yucatan." *Past and Present* (February 1982).

Coverdale, William. *Tadoussac Then and Now: A History and Narrative of the Kingdom of the Saguenay.* New York: Charles Francis Press, 1942.

Cox, J. Stevens. "News from Canada, 1628" in Canada's Huguenot Heritage, 1685–1985, ed Michael Harrison. Toronto, ON: Huguenot Society of Canada, 1987.

Davis, Natalie Zemon. *The Gift in Sixteenth-Century France.* Madison: University of Wisconsin Press, 2000.

———. "Iroquoian Women, European Women," in *Women, "Race," and Writing in the Early Modern Period,* ed. Margo Hendricks and Patricia Parker. New York: Routledge, 1994, 243–258.

———. "Polarities, Hybridities: What Strategies for Decentering?" in *Decentering the Renaissance: Canada and Europe in Multidisciplinary Perspective, 1500–1700,* ed. Germaine Warkentin and Carolyn Podruchny, Toronto: University of Toronto Press, 2001.

———. *Women on the Margins: Three Seventeenth-Century Lives.* Cambridge, Mass.: Harvard University Press, 1995.

Deffain, Dominique. *Un voyager francais en Nouvelle-France au XVII siécle: Étude littéraire des relations du Père Paul Le Jeune 1632–1641.* Tubingen: Max Neimeyer Verlag, 1995.

Delâge, Denys. *Bitter Feast: Amerindians and Europeans in Northeastern North America, 1600–1664.* Vancouver: University of British Columbia Press, 1993.

Delumeau, Jean. *Catholicism between Luther and Voltaire: A New View of the Counter-Reformation.* London: Burnes and Oates, 1977.

————. *Sin and Fear: The Emergence of a Western Guilt Culture, 13th–18th Centuries.* trans. Eric Nicholson. New York, St. Martin's Press, 1990.

Dickason, Olive P. "Campaigns to Capture Young Minds: a Look at Early Attempts in Colonial Mexico and New France to Remold Amerindians." *Historical Papers* 61 (1987): 44–66.

————. *The Myth of the Savage and the Beginnings of French Colonialism in the Americas.* Edmonton: University of Alberta Press, 1997.

Diefendorf, Barbara B. *Beneath the Cross: Catholics and Huguenots in Sixteenth-Century Paris.* Oxford: Oxford University Press, 1991.

————. "Houses Divided: Religious Schism in Sixteenth-Century Parisian Families." In *Urban Life in the Renaissance,* ed. Susan Zimmerman and Ronald Weissman, Newark, Del.: University of Delaware Press, 1989, 80–99.

Feest, Christian. *Indians and Europe: An Interdisciplinary Collection of Essays.* Lincoln: University of Nebraska Press, 1999.

Flood, David and Thaddée Matura. *The Birth of a Movement: A Study of the First Rule of St. Francis.* Chicago: Franciscan Herald Press, 1975.

Frame, Donald M. *François Rabelais: A Study.* New York: Harcourt Brace, 1977.

Frank, Steven. "Schools of Shame." *Time Magazine,* July 28, 2003, 31–39.

Gagnon, François-Marc. *La Conversion par l'image: un aspect de la mission des jésuites auprès des Indiens du Canada au XVIIe siècle.* Montreal: Bellarmin, 1975.

Goddard, Peter A. "Augustine and the Amerindian in Seventeenth-Century New France." *Church History* 67, no 4 (December 1998a): 662–681.

————. "Converting the Sauvage: Jesuit and Montagnais in Seventeenth-Century New France." *Catholic Historical Review* 84, no. 2 (1998b): 219–239.

————. "The Devil in New France: Jesuit Demonology." *Canadian Historical Review* 78, no. 1 (1997): 40–62.

Goulet, Jean-Guy A. *Ways of Knowing: Experience, Knowledge, and Power among the Dene Tha.* Vancouver: University of British Columbia Press, 1998.

Grant, John Webster. *Moon of Wintertime: Missionaries and the Indians of Canada in Encounter since 1534.* Toronto: University of Toronto Press, 1984.

Greer, Allan. "Colonial Saints: Gender, Race, and Hagiography in New France." *William and Mary Quarterly,* 3rd ser., 57 (April 2000): 323–348.

————. "Conversion and Identity: Iroquois Christianity in Seventeenth-Century New France." In *Conversions: Old Worlds and New,* ed. A. Grafton and K. Mills. Rochester, N.Y.: University of Rochester Press, 2003.

————, ed. *The Jesuit Relations: Natives and Missionaries in Seventeenth-Century North America.* Boston: Bedford/St. Martin's, 2000.

————. *Mohawk Saint: Catherine Tekakwitha and the Jesuits.* Oxford: Oxford University Press, 2005.

Greimas, Algirdas Julien and Teresa Mary Keane, eds. *Dictionnaire du moyen français: la Renaissance* (Paris: Larousse, 1992).

Haig-Brown, Celia. *Resistance and Renewal: Surviving the Indian Residential School*. Vancouver: Tillacum Library, 1988.

Hallowell, A. Irving. "Ojibwa Ontology, Behavior, and World View." In *Contributions to Anthropology: Selected Papers of A. Irving Hallowell*. Chicago: University of Chicago Press, 1976, 357–390.

Harrison, Michael, ed. *Canada's Huguenot Heritage, 1685–1985*. Toronto: Huguenot Society of Canada, 1987.

Harrod, Howard. *Renewing the World: Plains Indian Religion and Morality*. Tucson: University of Arizona Press, 1987.

Harvey, Graham, ed. *Indigenous Religions: A Companion*. London: Cassell, 2000.

Highway, Thompson. *The Kiss of the Fur Queen*. Toronto: Doubleday, 1998.

Iriarte, Lázaro. *Histoire du Franciscanisme*. Paris: Les Éditions du Cerf, 2004.

Jacquin, Philippe. *Les Indiens blancs: Français et Indiens en Amérique de Nord (XVI–XVIII siècle)*. Montréal: Éditions Libre Expression, 1996.

Jaenen, Cornelius. "Education for Francization: The Case of New France in the Seventeenth Century." In *Indian Education in Canada*. vol. 1: *The Legacy*, ed. Jean Barman, Yvonne Hebert, and Don McCaskill. Vancouver: University of British Columbia Press, 1986, 45–63.

———. *Friend and Foe: Aspects of Amerindian Cultural Contact in the Sixteenth and Seventeenth Centuries*. New York: Columbia University Press, 1976.

Jauvin, Serge, recorder and photographer. *Aitnanu: The Lives of Helene and William-Mathieu Mark*. Ed. Daniel Clement. Hull: Quebec Canadian Museum of Civilization, 1993.

Jenness, Diamond. *Indians of Canada*. Ottawa: National Museum of Canada, 1932. Bulletin 85.

Johnston, Basil. *Indian School Days*. Toronto: Key Porter Books, 1988.

Jouve, Odoric, et al. *Dictionnaire biographique des Récollets missionaires en Nouvelle-France, 1645–1645, 1670–1849*. Montreal: Bellarmin, 1996.

———. *Les Franciscains et le Canada*. vol. 1: *L'Éstablissement de la foi, 1615–1629*. Quebec, 1915.

Krailsheimer, A. J. *Rabelais and the Franciscans*. Oxford: Clarendon Press, 1963.

LaBras, Yvon. *L'Amérindien dans les Relations du père Paul LeJeune (1632–1641): Études sur la relation de voyage en Nouvelle-France*. Sainte-Foy, PQ, 1994.

LeBrun, François. *Histoire d'Angers*. Toulouse: Eduoard Privat, 1975.

LaFlèche, Guy. *Relation de 1634 de Paul Le Jeune: Le Missionaire, l'apostat, le sorcier*. Montreal: Les Presses de l'Université de Montréal, 1973.

Larin, Robert. *Brève Histoire des Protestants in Nouvelle-France et au Québec (XVI–XIX siecles)*. Saint-Alphone de Granby, Quebec: Éditions de la Paix, 1998.

Leahey, Margaret J. "'Comment peut un muet prescher l'evangile?' Jesuit Missionaries and the Native Languages of New France." *French Historical Studies* 19, no. 1 (1995), 105–131.

Lewis, D. B. *Doctor Rabelais*. New York: Greenwood Press, 1968.

Lomawaima, K. Tsianina. *They Called It Prairie Light: The Story of the Chilocco Indian School*. Lincoln: University of Nebraska Press, 1994.

Lutz, Hartmut. The Diary of Abraham Ulrikab: Text and Context. Ottowa: University of Ottawa Press, 2005.

MacManners, John. *French Ecclesiastical Society under the Ancien Regime: A Study of Angers in the Eighteenth Century*. Manchester: Manchester University Press, 1960.

Mailhot, Jose. *The People of Sheshatshit: In the Land of the Innu*. St. John's, NF: Institution of Social and Economic Research, 1997.

Martin, A. Lynn. *The Jesuit Mind: The Mentality of an Elite in Early Modern France*. Ithaca, N.Y.: Cornell University Press, 1988.

Martin, Calvin. *The American Indian and the Problem of History*. New York: Oxford University Press, 1987.

———. *Keepers of the Game: Indian Animal Relationships and the Fur Trade*. Berkeley: University of California Press, 1978.

McGee, John T. *Cultural Stability and Change among the Montagnais Indians of the Lake Melville Region of Labrador*. Washington, D.C.: Catholic University of America Press, 1961.

McGowan, Mark G. and David B. Marshall. *Prophets, Priests, and Prodigals: Readings in Canadian Religious History, 1608 to the Present*. Toronto: McGraw-Hill Ryerson, 1992.

Mihesuah, Devon A., ed. *Natives and Academics: Researching and Writing about American Indians*. Lincoln: University of Nebraska Press, 1998.

Miller, J. R. *Shingwauk's Vision: A History of Native Residential Schools*. Toronto: University of Toronto Press, 1996.

Millman, Lawrence. *Wolverine Creates the World: Labrador Indian Tales*. Santa Barbara: Capra Press, 1993.

Mills, Antonia, and Richard Slobodin. *Amerindian Rebirth: Recincarnation Belief among North American Indians and Inuit*. Toronto: University of Toronto Press, 1994.

Moorman, John. *A History of the Franciscan Order from its Origins to the Year 1517*. Oxford: Clarendon Press, 1968.

Morrison, Kenneth M. "Baptism and Alliance: The Symbolic Mediations of Religious Syncretism." *Ethnohistory* 37 (1990): 416–437.

———. "The Cosmos as Intersubjective: Native American Other-Than-Human Persons." In *Indigenous Religions: A Companion*, ed. Graham Harvey. London: Cassell, 2000, 23–36.

———. "Discourse and the Accommodation of Values: Toward Revision of Mission History." *Journal of the American Academy of Religion* 103, no. 3 (1985): 365–382.

————. *The Solidarity of Kin: Ethnohistory, Religious Studies, and the Algonkian-French Religious Encounter.* Albany: State University of New York, 2002.

Muel, Francis. *Front and Back: The Tapestry of the Apocalypse at Angers.* Nantes: Images du Patrimonie, 1996.

O'Malley, John. *The First Jesuits.* Cambridge, Mass.: Harvard University Press, 1993.

Ouellet, Réal, et al. *Rhétorique de conquête missionaire: le Jesuite Paul Lejeune.* Sillery, PQ: Septentrion Press, 1993.

Perdue, Theda. *Cherokee Women: Gender and Culture Change, 1700–1835.* Lincoln: University of Nebraska Press, 1998.

Pilatte, Léon, *Édits, Déclarations et Arrests concernans la réligion p. réformée, 1662–1751,* Paris: Librairie Fischbacher and Co, 1885.

Pouliot, Leon. "Que penser des frères Kirke?" *Le Bulletin Recherches Historiques* 44, no. 11 (November 1938): 321–335.

Principe, Charles. "A Moral Portrait of the Indian of the St. Lawrence in One Relation of New France." *Historical Studies* (Ottawa: Canadian Catholic Historical Association) 57, (1990): 29–50.

————. "Trois Relations de la Nouvelle France Écrites par le Père Paul Le Jeune (1632, 1633, 1634)." *Cahiers de l'Association Internationale des Études Français* 27 (May 1975): 83–108.

Pritzker, M. *A Native American Encyclopedia.* Oxford: Oxford University Press, 2000.

Proulx, Jean-René. "Acquisition de Douvoirs et Tente Tremblant Chez les Montagnais," Recherches Amérindiennes au Québec, vol. 28, no. 2–3, 1988, p. 51–59.

Richter, Daniel K. *Facing East from Indian Country: A Native History of Early America.* Cambridge, Mass.: Harvard University Press, 2001.

————. "Iroquois versus Iroquois: Jesuit Missions and Christianity in Village Politics." *Ethnohistory* 32, no. 1 (1985): 1–16.

————. *The Ordeal of the Longhouse: The Peoples of the Iroquois League in the Era of European Colonization.* Chapel Hill: University of North Carolina Press; Williamsburg, Va.: Institute of Early American History and Culture, 1992.

————. "War and Culture: The Iroquois Experience." *William and Mary Quarterly* 40 (1983): 528–559.

Richter, Daniel, and James Merrell, eds. *Beyond the Covenant Chain: The Iroquois and Their Neighbors in Indian North America, 1600–1800.* University Park: Pennsylvania State University Press, 1987.

Roest, Bert. *Franciscan Literature of Religious Instruction before the Council of Trent.* Leiden: Brill, 2004.

Samson, Colin. *A Way of Life that Does Not Exist: Canada and the Extinguishment of the Innu.* London: Verso, 2003.

Snow, Dean R., Charles Gehring, and William Starna, eds. *In Mohawk Country: Early Narratives about a Native People.* Syracuse, N.Y.: Syracuse University Press, 1996.

Speck, Frank. *Naskapi: The Savage Hunters of the Labrador Peninsula.* Norman, Okla: University of Oklahoma Press, 19535.

Trigger, Bruce G. *The Children of Aataentsic: A History of the Huron People to 1660.* 2 vols. Montreal: McGill-Queen's University Press, 1976.

——. *Natives and Newcomers: Canada's "Heroic Age" Reconsidered.* Kington, ON.: McGill-Queen's University Press, 1985.

Trigger, Bruce G., and Wilcomb E. Washburn, eds. *The Cambridge History of the Native Peoples of the Americas.* vol. 1: *North America, Part I.* Cambridge: Cambridge University Press, 1996.

Trudel, Marcel. *The Beginnings of New France, 1524–1663.* Toronto: McClelland and Stewart, 1973.

——. *Histoire de la Nouvelle-France.* Montreal: Fides Press, 1966.

Usureau, F. "L'Assemblée de la Baumette-les-Angers, 22 juillet." *Angdegaviana* 33 (1939): 276–277.

——. "Le Chapitre de la Cathédrale d'Angers avant la Révolution: Processions." *Andegaviana* 24 (1925): 64–70.

——. "Le Couvent de la Baumette-les-Angers." *Andegaviana* 28 (1932): 315–318.

——. "Le Couvent de la Baumette-lès-Angers." *Revue d'histoire Franciscaine* 8 (1931): 357.

——. "Le Couvent de la Baumette (1456–1791) in *Andegaviana* 26 (1928): 13–19.

——. "Le Couvent de la Baumette-lès-Angers, 1456–1791," *Andegaviana* 32 (1938): 48–64.

——. "Les Récollets dela Baumette-les-Angers," *Andegaviana* 16 (1915): 113–118.

——. "Un Recollet de la Baumette, missionaire au Canada." *Andegaviana* 22 (1921): 101–106.

——. "Le Sacred' Angers." in *Andegaviana* 30 (1934): 216–222.

——. "Le 'Sacre d'Angers' avant la Révolution." *Andegaviana* 17 (1915): 260–266.

Vecsey, Christopher. *Traditional Ojibwa Religion and Its Historical Changes.* Philadelphia: American Philosophical Society, 1983.

Wadden, Marie. *Nitassinan: The Innu Struggle to Reclaim their Homeland.* Vancouver: Douglas and McIntyre, 1991.

White, Richard. *The Middle Ground: Indians, Empires and Republics in the Great Lakes Region, 1650–1815.* Cambridge: Cambridge University Press, 1991.

Wrong, George M. *The Rise and Fall of New France.* Toronto: McMillan, 1928.

Index

Acadia, 109, 133, 270n15, 271n26

Adoption. *See* Captives

Adulthood, Innu: respect for elders in Innu culture, 33, 41; meaning of adulthood, 114–115; Pastedechouan's transgression of adult norms, 130; Jesuit shift to adult-focused missionization model, 155, 157, 163–164, 208; contemporary elders affected by assimilative education, 229. *See also* Initiation

Afterlife: Innu concepts of, 23, 27–28, 67; association with West, 27; with celestial realm, 28; simultaneous belief in reincarnation and afterlife, 27, 254n43; facilitates community cohesion, 28; not dependent upon moral fitness, 29; Milky Way as path to, 27–28; contrast with Christian concepts, 28. *See also* Heaven; Hell; Reincarnation

Alcohol abuse: of Pastedechouan, 140, 168, 171–175; motives for, 172–174, 229–230; in the contemporary Innu community, 229–232

Alcohol: Innu perception of, 171–172, 188–189, 192–193, 277n13

Amantacha, 265n96, 268n4

Ambivalence, religious: of Pastedechouan, 136–137, 139, 141–150, 155–156, 161, 166, 167–168, 170–172, 174–175, 181–182, 197–199, 212–213, 227–228; ignored historiographically, 212–214; of contemporary native individuals, 228; at the community level, 228–229

Anadabijou, 117

Angers, 81, 84; map of, 82; religious life of, 84; relationship with La Baumette, 84–85

Animals, 11, 12, 14, 15–16, 25, 29, 31, 32, 37, 61, 129, 165, 182, 185, 188; animal masters, 14, 32, 248n48; role in vision quests 34–35, 113, 130; depiction of in Christian art, 99–100, 212; Pastedechouan's description of family as "beasts," 105–106; contemporary descriptions of, 245n8. *See also* Other-than-human persons

Anthoynette of Bretagne: godmother of Pastedechouan, 90; signature on baptismal registry, 89; participation in baptism 87–90

Apostasy: fear of as shaping missionary approaches, 70–72, 75, 94, 154–155; Pastedecouan's flirtation with, 139, 182–187, 296–199, 203–204; Le Jeune's perception of Pastedechouan and his family as apostates, 167, 197, 199–202; Pastedechouan's nickname, "the Apostate," 168–169, 202, 214; Le Jeune's reflections on Pastedechouan's spiritual status, 140, 169–170, 181, 197–198, 201–202, 205; definitional problems with term, 200, 212–214, 275n73. *See also* Ambivalence

Atahensic, 48

Atcen, 14, 38, 52, 185, 229, 231; contemporary beliefs concerning, 251n64. *See also* Cannibalism

Backstreaming, 235, 239

Baptism: Innu reversion to traditional lifestyle following, 70; Innu regard as symbol of alliance with French, 72; Recollet restrict sacrament to dying children, 74–75; Innu perceive as deadly, 75; of Pastedechouan, 87–93, 120, 124–125; of aboriginal people in Europe, 90–91, 265n96; of Franks, 94; Recollet attempt to link to French citizenship to, 93–94; of Naneogauchit, 115–116; of Sasousmat, 127–128, 196, 200, 201; Jesuit shift to

Confessional tensions: in Canadian colony, 68, 111–114, 117, 120; in Europe, 122–123, 135–136; English burn religious buildings at Quebec, 128; on Canadian missionization policy, 135–136; as influence on Le Jeune's mentality, 136; Protestant traders refusal to teach missionaries aboriginal languages, 146, 149. *See also* Exclusivism; Protestants

Conversion, 63; Innu relativistic conceptions of, 71, 155–157, 175–176, 179–180, 185–186, 200; European exclusivistic conceptions of, 71–72, 94–95, 135–137, 212; historiographic difficulties with term, 212–214; bias towards study of exemplary aboriginal converts, 213. *See also* Baptism; Exclusivism; Relativism

Cordeliers, 83, 84, 86

Coureurs de bois. *See* Trouchemens

Cree, 129, 229, 244n6, 245n8

Davis, Natalie Zemon, 56, 216

Death: in Innu culture, 26–28, 30, 50, 61; Catholic death rituals, 103, 205. *See also* Cannibalism; Euthanasia; Illness; Torture

De Caen, Emery, 133, 140, 142

De Gagne, Mike, 228

Dene Tha, 244n6, 248n43, 250n59

Des Boves, Charles, 77, 78, 86; biographical sketch, 259n35

Diabolism, Jesuit perceptions of Innu culture as, 31, 49, 99, 176, 176–177, 196

Dictionaries authored by Pastedechouan, 103, 144, 235

Dieppe, 122

Dogs, 169; use in Innu hunting, 22; religious taboos regarding, 33, 188–189; Europeans perceived as resembling, 61, 189

Dolbeau, Jean, 68, 69, 70; takes Pastedechouan to France, 81; spiritual direction of Pastedechouan, 97–98; bio sketch, 257n16; letters and *Vita* as source for Pastedechouan's life, 236

Dreams: in Innu culture, 14, 23–25, 29, 30, 31; Pastedechouan's, 25, 181; contemporary Innu dream beliefs, 248n35

Dual-track ethic, Innu, 45–47, 49–51, 59–60

Du Plessis, Pacifique, 68, 69

Duplessis-Bochart, Charles, 140, 142, 273n43

Dupont, François Grave de, 79, 80

Easter, 147–148, 149, 150–151

"Eat-all" feast, 42–43, 125, 187. *See also* Feasting; Taboos

Edict of Nantes, 73, 110

Education, assimilative (in seventeenth century): 63–64; strategic use of isolation, 74–75, 78, 94–95, 107, 116, 120, 159–160, 163–164; as part of Recollets' child-focused missionization, 74–76; of Pastedechouan, 76, 86, 93–101, 103, 120; contrasted with Innu education, 96–97; children's reactions to, 106–108, 115, 159–160; Jesuit assimilative education, 133, 145–146, 153, 154–161; aboriginal critiques of, 154. *See also* Children; Jesuits; Recollets

Education, assimilative (modern): of aboriginal peoples, 220–221; intergeneration impact of, 220–221, 229, 232; similarities to seventeenth century model, 220–221, 227; differences from, 221–227; attendance of made mandatory, 226; code of silence around abuse at, 227; exclusivism at, 227–228; child-on-child violence at, 230. *See also* Innu, modern

Education, Innu (in seventeenth century): general contours, 18–21; gender specific, 21–23; during late teens, 32–34, 95–96. *See also* Children

Emotion: emphasis on emotional stoicism, 11, 18–20; negative emotions taboo, 44, 49; Pastedechouan breaks, 172–174; Le Jeune breaks, 178, 180, 188–189; association of negative emotions with illness, 44, 191–192. *See also* Illness; Innu; Shaming

Eucharist, 184; importance within Catholicism, 148, 184; Pastedechouan's refusal of, 148–149

Euthanasia, in Innu culture, 40, 42, 61, 158

Exclusivism, Catholic, 68, 71, 120; expressed in Pastedechouan's baptismal service, 94–95, in art, 99–100; molds Pastedechouan's outlook, 106, 120,